I0151891

"Troublemaker"
Memories of the Freedom Movement

Bruce Hartford

Westwind Writers
2019

Also by Bruce Hartford

The Ghandi Ring

The March on Washington for Jobs and Freedom

The Selma Voting Rights Struggle & the March to Montgomery

Voting Rights in America: Two Centuries of Struggle

ISBN-978-0-9778000-6-3

Library of Congress Control Number: 2019902212

Freedom Now! Series #3

Westwind Writers Inc.
San Francisco, California
www.wwwriters.com
bruceh@wwwriters.com
SAN 850-2730

Front cover photo: © John Phillips
(From left to right: Albert Turner, Bruce Hartford, Rev. Richard Boone.)

Rear cover photo: © Bob Fitch, courtesy of Bob Fitch Photography Archive, Department of Special Collections, Stanford University Libraries.
(Left: Bruce Hartford, right: possibly Nita Faison.)

Advance Praise for Troublemaker:

"Bruce Hartford, author of Troublemakers is a man who decided to do something and put his body on the line to fight evil. The book is Bruce's narrative that gives the reader a clear and exceptional understanding of what trying to change a White Anglo-Saxon Protestant (WASP) dominated America entails. Through the use of specific details about people, places, and dates, the author gives the reader a three dimensional view of what it was like fighting for fair housing, quality education, and employment in the North. The reader's three-dimensional view continues its journey South to the Edmund Pettus Bridge in Selma, Alabama, the March from Selma to Montgomery and the Mississippi March Against Fear.

Troublemaker provides a unique experience for the reader because the narrative begins with Bruce Hartford's parents fight for workers rights as members of the Communist Party in the 1930's and continues with the author's participation in the Freedom Movement as a member of the Congress of Racial Equality (CORE) and the Southern Christian Leadership Conference (SCLC) in the 1960's. His journey provides the reader the rare look and feel of the Freedom Movement in America through the eyes of two generations of troublemakers"

— COURTLAND COX, SNCC, Chair of the SNCC Legacy Board

"John Lewis told us to make 'good trouble.' We get a special gift in this tradition with Bruce Hartford's memoir, "Troublemaker." In telling about his life in the Civil Rights Movement, he gives us a feeling for what it was actually like to live through that period and he shares lessons so that we can learn what do to carry on those struggles today. Bruce's forceful, humble, warm, humorous character shines throughout. This is a book that helps us learn about history so we can shape it for the future. It is a joy to read."

— HEATHER BOOTH, organizer, and founder of Midwest Academy

"This is a must-read chronicle for anyone seeking to gain greater insight into the critical years of the Freedom movement, the civil rights movement, and the challenges of activism in America. The March on Washington, Selma, CORE, SCLC, SNCC, Martin Luther King, Jr. – all placed within a unique perspective. Bruce Hartford relates this important story with compassion, energy and a palpable sense of humor. It is his story, intimate and personal; but also his activist parents' story, and our collective story, no matter where we once were or where we are now on the political spectrum. Spanning multiple time periods and generations of activism, it should be read by anyone interested in learning more about what worked and what didn't in moving from the threatening atmosphere of intense racism and the McCarthy era to present day. Hartford demonstrates through this personal chronicle how one individual can indeed make a difference during his or her lifetime and leave a legacy to inspire others."

—JENNIFER LAWSON, SNCC veteran
and former Head of Programming for PBS

"Bruce Hartford's well-written and engaging memoir combines vivid detail with thoughtful analysis. His compelling account of one person's movement experiences is an important read and it will be of particular interest to those who look to the past as part of their struggle for justice today."

—EMILY CROSBY, author of "A Little Taste of Freedom" and editor of "Civil Rights History from the Ground Up"

"In Troublemaker, Bruce places you in the midst of the Civil Rights Movement. He places you within the working structure of the Southern Christian Leadership Conference. You see the personalities that were a part of SCLC. Bruce also takes us inside the homes of the people who dared to become involved. Specifically he takes us to the housing projects, into the home of the West family, a family who had very little but shared their food and their space with Bruce, as well as they did with me. He puts you on the March from Selma to Montgomery. You feel his fear. You feel his excitement. Bruce took me back to some of my experiences in the Movement. He forced me to relive the James Meredith march after Meredith was shot trying to walk across Mississippi. Reading "Troublemaker," I felt the burning in my lungs once again from the tear gas, choking and gasping for air. This is just one of the experiences that Bruce and I shared. Troublemaker provides an insider's perspective on a dark time in our country's history, and it humanizes those who were involved. It was a time when many people sacrificed a great deal and some gave their lives for the right to vote. We must never forget the price paid for this right."

—JOHN REYNOLDS, SCLC 1965-71, President, SCOPE50

"Inspiring. A gripping and emotional first person account of a young man's commitment and experiences in the Civil Rights Movement. Reading this book, I felt intimately connected with the highs and lows, as well as the fears and courage of those who participated in this period of our history. Hartford has provided an important story about how one individual, together with others of the same mind, can curve the path of history. As important in today's climate as it was in the sixties."

— JUDITH FRIEZE WRIGHT, Freedom Rider & CORE

Dedicated to the Winter Soldiers I served with:

Ken and Claire, Woody, F. Daniel, Gerry, Jay, Roberta, Fred, Michael, Mari, Richard, Robert, Josh, Lyn, the West family, Annell, Orange, Chuck, Havard, Cookie, Alphonso, Charlie & Dagmar, Alex, Joy, Jean, Chude, Wazir, Jimmy, Betita, Fred, Don, Hardy, Miriam, Mike, Marion, Gene, Cathy, and so many more.

> *Think where man's glory most begins and ends,*
> *and say my glory was I had such friends.*
> — William Butler Yeats

Acknowledgements

Cover artist: Vanessa Maynard
Cover photos: front, John Phillips, back, Bob Fitch
Editors: Pam & Michael Rosenthal, P&M Editorial Services
Commentators: Chude Allen, Heather Booth, Maria Gitin, Wesley Hogan, John Reynolds, and others

vi

Table of Contents

x

Preface

We're all shaped by our memories — accurate or not. These are memories of my four years service in the Civil Rights Movement, true as I remember them. So too are my retellings of tales told by my parents as I recall hearing them and as they shaped my life and activism.

No names have been changed in this memoir to protect either the innocent or the guilty. But this is not a muck-raking expose, so in some instances I've chosen to omit the names of a few folk whose very human failings I mention. A much larger number of names, however, are omitted because while I can remember events, names have been lost in the attic of my memory.

Some Language Notes

Elementary school gave me the impression that the meaning of words were fixed and immutable, each word and phrase meant what they taught me forevermore. Now as an old geezer — sorry, I mean *senior citizen* — I understand that the meaning and use of words are not set in stone but rather inevitably evolve and change like the meandering of a lazy river. And in some cases, language changes are the subject of social-political controversy and conflict. In my lifetime, for example, *"gay"* has evolved from a synonym of *"cheerful,"* to a positive identifier of homosexuality, to a generation-specific use as a pejorative (as in *"that's so gay"*).

As a general rule, I try to write in the language and vernacular of the times I am describing rather than the current common usages — though I do make some exceptions.

Civil Rights Movement vs Freedom Movement

As veterans of the Freedom Movement, we're constantly confronted by how the mass media and education system distorts our Movement. The very term *"Civil Rights Movement"* is itself a distortion. Many of us prefer instead to use *"Freedom Movement"* whenever we can.

Successful social movements usually address one or two specific issues as stepping stones toward broader goals. The Southern Freedom Movement focused on segregation and voting, but the Movement's vision was not limited to just the notion of achieving those two civil rights. The Movement was really about the overthrow of the entire system of feudal oppression and exploitation that had replaced slavery after the Civil War. So our songs and chants were, *"Freedom Now!"* Not *"Civil rights now!"*

By defining the Freedom Movement as a civil rights movement, the media limits its scope to that of a modest reform within a benevolent broader system. In reality, by demanding an end to segregation and restoration of voting rights for Afro-Americans and other people of color we were engaged in a fundamental attack on the existing political and economic power structure of the South — and on the national economic and political powers who accommodated and enabled race-based southern feudalism.

Negro, Black, Afro-American, African-American, and Nigger

In the 1950s and early '60s, *Negro* was the term of courtesy and respect for the descendants of African slaves, but today *Negro* is archaic with a connotation that is no longer positive. When directly quoting from the 1960s, I use *Negro* as it was intended by the speaker or author at the time. In writing this book today, I use the terms *Black* and *Afro-American* (both capitalized) interchangeably as we did in the later '60s and early '70s.

My usage of *Afro-American* follows that of SNCC veteran and author Charlie Cobb:

> I use *Afro-American* as a way of formally designating what I consider to be the ethnic group that over the past four hundred years has evolved in the United States from descendants of people from the African continent many of whom were captured and brought to the Americas as slaves. *African-American* more properly describes any former citizen of an African nation who has U.S. citizenship. — Charlie Cobb, *On the Road to Freedom.*

There is a subtle way in which a portion of white society uses *African-American* to gloss over social and political realities by seeming to equate the descendants of former slaves and Jim Crow segregation with ethnic groups who voluntarily immigrated to our shores (*Irish-Americans, Italian-Americans, Jewish-Americans,* etc). The implication being that ethnic immigrant populations overcame discrimination to lift themselves out of poverty and powerlessness by hard work and perseverance so if African-Americans have had difficulty doing so it's their fault alone.

I reject that false-equivalency. I believe the events and realities described in this memoir make clear that the oppression, exploitation, and racism experienced by Afro-Americans was (and still is) of a fundamentally different order than that experienced by white *hyphenated-Americans.*

For people of my generation — both Black and white — the word *"nigger"* is fraught with emotional trauma. To us it is a forbidden word of hate and anger and an explicit incitement to violence. It is a word that reflects an attitude of supporting racial subjugation, oppression, and exploitation and a word used to impose and reinforce that world-view. We do not use it, and most of us internally wince when we hear Afro-Americans of a younger generation casually toss it around as a colloquialism, and even more so do we cringe when younger whites act as if they are entitled to use it in a similar way. We know that for many people of color it is a word of such pain and ugliness that they do not want to read it, hear it, or allow their children to be exposed to it.

Yet I cannot truthfully convey the realities that we of the Freedom Movement faced without describing and quoting how that word was used by racists in the 1950s and '60s. So as a matter of honest history, this memoir quotes those who used it to maintain segregation and white supremacy. A context that I hope will illustrate why we still react so strongly against it when we encounter it so many decades later.

Latino, Rather Than Mexican or Chicano

In the 1960s, *Mexican* was the term commonly applied to Spanish-speaking inhabitants west of the Mississippi — the descendents of those who lived in the lands conquered by the U.S. in 1848. It was also used for *all* more recent immigrants from south of the border regardless of nationality. Later, *Chicano* became preferred (at least in California). Today, *Latino* is more inclusive of many nationalities and histories and I therefore use it in this memoir though at the time I and others mostly used *Mexican.* Note that statistics presented her for

"Latinos" were most likely labelled *Mexican* or possibly *Hispanic* in the original source.

Freedom Riders

The first racially integrated freedom ride — called a "Journey of Reconciliation" — took place in 1947 and ended with all the participants serving chain-gang prison sentences in North Carolina. The wave of Freedom Rides that began in 1961 were more successful and they ended legally-enforced segregation in inter-state travel. Those who rode the buses, braved mob violence and served their time in jail were known as "Freedom Riders."

I wasn't a Freedom Rider. At age 17, I read about them in the *Los Angeles Times* but had no thought that they had anything to do with me. When I arrived in Selma in 1965, however, I discovered that those rides had so impressed Afro-Americans living under the yoke of segregation in the Deep South that *freedom rider* had for them become a generic term for all civil rights workers who came from outside their community to support their fight for freedom. After several failed attempts to explain that while I was a freedom worker I hadn't been a Freedom Rider I accepted the title of *freedom rider* in the sense they intended and I use it that way in this memoir.

Ghetto is Not a Pejorative

In the 1960s, social-justice activists commonly used the word *"ghetto"* for Afro-American neighborhoods, particularly in the urban north, as a way of calling attention to involuntary residential segregation, economic exploitation, systemic poverty, police repression, and legal-social-cultural barriers hindering escape. For us, in many contexts *ghetto* was a term of defiant community pride and a rejection of deracialized, depoliticized euphemisms such as *inner city*. Today, *ghetto* is sometimes used as a disparaging pejorative, as in "that's so ghetto." In this memoir, *ghetto* is used as it was in the 1960s.

North & South, NorCal & SoCal

For Freedom Movement activists, the geopolitical term *South* referred to the former slave states. For us, the term *North* meant the not-South (in other words, all states *except* the former slave states). Though the terms *NorCal* and *SoCal* were not used in the 1960s, they are used here for convenience to refer to the Northern and Southern California regions.

'Frisco

For generations, sailors, longshoreman, teamsters, and other members of the working class used the nickname *'Frisco* to refer to San Francisco, a city that I love and live in. In the 1950s, elitist snobs led by newspaper columnist Herb Caen led a successful culture-war campaign to denigrate *'Frisco* as somehow socially unacceptable. I never bought into that, so I still use *'Frisco* from time to time (sometimes to the shocked consternation of others who think I'm being politically incorrect).

Acronyms

ACA: American Communications Association (1930s-1940s)
ACLU: American Civil Liberties Union
ASCS: Agriculture Stabilization & Conservation Service
AFL: American Federation of Labor
BoE: Board of Education (Los Angeles)
CIO: Congress of Industrial Organizations
CORE: Congress of Racial Equality (1942-late '60s)
CP: Communist Party of the United States of America
DCVL: Dallas County Voters League (Alabama) (1956-????)
FBI: Federal Bureau of Investigation
FSM: Free Speech Movement (UC Berkeley, 1964)
GCFM: Grenada County Freedom Movement (1966-1968)
HUAC: House Un-American Activities Committee, (1938-1975)
ILWU: International Longshore and Warehouse Union
LACMA: Los Angeles County Medical Association
MCHR: Medical Committee for Human Rights (1964-????)
MFDP: Mississippi Freedom Democratic Party (1964-late 1960s)
N-VAC: Non-Violent Action Committee (Los Angeles) (1963-1966)
NAACP: National Assoc. for the Advancement of Colored People
SCEF: Southern Conference Education Fund (1942-1985)
SCLC: Southern Christian Leadership Council
SDS: Students for a Democratic Society (1960-1969)
SNCC: Student Nonviolent Coordinating Committee (1960-late '60s)
SRA: Society of Research Administrators
SWAFCA: Southwest Alabama Farmers Cooperative Association
YCL: Young Communist League USA (1920-????)

Quotation Sources

1. Private email correspondence.
2. "Divided We Fail: Segregated and Unequal Schools in the Southland," UCLA Civil Rights Project, March 18, 2011. Orfield, Siegel-Hawley, Kucsera
3. *Fragile Roots*, Claire Hartford Hornstein, 2004.
4. "Nonviolent Training," Bruce Hartford, 2004 (www.crmvet.org)
5. "Operation Bootstrap: Beginnings," Jason Martineau
6. Claire Hartford Hornstein Oral History, 2003
7. *Selma, Lord, Selma*, Sheyann Webb & Rachel West Nelson, 1980.
8. *My Soul is Rested: The Story of the CRM in the Deep South*, Howell Raines, 1977
9. Letter to Lyn Busch, Bruce Hartford, 4/12/65
10. Article by Paul Montgomery, *New York Times*, 3/23/65
11. *Selma 1965: The March That Changed the South*, Charles Fager, 1974
12. "Our God is Marching On!" Dr. Martin Luther King, March 25, 1965
13. Kingman Brewster, *Yale Daily News* 12/3/62
14. Society of Research Administrators International website, 2018
15. Alabama literacy test, circa 1965 (www.crmvet.org)
16. Dr. Martin Luther King, *Trumpet of Conscience*, 1967
17. Eighth Report of the [Calif] Senate Fact-Finding Committee On Un-American Activities, 1955.
18. Rev. Andrew Young, *Voices of Freedom*, Henry Hampton & Steven Fayer, 1991
19. *Where Do We Go From Here: Chaos or Community?* Martin Luther King, 1967
20. *Down to the Crossroads: Civil Rights, Black Power, and the Meredith March Against Fear*, Aram Goudsouzian, 2014
21. SCLC field report, Bruce Hartford, August 2, 1966 (www.crmvet.org)
22. Don Jelinek oral history, 2005 (www.crmvet.org)
23. Mississippi Sovereignty Commission online archive
24. Letter to parents of Negro school children, Paul Brest, Marian Wright, Iris Brest 12/20/66 (www.crmvet.org)
25. Letter from Poor People's Committee to Dr. King, 1/19/68
26. *On the Road to Freedom*, Charles Cobb, 2008
27. Jean Wiley oral history, 2001 (www.crmvet.org)
28. Ron Bridgeforth, Looking Back 50 Years Later discussion group E (www.crmvet.org)
29. *Hands on the Freedom Plow*, SNCC woman 2010
30. *There is a River: The Black Struggle for Freedom in America*, Vincent Harding 1993
31. *You Can't be Neutral on a Moving Train*, Howard Zinn 2010

Song Credits

The Liberals Song, Jerry Farber
Berlin Wall,
Wade in the Water, adapted from traditional
Why Was the Darkie Born? James Bevel & Bernice Reagon
Mississippi Goddam! Nina Simone

In the CORE of LaLa Land

Dr. King and Rosa Parks inspired me to get in what I call good trouble, necessary trouble. And I think we're going to have generations for years to come that will be prepared to get in trouble, good trouble, necessary trouble. — John Lewis, SNCC.

If there is no struggle there is no progress. This struggle may be a moral one, or it may be a physical one, and it may be both moral and physical, but it must be a struggle. Power concedes nothing without a demand. It never did and it never will. If we ever get free from the oppressions and wrongs heaped upon us, we must pay for their removal. We must do this by labor, by suffering, by sacrifice, and if needs be, by our lives and the lives of others. — Frederick Douglas, 1857

FBI at the Door ~ 1953

I was born a "red diaper baby." That's not a medical term, rather it's the vernacular for a child born of lefties. My earliest political memory is of blocking a pair of FBI agents who had shown up at our door to interrogate my parents. I had to tell the two of them they weren't welcome to enter our home. I was nine or ten, which would have made it '53 or '54. I don't remember what the two agents looked like, just two grown-ups in suits.

"Are your parents home, son?"

"They don't want to talk to you."

"Can we come inside?"

"Uh-uh," shaking my head.

"Why not?"

I don't recall what (if anything) I answered. They were intimidating and I was scared — defying adults may be a favorite pastime of teenagers, but for kids it's a scary proposition. And these men were not just ordinary adults (though they looked pretty ordinary), they were FBI agents who, according to the TV, were heroic defenders of Truth, Justice, and the American Way (you know, like Superman).

They called me "smart" (not in a good way). I looked down at my feet. Eventually, they left.

My family — father, mother, younger brother, and me — were living in Los Angeles during the height of the Red Scare hysteria whipped up by Senator Joe McCarthy and his band of right-wing zealots. The Bertolinis — Ethel and Angelo Bertolini — were hiding out at our place in the Leimert Park neighborhood while their immigration case worked its way up through the appeal courts. I don't remember which of the anti-Red laws the Bertolinis were being persecuted under, but I did understand that if caught they faced arrest and deportation as "subversives."

Ethel Shapiro was a young Jew who had fled pogroms in Ukraine and legally emigrated to America in the 1920s as had her husband Angelo, a union activist who had been targeted by Mussolini's fascists in Italy. Like my parents, they were both Communists, "Reds" in the lingo of the time (and how strange I find it today that "red state" means Republican and that the logo of Macy's department store is the same red star that once identified Soviet tanks).

Of course, we're a nation of laws and rules. One of those laws prohibited police from entering your home without permission unless they either had a search warrant issued by a judge on the basis of "probable cause" or they had direct knowledge that some crime was being committed on the premises right at that moment. Under FBI rules as they existed then, had they asked my parents if the Bertolinis were inside, and been told "yes," that would have been admitting they were harboring fugitives (a felony) and the FBI could have entered to make arrests; if they lied by saying "no," that was also a felony, and if the truth ever came out it would be grounds for later arrest. "Catch-22," as we said in the '60s.

But another rule at that time prevented FBI agents from interrogating children unless their parents were present. So when they came looking for the Bertolinis and knocked on our door, I was sent out to answer while my parents and the Bertolinis listened and waited just out of sight.

As soon as the agents left, the Bertolinis were quickly moved to some other safe house. I suppose there must have been a network of safe houses sheltering folks threatened with arrest and deportation. Meanwhile, my brother and I were suddenly sent on a surprise "sleepover" with family friends. Which I realize now must have been because my parents feared the feebs might return with a search warrant. Eventually the Bertolinis' case reached the U.S. Supreme Court, which ruled in their favor so they were able to continue living in Los Angeles and be politically active for decades.

Back then membership in the Communist Party was not illegal. Nor was organizing labor unions, advocating for racial equality, marching in "Ban the Bomb" protests, supporting the United Nations, or holding similar unpopular beliefs a crime. But those *were* considered "subversive activities." Those who engaged in such subversive activities faced social ostracism, economic retaliation from both public and private employers, and in some cases physical violence. In many southern states, for example, the NAACP was officially designated a "subversive" organization. If you were a teacher or other government employee, being an NAACP member was grounds for immediate termination.

No one was immune from these political witch hunts. The great comedy actor Charlie Chaplin was forced to leave the country because, at President Roosevelt's request, he'd helped raise money for Soviet war relief during World War II. That made him a "pinko" in the eyes of the anti-communist zealots. It's not clear which they considered worse, his support for Red Russia or his association with FDR. Right-wing bigots even whipped up a hue and cry to deport Albert Einstein as an "undesirable alien" because he spoke out against the use of nuclear weapons and in favor of peace and the United Nations. Fortunately, the defense establishment squashed that effort — for obvious reasons.

Not that I knew much about any of that at the time. The Communist Party had an ironclad rule — well, all their rules were ironclad — that parents were not allowed to tell their children that they were Communists or to discuss political work where the kids might overhear. Supposedly, this was for "security reasons," because a child might innocently mention something that would then wend its way to the FBI. So I grew up surrounded by secrets, innuendoes, and questions that I knew only enough to know I couldn't ask about.

What I officially knew — as opposed to what I suspected but dared not utter — was that my parents and all their friends (such as the Bertolinis) were "progressives." Which meant that they went to meetings most evenings, participated in occasional protest marches, had lots of arguments with other grown-ups in our living room, signed petitions, passionately supported labor unions, opposed the Korean War, and read the *People's World* and *National Guardian* newspapers. If we visited someone's home and they had shelves jam-crammed with books, I intuitively knew they were "progressives" too, even though no explicitly Marxist books were visible where some stranger might see them. If they didn't have a ton of books, then they were merely ordinary neighbors or acquaintances with whom secrets must not be mentioned or shared.

Years later, my mom — Claire Brown Iceland Hartford Hornstein — told me why we had moved from our home in Altadena to the Leimert Park area of Los Angeles in the summer of '51 when I was seven years old and just starting second grade. Altadena was a suburb of Pasadena, which was itself a suburb of L.A. (good ol' LaLa Land, where even the suburbs have suburbs). Altadena was not incorporated as a city, so it was governed by the county Board of Supervisors, which passed a law that membership in a subversive organization was grounds for declaring you an "unfit parent," which meant that your kids could be taken away and placed in foster care. So all the Reds in Altadena had to get out of town — quick. Hence our move into Los Angeles proper.

At that age I knew none of the political background, nor was it explained to me why we were moving. Home was where we lived, school was where I had to go. Altadena or L.A., it made no difference to me and even less to my two-year-old brother Dan. I was, though, glad to get away from our next-door neighbor, a man who was mean and yelled at me for reasons I never understood. Of course, as a seven-year-old I usually had only the vaguest notion of why grown-ups did anything they did, nor did

I particularly care. It was only years later that I learned his antagonism was political, he considered us a family of "Red traitors" because my parents opposed the Korean War and supported labor unions.

I don't know whether the Party's edict against parents discussing politics with their kids helped keep the FBI at bay (personally I doubt it), but I know it greatly increased *my* anxiety. At night after I had been put to bed, I would occasionally creep downstairs to covertly eavesdrop on the adult meetings going on in our living room. I could sense their fear and tension as they discussed hearings, trials, and the imminent threat of prison and deportation. I was terrified that Mom and Dad would be taken away, and I feared I would be left alone. I did understand, though, that asking them anything about it, particularly what would happen to me, was forbidden — taboo. So I was left to endure those fears on my own. Today, I'm embarrassed to admit that "What will happen to me?" was my selfish concern. Perhaps if they'd been able to talk openly to me I'd have been less self-centered. Certainly I would have been less frightened.

Not surprisingly, I didn't have many neighborhood friends and my social world was mainly kids I knew from my parents' political circles — an interracial collection of other red diaper babies and their parents. As we grew up, it never occurred to us that having playmates of different races was strange or unusual, that's just the way it was. When our parents could afford it, Dan and I were sent to a lefty summer camp in the San Bernardino Mountains for a couple of weeks each summer. I forget what it was named — we kids called it "Commie Camp" — and for all I knew it might have been the only interracial summer camp in all of Southern California.

Some years after the FBI incident I was having a birthday party, I guess maybe I was 12 or 13, and that day the Bertolinis came by to talk to my parents about some adult stuff. For a birthday present they gave me an engraved steel letter opener — obviously something they'd just grabbed at the last minute, it wasn't even gift-wrapped. I was polite and thanked them, but what did I need a letter opener for? Nobody ever sent me mail. They sensed that their gift wasn't a hit. "It's from Italy," Angelo earnestly told me as if that would make a difference.

After the party I gave the letter opener to Ken, my father. My brother and I always called him "Ken," never "Dad" or "Pop," I assume because that was how he identified himself to us when we were first learning words. To this day in our family, we still refer to him as "Ken," but when discussing him with other people I use "Dad" just as often. Anyway, he used that letter opener for the rest of his life. When he died in 1972 it came back to me and I've been using it ever since — more than 45 years now. I can't remember a single toy or gift I got on that birthday, or any of my other birthdays for that matter, but every time I open a bill or fund appeal with that (now rusty) letter opener I remember the Bertolinis and the time I had to block the FBI at the door.

A Four-Nevers Jew ~ 1958

I started high school in the fall of 1958. Most Los Angeles high schools were sharply segregated by race, but Dorsey High where I went was one of the few exceptions. It was wonderfully integrated. It was one-quarter white, a quarter Black, a quarter Latino (or "Mexican" as we said back then), and a quarter Asian (mostly Japanese). The buildings were arranged in a way that they formed triangles of open space and each race adopted its own triangle. If you went into the wrong triangle you got pushed out or maybe beaten up. Unfortunately for me, the whites — or more accurately the white bullies — weren't completely convinced that Jews counted as fully "white." And, of course, I was not a normal Jew, I was a lefty-Jew. And even worse, I was the kind of weirdo who liked to read books rather than play sports. So I didn't really have any turf at all.

After school I kept mainly to myself, reading in my room. Comic books when I was in grade school, by high school I was devouring both novels and nonfiction books — history mostly. Books about the Holocaust like *Diary of Anne Frank* and John Hersey's *The Wall* had become widely available and I went deep into the Holocaust. Real deep.

And the deeper I got the angrier I became. At the Germans and Poles and French and other anti-Semites, but also at those who stood by and did nothing to halt the genocide. And not just against Jews, but also Gypsies, trade unionists, intellectuals, homosexuals, liberals, and, of course, Reds. I admired Churchill and Roosevelt for fighting the Nazis and I despised them for doing nothing about the death camps. And I particularly loathed Breckinridge Long, the State Department bureaucrat who, along with a posse of other government anti-Semites, did everything they could to bar Jews from reaching safety, sending them back to extermination without a qualm of hesitation.

By this time my parents were no longer members of the Communist Party, but they were still lefties at heart. My father grew up Christian (Presbyterian) in Kentucky and I think my mom's family was pro forma Jewish, probably some version of semi-Orthodox. But neither of my parents was religious at all. Or, I suppose more accurately, socialism and political causes were their religion. The only religious institution we ever (occasionally) visited was the First Unitarian Church — not for anything to do with God, but because under Rev. Stephen Fritchman it was a bulwark of resistance against McCarthyism, and he and his church provided support for victims of the witch hunts.

Neither I nor my brother Dan were ever baptized or Bar Mitzvahed, which was fine by both of us. (We were circumcised, though, because hospitals did that for all male babies as a matter of course, it had no religious significance to my parents or me.) But for our benefit, so we wouldn't feel alienated from the other kids and bereft of parental love in the form of loot — excuse me, I mean gifts — our family celebrated both Christmas and Hanukkah with both tree and menorah. Yaay — two sets of presents!

Dan was five years younger than me and when we were kids that was a gap too big to bridge. We had our usual sibling rivalries and conflicts, "my toy," "my space," "I want," "gimme," but though we somewhat grudgingly shared a home and parents, our lives and interests didn't really intersect much at all. I was nerdy, bookish, and wordy, while he took after our father, with interests in carpentry and mechanics.

For myself, I guess it was about the time I entered high school that I decided on my own to start considering myself a Jew, even though I'd never actually been inside a synagogue in my entire life — and had no desire or interest in ever doing so. Looking back, I'm pretty sure Leon Uris's novel *Exodus* influenced me quite a bit, both in terms of seeing myself as Jewish and drawing me deeper into reading and thinking about the Holocaust. But I saw myself as a cultural Jew, rather than a religious Jew.

Both my parents were skilled and effective political organizers — abilities which meant little to me as a kid. Mom, however, was also a world-class "worrywart" (my dad's term) and that affected my life a whole lot. Among the vast array of things she worried about — from world peace to the neatness of my room (neither of which she was ever able to do much about) — was my spending too much time reading alone rather than socializing with my peers like a "normal" kid. So she nagged me into joining the local B'nai B'rith Youth Organization (I think they just call it "BBYO" now).

Naturally, the other BBYO kids asked me what kind of Jew I was — Reform, Orthodox, Conservative, what? They were mostly Reform or Conservative, but I wasn't any of the recognized denominations and I only had the vaguest idea of what the differences between them were. So I started telling 'em I was a *"Four-Nevers Jew"* — *Never Forget, Never Forgive,*

Never Again, and *Never Stand By* while others are persecuted. Well, that set them back a bit — and also confirmed me as a real "oddball" outsider.

As the twig is bent, so grows the tree.

CORE? What's a CORE? ~ 1963

I was 19 years old in the spring of 1963, just finishing up my second year at Los Angeles City College (LACC). Back then it was a "junior college" but now they're called "community colleges," which I suppose sounds more erudite. Like many teens, I had no clue what I was doing with my life. I went from high school right into college because my parents insisted. Neither of them had any kind of higher education — my mom had a high school diploma, my dad only completed sixth grade — but they were adamant, I had to get that degree. They saw that piece of parchment as some kind of magic talisman that would somehow protect me from a life of hardship and poverty. As it turned out, I never did get one of those degrees they had such faith in, and so far at age 75 I've experienced no ill effects from its lack.

After classes I began hanging out at Pogo's Swamp, a beatnik coffeehouse on Melrose Avenue a short block from the LACC campus. It was only later that I learned that the Swamp had an unusual reputation as a "racially integrated" venue. As I recall, a Black guy named Levi ran it and the clientele was mixed — which, given my background, seemed quite normal and unremarkable to me. But it was considered strange and noteworthy by others.

One afternoon I was there minding my own business, reading or playing chess or something, and Levi said, "Hey, come by later tonight, a guy from CORE's gonna show movies from the Torrance protests." Well, I knew Torrance was one of L.A.'s many suburbs, but I had no idea what a CORE was. Turned out it was the Congress of Racial Equality. They had this *meshugana* idea that people should be allowed to buy homes and rent apartments wherever they wanted and could afford, regardless of their race or religion. Like so many L.A. suburbs at the time, Torrance was 100% white — and they were determined to keep it that way. Developers, realtors, bankers, homeowners, apartment landlords, and the federal government cooperated to prevent nonwhites from moving in. Some developments also barred Jews.

The CORE guy, Jim, showed up right on time with a 16mm projector and a portable screen. He was Latino, maybe a couple of years older than me. He had about ten or fifteen minutes of film showing CORE pickets at one of the housing tracts developed by Don Wilson, the huge real estate baron. There were a dozen or so CORE protesters with signs and leaflets — half Black, half white — walking back and forth on the sidewalk as permitted by the U.S. Constitution. They were outnumbered and under attack by members of the American Nazi Party in full swastika uniform. jackboots, armbands, stiff-arm salutes, "Heil Hitler! Kill the Jews! Down with the niggers!" The whole Nazi rigmarole.

"Holy shit!" I thought to myself. "What the fuck is this?"

When he finished I was the only one to go up to him afterward, "I don't know who you guys are, but if you're against the Nazis I'm with you. When's your next picket line, I'll be there."

He was pleased that I wanted to join them — that's why he was showing the film, after all — but there was a "but." A big "BUT." He told me they were "nonviolent," and that I had to agree to be nonviolent too. Nonviolent? What's that? He explained and gave me a nicely printed two-color brochure with a drawing of Gandhi on the cover. It was titled "CORE Rules for Action." I still have it more than 50 years later and a scanned image of it is displayed on the Civil Rights Movement Veterans website (www.crmvet.org).

"Okay, whatever," I told him. "When and where do I show up?"

The following Saturday I was on the line in Torrance. CORE picketed every Saturday and Sunday afternoon when people were looking to buy homes, and as it turned out, accepting nonviolence wasn't all that hard for me — I was one of those bookish, scrawny kids not much given to fighting. In any sort of conflict my natural weapon of choice was my mouth, not my fists. Which, I suppose, is one of the reasons I got bullied a lot. (If my mouth failed, I relied on swift feet to carry me out of danger — sometimes that worked, sometimes it didn't.)

The tract's official name was Southwood Royale, but we always referred to it as "Don Wilson." As required by CORE rules at that time, I signed in with the picket captain, a tall, thin, Afro-American named F. Daniel Gray, who everyone called "Danny." I recognized him as the leader right off because he was carrying the clipboard. In the early '60s, battery-powered bullhorns were too expensive for little civil rights groups, so the sign-in clipboard was the badge of leadership.

The Southwood Royale sales office was one of the homes in the middle of the development. About a dozen of us walked back and forth on the sidewalk in front of the office with signs calling for equality, justice, and fair housing. You know, really *subversive* concepts.

The Nazis were there too with their swastika armbands and brownshirt uniforms. "Kill the niggers! Gas the kikes! Seig Heil! Seig Heil!" They outnumbered us two to one.

These Nazis were scary. They weren't your handful of pathetic Nazis surrounded by a throng of anti-racist protesters, the way it might be today in most places. This was a band of racist thugs threatening a little CORE picket line. The Torrance police kept them at a distance so they couldn't physically assault us, but not so far that they couldn't hit us with thrown eggs and small stones from the beds of decorative gravel.

None of the sales agents, cops, home buyers, or bystanders seemed actively pro-Nazi, but they were definitely anti-us — anti-protest, anti-CORE, and definitely anti-Black. It was clear they considered us CORE members to be the "troublemakers." Which in my view was completely ass-backwards. *They* were the ones practicing racial discrimination. That was the real trouble, we were just trying to correct it.

Yet in another sense I have to admit it was true, we *were* "troublemakers." As I later learned when I attended my first nonviolent training session, it's a basic principle of nonviolent resistance that injustice and evil must not be allowed to carry out business as usual in silence. Our purpose was to directly call attention to what they were doing. To loudly and disruptively say, "*No! This is wrong. No! This is not acceptable.*" In other words, to raise a ruckus about it — to make trouble over it. "Troublemakers?" Yes, quite so.

For me, it was a tense and scary afternoon. It was also thrilling and uplifting. I knew no one else on the line (Jim wasn't there that day), but after a few minutes that didn't matter as eggs, rocks, and Nazi hate kept coming at us while people jostled and shoved us as they pushed past to go in and out of the sales office.

We responded by defiantly singing freedom songs. I didn't know any of the church-based songs like *We Shall Overcome, Oh Freedom,* or *This Little Light of Mine,* but those adapted from union picket lines — *Which Side Are You On, We Shall Not Be Moved* — those were the soundtrack of my childhood. Though I can't carry a tune to save my life, I joined in full voice. I was fascinated by the way the CORE song leader used different songs and verses composed on the spot to directly respond to and counter our adversaries. In those days, on a well-managed CORE action, the designated song leader was second in command, and it was a post of both skill and honor.

A police paddy wagon was parked nearby, and I realized it was there to haul us off to jail if we gave the cops the slightest pretext to arrest us. But so long as we remained nonviolent and picketed legally on the sidewalk they had no excuse to haul us away — as they clearly wanted to do.

I don't recall how long we picketed, probably most of the afternoon and then again the next day on Sunday. And back again the following weekend, alternating between Don Wilson and another segregated housing tract called Sun Ray Estates.

As the school semester wound down I spent more and more time with CORE, participating in nonviolent training sessions, attending meetings at CORE's office on Venice Boulevard at the edge of the ghetto, making signs, handing out flyers, and cranking the old mimeograph machine that we used to run off our leaflets. Some years later I saw *Fiddler on the Roof* — one of my favorite films. There's a scene where everyone is cooing over something that at first you assume must be a baby in a crib, but then discover is a pedal-operated sewing machine for Motel the tailor. The first time I saw that scene, I flashed back to how we all felt when L.A. CORE was finally able to afford a Gestetner electric-powered mimeo and we no longer had to crank that damned drum by hand. In the mid-'60s, if you were a serious political organization, you had a Gestetner.

I graduated LACC in June of 1963 with an Associate of Arts degree (my one and only academic achievement). It meant so little to me that I didn't bother to attend the ceremony. They had to mail it to me — well, actually to my parents, I had no interest in it. I was now a dedicated CORE activist, that's what was important to me.

This all occurred right at a time that the entire Freedom Movement was sweeping across the nation. Headlines were filled with Freedom Movement battles — Birmingham, Greenwood, 'Frisco, Durham, New York, Gadsden, Philly, Danville. North and South. The Movement was growing exponentially. As it turned out, those Torrance actions were the last time we were ever outnumbered by counter protesters. By the fall of '63, it was the Los Angeles Police Department (LAPD) we were confronting, not the Nazis. Personally, I preferred the Nazis. They were a lot more honest about what they were about — and less violent.

"Are You the Communists?" ~ 1932

My father, Ken, was born in 1908. He was a Kentucky boy, born and raised. Five foot ten or so, average build, with a friendly smile and a leathery face. I once thought that if I were casting an actor to play him in a film, Sam Shepard would be the best match in both looks and manner. As a child, he completed sixth grade — which as everyone from his neck of the woods knew was all the schooling anyone really needed, "'cepting them as had delusions of grandeur," of course.

Ken's father was a wayward son of the Kettringham clan of Houston Texas. He had run off to join a traveling carnival (or possibly it was a circus, opinions differ). He had no show business talent whatsoever, but he excelled at shady business, so he was the "advance man" who rented the land where the show set up, arranged publicity, bribed the appropriate public officials, and came to mutually beneficial arrangements with the local saloon owners, bordello madams, scammers, pickpockets, and general riffraff.

I guess he was considered a blot on the Kettringham escutcheon because his family back in Houston ordered him to change his name lest he bring such social shame on his sisters that they'd be unable to make suitable marriages. So he took the name "Hartford," perhaps because that's the city where the show was at the time. Eventually he married a Kentucky woman, fathered half a dozen kids, and then abandoned them all when my dad was five or six. They never heard from him again.

One of my greatest regrets is that my father died before I managed to evolve from rebellious teenager to good friend. So I never got to hear his tales of being a union organizer and Communist Party (CP) activist in the South. I knew bits and pieces of a few stories, but it wasn't until I was in my mid-30s that I began to hear my mom's stories in full rich detail, and by then my father had already passed. To this day, I blame my younger self for rebuffing my parents to protect a hard-won independence that I should have known they could no longer really threaten. Sometimes, I guess, it's harder to accept victory and make peace than it is to continue old habits of hostility and isolation.

I also continue to resent the Communist Party for their edict ordering parents to conceal from their children vital and important portions of their lives. Almost all of the heritage I should have heard and learned around the kitchen table was denied me — and to this day it still pisses me off.

One of the few stories Ken did tell me was how he became a union man. After finishing elementary school at the age of 11 or 12 he found work as a telegraph messenger boy in the "big city" of Cincinnati. I guess that must have been around 1919 or '20 — just after The Great War to End All Wars. I think he worked for Western Union, or possibly the rival Postal Telegraph. He was smart and diligent and soon worked his way up the ranks to become a highly skilled telegraph operator back in the days when it was done by hand — you know, *dot-dot, dit-dot, dot-dit.*

Decades later, when I was a kid, I came across the old telegraph key he used to tap out the Morse code messages across the wires. He had kept it all those years. I guess that like chefs with their personal knife kits and mechanics with their tools, telegraphers carried their personal key with them from job to job and shift to shift. I played with it as a toy, without the slightest understanding of what it must have meant to him.

When the Depression hit in 1929 there was mass unemployment, hunger, and desperation. Anyone who had a job held on to it for dear life. Aware of that, the company came up with a brilliant, cost-saving, profit-enhancing scheme, one worthy of a Stanford MBA. They built a shed of galvanized tin — freezing cold in the winter, sweltering hot in the summer — and furnished it with wooden benches. Then they laid off all the skilled operators and replaced them with high school kids at half the wages. The regulars waited in the shed until the kids screwed up the message queue, then the kids were laid off and the regulars brought back to clean up their mess. As soon as order was restored, the operators were laid off again and the kids put back on the wire. So Ken might get an hour or two of work a day — or more, or less.

One day he was sitting in the shed reading the city's main paper the *Cincinnati Daily Fascist* — okay, okay, I know that wasn't its formal name, but it accurately denotes their political bent — and he saw this article describing how loathsome Reds were trying to sabotage America's communications industry by forming a communist union of telegraph workers. (To the *Daily Fascist* all unions were "communist" by definition.) In a serious lapse of judgement, though, the article gave the name of the union and let slip that its headquarters were in wicked New York City — you know, *Jew York*, that foul Gotham of foreigners, that decadent wellspring of everything corrupt and un-American.

The next time my father was on the wire, he slipped in a telegram addressed to the American Communications Association (ACA), asking, "Are you the Communists?"

They quickly replied, explaining they weren't Communists, but rather simple trade unionists trying to win higher wages and better working conditions for exploited and abused workers.

My dad didn't hesitate a moment. "I don't care who you are. Please come to Cincinnati. We need you."

They did send someone. And as it turned out, a lot of the ACA leaders and organizers *were* Communists. My father organized the Cincinnati local for them and they organized him into the Party. And for the CP, he was a real treasure. Not only was he a crackerjack organizer, he was a native-born, white southerner in a party dominated by Jews, European immigrants, and Easterners. When he wanted to, he could talk "good ol' boy" with a slow southern drawl, and unlike so many southern whites, he wasn't noticeably racist — he got on fine with Black folk (not that there were that many of them working in the telegraph industry, of course).

Looking back on it now, I think the reason he was such a good organizer is that, like my mom, he approached people and dealt with them on a human, sharing level rather than with an ideological, rhetorical, "I'll set you straight" arrogance. He walked alongside those he was organizing, not ahead of them. Certainly he provided leadership, but it was leadership by example, and leadership as a kind of teaching, where he was *also* a student of the people he was organizing. A style of political work that I still aspire to, though sadly with but limited success.

When I later encountered the organizing ethos of the Student Nonviolent Coordinating Committee (SNCC) and their ideal of non-egoistic leadership, it seemed familiar to me because it reminded me so much of how my dad worked. Both Ken and Mom were highly effective organizers — each in their own way, she the inspiring spitfire, he the calm, rock-steady friend you turned to in need. They had that in common, and I think it's one of the reasons they were attracted to each other.

Unlike my mom, though, Ken was a voracious reader and a self-taught intellectual. He was one of the very few rank-and-file Party members who had not only read Marx, Lenin, Stalin, and the rest of the Bolshevik boys, he actually understood what he read (to the extent it was understandable by anyone at all).

The truth is, and I better own up to this now, I harbor considerable residual hostility against the Communist Party and similar Marxist organizations with which I, my parents, and my friends have had direct dealings in the course of my admittedly disreputable life. But not from enmity to Marxism's professed goals of social equality, economic justice, real democracy, and racial brotherhood — ideals I continue to share — but because the Party's real-life behavior fell so enormously short of those ideals as to be antagonistic to them.

Busting My Block ~ 1957

After I began working with CORE in the spring of '63, I realized that the Torrance picket line had not been my first experience with housing segregation.

For most of my childhood after we had to flee Altadena, we lived on Arlington Avenue just south of 48th Street. This was on the edge of the Leimert Park neighborhood not too far from Vernon and Western. Ours was a working-class block of single-family homes on modest lots. The men were mostly craftsmen and factory workers in jobs that paid union wages, blue- and white-collar civil service employees, owner-operators of very small businesses, and so on. The women either kept house or worked as teachers, typists, salesclerks, and waitresses. Everyone was white. Like most of L.A.'s working-class neighborhoods, ours was ethnically mixed — Irish, WASP, Italian, Polish, and so on — but all white, all the time.

When we arrived in the early 1950s, the border of the Afro-American ghetto was Western Avenue six blocks east of Arlington. That boundary line was sharp as a knife and referred to by civil rights activists as "the Western Wall." The blocks to the west of Western were all white, those to the east were all Black.

This was an era of great migrations. Blacks were fleeing the Jim Crow South in massive numbers, the new Immigration Act had recently opened up opportunities for Asians seeking opportunity in America, and employers looking for low-wage labor were luring Latinos to migrate *norte*. But as they flowed into Southern California they could only find housing in overcrowded ghettos, barrios, and "towns" (Chinatown, Koreatown, Japantown). Yet with so many nonwhites arriving every year, the Los Angeles ghettos had to expand — slowly, but steadily. Which is how I came to personally encounter residential segregation and the tender mercies of the real estate industry.

A few years after we moved in, the local real estate association decided to "break" the Western Wall and begin expanding the Afro-American ghetto in our direction. Over the next few years, block by block, the ghetto steadily advanced toward us. I was too young to pay much attention to any of that until I became a paperboy delivering the *Angeles Mesa News* two mornings a week. My delivery route took me into blocks that were now entirely Black and part of my job was collecting the subscription fee door-to-door. I sensed the suspicion of me as a white kid on the wrong side of the line. It was scary. I used to dread making collections on that portion of my route. Not because anyone ever actually harmed me, but because the hostility was palpable in tone of voice and angry stares that clearly demanded to know "What you doing here, white boy?"

As the ghetto boundary shifted closer and closer to Arlington Avenue, fear and hatred of Blacks by our white neighbors dramatically intensified — *They* were coming! Some of that white anger was aimed at us, because so far as I know my family and our next-door neighbors were the only Jews on the block, and we were certainly the only ones who ever had Afro-American guests or Black kids playing with my brother and me in the front yard.

On one or two occasions, one of those Black dinner guests was Paul Robeson, the famous activist/singer/thespian. Sadly, now, I have no real recollection of him. I was just nine or ten and my main concern was finishing the meal so I could watch my favorite TV show, *"Time for Beany"* (Cecil the Seasick Sea Serpent, Captain Huff'n'puff, and Tear-Along the Dotted Lion were my favorite characters).

Looking back on it now, it's hard to say how much of the hostility directed against us by our white neighbors was because my parents were known or thought to be "Reds," and how much was because we obviously favored integration.

Of course, the white kids echoed their parent's antagonism with regard to both Blacks and me. As the years went by, those who were bigger or older expressed their hostility through physical bullying — one time a gang of half a dozen or so surrounded me while I was riding my bike and stole my dad's leather saddle bags from his motorcycle days that I was so proud of. I was so ashamed that bullies had stolen them from me that I never told him. Other times, two or three bigger kids would verbally harass me and then escalate to punches and kicks until I was knocked down. Former playmates were ordered by their parents to avoid me, and most of the rest intuitively understood that I was a pariah and treated me accordingly. So I grew up lonely with no friends on the block.

Then one year in the mid-1950s when I was 12 or 13 and an inmate at Audubon Junior High, the realtors "busted" our block. Meaning they sold a home to an Afro-American family — to the horror and fury of our white neighbors.

As the older brother, I had the honor of mowing our front lawn every weekend. This was before lawn mowers had motors — they had to be pushed by resentful teenage boys. It was a hard, sweaty job that I absolutely loathed. So whenever a real estate agent would drop by uninvited — which they did constantly that summer, often two or three in a single day — I took the opportunity to malinger and eavesdrop as they stood at our door oozing insincere friendship as they talked to my dad (Mom wouldn't speak to them).

"Oh, Mr. Hartford, I am sure you're aware of what's happening to the neighborhood. I see you have children, I can't even imagine what's going to happen to the schools. And, of course, you know how much property values are going to plummet." (If I'd had a sister, I'm sure they would have played that card too.)

Then — out of the goodness of their hearts you understand, because they really wanted to help us — they'd offer to buy our home themselves (as a kindly service, you see). *Yes, sir!* Right then and there. They had checkbook and transfer documents with them for an immediate sale. The amount they offered, of course, was well below fair market price.

Nowadays we call them "speculators," but they were just real estate agents back then. They'd buy these homes for significantly less than what they were worth on the open market. Then within a week or so — two weeks at the outside — they'd sell at an inflated price (and a high-interest mortgage) to Black families trying to escape the ghetto. No muss, no fuss, hardly any work, and all the profit into their own pockets. Over the course of that one summer, just three months, every house on our block was flipped from white to Black except for us and one immigrant family from Sweden who didn't understand what was going on and saw no reason to sell their home at a loss.

Later, through my work with CORE, I learned more about L.A.'s well-organized mechanism of formalized residential segregation. Whites, Blacks, Latinos, Asians all had their assigned zones. It was an elaborate and complex system, managed and controlled nationwide by private real estate associations, commercial banks, and federal government housing agencies to explicitly control where different races lived. It came to be called "redlining" — a term that originated with the Federal Housing Authority system of color-coding neighborhoods for the specific and explicit purpose of denying government-insured loans to nonwhites, particularly Blacks. Similarly, the Home Owners' Loan Corporation (another federal agency) *required* that "restrictive covenants" forbidding sale to nonwhites cover all properties purchased with loans they insured.

The National Association of Real Estate Boards code of ethics stated it quite plainly: "A realtor should never be instrumental in introducing into a neighborhood ... any race or nationality, or any individuals, whose presence will clearly be detrimental to property values" — in other words no nonwhites and, in some areas no Jews. So on the white side of a redline border, no realtor would show a house to any nonwhite, no bank would grant a mortgage, no government agency would offer or insure a loan, and no landlord would rent an apartment. On the other side of the line, it would be just the reverse — no whites permitted. The result was ghettos so sharply defined that in some cases everyone living on one side of a street might be white while those living across the street might be entirely Black. Or Latino. Or Asian.

Today, mass media and our school systems present the overt, in-your-face racism of the 1950s as moral, psychological, and sociological issues — which they were. But they tend to gloss over the deep economic roots of segregation. For the real estate industry, it wasn't really about personal racial attitudes, because housing segregation was enormously profitable. By ruthlessly constricting the housing supply, the industry forced families who desperately needed a roof over their heads to pay premium rent for rundown, poorly maintained apartments and left them with no choice but to buy overpriced homes with predatory mortgages charging excessive interest rates.

I mean, do the math. There were 80 homes on my Arlington block. I was just a kid, I don't know what the actual numbers were, but suppose the realtors bought each house for $5,000 less than it was worth and sold it for $5,000 more than its fair market price. That's a $10,000 profit for little more than paper-shuffling. For 80 houses — well, 78 not counting us and the Strandbergs — that totaled out to $780,000 pure profit for just our one single block. (For comparison, $780,000 in 1957 is the equivalent of almost $7,000,000 in 2018.)

Sweet deal — for them. In a normal home sale the real estate agents get a small percentage of the sales price as their commission, but when they busted a block they bought the houses from the white owners themselves — and reaped the profits. Like sharks in a feeding frenzy, they ripped off everyone, whites and Afro-Americans alike. It didn't matter what the broker's personal feelings were toward Blacks, it didn't matter what their sociological or psychological attitudes were regarding race — a buck was a buck and ten grand was ten grand. Segregation was making them rich and that's why the real estate industry fought so fiercely against open housing legislation.

But it wasn't so sweet for the rest of us — Black or white. There was enormous racial tension. As our white working-class (former) neighbors saw it, they were being driven out of a neighborhood they'd grown up in and forced to sell their only real financial asset at a loss. As for the Black families coming in, they were encountering ferocious race hatred from the whites who were fleeing en masse. And for those who hoped to escape the ghetto, the ghetto was coming right on their heels.

Those racial tensions and hostilities flowed down to us kids. White kids beat up Black kids, Black kids beat up white kids. One day I was walking home from the bus stop at Vernon and Arlington when three Afro-American kids who I'd never seen before jumped me, hitting me with their fists and swinging a 2x4 at my head. Fortunately I was a fast runner, so I got away without noticeable damage. *"But why me? What'd I ever do to them?"*

Looking back on it now, I understand they were probably retaliating for something similar that had happened to them at the hands of white kids. In some vague way I might even have sort of understood that at the time. But that didn't erase the anxiety and shame I felt at having to run away. Years later, of course, I embraced running away as a valid and effective tactic of nonviolence. On at least one occasion it may well have saved my life, and I later took pride in my high-speed, evasive-driving skills. But that 13-year-old me in 1957 was deeply humiliated. So shamed that I said nothing about it to my parents. Not that there was anything they could have done. And so it went, hatred begetting more hatred.

Anyway, by the end of that year we were one of a small handful of white families still living in the ghetto on the wrong side of the border. Now we were the unwelcome white interlopers. As the redline moved past us to the west, racial tension on our block eventually eased off a bit — but it was always there to some degree.

We remained on Arlington for a few more years, but eventually moved because the neighborhood schools quickly deteriorated as they became more nonwhite. Their funding declined and the best and most experienced teachers were shifted to "white" schools elsewhere. Toward the end of the 1950s, we moved to Edgemont Street a block from Los Angeles City College — an area called "East Hollywood." Don't let that word Hollywood fool you though, it was another white working-class area. But unlike Arlington Avenue there was a sprinkling of Bohemian types — college students, writers and intellectuals, struggling actors waiting table and driving hack. And in addition to such artsy riffraff, the neighborhood did include some Blacks, Latinos, and Jews. Pogo's Swamp, where I later encountered CORE, was just around the corner.

Fighting for Fair Housing ~ 1963

The 1963 protests against segregated housing by Los Angeles CORE were not unique of course. Throughout the 1950s and '60s, battles against housing discrimination flared across California and the nation. While L.A. CORE was protesting in Torrance, the NAACP and Northern California CORE chapters were waging a legislative battle in Sacramento for the California Fair Housing Act — commonly known as the "Rumford Act" — a law that would outlaw redlining and other forms of housing discrimination statewide.

Our demonstrations in Torrance were also intended to support that legislative fight. On one occasion we protested outside a Real Estate Board meeting which was being held at a suburban Ramada Inn. First we picketed outside. Then, once their meeting began, our line of about a dozen CORE members entered the building without permission and we sang as loud as we could while we marched down the hallway past the room they were using. We left before the cops arrived to arrest us for trespass. I was thrilled by our brazen defiance of the laws prohibiting protests on private property. At the same time, I was anxious about being arrested and so I was quite relieved when we safely exited and resumed our legal sidewalk protest.

For three weeks up in Sacramento, NorCal CORE members staged a round-the-clock sit-in on the marble floor of the Capitol Rotunda to demand passage of the Rumford bill. It was a fierce fight. Republican legislators who worshiped at the altar of Private Property ferociously defended the absolute right of owners to freely do whatever they wanted with their real estate regardless of broader social or economic consequences. In their opinion, that included the right to racially discriminate and maintain all-white neighborhoods. It wasn't until the last minute of the last session, on July 21, 1963, that their opposition was overcome and the bill was passed. Governor Edmund Brown — father of Governor Jerry Brown — signed it into law.

There was joyous celebration in the L.A. CORE office. We all basked in the satisfied glow of a great victory in a righteous cause an in the course of some serious partying I was introduced to something called a "tequila shot." I'm pretty sure we had a lot of fun that night, but the details are somewhat blurry.

Our victory didn't last long though. The California Real Estate Association, which had been fighting the Rumsford bill with every dollar and dime at their disposal, immediately launched a well-financed initiative campaign to repeal it. They had no trouble getting thousands of whites to sign their petition. In November of 1964 voters overwhelmingly passed Proposition14 by a two-thirds margin.

That emphatic embrace of racism and repudiation of integration by the great majority of white voters was a low point in my life. It depressed and discouraged me. And it showed me how little progress we had made in 18 months of nonviolent protest and direct action. In my initial naive idealism, I had assumed that all we had to do was expose the injustice, unfairness, and un-Americanism of discrimination and segregation for people to reject it — that once we exposed the cruel reality, folks would stand on the side of justice. Nope. Now I knew better.

Two years later, in 1966, the California Supreme Court overturned Prop 14 on constitutional grounds, restoring the Rumford Act. Again there were court challenges delaying its implementation. Then, in the wake of violent ghetto revolts in more than 100 cities across the country after Martin Luther King was assassinated while supporting the sanitation workers' strike in Memphis, Congress passed a national Fair Housing Act in 1968.

California's Rumford Act and the federal Fair Housing Act outlawed most (though not all) overt, explicit forms of housing discrimination. But over the decades since, many in the real estate and banking industries continued to covertly evade those fair housing laws by various stratagems and subterfuges. And to this day, some local governments use zoning rules, building permits, urban renewal projects, municipal ordinances, subsidies, set-asides, and highway-planning schemes for the same purpose.

After the fair housing laws went into effect, whites migrated farther out from the city center as the nonwhite inner-city population expanded. As a result, many of the formerly all-white middle and working-class areas where we of CORE protested eventually become racially mixed or predominantly nonwhite. For example:

L.A. in 1960: roughly 70% white, 13% Black and 10% Latino.
L.A. in 2010: roughly 30% white, 10% Black, and 50% Latino.

Torrance in 1960: almost entirely white.
Torrance in 2010: 51% white, 3% Black, 16% Latino, 34% Asian.

Inglewood in 1960: almost entirely white.
Inglewood in 2010: 5% white, 44% Black, and 50% Latino.

Still, today in the 21st century, *affluent* nonwhites can usually live where they want — if they're doggedly persistent and willing to push through and overcome discriminatory obstacles and in some cases racial hostility from neighbors and suspicion on the part of cops in patrol cars. But most people of color in the urban North still live in racially defined neighborhoods, though the boundaries of those districts are now blurry and no longer delineated with the knife-edge sharpness they had in the 1960s.

Meanwhile, over the last half of the 20th century, many major American cities have become "majority-minority," with nonwhites outnumbering whites within the city limits which resulted in the election of nonwhite mayors and city councils. Now, however, a "gentrification" wave is bringing affluent whites, mostly young professionals, back into the inner city, while the inner ring of older suburbs are becoming the new nonwhite zones. Yet in all this ebb and flow of whites and nonwhites two things have remained constant — persistent racial attitudes of *them versus us* held by a significant segment of the American population, and the deliberate, profit-motivated exacerbation of residential racism practiced by individuals and institutions who financially benefit from housing segregation.

Marching on Washington ~ 1963

CORE was not the only big change in my life. Somehow I'd managed at LACC to scrape together grades good enough for admission to UCLA as a transfer student for the fall '63 semester. (They must have been desperate for students.)

At the beginning of 1963 my father had gotten a new job in Connecticut and was now living just outside of New Haven. In June my mom and younger brother moved east too. My parents urged me to join them for the summer before starting UCLA, but at age 19 I wanted none of that. I was in the thick of CORE actions and eager to be free of parental control, influence, and (to be honest) their mere presence.

So long as I was enrolled in college, my parents provided me with a small stipend — $50 a month as I recall, equal to about $400 in 2018. Combined with my part-time job as a fry cook in a local chicken shack, that was enough for me to survive on. I rented a tiny one-room apartment in an old building on Hamilton Way overlooking Sunset Boulevard at the edge of the Silver Lake district. It was a crummy crib with a pull-down Murphy bed, but it was all mine and I loved it. Across the hall in a larger space lived a trio of call girls — drop-dead gorgeous each and every one of them. They were lesbians. They had to explain to me what that was.

CORE was going strong, and outside of work my summer hours were entirely consumed by the Freedom Movement. Our picket lines were growing larger, and by now we well outnumbered the Nazis when they even bothered to show up.

In a planned act of nonviolent civil disobedience, a number of CORE members sat down on the driveway of the Don Wilson housing tract office. It wasn't being used for cars and they weren't blocking anything, but they were on private property and therefore subject to arrest for trespassing. They went limp, the Torrance cops picked them up and carried them to the paddy wagon, and off they went. It was all quite civilized compared to the overt, almost pathological hostility of the LAPD that we later encountered at protests within the city limits.

I didn't sit down and I wasn't arrested. I wanted to — but I was afraid. Both Mom and Ken were laying it on thick and heavy. "Finish college, get your professional degree, secure your economic future, then you can really help others more effectively." They weren't politically opposed to integration or to CORE, I think they were secretly proud of what I was doing, but they were emotionally and economically scarred by the Red Scare persecution and they feared for my future if I became a radical with an arrest record. I wasn't entirely buying their line — but neither was I rejecting it.

Then in July — savvy and experienced organizers that they were — they made me an offer I couldn't refuse. Greyhound bus fare across the country, stay with them in Connecticut for a couple of weeks, participate in the upcoming August 28 March on Washington, and then return to L.A. in my mom's hand-me-down car. Okay, it was a crappy Renault Dauphine at the ragged end of its short shelf life — but it was a car! Of my own! The next day I was riding the dog east on Route 66.

Orange, Connecticut was pleasant in a very suburban way. Ken's new job at Yale paid much better than anything he'd ever earned before, and my parents' new two-story home was set on a half-acre, tree-shaded lot. A nice place to visit, no doubt, and it was good to see them all, but I was a city kid and suburbs bored me.

I soon made contact with the New Haven CORE chapter and arranged a ride down to DC on one of the four buses they had chartered. We assembled at the train station the night before the march and around 10pm headed south on I-95.

I didn't know any of the other folk on the bus and nobody was talking much anyway. Everyone was tense. Today, history knows how the march turned out, but as we rolled south that night we had no clue what we were headed into. A significant portion of the news media was in full panic mode over the march. "Call out the National Guard! Alert the 101st Airborne! Close the liquor stores! Hide the white women!" I'm not joking (I'm not even exaggerating very much). And it wasn't just the press. Members of Congress were literally saying crap like that and so were some of TV's talking-head pundits. It was like they thought the Mongol hordes of Gengis Khan were descending on the nation's capital to rape, ravage, and pillage.

Having by now learned quite a bit from CORE, I understood that such nonsense came from deep wells of racist fears and fantasies. But we'd just had Birmingham and Gadsden and Greenwood, where nonviolent demonstrators had been savagely clubbed, beaten, gassed and arrested, where fire hoses and police dogs were used to attack children for peacefully marching — just as we planned to do in DC

For some people on the bus this was the first public protest they'd ever participated in and they were scared. I was experienced enough in nonviolent direct action to be fairly certain we wouldn't encounter mass arrests or large-scale police violence. But whether the march would be a success or not — that none of us knew. We hoped — but we didn't know. A lot of the media had been running stories that only a small number of people would show up, that the Civil Rights Movement was a hoax, that it was just a handful of malcontents, outside-agitators, and so on, *yada, yada, yada*.

It was deep in the night, pitch dark, when we got our first inkling of what we were about to become part of. We were on some big bridge, maybe the one over the Delaware river, maybe the Susquehanna. The bus began to slow and I could see a red glow, like some kind of fire burning up ahead. As we came off the bridge we passed 20 or 30 people on the embankment with flaming highway flares and signs saying, "We're With You," "God Speed," "March For Us." They were cheering the buses on. We instantly realized they were folks who couldn't participate in the march because it was a weekday — a workday — but they'd gotten up before dawn to show their support. I can't describe how emotional that was for me, but I know it's a memory I'll treasure to day I die.

Not long afterwards, the horizon to the east began to grow lighter with the approach of dawn. As the sun came up over the Eastern Shore, we could see that the whole freeway was just buses, the whole damn road, just buses flowing into DC bumper to bumper. And we we're still miles out. Nothing but buses, solid buses. That's when we knew.

By 10am we were off the bus and march marshals were guiding us to the Washington Monument where everyone was assembling. Peter, Paul and Mary were singing *This Little Light* up on a platform, and a huge crowd of people — 80% Black, the rest white — were pouring in from all directions. Call us what you will, "freedom fighters," "freedom riders," "shit-disturbers," or just plain ol' "troublemakers," we were all there together, united for the same purpose. I was thrilled and excited by the power of our numbers and the sense of welcome and solidarity that everyone shared.

The scheduled start time for the march came and went. The leaders were meeting with members of Congress and as usual were running late.

The Lincoln Memorial was easily visible and the route was obvious. Folk started singing, feet started walking, and without any formality or conscious decision the march was spontaneously on its way, flowing like twin rivers down Constitution and Independence Avenues. The "leaders" never did catch up to the front, they had to stop the flow somewhere in the middle so they could link arms and pretend for the photographers that they were at the head of the line. I thought that was so cool, the people leading the leaders.

The day was oven-hot, hot and muggy, but the oppressive heat did nothing to diminish the joyful spirit. We had no idea how many of us there were because only someone in a helicopter, or maybe on top of the Lincoln Memorial, could see the whole crowd, but we knew the turnout was vast and the protest an enormous success. People were proud — in some cases proud to the point of tears — of what we had collectively accomplished. And not just our huge number, but the atmosphere of friendship, solidarity, and determination. Determination to peacefully demand freedom and justice. Determination to give the lie to all those who had decried the march as an invitation to riot and rampage.

The speakers' platform was built up on the steps of the Lincoln Memorial, but from where I sat on the grass at the far end of the reflecting pool it was too distant for me to visually identify anyone. Big loudspeakers on portable stands carried their voices to even the farthest outskirts of the crowd. I remember a moment of silence in honor of W.E.B. DuBois, who had passed away that very day at the age of 95 in African exile, driven from the country by the Red-baiting witch hunts of the McCarthy era. And I still remember the electric power of Mahalia Jackson singing *I've Been 'Buked, and I've Been Scorned*.

There were many good speakers that day, but the two I remember most vividly 55 years later are John Lewis of the Student Nonviolent Coordinating Committee (SNCC) and Dr. King of the Southern Christian Leadership Conference (SCLC). John castigated the federal government and the Kennedy administration for their lethargy, their inaction, and their politically expedient complicity with segregationists. He spoke for us young militants in SNCC and CORE when he declared, *"We want our freedom and we want it now ... For we cannot stop, and we will not and cannot be patient."*

King spoke toward the end of the program. Today, the first part of his speech where he raised issues of poverty and economic justice are hardly ever mentioned, but the "Dream" portion continues to be widely quoted and replayed. It still has the power to move me as it did when I first heard it thundering across the reflecting pool, with Mahalia Jackson and others on the platform backing him up with the traditional affirmation of the Black church, *"My Lord! My Lord!"* and the enormous shadowed statue of the compassionate Lincoln gazing down on us all. *"Free at last, free at last. Thank God Almighty, free at last,"* and tears were streaming down my face. And not mine alone.

A. Philip Randolph then led us through the ten demands of the march and we pledged our dedication to continue the struggle until all of them were met. Now, more than 50 years after, some have been achieved and some we're still fighting for. The $2 per hour minimum wage we were marching for in 1963 was equal to about $16 in 2018 — and as I write these pages we are *still* fighting for a $15 per hour minimum wage.

Benjamin Mays of Morehouse College gave the benediction and then all of us in our hundreds of thousands clasped hands with whomever was next to us and fervently sang *We Shall Overcome*. I didn't know the Black man and woman on either side of me whose hands I held, nor did it matter, for that day we were one.

Someone once asked me whether the mood was jubilant on the bus returning to New Haven. The truth is I don't know. I was so exhausted I fell right to sleep and didn't wake up till we unloaded around midnight at the New Haven train station.

The next day, though, I remember being surprised at the amount of attention the media bestowed on the march — print, TV and radio, domestic and international, it was *the* major story. Up to then, press coverage of the Freedom Movement had been almost nonexistent, or at best understated and under reported except for a few brief flash points where there had been dramatic violence — the Freedom Rides, Meredith at Ol' Miss, Birmingham, and so on.

But more than surprised, I was furious at how completely the media missed the point and distorted the meaning of the march. I'm not referring to the southern press — we knew they'd downplay, distort and condemn. I'm talking about the northern "mainstream" media, particularly the "liberal" press. Did they focus on the issues we were raising? No. Did they report on the civil rights bill being debated in Congress? No. Did they explore the failings of the Kennedy administration? No, not a word. Instead they expressed their astonishment that hundreds of thousands of Afro-Americans ("Negroes" in the parlance of the time) could peacefully gather and protest in the nation's capital without violence and drunkenness, looting and rape. To them, that was the great revelation of the march. To me, it was evidence of their ingrained cultural racism.

To a man (and they were almost all men), the members of Congress stridently proclaimed that the march would not influence their legislative votes one iota. But as my father was fond of telling me, "the proof of the pudding is in the eating" (he loved a good cliché). Reconstruction had ended 86 years earlier and in those 86 years, not a single piece of effective race-related civil rights legislation had been signed into law. (The Civil Rights Acts of 1957 and 1960 were watered-down shams.) But in the two years after the March on Washington the two most far-reaching and effective pieces of civil rights legislation ever enacted — the Civil Rights Act of 1964 and the Voting Rights Act of 1965 — were passed. Not due to the march alone, of course, but to the entire Freedom Movement as a whole. Yet it was the march, I believe, that showed wavering northern legislators that their constituents — both Black and white — not only cared about civil rights but were watching how they voted.

The march also had another beneficial effect, less clearly understood, perhaps, but no less significant. In 1963, fear of Communism still dominated the political thinking of a great many whites. Most Afro-Americans had long since dismissed "red menace" and "Communist plot" smears against the Civil Rights Movement by racist segregationists like FBI Director J. Edgar Hoover and Senator Strom Thurmond of South Carolina. But those kinds of Red-baiting attacks still influenced a large number of whites. Now, at least for some of the millions who watched the march and King's entire 19-minute speech live on national TV — and heard for the first time, not just a few sound bites but the full content of a freedom sermon — slanders of foreign subversion and secret Soviet plots begin to lose their credibility.

For me personally, the march had a profound effect. It solidified my commitment as a full-time civil rights activist, and it set me on a lifetime path of political activism. I entered UCLA as a junior a couple of weeks later, but I had no intention of letting classroom studies or term papers interfere with my Movement work. Like cigarette smoke blown away in the wind, my hesitation (okay, fear) about engaging in civil disobedience and courting arrest were gone. I wasn't eager to be arrested, I didn't seek out opportunities, but I was no longer reluctant. Over the following 12 months I would be jailed four times for protesting. My mom fretted over what she saw as great risks to my future economic stability that I was running but I think she was also proud of me — and I know my dad was. As it turned out, so far as I know what eventually became a lengthy arrest record never affected my employment history at all.

Five-Foot Firecracker ~ 1931

From the stories she told me as a child and later the oral history I recorded with her, I know that my mom, Claire Brown, grew up in wealth and luxury. Her father immigrated to America around 1885, changing his name from Burech Bercovici (the Romanian form of "Berkowitz") to Bernard Brown. After he achieved financial success in the garment industry, he married Rose Mutterperl, the beautiful young widow of a rabbi and a Romanian immigrant herself. He bragged of owning seven raincoat "factories," something my mom still sounded proud of decades later. When I was a kid, "factories" implied to me huge buildings belching smoke from multiple smokestacks and hundreds of workers pouring in and out. Later in life I learned that his "factories" were dimly lit Brooklyn sweatshop lofts.

When my mom was a kid, her father moved them all, wife and three children, into a large mansion in the posh resort town of Saratoga Springs. She was the middle child with both an older and younger brother. They had two "Colored" servants and a chauffeur-driven limousine — but they didn't have much of a dad.

With his wife and kids stashed upstate in a "proper" Jewish home, Bernard enjoyed the life of a Broadway *bon vivant*. Eventually, he took up with a Philadelphia actress by whom he also had children. Years later, after it all came apart, Mom's mother Rose bitterly told her, "I thought he'd take me to cabarets, theater, opera, that I'd meet his friends and live an exciting life. But all he wanted was someone respectable to bear his children. Your father had plenty of excitement and pleasure in life — but none of it with me. He had other women."

Though he was rarely at home, my mom adored her vibrant, flamboyant father. And as her mother Rose descended into enervating depression, more and more it was young Claire who had to take charge of household matters in her mother's place. *Take charge* became her way of life.

She was 15 in early 1929, living the life of a Jewish-American princess. Five foot one, long black hair, a slender figure, and a beautiful face with dark flashing eyes. Fifteen must have been a really big year for her. She fell in love and started having sex with her boyfriend, Ben Iceland, who was working that summer in his uncle's hotel. She married him a few years later, and then eventually left him for my father. She also began smoking a pack a day, a vice she continued for the rest of her life, and it's possible, I suppose, that smoking may have contributed to her death from a lung disease at the age of 98 in 2012, a couple of years after her third husband, Aaron Hornstein, passed away — possibly from exhaustion.

Her good life came crashing down on "Black Thursday," October 24, 1929, when the stock market collapsed. By early 1931, when my mom was a 17-year-old junior in high school, all of her bankrupt father's assets had been seized — mansion, limousine, "factories," everything. He moved the family into a three-story Brooklyn tenement building that Rose had inherited from her first husband and owned in her own name. The rooms were cramped and airless, "El" trains rumbled and roared past their second-floor windows, and the single filthy, pull-chain toilet was "down the hall."

Shamed and humiliated, Bernard disappeared into intermittent homelessness, dementia, and institutionalization, leaving his hapless wife and children to fend for themselves. Meager rents from the building's other two tenants and older brother Leon's long hours as a garment industry "cutter" barely brought in enough to keep food on the table.

Mom enrolled in Washington Irving High, a girls' school a block from Union Square in Manhattan. She faked a Manhattan address to gain admission and rode the subway — half an hour each way, ten cents round trip. Her mother didn't understand why she refused to go to the local high school in Brooklyn and Claire chose not to explain that she insisted on going to Irving because it was close to New York University (NYU) where her lover Ben was studying Latin and philosophy. After class they could meet together.

Ben was a leftist — he hung around the Young Communist League (YCL) at NYU though he wasn't actually a member. He tried to interest Mom in Marxist analysis and theory, but his books and pamphlets simply put her to sleep. Ben's older sister, Rebecca, was also something of a lefty though not so much as her brother — a "parlor pink" in the lingo of the day. She was older than Ben, already a college graduate and a newly hired elementary school teacher. One day in early 1932, she tried to assert her intellectual superiority and worldly sophistication by scorning Claire's youth and social ignorance. "Don't you know about the Scottsboro Boys? What about the striking coal miners who've been driven from their homes by gun thugs? What have you done to help?"

Leftist theory bored my mom, but peoples' hardships and sufferings brought her compassion and anger alive, emotions that for her knew no bounds — then or ever. Immediately after school the next day, before meeting Ben in Washington Square, Mom showed up at the YCL office.

At that time, CP headquarters were in a former garment industry building at 35 East 12th near University Place, just a few blocks from Irving High (today it's luxury condo lofts). She found a small group of college-age kids stuffing envelopes in a desultory fashion while carrying on an animated argument about some point of political analysis or current events. They weren't sure what to make of her. She was still in high school, she didn't know their jargon or much about their issues — and nothing at all about their organization. But she told them she wanted to help the starving coal strikers, so they handed her some brochures and a petition addressed to President Hoover. "See if you can get some signatures and maybe collect some support money."

The following day she returned with a full sheet of signatures and $1.35 in donations (equal to about $23 in 2018), which was damn good for 1931 in the depths of the Depression. It turned out she was a natural organizer — a "five-foot firecracker" as someone later described her. Unlike intellectual leftists, she didn't approach people with rhetoric or theories or complicated political analyses, instead she connected on a human level of pain, suffering, and common experiences, like how hard it was to find a job. (And, of course, being a petite, brown-eyed beauty didn't hurt at all.)

An Indifferent Bruin ~ 1963

I enrolled as a UCLA junior in the fall of 1963. After World War II, California progressives had waged an aggressive political campaign to make college affordable. They won a huge victory in 1960 by forcing state government to enact the "Master Plan for Higher Education." Under that set of laws, California residents paid no tuition at all at any public university or college in the state. None. Zip. Nada. At UCLA we did have to pay student government and registration fees totaling $356 per year (equal to about $2800 in 2018). Since I had remained in Los Angeles when my family moved to Connecticut, I was still legally a California resident, and with my father now employed by Yale University as a business manager my parents could easily afford such a moderate cost.

Luckily for me, my college years happened to coincide with what turned out to be a short "tuition-free" period. Though the Master Plan was never officially repealed, Governor Reagan's administration began circumventing it in the late '60s by charging students tuition disguised as phony "incidental fees." (I call them "phony" because those "fees" were used to pay university expenses that all other colleges funded through tuition.) Since 1967, Sacramento politicians from both parties have continued to ignore the Master Plan by steadily increasing the amount students have to pay. Today in 2018, UCLA tuition for California students is more than $13,000 a year.

As it turned out though, accommodating myself to UCLA proved more difficult than I anticipated. Our family had lived only a block from LACC and for me as a student it just seemed like a really big high school — high school on steroids, as it were. I think LACC's enrollment at that time was around 8,000 students, but a lot of them were working adults in evening programs, so as a day student I didn't encounter them. While the courses were both more challenging and more interesting than high school, class size was not that much different from Dorsey High (which, admittedly, was over capacity). And they were in normal size classrooms with individual high school–type desks. Most important, the professors were accessible, you could talk to them, ask questions, and engage in dialogue.

Not so, UCLA. Depending on traffic, it took me more than an hour to drive from my pad on Hamilton Way to the Westwood campus. With 30,000 students, UCLA was four times the size of LACC, the campus was huge and complex, classes were attended by hundreds of students in large, tiered lecture halls, and the professors had no time for lowly undergraduates like me.

During a full year at UCLA, I only remember two professors (though not their names). One was a cold, arrogant, narrow-minded experimental psychologist whom I detested. As I recall, he later became department head. The other prof was a marvelous American literature teacher who engaged, challenged, and stimulated his students — there was always a long wait-list for his courses. I thought he was so terrific that I actually made an effort to attend his classes. He was dismissed the following semester — in part I suspect because he taught racially controversial works such as *Invisible Man*, by Ralph Ellison. Today, that book is taught in many high schools, but back then it was "too radical" for UCLA administrators and their Sacramento overseers.

To be honest, though, except for that one lit class my real problem at UCLA was lack of interest. I hadn't gotten involved with CORE until just a few months before I graduated from LACC, so until the last half of that last semester I had plenty of time to devote to schoolwork. After I came back from the March on Washington, the only aspect of university that held much interest for me was UCLA's CORE chapter. At UCLA, everything was named "Bruin," the sports teams, the campus newspaper, the coffee mugs, the T-shirts — everything was "Bruin this" and "Bruin that." So, of course, we called our CORE group "Bruin CORE." The campus jocks were not amused, but that was their problem, not ours.

Actions of the "Action Faction" ~ 1963

What with registration and new classes, Bruin CORE didn't become active until the end of September, so my main focus upon returning to the city was resuming work with the main L.A. CORE chapter, which at that time was growing rapidly — the monthly general membership meetings were by then drawing 50–75 activists.

Over the years, I've noticed that when faced with new circumstances people usually go with what they know rather than inventing something entirely new from scratch. CORE was founded by pacifists and integrationists in the early 1940s when the labor movement was actually a real social movement. CORE's founders were familiar with trade unions, so that was the organizational form they adopted. Twenty years later, CORE chapters were still structured like union locals, with constitutions, elected executive committees (and therefore, internal electoral politics), various working committees — Membership, Publicity, Fundraising — and even a Sergeant at Arms (who never did anything).

CORE membership meetings were run like union meetings, with officers on a platform before a seated audience, a chairman with a gavel in his hand, and a formal agenda:

Pledge of Allegiance
Reports from president, treasurer, and committee heads
Old business
New business
Good & welfare

But rather than strikes, CORE engaged in "actions." For me as a child of union organizers, all this seemed quite normal and natural. So imagine my surprise (and fascination) when I started working for SCLC in Selma Alabama in early 1965 and discovered that the southern wing of the Freedom Movement was organized and run like an Afro-American church. There were "mass meetings," not membership meetings. Those mass meetings were modeled on church revivals and were *nothing at all* like union meetings. Amen.

As I saw it, protests were the essence of CORE. So I naturally gravitated to the Action Committee which was responsible for organizing demonstrations. Its leaders were three Black men — Woodrow (Woody)

Coleman, F. Daniel Gray, and Robert Hall. They were my role models far more than the chapter chairman and the other Executive Committee officers who I rarely encountered. The Action Committee's stalwart nonviolent warriors — Mari Goldman, Richard Thompson, Jerry Farber, Jay Frank, Annette Becker, Danny Grant, Roberta Krinsky and her brother Fred, Lea Arond, Michael Robinson, Charles Bratton, Scott Van Leuvan, Sue Kovner, Candy Brown, Le Faucette, Bob Freeman, Jackie King, Jean Dalbert, and so many others were my comrades in arms — except, of course, that we were nonviolent and therefore armed with nothing more than songs, leaflets, and cardboard signs.

It was from the Action Committee that I acquired my commitment to and understanding of nonviolent direct action. I studied the tactics and techniques — as opposed to the philosophy — of nonviolent resistance far more diligently than whatever it was I was supposed to be learning at UCLA. And by that fall of 1963 I had participated in so many demonstrations that I was considered an expert protester. Not that anyone ever praised or complimented me. Affirmations, acknowledgements, and "touchy-feely" human relations simply weren't part of our task-oriented organizational culture, but I knew I was respected and valued because they gave me increased responsibilities and trusted me to carry them out.

Another thing I've noticed in life is that promotions come amazingly fast if you're willing and able to do the work — and the job don't pay nothing. By October of '63, I was head of a tiny subcommittee consisting of Jay Frank, Jerry Farber and me. We were in charge of training picket captains and march marshals, and on occasion I led small actions myself (larger demonstrations were led by Woody or Danny, with me and other marshals assisting them). I was proud to be placed in charge of Action Committee training sessions, and I took the work seriously.

In the larger scheme of things however, L.A. CORE was dividing against itself, and the Action Committee and its various allies — colloquially referred to as the "Action Faction" — were becoming more and more pissed off at those we considered the "Conservatives." At root was a conflict between two different visions of what a CORE chapter should be doing. In essence, we of the Action Faction saw CORE as primarily a direct action organization whose committees — Publicity, Fundraising, Outreach, etc — existed to support militant and if necessary disruptive protests to demand immediate changes.

I don't know how the other faction thought of themselves, — we scornfully labeled them "conservatives" — though, of course, I'm sure they didn't think of themselves that way. No doubt they saw themselves as realistic and responsible moderates in opposition to us wild-eyed radicals, so I'll refer to them here as "moderates." Looking back on it now, I think the moderates saw CORE as a public education, community relations, negotiate-compromise, racial healing–type organization. One that sometimes might have to reluctantly use nondisruptive protests to further the work of persuading individuals, organizations, and businesses to accept the moral justice of integration by ending school segregation and adopting fair hiring and fair housing policies.

In reality, I was still so new to CORE that I didn't fully grasp the issues and all of their ramifications. But with all the passion and commitment that a 19-year-old can muster, I stood with my Action Faction compañeros. What's that song from *West Side Story*? — *"When you're a Jet, you're a Jet all the way...,"* sorry, my mind wanders sometimes.

In any case, we of the Action Faction were usually outnumbered in membership meetings by the moderates who dominated the elected leadership and most of the committees. But they rarely showed up on protests. We were the ones on the picket lines confronting the Nazis and the cops, and it was Action Faction folk who were committing civil disobedience and going to jail. Which for us, meant that we were the *real* CORE, and we deeply resented the fact that they who did so little held the power to restrict and restrain those of us who were putting our bodies on the line.

While I was in Connecticut and marching on Washington, a crisis between the two factions had erupted around the housing protests. As I later understood it, some 50 or 60 people had been arrested for sitting down on the sales office driveway. CORE had no money to bail them out, a repressive injunction was imposed by a local judge, and there was a big media controversy over the sanctity of Private Property (meaning that empty driveway that had briefly been sat on by nonviolent protesters).

Somehow a mysterious agreement had been negotiated that required CORE to halt the Don Wilson protests in return for charges being dropped against those arrested in the sit-ins — but without any concession from Don Wilson that he would halt racial discrimination at any of his housing tracts. There had been no acknowledged meetings between Don Wilson and CORE, so no one seemed to know who had negotiated the agreement. It was all very murky. Nevertheless, the CORE Executive Committee endorsed it. The Action Committee, which had been organizing and running the housing protests, were not consulted at all. When the picket lines were halted we cried, *"Sellout!"*

The moderates countered that the Action Committee had had no authority to engage in large-scale civil disobedience without approval from the Executive Committee (which they would never have given) and that doing so when CORE had no funds for bail was "irresponsible." Action Faction proponents argued that L.A. CORE's constitution gave the Action Committee power to call and run demonstrations — that's why it was called the "Action Committee." And most of those in jail were Action Faction supporters who had known they wouldn't be bailed out right away. Now they all felt betrayed by a settlement that freed them without achieving any of what they were fighting for.

On a deeper level, those in the Action Faction more experienced than I saw the widening split in broader, more sinister, political terms. They were convinced that some of the moderate CORE leaders were politically aligned with the liberal wing of the Democratic Party. Democratic insiders — politicians and their campaign managers — feared that militant civil rights protests would alienate white voters and benefit conservative Republicans. Action Faction militants believed that some moderate CORE leaders were trying to rein in demonstrations for the benefit of the Democratic Party in the upcoming '64 elections, which were more than a year off. (At that time, Republicans were still strong enough in California to frequently win not only local and statewide offices but even presidential campaigns.)

As the Action Faction saw it, CORE's goal was to win racial justice, not to elect liberal politicians. For us, the whole point of CORE was using nonviolent direct action to provoke crises that would disrupt the quiet status quo — there were other organizations dedicated to tedious (and ineffective) moral education and humble pleas for justice and redress of grievances. We were putting ourselves on the line to end segregation and we held no brief for tokenism, lip service, or soothing moderation — nor should we have.

Some of the moderate CORE leaders were said by Action Faction adherents to be either members of the Communist Party or influenced by their leadership. As was well known among political activists on the left, the CP had long since separated its actual political work from its Marxist rhetoric, and by the early 1960s their strategy was to align with liberal Democrats against Dixiecrat segregationists and Red-baiting McCarthyite Republicans. In other words, they were "revolutionaries" who spent most of their time supporting the liberal wing of the Democratic Party (which they in no way controlled or even had much influence with).

After growing up in a Party family and seeing what they did to my parents, I had little love and less respect for the CP. And I had scant patience for the Party members and ex-members — including my parents and our family friends — who were all in my face (some politely, some arrogantly) telling me (from the safety of their living rooms) that we had to "go slower," and that the Civil Rights Movement was pushing "too far, too fast."

It constantly irked me that reactionaries and segregationists tried to slander the Freedom Movement as "Communist dominated" — and therefore dangerously revolutionary — when everyone inside the Freedom Movement knew that very very few Party members were actually active, and those who did take part were among the *most* conservative and *least* militant. The great majority of Marxists I encountered in Los Angeles were not only not active in the Freedom Movement at all, they stood to one side, criticizing us for "only putting a Band-aid on a diseased society" that in their view could only be cured by a socialist revolution — which they weren't doing squat to bring about.

Looking back on this factional conflict now, I suspect that the moderates were more amorphous and varied than we assumed at the time. I'm sure some of those in CORE leadership were exactly who we thought they were for precisely the reasons we assumed, but most were probably not. I now think many were simply liberals who sought racial justice yet were repelled by — in fact terrified of — turmoil and conflict. Demonstrators today often chant, *"No justice, no peace!"* But over the course of a long political life, I've encountered no small number of well-meaning folks whose actions — or lack thereof — quietly affirm, "Peace and tranquility first, justice second."

Engaging in political conflict through parliamentary maneuvers and dueling polemics, however, wasn't really our Action Faction thing. Instead we verbalized how we felt through song. Jerry Farber put new words to the popular calypso tune "Marianne," and others added their own verses until there were a dozen or more. We called it "The Liberals Song," and sang it often. The first verse and chorus went:

> *Walking on the picket line*
> *Carrying my freedom sign*
> *Up came a liberal anxiously*
> *These are the words he said to me:*
>
> *You're only hurting your cause this way*
> *That's what all of us liberals say*
> *Nobody likes things the way they are*
> *But you're going too fast, and you're going too far.*

"I'm Going to Marry That Little Gal" ~ 1938

Thinking about those L.A. CORE meetings reminds me of a story Ken, my father, once told me. But first I need to explain about his motorcycle and "Unk." During the Depression years a car was way beyond the economic reach of a telegraph operator. My dad did manage, however, to somehow acquire a rugged old Indian Chief motorcycle. He was a good mechanic and managed to keep it running from one coast to the other.

Years later my brother Dan wrote me:

Concerning Ken's motorcycle, when people mention that model they usually tack on, "with a suicide shift" to the end of the name. You shift most motorcycles by nudging a lever up or down with your foot after engaging the clutch. The shift on those Indian bikes was a lever that stuck up next to the gas tank between your legs. So, to shift you had to let go of the handle bars with one hand, then reach down between your leg and the gas tank to move the shift lever. In addition, that shift lever — being between your legs — was precariously close to the family jewels, so to speak, so great care was required when mounting or dismounting the bike — and forget it if you got in an accident.[1]

Don't think of my father as some kind of Hells Angel biker type — quite the contrary. The Chief came with a sidecar for his mother Ida Belle Hartford, whom everyone called "Unk" (no one now living knows why they called her Unk). Anyway, he also built a little two-wheel trailer for their camping gear and he and Unk would ride the highways and byways, he on the bike, she in the sidecar, the little trailer tagging along, and sometimes his younger sister on the seat behind him. Out to California, up to Beantown, down to Tampa, camping by the side of the road. Unk loved those trips — anywhere, any place to get out of the Kentucky sticks.

In 1938, the American Communications Association held its convention in New York City at a hotel across the street from Van Cortland Park in the lower Bronx. ACA was the CIO union for communication workers, and at the ripe old age of 30 Ken was president of the Cincinnati local and a delegate to the convention.

As you would expect, the union provided all the delegates with train tickets and hotel rooms. But that wasn't my dad's style. Instead he came on up from the South on his bike with Unk in the sidecar. He drove onto the park grass across from the hotel and while he signed in at convention registration to pick up his credentials Unk unpacked the trailer, set up a canvas tent, and got the campfire going with a cookpot over it on a tripod — all right, tight, and Kentucky fashion.

A cop ordered them off — *"No camping in a public park!"*

Unk and Ken refused to move. A reporter from the *Daily News* photographed them for a "human interest" article about the hillbilly hick and his mom who were camping outside the union meeting because (of course) they were too dumb to know what hotels were.

In 1938, war production had not yet lifted the nation out of the Depression, and everyone knew that unemployed homeless men discreetly slept in the park's wooded areas, so I suppose officials decided not to risk stirring up uncomfortable questions in the press by arresting Ken or Unk. So they continued camping until the meeting ended.

I love that story about my dad and his mother camping in the park for the union meeting, but that's not why the '38 convention was important to me. During one of the sessions he made a motion arguing that "most of the country is made up of little cities, towns, and villages spread around from hell to breakfast," all of which had telegraph offices that the union should try to organize because in the aggregate those workers outnumbered the operators in the big city centers by a wide margin.

Claire Brown, the 24-year-old Midwest Region organizer, then got up and utterly eviscerated his plan on strategic, practical, and cost-benefit grounds. "It's good that the Kentucky delegate is reminding us of the hinterlands, but isn't he aware that we haven't the resources to send organizers to all the little places in the country? If we could, we would. Our strategy is to win the biggest cities and once we get a national contract, that will cover the boondocks."

Slender, hazel-eyed, with a delicate face, she stood all of five foot four in her three-inch heels, and by every account she was quite the looker. My dad was totally smitten, and he later told me that he said to himself, "I'm going to marry that little gal."

Easier said than done, of course. They worked in different regions of the country. He was pure Kentucky and she was Brooklyn Jew by way of Saratoga Springs. And he soon learned that she was already married to a soldier fighting in Europe (and, yes, I do have my dates correct). But it turned out there was a mutual attraction, and while Ken didn't have much schooling he was self-educated and wicked smart — smarter than my mom, truth to tell. Whenever they were at the same union meeting or convention, he let her fix him up with her friends, and arrange outings, and so on. And so on. And so on ...

Mom and her first husband, Ben Iceland, eventually agreed to a more or less amicable divorce. She and my father were married in 1943 by a Kentucky justice of the peace who was quite reluctant about the whole idea. Back then Kentucky had anti-miscegenation laws prohibiting interracial marriage, and in his view hitching this good Gentile boy to some Jewess from "Jew York" was pretty close to that line. He did give her a stern lecture about a wife's proper role. One she still remembered — and was still fuming about — 65 years later (Mom was a world-class fumer, and no slouch when it came to fulminating either).

After my dad and Mom started seeing one another it was she who accompanied him on various travels — in the sidecar for a short while until she convinced him that as a union official he could afford to buy an real car with a roof and glass windows and seats with cushions.

To the day she died, Unk never forgave my mom for replacing her as Ken's traveling companion.

As for him, I think he missed that old bike.

Bruin CORE and the DuBois Club ~ 1963

Over the decades since the 1960s history has bestowed on the Civil Rights Movement a glow of social admirability — but that was not the case at the time. Most definitely not. CORE, SNCC, and SCLC were widely seen as dangerously radical and potentially subversive. In November of 1963, for example — just before President Kennedy was assassinated — the University of Southern California (USC) barred James Farmer, CORE's nonviolent leader, from speaking on campus because he was "too controversial." I guess they felt their intellectually innocent students had to be shielded from his dangerous ideas (or, perhaps, it was the endowment fund that had to be protected from the ire of conservative alumni).

UCLA administrators, of course, were no less determined to avoid political controversies that might provoke retaliation — in their case mainly from conservative state legislators who controlled the UC budget. But as a public institution they had to carefully balance political pressures from Sacramento against potential negative consequences if they blatantly violated students' constitutional rights of free speech and association. (A year later, UC Berkeley misjudged that balance and sparked the Free Speech Movement, which rocked not only Berkeley but every college and university in America.)

So in the fall of 1963, questionable student groups like Bruin CORE were allowed to exist at UCLA so long as we strictly obeyed an extensive set of rules and restrictions and refrained from inviting "controversial" outsiders to speak on campus.

Classes started in mid-September, and as I recall it took a few weeks for Bruin CORE to pull together its first meeting of the new semester. Black students at UCLA were few and far between in 1963. So rare that some of them complained they were mistaken for janitors or kitchen help by faculty members who questioned what they were doing in the classroom — I kid you not. So it was no surprise that the CORE chapter was almost entirely white, though a young Black woman named Berenice Powdrill was both chair and one of our two main spokeswomen — the other being a leftist graduate student named Marlene Dixon. Both of them were primarily interested in the sociology and politics of racism, so I stepped into the role of chapter picket captain and nonviolent tactics instructor.

Bruin CORE and the W.E.B. DuBois Club were the two main radical groups at UCLA that fall (if there was an SDS chapter I wasn't aware of it). Leftists were even rarer on campus than Afro-Americans that year, and we were heavily outnumbered by the Young Republicans and the extremist John Birch Society, with their calls to impeach Chief Justice Earl Warren and their accusations that Martin Luther King was a "Soviet agent." So to a certain extent there was a mutual "everyone's against us" affinity between Bruin CORE and the DuBois Club.

Both groups occasionally set up literature tables on a little plaza outside the student union cafeteria and we were sometimes physically attacked by men we referred to as "jocks." Whether they actually were school athletes we really didn't know since we didn't attend football games or participate in pep rallies like "normal students."

My feelings about the DuBois Club were quite mixed. The DuBois Club claimed they were independent of any "parent" group, but everyone knew they were closely associated with the Communist Party and I knew a couple of Club members through my parents. However, since both my father and mother had resigned (or been expelled) from the Party some years earlier, that created a bit of awkwardness.

On the other hand, it was reassuring to at least know *somebody* on that vast and crowded campus. And, of course, DuBois members sometimes participated in our CORE actions, we sometimes attended their public programs, and all of us faced the hostility of aggressive conservatives. Sharing those activities and common enemies drew me closer to them, but at the same time I was increasingly at odds with the moderate faction of L.A. CORE, whose cautious "go-slow" political views were dutifully echoed by the DuBois Club leadership.

Politics aside, however, my academic career was not going well. Participating in the Freedom Movement left me with scant time for classes, homework, labs, or term papers. Yet I was learning an incredible amount about racism, economics, practical politics, government institutions, mass media, social interaction, and human psychology (technically I was a psych major). Unfortunately, none of that was in the course syllabus or final exams. Yet I was thriving and growing as a person, becoming more self-confident and increasingly competent as an activist and demonstration organizer. So in that sense I considered myself a highly successful university student — despite my abysmal grade point average.

School Segregation, L.A. Style ~ 1963

At that time, American schools were segregated in two different ways. In the South there was "de jure" segregation — dual separate (and unequal) white and Colored school systems that were formally and legally segregated. In the North, including California and Los Angeles, there was what we referred to as "de facto" segregation. This northern-style segregation was imposed by the careful drawing of school district boundaries, use of racially biased academic tracking programs, and disparities in resource allocations and teacher assignments.

The white authorities overseeing de jure segregation in the South boasted about it: *"Segregation now, segregation forever!"* Those in charge of imposing segregation in the North denied any racial discrimination on their part at all. They positioned themselves as champions of neighborhoods and neighborhood schools, though as modern historians are now exposing northern residential segregation was *legally required* and *enforced* by federal housing policies starting with the New Deal and continuing on into the 1950s and '60s.

Residential segregation and school segregation were (and still are) inextricably linked. The proclaimed value of "neighborhood schools" was the justification for northern school segregation, and providing "good" (meaning "white") schools for their kids was the main rationale used by those who fought to maintain white-only neighborhoods by opposing open housing laws. So it's no surprise that battles over school segregation raged in parallel with struggles over segregated housing throughout the North — in Los Angeles, Boston, New York, Chicago, and elsewhere.

When I was growing up, the Los Angeles Unified School District was the third largest in the country, and under their system of covert segregation the disparities between white and nonwhite schools in resources, quality of education, and graduation rates were both stark and undeniable. Though there were a few integrated schools like Audubon and Dorsey where I went, most L.A. schools were segregated — either overwhelmingly white with perhaps a few token Blacks, Latinos, or Asians, or overwhelmingly nonwhite with perhaps a handful of whites.

Everyone in Los Angeles County — and especially all us kids — knew that the white high schools were the "good" ones and the Black, Latino, and integrated schools like Dorsey were the "bad" ones. Almost all of the district's Black students were in 93 underfunded, overcrowded, overwhelmingly segregated schools while the remaining 400 or so schools were either all white or had just a token handful of nonwhite students.

Three-quarters of all L.A. elementary schools were overwhelmingly white, but 90% of the elementary schools forced by overcrowding to limit children to half-day sessions were among those that were Afro-American or Latino because that's how the Board of Education (BoE) chose to allocate resources and assign students. Personally, I loved being on half-day sessions because I hated school, but my parents seemed to think there was something wrong with it. Go figure.

Inspired by *Brown v. Board of Education* and Freedom Movement successes in the South against de jure segregation, Black parents in L.A. began to demand that something be done to significantly improve their children's education. The NAACP, Afro-American community leaders, and local ministerial groups had been studying the situation, issuing reports, and negotiating with the BoE and City Council for years — to no avail.

When Black parents in Los Angeles asked the Board to end segregated schools in 1962, officials piously denied any racial intent on their part. They claimed they were just neutrally administering a system based on "neighborhood schools." But BoE members ran for election on explicit, openly stated anti-integration platforms, and they adamantly refused to collect or release relevant statistics while they stonewalled desegregation demands by CORE, NAACP, and others. Which is precisely what most white voters and public office-holders wanted — and in 1963 well over 70% of Los Angeles voters were white.

Most white parents feared their kid's education would suffer if they had to share classrooms and hallways with significant numbers of Black or Latino kids. A few token nonwhites they could accept, but more than that — no way! They also worried about crime and violence (though not so much about drugs, because this was before Nixon's War on Drugs turned narcotics into a major growth industry).

On an even deeper level, integrating schools raised white fears of interracial dating, sex, and the perceived horrors of "miscegenation." (Unbeknownst to any of us at that time, a child of just such an interracial marriage had been born two years earlier in Honolulu who would go on to become President of the United States — a reality that a good number of whites are still unable to cope with to this day.)

Afro-American demands for school desegregation put liberal Democrats in a bind. Conservative Democrats against whom they competed in primaries were solid backers of the segregated status quo. They enthusiastically exalted the sanctity of "neighborhoods," as did the Republicans who they ran against in the November general elections. Yet almost ten years after *Brown*, liberal politicians had to publicly support the theoretical concept of integration — with, of course, "all deliberate speed," "in due time," "as conditions mature" — or risk alienating their base among Black, Latino, Jewish, and liberal white voters.

Political campaign managers, however, were terrified that if Afro-Americans pushed too hard for school integration they would arouse furious resistance — the kind of reaction that would soon be referred to as the "white backlash."

Enter CORE and the "Action Faction."

Sitting-In at the Board of Education ~ 1963

By the time I resumed working with L.A. CORE in September of '63, the housing protests had been hobbled by the moderates and their mysterious agreements with Don Wilson. And those aligned with the Democratic Party were increasing their opposition to further direct action of any sort. We of the Action Faction, however, were determined to push full speed ahead for "Freedom Now!" Regardless of electoral consequences.

With the 1963-64 academic school year commencing in September, L.A. CORE's Action Committee shifted its attention from housing to the equally controversial issue of school desegregation. Though I didn't realize it at the time, an action campaign for school integration would inevitably bring L.A. CORE's internal conflict to a head.

At our urging — and over the objections of the moderates — CORE's general membership meeting that September voted by a narrow majority to commence protests against segregation and racial discrimination by the L.A. Board of Education (BoE). The campaign began with eight CORE members participation in a week-long fast at the BoE headquarters, followed by a six-mile protest march to the BoE by some 500 students from the heart of the ghetto.

Meanwhile, out at UCLA in Westwood, Bruin CORE was starting up for the semester. Chapter leaders Berenice Powdrill and Marlene Dixon focused their energies on campus education and outreach efforts around race and discrimination, while I concentrated on recruiting and leading UCLA students to participate in protests at the BoE beginning in early October.

The first such actions were called "study-ins." A study-in was a kind of low-key sit-in. The Board met every Thursday afternoon, so around four o'clock, *Black and white together*, we marched into BoE headquarters at the corner of Sunset and Grand, lined the hallway, and then sat down, leaving open space in the middle of the corridor and in front of each doorway so that no one was blocked from entering or leaving.

We called it a "study-in" because we wanted to counter segregationists who seemed to fear some horrible racial catastrophe if Afro-American and white students studied and learned together. As we conceived them, the study-ins were not civil disobedience. Our plan was to peacefully leave if told to do so. Of course, we knew that ordering students to stop doing school work under threat of arrest would be politically embarrassing to the elected BoE members. Which they obviously also understood, since they stoically suffered our presence.

In the early 1960s, CORE demonstrations were highly disciplined. They were not excuses for protesters to act out their personal rebellions, "do their own thing," or self-aggrandize their egos. If someone refused to accept that, they were asked to leave. And everyone understood and accepted this because we wanted to win and we understood that victory required self-discipline. So there was little risk of arrest on the study-ins, and participants trusted CORE monitors and picket captains like me to maintain the discipline that kept everyone safe.

We held four Thursday study-ins during October with from 200–400 participants — mainly students, most of them college age, some from high school. It was an hour's drive from UCLA to the BoE, twice as long on the bus, yet I would guess that between a quarter and a third of the study-in participants were mobilized by Bruin CORE, primarily from UCLA, plus a few from Santa Monica College and University High School.

As our actions continued and grew larger, so did media controversy and opposition from angry whites who furiously objected to their children attending class with Afro-Americans and Latinos. The growing furor dismayed the CORE moderates who stepped up their opposition to "provocative" direct action. They argued that petitions and educational outreach programs aimed at persuading whites that segregation was morally unjust were more effective than demonstrations that stirred up anger and hostility. We, of course, disagreed — passionately.

For their part, the Board of Education knew they had the solid support of both white voters and white elected officials. So rather than threatening mass arrests or using force to clear the building, which would have resulted in greatly increased media attention and controversy over their segregation policies, their strategy was to wait us out while vilifying us in the media as "impractical," "irresponsible," "divisive," and "disruptive."

We of the Action Faction and Bruin CORE considered ourselves nonviolent warriors — adapting Gandhian strategies to American realities. One of Gandhi's precepts was that "the function of a civil resistor is to provoke a response and continue to provoke until they respond or change the law." So since the BoE was simply waiting out the study-ins, we decided to discontinue them and escalate toward civil disobedience.

One could argue — as we did — that it was no violation of law for students to sit in a Board of Education hallway on a Thursday afternoon without blocking any doors or hallways while reading books and doing homework. But an all-night sit-in after closing hours might well be construed as a form of trespass, certainly so if they told us to leave and we refused. At the end of the last study-in on October 24, about 150 of us remained in the building for what we called a "vigil." All of us understood and agreed that we would refuse to leave if ordered to do so and submit to arrest if necessary. As it happened, we must have taken the BoE by surprise because they made no effort to evict us, and we left in the morning as the office workers were arriving.

The BoE told the press that we had broken into an office and stolen hypodermic needles (untrue) and they claimed we had engaged in "licentious behavior" in the halls — meaning, I suppose, that some official saw some snuggling and possibly even some kissing. Apparently it astonished — horrified — whomever it was to observe such behavior by high school and college-age students. The CORE moderates echoed the BoE's nonsense, not because they believed it but because it suited their political purposes to paint us as out of control "radicals." We expected lies from the BoE we were protesting against, but hearing slanders from our fellow CORE members enraged us.

The moderates also falsely charged that we had violated CORE process when we canceled the study-ins and commenced the all-night vigils. And it was "irresponsible," they added, to court arrest for 150 people when CORE had no money for bail. We argued that we followed the correct internal procedures because the Action Committee had the power to initiate protests. And we countered that everyone understood they might be in jail for some time, that the dramatic arrest of such a large number of protesters would force the BoE to respond, and once we were in jail bond money could eventually be raised — which was, in fact, the standard CORE approach everywhere in the country.

After a fierce political fight the CORE Executive Committee narrowly approved a second vigil for October 31st.

The Los Angeles Unified School District had their own well-trained and well-disciplined police force, which meant we weren't up against the racist, violence-prone LAPD. When we attempted to enter the BoE for the second vigil just before closing time, the school cops tried to lock the doors and block us. About 30 of us managed to get inside, leaving a larger group locked out. This was long before cell phones, so communication between those of us inside and the others outside was almost impossible except by shouting out the restroom windows (the offices were all locked and we made no effort to break into them).

Those of us on the inside found a set of unguarded doors, opened them, and then sat down in the doorway to keep the school police from closing them while outside protesters scrambled over us to get in. The cops roughly forced their way through, dragged us away, arrested three people, and managed to get the doors closed and locked, though not before a number of additional protesters had managed to enter the building.

Jerry Farber, Jay Frank, and Scott Van Leuvan were the three arrested. A couple of months later they were convicted on a minor misdemeanor and sentenced to three days in city jail. They began serving their sentence on January 30, 1964, and as both a gesture of solidarity and continued protest we began an around-the-clock sit-in in the Hall of Justice lobby, which was open around the clock. Apparently we made such a nuisance of ourselves — my tone-deaf singing no doubt a major contribution — they let our people go a day and half early just to get rid of us. A victory to be celebrated.

Compared to what we had experienced from the Nazis in Torrance and would later receive at the hands of the LAPD, the roughness of the BoE cops that afternoon was minor. And compared to what protesters in the Deep South were enduring it was trivial. But some of the UCLA students were shocked, indignant, and outraged at being manhandled and shoved aside. A third vigil was held on the night of November 7. The school cops made no attempt to block us this time and it was clear the BoE had returned to their waiting-us-out strategy. Perhaps they knew CORE's internal conflict would soon solve their pesky protesters problem. They were right.

By now CORE membership and committee meetings had become increasingly bitter political battles as the two factions put forward rival motions and used parliamentary maneuvers to either curtail or push forward the school protests. As it turned out the moderates on the chapter's Executive Committee were far more skilled at political infighting than we were. They called two special membership meetings to revise the chapter constitution and bylaws, each meeting carefully scheduled to take place during one of our vigil actions at the BoE, when Action Faction supporters would be demonstrating rather than debating bylaws language.

With most of the Action Faction engaged in action, the moderates were able to rewrite the rules and revoke the Action Committee's authority to call and organize protests or make statements to the press. That gave them the power to slam on the brakes. Under the new procedures, a complex committee process was required to mount a protest. We had been in action at the BoE during every one of their regular Thursday meetings since mid-September, but on Thursday, November 14 nothing had been approved through the process, so nothing was done.

The following Thursday, November 21st, was the date for chapter elections. More than 100 members attended the meeting and both factions nominated candidates. The moderates decisively defeated us. Most of our votes came from people who had consistently been on the line in Torrance and risked arrest at the Board of Education. Most of the moderate votes came from CORE members we had never seen on a demonstration and many we had never seen at all, not even in committee meetings.

The next day, November 22nd, President Kennedy was assassinated in Dallas. There was no question in our minds — moderates and Action Faction both — that he was killed by white racists because of his perceived support for Afro-American civil rights. National CORE leaders in New York responded by ordering a month-long moratorium on civil disobedience until after Christmas. The new L.A. CORE officers expanded that into a moratorium on *all* protests of *any* kind.

After the moderates won the chapter elections and declared their expanded moratorium, CORE never resumed direct action protests against the Board of Education. The moderates continued to petition and plead for years — with no noticeable success at all.

But that didn't end the struggle against segregated education. Just as Afro-Americans were forced into overcrowded, highly-segregated schools, so too were Latinos living in East Los Angeles. The four Latino high schools, Garfield, Lincoln, Roosevelt, and Wilson, were notorious for their high dropout and low college-admittance rates, for penalizing students for speaking Spanish with their friends, and for using corporal punishment (swats with a wooden paddle). In 1968, students at those four schools organized a series of student strikes they called "walkouts" to protest conditions. Students at Roosevelt nonviolently sitting in on the school steps were brutally attacked by L.A. police in riot gear, who beat them with clubs, putting a savage end to such student protests.

In 1970, Judge Gitelson ruled that the Los Angeles Unified School District "knowingly, affirmatively, and in bad faith" deliberately segregated L.A. schools. He ordered them to desegregate the predominantly Black and Latino schools by 1972. Angry whites immediately voted him out of office. President Nixon and Governor Ronald Reagan condemned his ruling, which was quickly appealed, blocking the judge's 1972 deadline.

Finally, in 1976, the California Supreme Court ruled that L.A. had to desegregate its schools. Again the BoE, white parents, and their loyal politicians resisted. Anti-integration forces put Proposition 1 before the voters, who passed it in 1979 by another two-thirds majority. That proposition changed the California constitution so as to block all court-ordered school integration plans. Capitulating to the political winds, the California Supreme Court choose not to overturn Prop1. Los Angeles thus became the first city in America to eviscerate and completely eliminate court-ordered school desegregation. Today, school segregation in SoCal is worse than ever. According to a 2011 report by the UCLA Civil Rights Project:

"Southern California schools show profound segregation by race, poverty, and language status, all of which are visibly related to disparities in educational opportunity and outcomes. ... Over twice as many intensely segregated secondary schools were identified by the state as critically overcrowded compared to predominately white and Asian schools ... less than 50% of Grade-9 students in intensely segregated schools graduated on time. In schools educating a majority of white and Asian youth, 81% graduated on time. ... students in intensely segregated schools were close to three times as likely to have a teacher lacking full qualifications than students attending majority white and Asian schools." — UCLA Civil Rights Project report, 2011[2]

Expelled From Los Angeles CORE ~ 1963

Defeat in the CORE election didn't end the Action Faction. We decided to set up a new CORE chapter, one dedicated to direct action, one where no one could vote in any meeting unless they had participated in at least one recent protest action. We called it "Central CORE" after Central Avenue, the major artery of the main Los Angeles ghetto and the street on which we opened a tiny storefront office. Since National CORE had already chartered several satellite chapters in the Los Angeles area — Long Beach, Pasadena, Pacoima, Venice, and so on — we assumed we had a right to set up a new chapter too. The moderates now in firm control of L.A. CORE did not see it that way, and National CORE eventually sided with them against us.

Those of us who had tried to set up Central CORE were then charged by L.A. CORE leaders with violation of various rules and regulations, all of which boiled down to attempting to start a rival chapter. In all, 17 of the most vocal Action Faction members — including me — were expelled from L.A. CORE for our nefarious crimes. Since none of us had any interest in continuing to work with the moderates, our expulsion was entirely symbolic with little practical effect. My commitment and allegiance was to the Movement and to the other members of the Action Faction, not to a particular organization, so being expelled had little effect on me. Nor did it have any effect on Bruin CORE, with which I remained quite active.

Since we were barred from using the CORE name, we formed an independent civil rights organization — the Non-Violent Action Committee (N-VAC). To some degree we chose that name in honor of the Nonviolent Action Group at Howard University in Washington DC and the Cambridge Nonviolent Action Committee (CNAC) in Cambridge Maryland, both of which we greatly admired from afar for their militancy. But mainly the name denoted our determination to push nonviolent direct action as far as we could take it.

N-VAC's three co-chairs had been the main leaders of the Action Faction. First and foremost was Woodrow Coleman — everyone called him "Woody." He was our heart. At 29, he was ten years older than me. Originally from Texas, he was one of the many Afro-Americans who joined the Great Migration out of the South and out of legally enforced segregation. He first got involved with the NAACP and CORE in 1960 during the Woolworth pickets in support of the student sit-ins, events that convinced him of nonviolent direct action's potential power. I don't know how many times he was arrested, more than a dozen at the time I first met him. He was a brilliant, self-taught innovator of nonviolent tactics and in 1962 he led a successful 33-day sit-in that desegregated an all-white Monterey Park neighborhood that had refused to sell a home to a Black college professor. Though he always wore a dark suit and tie on protests, Woody was stone working class, a construction laborer working out of Laborer's Local 300. He was then, still is, and will ever be, my picket captain.

F. Daniel Gray ("Danny") was our political strategist and along with Woody our main direct action leader. Tall and thin, originally from Brooklyn, a Black intellectual carrying on the tradition of the Harlem Renaissance. He was our head. One of the few Marxists actually active in civil rights protests, he knew all the currents, backwaters, and factions of the thoroughly splintered Los Angeles left. He had been one of L.A. CORE's most prominent leaders since at least the 1960 civil rights protests outside the Democratic Convention.

Robert Hall was N-VAC's soul. A snappy dresser with a thin mustache and a narrow-brimmed fedora, he was a former car salesman with the high-energy air of a born street hustler. He knew the ghetto, the walk, the talk, and the bitter anger, and he carried himself with the panache of a natural-born community organizer. He was a private person and shared little of his past with me, so I don't know how he got involved in CORE or Freedom Movement protests.

By obvious and common consent those three were our leaders. They were leaders by example because of their actions — not their verbal manipulations, political maneuvers, or sense of class entitlement.

Tikkun Olam

During one of those Thursday afternoon study-ins at the Board of Education I got into a conversation with one of the BoE staff. He actually asked me, "What's a good Jewish kid like you doing mixed up with all these troublemakers?"

At the time his question simply irked me and I answered him with what amounted to rhetoric and slogans. But it stuck with me for quite a while. Why was I there? What was I doing? Yeah, sure, I'd gotten involved in civil rights as a way of striking back against the Nazis, but by that fall they were no longer a factor, and yet there I was still picketing, sitting in, marching, handing out leaflets, arguing in meetings, getting expelled from CORE, and so on.

And when I began teaching nonviolent training sessions, some guys (it was always men) would say (well, boast, really) they couldn't be nonviolent in the face of provocation or attack — it was just too impossible for them to contemplate. But as I grew more experienced I came to understand that remaining nonviolent in the face of violence was not the hardest part of engaging in nonviolent resistance. Once there was a will to take a stand and do something about injustice, training and group solidarity could solve the problem of maintaining nonviolent self-discipline.

The hard part was first overcoming apathy, discouragement, and despair enough to commit yourself to take action. Our bias against taking social/political action is deeply rooted in our culture, and our cultural language is so filled with reasons not do anything about inequality injustice, and exploitation that they've become clichés:

"You can't fight City Hall."
"I have no power or influence."
"There's nothing I can do"
"Nothing ever changes, the rich get richer and the poor get children."

It turns out that ain't a new problem. Nor is it uniquely American. I never formally studied Judaism, but I did read Jewish history and literature. One time I came across a story in the Talmud that remained with me all my life. Almost two thousand years ago, Rabbi Tarfon was teaching a class in Jerusalem on the subject of Tikkun Olam — Hebrew for "healing the world."

"You are not required to complete the task [of healing the world's ills]," he told his students, "but neither are you free to avoid it."

Now at that time, their world was in a world of hurt:

The Jewish revolt against Rome had been crushed.
Jerusalem had fallen, the city burned, the Temple destroyed.
Tens of thousands had been slaughtered, gutters ran red with blood.
Hundreds of thousands of Jews & Christians were enslaved.
Thousands were being tortured to death in the Coliseum.

There was enormous despair. Yet Tarfon's response was, "You are not required to complete the task, but neither are you free to avoid it."

Somewhere else in the Talmud (or maybe some other book), I came across a commentary from a different rabbi a century or two later, who was teaching his students about Tarfon's dictum. I can't find that quote, so I'll have to paraphrase it. One of his students asked, "But Rabbi, what can one person do?"

The rabbi's answer was, "You don't measure your individual contribution against the totality of the task. You measure your contribution against the totality of your life."

I understood that. Measured against the pain and injustice that exist in the world, the contribution of any individual — even the greatest individual — is infinitesimally small. We don't have control over the world, but we do have control over how we lead our lives. Tikkun Olam can form:

No part of your life, or
A small part, or
Fighting for justice can become a life focus.

Which is why I found myself sitting in a Board of Education hallway one afternoon when a bureaucrat asked me, "What's a good Jewish kid like you doing mixed up with all these troublemakers?"

But don't think for one moment that I reasoned all that out or came to some epiphany-type decision about the course of my life to come. It doesn't work that way — or at least it didn't for me. For me, becoming a political activist was simply the sum of a thousand daily decisions, one after another, each one made without deep thought at all. Should I go to the movies this afternoon or down to the CORE office to crank that old mimeograph? Should I go to my friend's party this evening or to the CORE membership meeting to argue with the moderates? Do I sit in at the BoE and risk getting arrested and ending up with a police record or should I focus on my UCLA classes and future career prospects? Do I stand with my compañeros on the line, or do I turn away? Each choice I made, day after day, was a step on a long road. A road I travel to this day.

Freedom Now!

Kennedy & the Freedom Movement ~ 1963

My feelings about President Kennedy were quite mixed. His rhetoric was inspiring, yet as a child of progressives I had supported Adlai Stevenson during the 1960 primaries — one of the very few to do so at Dorsey High — and I resented Stevenson's defeat at the hands of the Cold Warrior from Massachusetts. I admired JFK's youth and energy, but his posturing and brinkmanship during the 1962 Cuban Missile Crisis alienated and, frankly, terrified me. It was obvious that Los Angeles would be a prime target in any nuclear war with the Soviet Union. All through grade school, in addition to fire drills we'd had "drop drills" where we practiced cowering under our desks — as if that would somehow protect us from a nuclear blast. Even as a kid I could spot bullshit of that magnitude — or should I say "megatonnage?"

After he was elected, the mass media portrayed Kennedy as a civil rights champion, but once I started working with CORE I came to understand how false that image was. The tepid and limited actions he took towards racial justice were the absolute minimum he was forced to do by political pressure mobilized by the Freedom Movement.

It was only reluctantly and with great hesitancy that he finally enforced Supreme Court rulings during the Freedom Rides, and his use of federal troops to protect James Meredith from a savage white mob instigated and inflamed by Mississippi politicians was tardy, half-hearted, and as conciliatory as possible towards the racist rioters — even to the extent of humiliating and disarming Afro-American soldiers so that the sight of armed Black men enforcing the peace would not upset white supremacists. He had no qualms sending Afro-American GIs to fight and die in foreign wars, but he wouldn't allow them to defend a Black man in Mississippi from a lynch mob.

It was the furious rage of segregationists at the minimal steps he was forced to take that made him appear to the public — both white and Black — as if he was a Freedom Movement supporter. He wasn't.

For me personally, I was most affected by discovering that in order to curry political favor with the southern white Democrats he and his brother Bobby had falsely prosecuted Freedom Movement activists in Albany, Georgia on phony federal charges. One of them was Joni Rabinowitz, a red diaper baby just like me. I didn't know her personally, but I knew of her father, a famous radical lawyer. I identified with her, and felt her persecution as my own.

Most American adults living today can tell you exactly where they were when they heard about the 9/11 terror attacks and, though we're all in our 70s now, my generation has equally searing memories of the Kennedy assassination. Some of us from Bruin CORE and the DuBois Club were in the UCLA Student Union cafeteria about an hour before noon on November 22, 1963 when loudspeakers in the ceiling suddenly announced, "The President has been shot in Dallas Texas."

We — everyone — were stunned and shocked. Some students were crying, others were saying over and over, "This is America, this can't be happening here." But it could. And it was.

Like everyone else I was shaken by JFK's murder. A dozen or so of us retreated to a Westwood apartment shared by a couple of the DuBois Club members. There we watched the unfolding drama on a grainy black and white TV.

We were convinced beyond a shadow of doubt that the killers were racist right-wing extremists opposed to the Civil Rights Movement. It was obvious. For days, Texas segregationists had been vilifying him (falsely) as a "race-mixing integrationist." Anti-Kennedy zealots shouting racist chants lined the motorcade route, and the *Dallas Morning News* ran a black-bordered, full-page advertisement attacking him for being, "... soft on Communists, fellow travelers, and ultra-leftists in America." Before his arrival, thousands of "Kennedy Wanted for Treason" leaflets had been distributed by right-wing hate groups who accused him of being a Communist sympathizer — just as they claimed Martin Luther King and the entire Freedom Movement were subversive tools of the Soviet Union paid for by Moscow gold. I kid you not — they really said nonsense like that. Worse, they actually believed it.

That it might have been a CIA hit motivated by foreign policy issues did not occur to us. In 1963, Vietnam rarely made even the back pages, and most Americans couldn't find it on a map. We had no way of knowing that JFK was secretly contemplating a significant reduction in military and covert aid to the Saigon generals. Nor did we have any concept of the bitter hatred directed against the Kennedys by anti-Castro zealots who were convinced he had betrayed them by not invading Cuba and using military force to overthrow Fidel Castro and suppress the Cuban revolution.

In the decades since the Kennedy assassination a cottage industry of conspiracy theories asserting a wide range of various killers, plots, and motives came into being. Some of them plausible, others not even close. My personal belief is that there certainly was a broader conspiracy, including individuals associated with either the police or intelligence agencies or both. A conspiracy motivated by white-supremacist racism or foreign-affairs anti-communism or both.

Some of us watching the TV news that afternoon had parents who had been victims of Red Scare persecutions. We feared the assassination would be falsely blamed on leftists, and that, like Hitler's Reichstag fire, it would spark a political pogrom of smears, harassment, and arrests targeting liberals, progressives, and Freedom Movement activists on phony "subversion" charges. And for a time it seemed like that might become the case. As soon as Lee Harvey Oswald was arrested the media instantly labeled him a "Marxist." He was then murdered on live TV in a police station — to prevent him from naming others in the conspiracy, we concluded.

Given their hopes of positive social change through the liberal wing of the Democratic Party, the DuBois Club members were devastated by Kennedy's murder, politically despondent and bereft. Those of us from Bruin CORE were already becoming disenchanted with liberal electoral politics — a trend that would accelerate through 1964 and later. We were far more attuned to, and fearful of, racist violence — the Birmingham Church bombing was still fresh in our memories, as was the assassination of Medgar Evers and the mob attacks on the Freedom Riders and James Meredith.

The DuBois members started collecting money for a beer run to ease their depression and drown their fears. Those of us from Bruin CORE removed ourselves to the apartment of Lynn Busch where we carefully locked the doors and drew the shades before rolling joints and smoking pot for the same purpose. (Dubois Club members did not approve of marijuana use because it might offend the working class — which shows how little they knew about the working class, or at least its younger members.)

Eviction Fight ~ 1932

In the spring of '32, my mom was a high school senior. By then she was far more involved in the Young Communist League (YCL) than her college-student boyfriend, Ben Iceland. New York City was suffering through the depths of the Depression with mass unemployment and thousands of families being evicted from their apartments. Leftist groups of all kinds — Communists, Socialists, Catholic Workers, Jewish War Veterans — were all attempting to organize tenant unions and rent strikes to resist evictions.

As part of that effort, the YCL recruited students to pass out leaflets in the slums of the Lower East Side and Brooklyn. Fearing that her mother Rose would find out, Mom avoided leafleting in Brooklyn. One day, though, when she returned home to their tenement flat she found her mom clutching a rent strike flyer and frantic with worry. Her son Leon's garment industry job couldn't support all four of them, and their now fatherless family relied on the paltry rents paid by their three tenants. How would they survive if the renters stopped paying? For once, my mother bit her tongue, saying nothing about her own efforts to combat "greedy landlords" and the "rapacious capitalist class."

"It'll be all right Mother, we'll get by. In June I'll graduate, and somehow find a job."

A few days later she was in the YCL office picking up more leaflets when one of the boys told her, "There's going to be an eviction at 18th and First Avenue tomorrow morning. We're going to be there. Don't be surprised if there's some arrests and beatings by the police."

She knew that meant they were going to try putting the furniture back in the apartment in defiance of the sheriff's bailiffs. The way he said it made it a test of her commitment, and she knew she had to go. But if she were hurt or arrested her mother would be hysterical. Her beloved father though — as he used to be before he was crushed by the Depression — would expect her to stand by her principles. He despised cowards. If she truly believed in helping workers fight injustices, she had to do her part and not think of the consequences. Slowly she nodded her head. She would go to the eviction.

It was only four blocks from Irving High, so she cut class the next morning and joined the crowd. They were held back by police, some of them mounted on horseback. More than 70 years later my mom still remembered — and wrote about — how afraid she was:

Two mounted police kept the traffic moving while several police on foot confined the crowd to a small area. The leader of the Tenants' Union mounted an empty crate and blasted Tammany Hall for doing nothing to stop the eviction of a family with small children. As indignation mounted, the crowd growled and taunted the deputies. A few moments later when two burly men emerged from the building carrying a threadbare sofa, followed by a weeping woman and three small children, the crowd suddenly surged forward. Immediately the mounted police charged onto the sidewalk, rearing their horses to force people closer together.

I was terrified of the huge animals and tried to make myself smaller, to become invisible. I couldn't see over people's heads but heard them shouting, "They got the sofa away from the sheriff." Then suddenly the police were wildly flailing their clubs amidst a bedlam of screams and curses. "Bastards!" "Cossacks!" "This is America. We have rights —"

As people surged away from the nightsticks and rearing horses, I was swept along with them. I looked for my YCL friends but couldn't find them. I saw a policeman methodically clubbing a woman to the ground. I started towards the woman but suddenly my arm was seized by a stranger who told me, "Get going. It won't do any good. Run to the subway."

With tears streaming from my eyes, I ran to the subway and leaped down the steps two at a time. Luckily a train had just arrived and the doors were being forcibly held open by other demonstrators, all cursing the police brutality. We squeezed inside. ₃

When I was a teen in the late 1950s, I once overheard my father say something to her one morning during breakfast that made me realize she still suffered nightmares about that rearing horse and those club-swinging cops.

Nevertheless, the very next day my mom signed up as a member of the Young Communist League. Formally putting your name on paper to join a Communist organization was a risky move, so most YCL members used aliases. My mom, the petite, dark-haired Jewish daughter of Romanian immigrants living in the slums of Brooklyn, chose "Donna Ames" because, as she later told me, she thought it sounded "so graceful, connoting a tall, blue-eyed blonde with a college degree and a long lineage of American-born parents."

Nonviolent Bootcamp ~ 1964

By January of '64 most of us who had formerly been part of L.A. CORE's Action Faction were now members of the newborn Non-Violent Action Committee (N-VAC). Some who hadn't been expelled remained active with both. From our cramped storefront office on Central Avenue we were ready to roll with the new year.

Our relations with the moderates who were now in uncontested control of L.A. CORE were chilly. But since they did little protesting and we in N-VAC did little else, our paths rarely crossed. N-VAC and Bruin CORE, however, became firm allies, both of us committed to aggressive direct action. I was the bridge between the two organizations.

Back in those days, bumper stickers were an important source of both income and public outreach for civil rights groups. The ones L.A. CORE sold read "We Shall Overcome," those from N-VAC and Bruin CORE proclaimed "Freedom Now!" It wasn't that we rejected "We Shall Overcome" as a slogan or a song, we still sang it as the anthem that more than any other bound us together — every meeting ended with it. But we were no longer willing to settle for overcoming *some day*, we wanted freedom *now!*

N-VAC was democratic in its meetings and decision-making, we discussed, debated, argued, and disagreed. But out on the line we maintained — and expected others to maintain — the self-discipline of soldiers. Our discipline was self-discipline because, other than telling problem children to leave, we had no punishments with which to enforce it. Yet we almost never had to remove anyone because of their behavior — to tell the truth, I can't recall a single instance of that ever happening, though I suppose it must have at one time or another.

For us, you either put your body on the line with seriousness and discipline — or you didn't. It was your actions that counted, not your motives, psychology, verbal statements, political ideology or class consciousness. Rhetoric and bullshit didn't cut it. Later, when I was working for Dr. King's organization, the Southern Christian Leadership Conference (SCLC), in Alabama and Mississippi, it was pretty much the same with them — and with SNCC and CORE too.

When we were in action, the designated captain was in charge, usually assisted by a song leader and sometimes depending on the number of people involved one or two monitors or picket posts. On a big march there'd be a whole team of marshals organized into a structured unit. When new people showed up at a protest, we explained what we were about, and since all the N-VAC regulars were modeling disciplined behavior, everyone accepted self-discipline as the way it was. Which is not to imply that N-VAC actions were dour, regimented, militaristic affairs — far from it. Most N-VAC actions, even civil disobedience, were energetic, uplifting, sometimes humorous, often joyous. And always filled with singing.

On N-VAC actions I was frequently chosen to assist the picket captain as a monitor (though never as song leader). Outside of actually protesting, my main ongoing job for was printing our leaflets on my father's old 1930s-era hand-cranked mimeograph and running the nonviolent training sessions for new N-VAC recruits and Bruin CORE members. The training sessions I ran replicated how I had been trained by Woody and Danny, which was long on the tactics and strategies of direct action and short on nonviolent philosophy as a way of life.

In the Freedom Movement of the 1960s, two different kinds of nonviolence being put into practice (and argued over) — *Philosophical* and *Tactical*. (Today, Philosophical nonviolence might be referred to as *Principled*, and Tactical might be called *Strategic*.)

Philosophical nonviolence was the nonviolence of Dr. King, James Farmer, Bayard Rustin, and other well-known leaders and activists. It emphasized love, reconciliation, and winning over one's enemies through compassion and redemptive suffering. For its advocates it was a way of life. Though the mass media focused its attention on this kind of nonviolence, its adherents were always a small minority within the Movement.

Most Movement activists were tactically nonviolent. Rather than changing hearts, our focus was on changing racist behavior — through persuasion if possible, but if not, then by coercion through legislation, court rulings, nonviolent disruption, and cultural pressure. For us, nonviolence was not a way of life but rather a means to an end — we used nonviolence because we wanted to win.

As we saw it, violence as a social change strategy simply would not work in modern America — it was self-defeating. We knew there was no certainty that nonviolent tactics and strategies would achieve significant victories, but it offered the best chance of creating social change. By 1963, the great majority of Freedom Movement activists in all the main groups — CORE, SNCC, NAACP, and even SCLC — were tactically nonviolent rather than philosophically nonviolent. But the mass media portrayed Philosophical nonviolence as the only kind there was. That's still pretty much the case today.

On picket lines, sit-ins, marches, and other kinds of protests where we were confronted by violent racists and cops with their guns, badges, court systems, and jails, it was hard to tell Philosophical and Tactical adherents apart because our actual behavior was pretty much the same. The big argument between the two camps was over self-defense against white terrorists like the KKK when we were *not* engaged in public activity. Philosophicals argued for remaining nonviolent at all times in all situations. Tacticals under attack by the Klan might respond with either defensive violence or some form of nonviolence depending on their reading of the situation. This sounds like a minor theoretical difference, but we spent an enormous amount of time in passionate debate over it.

In real life situations, however, there was rarely any divergence in actions. Both Philosophicals and Tacticals agreed that most times nonviolence was more effective — and safer — than violence. It was more effective in winning supporters and achieving end goals, and safer in terms of arrest, injury, or death. During my first six months in Alabama working for SCLC, I came under direct deadly threat from the Ku Klux Klan on five different occasions. On three of those occasions — four if you count running like hell as a tactic of nonviolence, which I do — I escaped without serious injury through nonviolent techniques. On one of those occasions we returned fire against KKK nightriders and scared them off.

N-VAC's leaders — Woody Coleman, Danny Gray, and Robert Hall — believed in serious training for serious action, and our N-VAC training sessions concentrated less on the "why" and more on the "how." Today, our kind of hands-on, boot-camp-style training in the discipline and methods of protest is not much seen, it's gone quite out of fashion. Nowadays, most nonviolent training is oriented towards Philosophical nonviolence, and the trainers use dialogue, discussion, personal role playing, and exercises in understanding the other person's point of view to impart concepts of nonviolent philosophy and communication, nonviolence in thought, word, and deed, social alternatives to violence, nonviolent conflict resolution, compassion training, and so on.

All that is no doubt valuable — but it doesn't teach people how to mount effective nonviolent protests. Our N-VAC training sessions taught the techniques and subtleties of how to picket and sit in, how to organize and direct a mass march, what to do when arrested (we had no illusions on that score), techniques for preventing and de-escalating hostility or violence from adversaries, and how to nonviolently protect yourself from violent physical attack if our de-escalation techniques failed.

Underlying our form of nonviolent training was a saying we took from the U.S. Marine Corps, "When the shit hits the fan, people don't rise to the level of their expectations, rather they fall to the level of their training." That was certainly true in my life. When the head of the KKK in Crenshaw County, Alabama put a .38 to my head and told me he was going to blow my brains out, my training in Tactical nonviolence may well have saved my life. When a mob of white racists attacked me in Luverne, Alabama, I didn't have time to ponder, "Hmmm these people want to stomp and beat me, I wonder what I should do?" And even if I'd had the time — which I didn't — I was too freaked to do that kind of abstract analysis anyway. What I did was what I was trained to do — nothing more, nothing less.

Each of our training sessions would take a whole day (two days if it was for people who were going to be acting as captains and monitors). There were usually a dozen or so trainees — men and women both — plus me, Jay Frank, and sometimes Jerry Farber as instructors. We discussed and analyzed, then we practiced and drilled. We role-played protesters keeping their cool while hecklers screamed insults and racial epithets in our faces. We practiced maintaining the picket line while being pelted with eggs and water balloons. We drilled in the various methods of going limp when being dragged off to jail, the techniques of sitting in to block an entrance, and the discipline of action in hostile environments. And, of course, we taught and practiced the songs — perhaps the single most important element of the training session.

We took care not to really hurt anyone, no acid was thrown in anyone's eyes, no burning cigarettes ground into anyone's cheek, no heads cracked by hard-swinging billy clubs. But we were rough because we were training for real dangers. People are often paralyzed when confronted by sudden violence, both from surprise and from simply not knowing what to do — hence our training.

At the end of the day, we were tired, filthy, somewhat sore, and in some cases bruised. A few people decided that nonviolent direct action was not where they wanted to put their energy, but those who endured a full-on N-VAC training knew how to protest effectively and what to do when shit hit the fan. More than that, I think our training sessions were a rite of passage into the solidarity of the Freedom Movement family — as my first training had been for me in early 1963.

You may wonder, I suppose, if such rough, hands-on training was really necessary (or even wise). Back then, it was. In the early '60s, protesting for or against anything was considered suspicious, if not downright subversive, and violent, aggressive racists were not confined to the Deep South. I still have the syllabus notes from a training session I ran in early 1964 and it listed some of the actual situations that I and my fellow CORE and N-VAC protesters had recently faced in Los Angeles:

> Verbal abuse of many kinds
> Being spat upon, shoved, jostled, and punched
> A teenage girl dragged across the floor by her hair
> Another had her loop earring bloodily ripped from her pierced ear
> Beatings by white vigilantes with fists and chains
> Rocks, bricks, manure, eggs, and exploding firecrackers thrown at us
> Being kicked and stepped on during sit-ins on lobby floors
> Sit-in participants being rolled down a flight of stairs
> Cars attempting to run over pickets
> Police cracking heads with their billy clubs
> Choking by police (the infamous "choke hold")
> Hot tar poured over a man's head
> A knife stabbing (fortunately not serious)
> An attack with a can of hair spray used as a flame-thrower[4]

That list above reflects "liberal" California in the early 1960s. Violence against protesters in the Deep South was much, much worse.

White Mob Comes to Watts ~ 1963

From our tiny N-VAC office on Central Avenue we were determined to test the limits of militant nonviolent action in the ghetto. Our focus was job discrimination.

At that time, employment discrimination was explicit, overt, and widespread — as it had been for generations past. Entire occupations were commonly understood to be "white jobs," or "Colored work," or "women's work." It was so normal that most Los Angeles whites never spared a moment's thought about it, at least not until they personally encountered, or heard about, a jobs-related protest.

Newspaper Help Wanted ads were how most people looked for work when personal connections failed. Many papers divided their employment notices into three sections: "White Men," "White Women," and "Colored," or sometimes "Colored Men," and "Colored Women." People seeking work searched the classified ads in the section appropriate for their race and gender. And individual job postings might explicitly state racial requirements. I still have one snipped from the local Westwood paper reading: [SECOND COOK, white, for sorority house, UCLA.]

Though it's little noted today, the March on Washington that so strongly moved me was a march for "*Jobs* and Freedom" Three of the ten march demands were related to employment discrimination. And by the later part of 1963, Freedom Movement direct action protests were increasingly targeting occupational inequalities.

N-VAC's first direct action campaign began in December of '63 when we were still calling ourselves "Central CORE." It was against the two Wich Stands ("*Wich*" as in "*sandwich*"). The original Wich Stand was a drive-in burger joint at Florence and Figueroa, an area now commonly referred to as "Watts." (Technically, it was in the South Central district, not the Watts neighborhood, but after the 1965 rebellion most people used "Watts" to refer to the entire Black community of central Los Angeles.)

The first Wich Stand had spaces for about 15 cars served by carhops and inside maybe a dozen or so counter seats with a small bar on the side. It had opened in 1939 when the neighborhood was white working-class. Realtors later "busted" that area, annexing it to the rapidly growing Afro-American ghetto. At the time of our campaign, 95% of the Wich Stand #1's customers were Black. All of its employees were white. Every. Single. One.

Wich Stand #2 was newer and much larger. A drive-in diner (as opposed to a burger stand), it was able to accommodate twice as many more cars, plus it had inside table seating and a full lounge-bar. Located at the corner of Slauson and Overhill a block or so north of Inglewood, it was a hangout for white, "car-culture" teens who made it crystal clear that Afro-Americans were unwelcome. Together, the two Wich Stands employed almost 100 people — all of them white, even the janitors.

As was standard CORE policy, an N-VAC team composed of our most diplomatic members — not me, obviously — attempted to negotiate with the owners over their hiring practices. We asked that they immediately hire at least one Afro-American at each location and agree to stop discriminating against Black job applicants. Not an unreasonable position given that the clientele at Stand #1 was almost entirely Black.

We also wanted them to adopt a program of "compensatory hiring." Meaning that they would favor Black applicants until the percentage of Backs in their employ roughly matched that of surrounding area. Again, not an extreme redress for more than 25 years of explicit, overt racial discrimination.

They were not receptive. They did, briefly, hire one Black carhop at the ghetto location, but she quit after three hours because of harassment from the white employees. After that, the Wich Stand managers stonewalled us.

So early in December we began to picket the ghetto Wich Stand. It was mainly a dinner joint, and every day we would picket from four in the afternoon until midnight — 2am on weekends. No Afro-Americans crossed our line. None. Zip. Nada. People from the neighborhood would come up to us saying, "Oh we're so glad someone is finally doing something about this. We've been angry about this for years." Folk would bring us fried chicken, cake, coffee, and other expressions of community support.

Looking back now, I'm both surprised and self-critical that we made no real attempt to organize the local community. I believe some N-VAC members did distribute leaflets along the adjacent streets during the day while I was at UCLA, and (I hope) they explained to people why we were picketing. Given the neighborhood support for our action, we could have — we absolutely *should* have — organized an ongoing community-based civil rights group. But our minds were fixed on direct action, not community organizing.

Our failure in that regard reflected our CORE roots. CORE mainly saw itself as a small force of highly trained nonviolent warriors who fought the good fight on behalf of the broader society. Community organizing, mass action, and building a broad mass base for political campaigns were just not part of CORE's organizational DNA. At least not in the North. In the South, CORE projects were influenced in a community-organizing direction by the success of SNCC's Mississippi and Southwest Georgia projects, but that didn't carry over to the northern or western CORE chapters — at least not those in SoCal.

Early on we tried picketing what we referred to as the "Inglewood" location, but without success. None of the white teens respected our line or sympathized with the issues we were fighting for. They did enjoy harassing us and calling us "niggers" and "nigger-lovers." Since it was clearly a waste of our time we decided to ignore Wich Stand #2 and concentrate on the ghetto location where we could really affect their business. Four to midnight picket, seven days a week. Maybe once or twice a night a white customer might come through our line, usually headed to the bar. Essentially their business was dead so long as we were there.

By midnight we were exhausted but still emotionally wired, so a group of us usually retired to someone's pad where we drank tequila shots with salt and lime until we were drunk enough to crash. By mid-morning we'd wake up hung over and grouchy, go about whatever errands and business we had for the day (in my case going to UCLA where I pretended to be a student). Then back on the Wich Stand line by four.

After a few weeks of that regime I realized I didn't like getting drunk and I liked the hangover even less. Marijuana, it turned out, was my relaxant of choice. So I stopped drinking alcohol and never resumed, becoming instead a dedicated pothead for the next 50 years (except when I was in the South or some other place where it was too dangerous, arrest-wise).

The Slausons were a large Afro-American street gang and Wich Stand #1 was on their turf. At that time L.A. had five major Black gangs — Slausons, Businessmen, Gladiators, Watts, and Comptons. They were big gangs with hundreds of members. But this was before Nixon's War Against Drugs turned narcotics into a billion-dollar business, so they weren't the narco gangs we see today with drive-by shootings, murder, mayhem, and kids dying with needles in their arms. Yes, they were sometimes violent, they committed petty and some not so petty crimes, they smoked weed and some of them sold it. But mainly they protected their hood from outsiders, hostile gangs, and to the extent they could, the LAPD.

Like the hood as a whole, the Slausons were quite friendly toward us. They supported our fight for racial justice, though they found the notion of nonviolence incomprehensible. We never preached nonviolence as a way of life to them, nor did we diss their gang culture, but we were firm that nonviolence was our *strategy* because that's what we thought could *win*. They respected that.

Every once in a while, for a lark, some of the gang members might walk the line with us for a few minutes. "Hey! Look at me! I'm being nonviolent!" And they'd all laugh and have a good time. Which was cool with us, we got a kick out of it too. N-VAC co-chair Robert Hall later told an interviewer:

> They would come down and walk the picket line. When they'd get on the line they'd tell you, "I don't believe in nonviolence," and I'd say, "Okay baby, give me your piece [gun] now, and if you get mad or something like that just step off the line." Sometimes I used to be standing around at the Wich Stand, Jerry Farber and myself, and I'd have as much as fifteen knives, three or four guns. ... And the guys would walk the picket line. Then they'd come up and say, "Okay baby, I'm ready to go." We'd give 'em the knife or gun or whatever they had. And we'd say, "See you tomorrow" and they'd come down.[5]

Though our action was strictly legal and we gave the LAPD no excuse to break us up with arrests or violence, they kept us under a close and hostile watch — passing by at frequent intervals and giving us the hard eye. They repeatedly stopped, got out of their squad cars, and demanded that we identify ourselves — the same cops demanding our same IDs over and over, day after day. Their obvious antagonism, however, was a mark in our favor with the Slausons. There was bitter, unrelenting enmity between the LAPD and the youth gangs — Black and Latino both — and in truth the cops acted like an enemy gang — a blue gang that used their guns and badges to humiliate and dominate nonwhite communities.

As both the street cops and Police Chief William Parker saw it, their job was to enforce the social status quo of Jim Crow and racial subservience. Parker had a policy of recruiting white southerners because of their racial attitudes and their supposed "expertise" in controlling Blacks. He hired white Texans for the same reason with regard to Latinos. On the street their attitude clearly articulated their intention "to keep the monkeys in their place," as one police official so charmingly expressed it.

The LAPD's dedication to social and political control ran from trivial to brutal. I was (and still am) a good driver with nary a ticket. One month I attached a "Freedom Now" bumper sticker to my car and within six weeks collected four moving violations. I removed the bumper sticker and never got another ticket. For me it was just traffic tickets, for nonwhites the police policy was stop, harass, humiliate, and in some cases shoot first and fill out the paperwork later. There's also no question in my mind that they yearned to crush the Black and Latino street gangs — and the Freedom Movement.

One chilly Saturday night in late early January of '64 a dozen or so of us were on the line, maybe five of us white, eight or nine Black, and we were walking slowly back and forth on the sidewalk, talking quietly and singing our freedom songs from time to time. Just routine. Familiar. Boring.

Suddenly a car came crashing through the line, almost running over Roberta Krinsky and her brother Fred. Then more cars came screeching in, a dozen or more, and they were all filled with white teenagers — mostly boys, a few girls. There must have been more than 50 of them. "What the fuck is this shit?" I thought.

They got out and started up with all this racist crap, singing "Dixie," making racial jokes, shouting, "Jiggaboos, niggers, nigger-lovers." Some of them pretended to be monkeys — you know, dancing around and scratching under their armpits, as if to mimic us as monkeys.

They had a crate of eggs, whole flats of them, which they began to pelt us with. We recognized a few of the most aggressive from the time they had harassed us at Wich Stand #2, so we understood that somehow the owner had convinced them to come teach us a lesson in white supremacy. I doubt he paid them money, they probably said to each other, "Hey, what a kick! Let's go mess with the niggers!"

Keep in mind that this was before the large-scale urban violence of the mid-'60s. It was a year and a half before the Watts revolt, and the ghetto was not yet a scary place for whites. For some whites, especially a large pack of teenagers, Blacks were people you humiliate, people you make racist jokes about, people you look down upon — not people you fear — not if you were in a mob with others of your kind.

Of course, we were deep into nonviolent training and discipline. We were determined to hold our line, "come hell or high water" as the old saying went. We kept on picketing, walking steady, keeping our intervals, and singing our hearts out — dodging eggs when we could, getting hit when we couldn't.

The Afro-American neighborhood, however, was most definitely NOT into nonviolence. A crowd quickly began gathering, at first across the street, then edging in closer as it grew larger. In a strange kind of way, they considered us *their* freedom fighters. They liked us, they were even proud of us. They reacted to the whites attacking us as if we were family and they ready to take care of business. Soon we had 50 white teenagers shouting racist epithets on one side of us, and almost 150 furious Blacks on the other side. Standing between them were our dozen or so nonviolent pickets singing freedom songs. And these idiot white kids had absolutely no clue the danger they were in. They're throwing eggs at us while we were trying to save their lives.

I remember clear as yesterday, a few minutes after the white teens first arrived this cool cat and his girl came walking down the street. Dressed. Obviously out on the town. Saturday night. She had on a green sequin sheath. He had on a dark suit with a turtleneck — no tie. Spiffy. Way cool. They must have seen the commotion and came over to find out what was going down. She got an egg right in the chest, splattering her sequin dress which is almost impossible to clean. They didn't say a word. They just looked at each other and walked away.

Then the Slausons came rolling in, more and more of them. The *word* had gone out.

"Please don't cross our line," we kept telling the gang kids and neighborhood folk. "That's what they want. We don't care what you do anywhere else, but this is our action. We have to keep it nonviolent. That's how we win. If they can provoke violence, then they win."

As I recall, Danny Gray was our picket captain that night (Woody was working). He was spending most of his time with a guy named Skillet who we knew to be the Slausons' war chief (their term) from the times he'd come by the line before. So it was up to Jerry Farber, Jay Frank, and me to hold the line together. And no police anywhere in sight. Any other night, they were always driving by giving us the eye, looking to harass us — but not that night. No. No, not that night.

As the gang kids rolled in, they would report to Skillet and Danny. "Four carloads of" — we didn't call them "pigs" in those days, that was later — we called them "fuzz." "Four carloads of fuzz over at... Three carloads up by... A whole Tac Team in such-and-so parking lot." In a three- or four-block radius, completely surrounding us, there were probably more than 100 cops, all of them arming up for heavy action. All of them carefully out of sight. Waiting. Just waiting. Waiting for some violence on the part of the neighborhood Blacks or the gang members so they could swoop in to "protect" those dumb white kids.

By now members of other gangs were showing up — Businessmen, Gladiators, Watts, even a few Comptons. Danny was the one who responded. "It's a trick," he told them. "It's a trap." The gang members were organized and disciplined. They understood what we were saying. The crowd did too — mostly. Intellectually. But it was emotionally hard. Every once in a while something would happen, someone would get hit with an egg, or the white numbskulls would do something especially provocative, and the crowd would kind of surge forward. We'd rush in front of them to put ourselves between them and the white kids who were still shouting insults and throwing eggs at us.

What allowed us to keep the teenagers from physically assaulting us and the Blacks from charging through us to get at the racist whites was our discipline, our training, and above all our freedom songs. There's not a doubt in my mind that we held the Wich Stand line that night with our songs. Somehow our singing created a psychological barrier that prevented those white teens — who outnumbered us four or five to one — from taking a few steps forward into our midst and beating the crap out of us as they so clearly wanted to do.

And at the same time, our songs created an invisible but emotionally-palpable social border that the furious Afro-American crowd respected and honored despite their anger. I cannot explain the psychology or sociology of the how or the why, but I saw it happen — and not just at the Wich Stand either, but again and again in similar situations I later encountered in Alabama and Mississippi. It's certainly what saved our asses that cold night at Florence and Figuroa.

That cool cat and his girl came back. Dark shirts and jeans. They passed by Danny and came up to the line where he showed me the sawed-off shotgun concealed by his long trench coat. She had a big purse slung across her shoulder, her right hand resting inside it. Very politely, he asked me to step aside.

"No, brother no!" I told them. "It's a trap, it's a trap!" Somehow I convinced them. They didn't leave, but they didn't start shooting.

Those white kids didn't know they were being used as bait to start the Watts Riot a year and a half early. I'm convinced that Chief Parker saw his opportunity to kill two birds with one stone. As soon as the "unruly crowd of Negroes" violently attacked the "innocent white children," those cops would've come swarming in, just as they did in a year and a half later when Watts blew and they shot 34 people to death. They would have brutally smashed and arrested Slausons and community folk alike while providing a media pretext to smear and discredit the entire Civil Rights Movement. No reporters were present, so the cops could have spun the tale any way they wanted, and since this was long before cellphones with cameras existed, their version would have been accepted as the gospel truth.

But that scheme didn't take into account N-VAC's disciplined nonviolence. Somehow we managed to hold that line for what seemed like an eternity (probably no more than 45 minutes). Protecting these racist idiots who were taunting us with verbal abuse and pelting us with eggs. A very weird night, very weird indeed.

Eventually, I guess either the white kids finally looked out and saw they were surrounded by what by then had grown to 300 or more angry Blacks, or they ran out of eggs, or something, because they abruptly jumped back in their cars and came smashing out through our line, driving through the crowd, almost running people down before they got out onto Florence. They raced back toward Inglewood, with people running after them and pounding on their cars with fists. The gang kids ran for their cars and gave chase. According to what we were told afterwards they caught some of the white teens and beat the shit out of them. Our attitude was that whatever happened away from our nonviolent action was not our concern — and if they got what was coming to them so be it.

The next day, of course, we were back on the line as usual. Skillet came by, kind of sheepish, "I want to apologize for what happened" he told us. "We weren't prepared. But don't worry, if they come again, we're copacetic. Look there." He pointed down the street to a house that had half a dozen or more cars parked on the lawn and a bunch of folk hanging around on the porch. "Every minute you're here," he told us, "we'll have 50 brothers standing by. We got your back. We've made a deal with the Gladiators." They were the gang that held territory between the Slausons' turf and Inglewood. "If they [the white kids] come back again, they'll never get back to Inglewood alive."

"As long as you don't do violence on our picket line," was our response.

"Yeah, yeah, we know. You people are nuts [laughing]. But you stand behind what you believe, and we respect that. But dig, those ofay motherfuckers won't get back to Inglewood alive." Fortunately, the idiot white kids never came back.

Not long after that, the Wich Stand owners tried to get an injunction against our picket line. We were stone broke as always, but Al Wirin, the famous ACLU attorney, agreed to represent us pro bono. He tied them in such knots they gave it up. Rather than hire Afro-Americans, they closed down Wich Stand #1 and sold the lot to Chevron for a gas station. Today, a McDonald's stands on that corner. I don't know how long Wich Stand #2 remained in business — probably quite a while — but now their old building is a health food restaurant.

All the Secrets of Saturn ~ 1933

In so many ways my mom never completely cast off the 1920s mindset and mores of the traditional, "good Jewish girl" upbringing that shaped her childhood and adolescent years until her father went bankrupt in 1930. Nevertheless, she somehow acquired a deep and abiding resentment of the limits society tried to impose on her as a woman. And in her own personal way — in those days there was no organized women's movement as such — she fiercely resisted what she termed "male chauvinism," and my generation would later call "sexism." In a recorded oral history, she once told me:

> "I didn't know I was a feminist. There was no such thing as being a feminist then, but I was innately so. I wanted absolutely to be accepted as their equal, and I must tell you, I never was. At any rate, I fought that fight long before it was popular."[6]

For her, this was not a theoretical battle of abstract ideology. Rather, it was one of immediate practical consequences — from being considered inconsequential because of her gender to constantly having to fend off casual, self-entitled lechery from men who assumed the only reason she was in their occupational world was for their sexual use. So she used the weapons she had. When you're a beautiful young woman, men open doors for you — both literally and figuratively. As she became more active in the YCL she soon caught the eye of men high up in the Communist Party (CP) hierarchy, and she seized the opportunities that brought her way.

In the early-1930s, "free love" and "smashing bourgeois mentality" were the official CP line (though that later changed). In practice, what that usually meant was that men were free to cat around all they wanted but they expected their wives and girlfriends to walk a more traditional, monogamous path. The arcana of Marxist ideology wasn't Mom's forte, but she clearly understood that if free love applied to the boys it should apply to her as well — whether they liked it or not. Though in actual fact I'm pretty sure she didn't step out on her boyfriend Ben — or, at least, not too much.

A deeper and far more fundamental principle of the Party was that "the end justifies the means." That dictum was drilled into every member's bones, even hers. For Party members, the proletarian revolution to overthrow capitalism was the ultimate great and shining goal, the Communist Party was the *sole* instrument of that revolution, and therefore *whatever* the Party ordered was — by automatic definition — not only justified, but necessary and required.

When Mom graduated Irving High in June of 1932 she entered an economy still reeling from massive unemployment. Jobs were almost impossible to find. Through a relative she eventually found work as a receptionist in the office of a middle-aged dentist with wandering hands and lecherous intent — he was "old and repulsive," she later told me. She couldn't afford to quit, though, so she quickly became adept in dodging and deflecting him.

Of course, as a good member of the Young Communist League, as soon as she landed the receptionist job she joined the Office Workers Union that the CP was organizing. A woman who went by the Party name "Laura" was a low-level CP official and executive director of the union. One day late in 1932, she visited the YCL office, introduced herself, and took my mom aside for a private conversation. After carefully looking Claire over, she told her that the Party district chief at the main CP offices wanted to meet her about a "special assignment helping to organize telegraph workers."

The Party boss also carefully inspected her and then plied her with questions about her background and why she had joined the YCL. Apparently she passed his test because after cautioning her about the need for secrecy he told her that a senior officer of Western Union was a clandestine Marxist. He'd been a shipboard marine radio operator who had later gotten a university degree in business administration and worked his way up the corporate ladder. He still sympathized with the working class, though, and was willing to provide the CP with inside information to help them organize a union. Frequent phone contact was too risky for him, and he couldn't be seen meeting with suspicious characters, so they needed a safe way for him to pass on his info. His code name was "Saturn."

Mom had just turned 19 and she still had fine clothes from when her family was affluent. She was familiar with — trained in, actually — the social graces of the upper classes. Her "special assignment" was to meet with this guy at fancy restaurants and similar venues where everyone would assume she was his young mistress. Saturn would pass information to her and she'd deliver it to Party and union organizers.

"Were you ordered to sleep with him?" I once asked her. "No," she assured me. Then quickly added that she never had. To this day I don't know how true that was, but she clearly found him to be an impressive guy. In his 40s, yes, but still good-looking, and quite charismatic. As she descried him:

> He was big and well-built, dressed marvelously. Fascinating man. He was more informed than any person I had ever met. He knew everything. He was so well read. He knew operas; he knew — no matter what it was, he knew it.[6]

And Saturn found her quite attractive as well. She continued to meet with him after she married Ben Iceland, and Ben did not like it one bit. But the Party line was "free love" and "ends justify the means," so there wasn't much he could do about it. Anyway, their — I'm not sure "relationship" is the correct word — continued for some years, she meeting with him at upscale locations, he passing inside info to her.

One time he arranged for them to meet for a weekend at a mountain summer camp, but instead of Saturn it was Saturn's wife who showed up.

> I was given the key to a cabin where I was going to sleep and a woman was there. She said, "Are you Claire?" I said, "Yes." She says, "I'm the

wife of — "and it was his wife. She had found out about it. He wasn't there, but she had come. She looked me up and down. She said, "You're nothing but a child." I looked very young. I said, "You know, you really don't have to worry. I wouldn't think of having — of being in love with your husband. You know, I'm not competing with you in any way. He's like a father. He's like an old man to me." So she was reassured, and she realized that we had nothing to fight about.₆

Mom once admitted to me, though, that she did have affairs with other men while married to both Ben and later my father. Whether Saturn was one of them I don't know — nor do I care. She was who she was, and the prices she paid in guilt and angst throughout her life were far higher than anything she deserved.

Any way, at that first meeting in December of 1932 Saturn gave her a list of company pay scales for all the different job classifications — confidential information that management tried to keep secret by ordering employees never to discuss with others what they were paid.

When she brought the info back to the Office Workers Union she suggested they leaflet the bike messengers, because at 25 cents an hour (equal to about $4.75 in 2018) they were the lowest paid and they also had to provide and maintain their own uniforms and bicycles. Both the union and Party leaders — pretty much one and the same — were focused on organizing the skilled operators and linemen, and the big department stores like Orbach's and Klein's. They didn't want to be bothered with teenage bike messengers, so they told her to write up a flyer and they'd have some other YCL members distribute it in front of the telegraph offices since they didn't want to blow her cover — her leafletting days were now over.

Other than schoolwork my mother had never written anything in her life. She must have learned pretty quick because 50 boys — most of them between 10 and 16 years old — responded to her leaflet by showing up for a meeting. She asked Dick Lewis, the union president, and "Laura," the organizer, for help — she'd never run a meeting before either — but they were tied up with matters of importance. "Claire, we're busy organizing. You have to handle it yourself." She was on her own, just turned 19 — and merely a girl.

The boys were all horsing around, shouting and shooting rubber bands at each other, paying no attention whatsoever to her polite attempts at calling them to order.

"Shut up, you guys!" she finally shouted as loud as she could. "Take your seat or get out of here now. If you want to do something about your wages and conditions you damn well better get down to business." They did. She proposed they form a group and elect officers to plan their next steps. They did that too.

By the time Roosevelt was inaugurated in March of 1933, Mom had been transferred out of the YCL and been promoted to full Communist Party membership. She was assigned to a branch (cell) of union leaders and activists.

Tilting at Blue Windmills ~ 1964

Rather than hire Blacks, Wich Stand #1 shut down in February of 1964. While that wasn't a victory, we didn't interpret it as a defeat. As we saw it, we had effectively drawn a line in the sand, making it clear that no business operating in the ghetto could get away with an all-white workforce. Having therefore not totally failed against a small, family-owned company with less than 100 employees, we decided to tackle a significant national corporation with 1,200 employees in the Southern California area alone. Clearly, the concept of "hubris" did not weigh heavily on our thoughts.

Van de Kamp's Holland Dutch Bakeries had been doing business in SoCal since 1915. Their logo was a blue windmill. In the mid-1950s, the company was bought up by the much larger General Baking Company of New York, though they continued to operate in California under the Van de Kamp brand. By 1964, Van de Kamp's SoCal operation had 240 retail outlets selling cakes, pies, and other baked goods inside supermarkets, a line of frozen foods that were also sold in grocery stores, and five large restaurants with attached stores.

Their frozen food products were sold in grocery freezers just like other frozen foods, but their bakery goods were marketed through concession spaces they rented from markets like Safeway and Vons. Stores with a Van de Kamp's concession had blue windmills on the outside, and they were staffed by bakery employees wearing cute blue and white "Dutch Girl" costumes rather than grocery store workers.

The majority of Van de Kamp's 1,200 or so employees were women. Half of them worked in the industrial bakery and food-processing factory, the other half served customers as waitresses, cashiers, and concession tenders. Women who dealt with the public were all required to wear the "Dutch girl" costumes. Male employees wore business suits. Our investigation indicated that fewer than 1% of their workers were Black,

Latino, or Asian, and those few were limited to the most menial positions such as janitor and busboy.

Following standard CORE procedure, N-VAC leaders met with Van de Kamp's managers to ask that they provide us with figures on the racial makeup of their work force and agree in writing to end discrimination in their hiring policies.

In response, they hired a "labor relations specialist" — the kind that corporations bring in to block unions — who assured us that Van de Kamp's did not in any way practice racial discrimination. He told our negotiators that no "qualified" Blacks or Mexicans had applied for the unionized factory and bakery jobs. And since the company based its marketing on a "Dutch" theme, all employees dealing directly with the public had to look like they were from Holland, which naturally precluded hiring dark-skinned people. Of course, with the Civil Rights Act of 1964 being debated in Congress, he didn't say it that explicitly or crudely, but that's what he meant.

We didn't find his "no-qualified" and "Dutch-theme" arguments persuasive. Other Los Angeles employers had no problem finding qualified Latinos and Afro-Americans for bakery and factory jobs. People of Color in Los Angeles worked as waitresses and sales clerks too. And he was apparently unaware that because of their colonial empire, which at one time included South Africa, the Netherlands had had an Afro-Dutch population since the1600s. We told him that anyone could put on a "Dutch Girl" costume regardless of their skin color. He refused to budge.

The labor relations expert proposed referring the matter to the county Commission on Human Relations or the United Civil Rights Committee (UCRC) for study. The commission was under the control of the same white politicians who were backing residential and school segregation. The UCRC was an umbrella coalition of the NAACP, L.A. CORE, and ACLU — N-VAC had not been invited to participate. So we saw his proposal for the stalling tactic that it was. So much for negotiations.

We began direct action against Van de Kamp's in mid-February of 1964. Their big restaurant-stores were all in white neighborhoods, but their grocery store concessions were spread out all over SoCal including 15 locations in the ghetto. We figured that if a boycott cut into their baked-goods business in the Afro-American neighborhoods, and we discouraged some patronage by picketing their restaurants, they might hire some Afro-American "Dutch Girls" along with some factory and bakery workers simply to get rid of us.

In order to effectively boycott a store — or in our case certain products within a store — we really needed two or three people covering each location with leaflets during all the hours they were open — 16 hours a day in most cases. But handing out boycott leaflets is really boring, and we simply couldn't mobilize the numbers we needed. And besides, we were N-VAC. We were "militants" dedicated to cutting-edge action and civil disobedience — leafleting was so mundane that even those stuffy NAACP folk sometimes did it. So we adopted a guerilla strategy of moving our actions from place to place — shifting back and forth between the ghetto stores and the restaurants. While we hoped for some media attention, we knew that was unlikely, so our plan was to generate word of mouth through bold, provocative actions.

Early in March we began "shop-ins" at the ghetto stores — an idea we adapted from the successful shop-ins conducted by the San Francisco Bay Area CORE chapters against Lucky Markets a couple of months earlier. We so envied the Bay Area (sigh). Where we struggled to find 25 people willing to sit in, they could mobilize hundreds for mass arrests. They were not only militant, they had panache — a flair for dramatic action we could only dream of.

Unlike the Bay Area shop-ins, ours were quick guerilla raids. Usually about 10 to 15 of us would drive to a ghetto store, hang signs around our necks, march single file into the store singing as loud as we could, find the Van de Kamp's space, remove all their goods and place them in shopping carts, scatter boycott leaflets on the now empty shelves and counters, and then get out of Dodge before the cops showed up. Then we'd drive to the next store and repeat. We often hit four or five stores in a single evening. Because we had school or jobs, most of our actions were after work or on the weekends.

Mari Goldman, an N-VAC mainstay, was our press-person. Though she was now a naturalized American citizen, she had been born in Britain and still spoke with an elegant English accent. She tipped off the media to our first shop-in and we did garner some newspaper and TV coverage. Which, of course, sparked controversy exactly as we intended. We hadn't stolen anything, nor had we deliberately damaged any goods, but some cakes and pies at the bottom of a shopping cart pile might have gotten a bit squashed by the weight of other goods on top of them — those thin boxes were so flimsy they didn't stack well.

In some quarters this "malicious property damage" caused great consternation, which we contrasted to lack of concern over lives crippled by pervasive racial discrimination — what's more important, a crushed pie or a crushed life? In the Los Angeles of 1964, if the life in question was

Afro-American it seemed the pie (or more accurately, the pie's owner) got far more sympathy.

My dad had taught me to read and love maps, a skill I still find useful even in this Google age. I scouted all of Van de Kamp's ghetto locations and taped an AAA street map to a corkboard with colored pins showing the location of different types of stores. That was our low-tech targeting system, and I was responsible for directing our little car caravan as it darted back and forth across the ghetto in routes designed to confuse and foil the cops (if any were after us).

Once or twice the police did arrive before we got away. But we hadn't touched any of the grocery's goods or caused any extra work for them since they weren't responsible for Van de Kamp's shelves, and the market's night managers were smart enough not to anger their Afro-American customers by filing charges against civil rights demonstrators. With the "Dutch Girls" gone home for the day, that left no one willing to file a complaint against us, so we weren't arrested.

By this time we had about 20 dedicated N-VAC members, plus another 30 or so from Bruin and other CORE chapters and Friends of SNCC we could count on to sometimes participate in our actions. But given people's work and school schedules, our weekday evening protests rarely had more than 15 participants. For the weekend demonstration outside one of the Van de Kamp's restaurants we usually had 30 or more.

Our first restaurant sit-ins were on a Saturday and Sunday in mid-March at Van de Kamp's large Glendale establishment. Glendale was notorious as an all-white "sundown town" — so named because a local ordinance had once required all nonwhites to be gone from the city by sundown. Federal courts had overturned such laws, but the concept was still aggressively enforced by the Glendale cops. If you were Black or Latino and they caught you in Glendale after dark they would find some pretext to charge you with some crime — or simply school you on the error of your ways by "tuning you up" with their nightsticks (or "nigger-knockers" as some lawmen referred to them).

About two dozen of us set up a picket line outside the restaurant's main entrance. Then about half went inside and sat down on the floor of the lobby area, forming a half-circle line, shoulder-to-shoulder, blocking entry into the restaurant and the baked-goods store. The other half maintained the picket line so that customers would see there was a protest going on, receive leaflets explaining it, and have to choose to cross the line before they encountered the lobby sit-in. My assignment those two days was to take photos, so I didn't sit in.

This being Glendale, all the customers were white. While some turned away rather than cross our picket line, most forced their way through the sit-ins, stepping on them and kicking them for good measure. An angry customer stabbed Richard Thompson in the back with a fork, and others on the sit-in had hot coffee poured over their heads. White patrons also dragged Annette Becker and Sue Kovnor across the floor by their hair, while Jerry Farber and Jay Frank were dragged out of position and repeatedly kicked. (Van de Kamp's employees took no part in any violence against the sit-ins, they left that to eager volunteers among their customers.)

Both Sue and Annette had been active members of L.A. CORE and my recollection is that, like me, Annette was also the child of leftist Jewish parents. I think she was employed as a social worker at the time, and whenever we had an evening or weekend action she was always on the line and in the thick of it. Though I hadn't really been that conscious of it at the time, most the whites active with N-VAC were from Jewish backgrounds, though not necessarily observant — Mari, Jerry, Jay, Annette, Sue, Lea Arond, Roberta and Fred Krinsky, myself, and a few others. I don't believe that Richard Thompson, an N-VAC stalwart, was Jewish, nor was Scott Van Leuvan, I don't think, but most of the other whites were Jews.

Eventually, the police arrived in force at the Van de Kamp's restaurant and the white violence subsided. I guess we must have taken them by surprise because on Saturday no one was arrested — I suppose the manager needed to check with the front office to see how they wanted us handled. After sitting in from 4pm to 8pm we left.

The next day, Sunday, we were back, same time, same place, same action, sitting on the lobby floor. This time they were ready for us. More patrons roughly climbed over our sit-ins or kicked their way through the line — so many more that we concluded some local Glendale whites had come by just for that express purpose. The level of violence quickly escalated until a white teenager with a big can of hair spray approached the sit-ins. He pressed the button and lit the spray with his cigarette lighter to create a homemade flame-thrower.

Fortunately, just at that moment a uniformed fire marshall showed up with a team of cops. To our relief — and no doubt that of the Van de Kamp's manager — they took the firebug into custody. None of us were ever called to testify against him so I assume he wasn't charged with anything.

The fire marshall and his assistants took photos of our people sitting on the floor and then announced the sit-ins were "blocking a fire exit." We told him that if a fire broke out everyone would simply get up and leave along with all the customers and employees. That seemed pretty obvious to me, but he didn't seem to grasp it. He ordered the sit-ins to leave. As planned, they refused and were placed under arrest. They went limp and had to be carried or dragged out to the waiting paddy wagon.

The next Saturday, March 21st, our protest was at the Van de Kamp's restaurant on Laurel Canyon Boulevard in the Van Nuys area of the San Fernando Valley. Since someone else was assigned to photo duty, I knew I'd be arrested this time with the other sit-ins. Despite my determined commitment I was a trifle nervous — okay, I was scared. Becoming a "criminal" with an arrest record — a "rap sheet" as they say — was a big step in my life. Still, though frightened, I was game.

We in N-VAC didn't like to routinely repeat ourselves, that was way too boring. So for the Van Nuys sit-in we came up with a new wrinkle. As we had in Glendale, we sat on the floor of the lobby blocking the way into the restaurant. The police and fire marshall showed up, took their evidence photos, ordered us to leave and then declared us all under arrest. I'll confess now (as I would never have admitted at the time) that my heart was pounding with excitement — and fear.

As soon as we heard "under arrest," we took out heavy chains that we had concealed in purses and pockets, quickly wrapped them around our ankles and padlocked them in such a way that each person's leg was chained to the leg of the person on either side — except for Mari. She was on the end of the line wearing skirt and stockings and she chained her wrist to Robert Hall's. We had carefully rehearsed this operation in advance because it isn't as easy as it sounds to accomplish so quickly that the police didn't have time to stop us.

The purpose of the "chain-in" was to delay for as long as possible being carted off to jail and thus prolong the disruption to Van de Kamp's business. And it worked — it took them half an hour or longer to obtain a bolt cutter large enough to break the locks. Fifteen of us were arrested on charges of trespass, disturbing the peace, and violation of that fire ordinance. It turned out that they must have gotten some good legal advice, because when we eventually went to trial we were only convicted of violating the fire ordinance.

Once the chains were off, we all "went limp." I was dragged by my arms to the wagon. By now we were running low on bail money — or more accurately the amount of credit Celes King Bail Bonds was willing to advance us — so in order to get lower bonds we remained in jail over the weekend until we were arraigned the following Monday, on bond of $100 each for those like me who had only been arrested once [equal to about $800 in 2018] and $250 for those who had also been arrested in Glendale.

But now unpleasant truths and hard realities began to bite. The more often someone was arrested the higher each successive bond became as the system used bail as a means of punishment-before-conviction. And, of course, we knew we would eventually be convicted and that multiple offenders would ultimately receive longer sentences.

Of more immediate concern, the 10% fees we owed Celes King for each bond were mounting higher and higher. We simply didn't have the money. Celes King, the Afro-American bondsman, was a great guy. He always bailed out civil rights demonstrators on credit because he supported the Movement and he knew we wouldn't skip town on him. But he was running a business and eventually we had to pay his fee.

All of which meant that the same people couldn't keep getting arrested over and over without end. In order to continue our civil disobedience sit-ins we had to find *new* people willing to be arrested. But they weren't coming forward — for some reason people were reluctant to get arrested and go to jail even for a good cause. Weird, but there it was. We had been arrested in Van Nuys on Saturday, and on Sunday N-VAC couldn't scrape up enough people willing to sit in at the Laurel Canyon restaurant to make it effective. We weren't quite ready to admit it yet, but the truth was we were beginning to encounter the limits of militant nonviolent direct action.

So we got creative. For the rest of March and into April, we shifted to a "raid" strategy. We went to a restaurant, sat in, remained until the cops and fire marshal showed up, then got up off the floor and drove to another location, maybe a restaurant, maybe a store for a shop-in. Again, using my trusty corkboard map with its push-pins, I did the targeting.

By early April, we were engaged in a cat and mouse game with Van de Kamp's, and the cops. One day we showed up at the first restaurant on our list and saw they were already waiting for us. We aborted that sit-in. When it happened again, we became suspicious, so the next day I and a few of the other hard-core N-VAC member "planned" a fake sit-in entirely and only over the phone. Sure enough, when I drove by that location the police were waiting nearby for a protest that never materialized.

Today, people are no longer surprised to discover their calls and emails are being tracked and monitored by an alphabet soup of police agencies, advertising marketeers, and organized crime gangs. But back in the early '60s it was shocking — and infuriating. After that, rather than telling supporters to meet us at the first target location, we designated an assembly spot where we all gathered before telling people where the initial sit-in would take place. That way the cops wouldn't be ready and waiting for us.

Eventually, on April 18, a Saturday night, a couple of squad cars caught us coming out of a shop-in at the Thrifty Mart at Vermont and Adams in the West Adams ghetto. It was the last one of the evening, and by then there were only nine of us left, all well-trained N-VAC veterans. A couple more cop cars showed up, but they couldn't seem to decide whether to arrest us or not. I guess the store manager was reluctant to press charges against us while his neighborhood customers were watching. Meanwhile, we're standing on the sidewalk singing our freedom songs with our signs hanging from around our necks with a small Afro-American crowd looking on.

After a long conference with the manager they finally ordered us into the back seats of their cop cars — which we assumed meant we were under arrest. As per our training, we immediately sat down on the sidewalk and locked arms. As devotees of nonviolence we would not fight back or violently resist arrest, but neither would we in any way cooperate with what we saw as unjust police repression in support of racial discrimination. They would have to pull us apart, at which point we would go limp, forcing them to drag us and lift us into the cars.

They, however, interpreted our action as "Contempt of Cop" — that most heinous of all crimes. Now they were really pissed at us. They went after the women first and managed to drag off Mari Goldman. Robert Hall and I were on either side of Annette Becker and they used the infamous and extremely painful "choke hold" on Robert and me to break her loose from our grip. As the pain in my neck became excruciating and my breath ran short I saw the proverbial stars so beloved by comic book illustrators and cartoon animators. It turns out that you really do see stars just before you pass out.

Anyway, at this point a police sergeant showed up. He told us that if we cooperated by giving our names (as everyone is legally required to do) we would not be arrested. Fine by us. Mari and Annette were let out of the police car and we all went home.

We had planned and publicized what we intended to be a large rally in South Park on Avalon Boulevard in the middle of the South Central ghetto for the following Sunday, April 26. We suspended shop-ins and sit-ins in order to leaflet and organize for this rally. An hour before it was to start, the cops raided our N-VAC office, arresting people on warrants. Others of us were picked up while leafleting or approaching the park. The warrants were for charges related to that Thrifty Mart shop-in the previous week. I assume the manager had been convinced to file charges once our arrest wouldn't be visibly connected to his store. The warrants could have been served at any time after they were issued, but they'd been held back until they could be used to disrupt the rally.

I was busted while making a phone call from a pay phone to the CORE office where we knew James Farmer, the national head of CORE, was meeting with the leaders of SoCal CORE chapters. Jerry Farber, who hadn't been on the shop-in and therefore had no warrant out on him, started the rally, which was soon joined by Farmer and other CORE members who had immediately halted their meeting to come to our support — Farmer was deep into Philosophical nonviolence, but he was most definitely not a "moderate." The rally was cut short and about 40 to 50 N-VAC and CORE folk went to picket the Newton police station a few blocks away as a protest against police repression.

Danny Gray, Robert Hall, and I were taken to L.A. police headquarters — known as the "Glass House" — where we were held for a while. Then we were put in with other prisoners and taken by bus to Lincoln Heights Jail. Known to generations of Angeleno inmates as the "Graybar Hotel," the hulking five-story concrete building was the main city lockup and drunk tank. You've no doubt seen it on-screen. For many years Hollywood film and TV studios used it for shooting prison scenes. As we got off the bus we started singing freedom songs, and some of the other prisoners joined in as we all marched inside with pride.

For some reason the guards did not consider that proper demeanor, so Danny, Robert, and I were invited to enjoy the facility's solitary confinement accommodations until we were bailed out later that night. Sadly, I cannot give the Graybar Hotel a "Like." The room was so small I might almost call it "cramped," and it was totally lacking in even the most minimal of amenities.

Busted Down in Reno ~ 1959

I guess I should confess that the Van de Kamp's sit-in arrest was not my first brush with the law. That occurred in 1959 when I was 15, making me, I suppose, a juvenile delinquent on a life path toward hardened criminal. Or some such nonsense.

When I was growing up we didn't have a lot of money. It was hard for my parents to hold a job because the FBI would always come 'round to make sure the employer knew he had a "commie" on the payroll. That usually resulted in a quick dismissal. My folks, though, wanted to provide a "normal" middle-class life for me and my brother Dan, but they had to do it on a tight budget. So they looked for bargains.

Back in the 1950s, summer camp was an essential component of a middle-class childhood. Yet it was expensive. Some years my parents were able to afford a two-week stint at an overnight camp for my brother and me, other years it was just day camp, and some years there was nothing but hanging out on our own at a neighborhood park. In '59 they came across a great deal — a car-caravan camping trip from L.A. to Alaska at an amazingly low price.

They weren't fools, they did what they could to check it out. They met with the guy, Wallace if I remember his name correctly, and he assured them he did the same trip every year. Ken looked him up in what little information there was available in those days about someone's background and found no red flags, so the deal was made. To his disappointment, my 11-year-old brother Dan was too young to be included.

Wallace — "Wally" we called him — was stout with a crewcut. He wore khaki pants and I thought of him as really old. Like in his 50s or something. I'm now 75, but back then I considered anyone over 50 to be ancient and decrepit.

Early in July, off we went. About 15 or so boys in four cars, a '51 Chrysler and three old Hudsons from the late 1940s. The four oldest boys were 16. They were the camp "counselors" and drivers. The youngest campers were 12. We had boxes of dry, backpack-type camp food, sleeping bags, and everyone but me had a tent (I didn't like tents). As it turned out, what we didn't have was adult supervision. Wally was none too bright, sickish a lot of the time, and not exactly together even when he was feeling at his best.

I forget the name of the kid who drove the car I was in, but as soon as we hit those long straight stretches of two-lane desert blacktop (this was before the Interstate) he managed to get that old Hudson Hornet up to 110mph — scaring the shit out of nerdy me. When the car started to shimmy and shake he brought it down to a safe and sane 85. The legal speed limit being, I think, 55.

If a free public campground was available that's what we used, if not we just pulled off the side of the road for the night. Since camping was the only kind of family vacation we could afford — and my Dad *loved* camping — by age 15 I was quite experienced in roughing it. Experienced in the fun part of camping, that is. My mom — who hated camping — did all the cooking and cleaning, while Ken did all the setting up, taking down, equipment maintaining, and securing food from bears.

I never liked tents, they were stuffy and I wanted to be able to see the stars, so I just inserted my sleeping bag between the folds of a waterproof tarp, rolled it all up, tied it into a thick bedroll in the morning, and then unrolled it again at night. If it rained, or even if it snowed, I just pulled the tarp-flap over my head and slept sung as a bug in its cocoon. Wally and the other kids, though, all shared tents.

The boy driving the Chrysler (our newest and fastest vehicle) managed to flip it off the road and roll it three times near Kemmerer, Wyoming — a total wreck. Even though this was before cars had seat belts, by some miracle a broken arm and bruises were the worst injuries suffered. Three of the kids went home at that point. What can I say? Some people are just quitters. While that was all being sorted out we were stuck for several days in a mosquito-infested campground between Kemmerer and La Barge. One of the boys tried to set the place on fire — he was a little strange, so we weren't surprised — and he was sent home too. That left about 12 of us in the three old Hudsons.

We pushed north to Yellowstone National Park where we were asked to leave by the Rangers for some reason that was never entirely clear to me. Then it was up and over Going To The Sun pass in Glacier which was awesome, an accolade I almost never use. From there it was into Canada, no passport needed, no border check point of any kind, just a "Welcome to Canada" sign as we drove across the border.

Our goal was to reach Alaska via the Alaska-Canada Highway — the "AlCan" as it was known — but by the time we reached Calgary food was already running low and cash too. The drivers had been given gas-company credit cards, but you couldn't use them to buy food, and general-use cards like Visa did not yet exist. Clearly, we were not going to make it to Alaska.

We turned west on Canadian Highway 1 to cross the Canadian Rockies and then head back south to California. While waiting for a repair part for one of the Hudsons, we had to spend a couple of days at a campground on the shores of Barrier Lake west of Calgary, and the Mounties very politely asked us to move on. I don't recall why, most likely our general rowdiness or possibly our body aroma — regular showers not being high on Wally's leadership agenda, and certainly not something we boys considered to be of any importance.

By this time we had been on the road for almost three weeks and were heartily sick of dried camp food, which we now had to ration. One of the boys had swiped a full-color, plastic menu from a highway diner and we wished over it, dreaming about and arguing the merits of different dishes. I favored a cheeseburger with hash browns and a salad heavy with Roquefort dressing.

Highway 1 is Canada's main transcontinental road, but it wasn't completely finished in 1959. The part over Logan Pass through Canada's Glacier Park was still under construction. So to get from Golden to Revelstoke we had to take a 180-mile detour on the notorious Big Bend bypass, which was the only way around the Selkirk Mountains.

Today, driving between Revelstoke and Golden on Highway 1 is a gorgeous and pleasant 90-minute jaunt on a smooth paved road. In 1959, the "Bend" was fifteen hours of dirt road through mountain rain forest, intermittent downpours, fog, and mist. All the while dodging heavy long-haul trucks on rickety, narrow wooden bridges over rushing white-water rivers. Knowledgeable Canadian tourists who could afford it loaded themselves and their cars onto a train and rode the rails between the two towns rather than drive the Bend.

That wasn't an option for us, of course. Somehow, we made it through The Bend, but were stuck for another couple of days in Revelstoke waiting for another car-repair part (Hudson parts not being readily available).

Much of our waiting time was spent sharing with each other our vast trove of sexual misinformation and mythical rumors. And making utterly false boasts, since none of us had ever actually had sex with a real — as opposed to imaginary — girl. A tattered Playboy that someone had boosted from a magazine rack was passed around from car to car — don't worry, though, you can rest assured that we only ogled the photos and drawings, we never read any of those socially-relevant and potentially subversive articles.

We re-entered the States on US 395 and followed it all the way south to Reno, Nevada. By now we were hungry, ragged, filthy — and utterly broke. But our fearless leader Wally had a plan. He had prepared for just this kind of eventuality. In the trunk of one of the Hudsons was a cardboard carton filled with little boxes of Christmas cards. So in the blazing heat of early August he set us going door-to-door in one of Reno's nicer residential neighborhoods, selling Xmas cards to raise money. All my life I've hated fundraising — and this was no exception.

The cops swooped in, rounded us up, and took us to the Reno jail. They thought Wally was some sort of criminal Fagin type up from wicked Los Angeles with his gang of urchin thieves using the Christmas cards as a pretext for casing the neighborhood before robbing the good citizens of Reno. It took them several hours to sort it all out and we enjoyed a hot meal that, while not up to casino standards, was way better than dried camp food. They had no valid charges against us, so rather than lock us up (and continue to feed us) they told us to camp in the empty Washoe County fairgrounds.

Of course they notified our parents. I had been very careful to send home marvelously circumspect "Everything great, having wonderful time" postcards, and I'm pretty sure the other boys had been doing the same, so it must have been quite a shock for the folks when they got a call from the Reno PD and discovered that perhaps Wally's adventure road trip wasn't all it was cracked up to be. They wired bus fare, we rode the dog home from Reno, and our parents picked us up at the Greyhound depot.

I guess the Reno cops must have shared contact info between parents because they were all there and in quite an uproar when we got off the bus. Turned out a story was going 'round that Wally was a pedophile. Whether that was true or just a rumor I never found out. Back in the 1950s, sexual abuse of any kind was never openly discussed, particularly in the presence of children. Since no one knew much about sexual predators no one worried about them. And, of course, there were no sex-offender registries of any kind.

I don't know what happened to Wally. He was feckless and incompetent for sure. But I never saw any indication he was any kind of child abuser. He never touched me or bothered me in any way. But, of course, I was sleeping under my tarp. I wasn't in any of the tents, and certainly never in *his* tent like some of the younger boys. I suppose it's possible that he abused one or more of them, but I never saw any evidence of it (not that I was looking for it or knew what to look for even if I was — which I wasn't).

Anyway, truth to tell and shame the Devil, I have to admit that for me — bar none, without question — that 1959 road trip was the best childhood summer vacation I ever had.

Trials and Tribulations ~ 1964

Early in the spring of 1964 I signed up to participate in the SNCC/ CORE Mississippi Summer Project — "Freedom Summer," as it became known. But with two protest trials scheduled for July and August, I was barred from leaving the state.

By May of '64, N-VAC was at low ebb. Those arrested on the first sit-in at the Glendale restaurant were on trial for over a week, and as a show of support we all attended whenever we could, which left little time for protesting. Charges against the six juveniles were dropped, but the four adults — Woody Coleman, Annette Becker, Jerry Farber, and Jay Frank — had to stand trial.

Jerry Farber was a popular and creative English professor at Los Angeles State College (he later taught at San Diego State and UC San Diego). He had a streak of irreverent humor and a sharp sense of social satire. He was tall, quite thin, and had a swarthy "Mediterranean" complexion. Of the other three defendants, Woody was coal black and the other two were quite white. One day during jury selection the judge started to ask a prospective juror if having a Black defendant would affect her verdict, when he stopped himself and asked, "Mr. Farber, are you Negro or white?"

Without missing a beat, Jerry replied, "On Mondays, Wednesdays, and Fridays, I'm white. On Tuesdays, Thursdays, and Saturdays, I'm Negro. And on Sunday I just don't know." As I recall, the whole courtroom cracked up in laughter including the judge — that was Jerry for you.

All four were convicted of violating the fire ordinance but not disturbing the peace or trespass. The cops identified Woody as the leader, so he was sentenced to $150 fine or 15 days in jail, the others got $100 or 10 days. I don't remember why the verdict wasn't appealed — most likely we couldn't afford the legal costs even though the lawyer was representing us pro bono. One hundred dollars in 1964 was equal to about $800 in 2018, so the total fines were the equivalent of around $3600 today. We didn't have that kind of money, but even if we did, none of us would have contributed funds to support a "justice" system dedicated to maintaining racial discrimination.

During the trial we held a couple of weekend picket lines at Van de Kamp restaurants, but people were tired and turnout was poor. Between Bruin CORE on the Westside and N-VAC and Van de Kamp's in Central L.A, I was being run ragged. Oh, yeah, it was also the end of the semester, and I believe UCLA was expecting me to turn in completed term papers and pass some sort of final exams.

By this time though we had developed an "N-VAC Way," a mystique we created and embraced. When spirits flag — get creative. So in June, we came up with a new tactic — "sip-ins." On a Saturday afternoon we set up a picket line and handed out leaflets at the Van de Kamp's restaurant on Wilshire — a large establishment in the heart of the

"Miracle Mile" shopping district a couple blocks from the La Brea Tar Pits. What with shoppers and tourists, weekend afternoons were quite busy for them. Once the picket line was up, most of us went inside, spread out one or two to a table, ordered a cup of coffee, and then sipped it very, very, very slowly.

Some of us carried our signs inside and propped them against the side of the table. "Oh, no, officer, we aren't trespassing or protesting, we're just having a nice cuppa joe." We stayed for more than four hours, and with 75 or so participants we put a serious crimp in their business as other customers got tired of waiting for a table. The manager did not seem to appreciate our patronage, and table service became somewhat frosty.

Next Saturday we went back, this time sipping from noon to eight with about the same number of people, and again the manager was quite cool to us — after a couple of hours he started asking us to leave. We told him we would leave when Van de Kamp's stopped discriminating against Black and Latino job seekers. He did not seem to find that satisfactory.

On June 15th, the convicted miscreants who had sat in at Glendale began serving their sentences, Annette in the women's lockup and the three men in Lincoln Heights Jail. On Thursday the 18th, we jammed up the Wilshire restaurant with an evening sip-in. They were quite crowded and the manager was by now very annoyed, even though we only had about 50 "sippers." Two cameramen working for Van de Kamp's carefully took photos and movies making sure to note each time we were asked to leave. Wise as we were in the intricacies of law, we knew that meant an injunction was on the way.

Annette, Jerry, and Jay completed their 10-day sentences on June 24th, but Woody still had five more days. So Jerry and Jay refused to leave their cells unless Woody was released too. The guards were quite taken aback, no one had ever refused to be set free before. But policy was clear, when your reservation at the Graybar Hotel was up you had to leave. The two from N-VAC refused. When the correctional officers pulled them out of the cell, Jay and Jerry went limp. They were dragged out, stripped of their jail uniform, dressed in their street clothes, and deposited on the front steps where N-VAC and CORE supporters were waiting for them. We then commenced an around-the-clock sit-in on the jail steps for five days and nights until Woody's sentence was finished. Back in those days, when we used to sing "Solidarity Forever," we meant it.

There was, however, a downside to the refuse-to-leave plan — at least in insofar as I was concerned. Whoever in N-VAC came up with the idea decided it had to be kept "top-secret," not just from the cops but from everyone — including me. Yet they had to tell Movement folk that something was about to go down, so everyone would be waiting outside of Lincoln Heights when Jay and Jerry were released. So it was a case of "We've got a secret — but we won't tell you." I was quite hurt that they didn't trust me. It felt like a betrayal and a dismissal of all I had done with CORE and N-VAC. It was painful and corrosive. It was also stupid. Keeping it secret gained nothing. Jay and Jerry would have refused to leave their cell regardless of whether the guards had advance knowledge. That's one of the strengths of nonviolent tactics, they don't require secrecy. In this instance, the only purpose secrecy served was boosting the egos of those "in the know" *vis-à-vis* the rest of us. It still pisses me off.

Early in July, a judge issued a TRO (temporary restraining order) requiring us to suspend the sip-ins until he had pondered the case and made his final ruling. Though he ordered us to halt our sip-in protests, he said nothing at all about, or even took note of, racial discrimination by Van de Kamp's, so we had no illusions as to what his eventual ruling was going to be. To us, he was just one more enabler of a racist system. We immediately violated his order by conducting another sip-in, and shortly thereafter we were served with contempt of court notices. Though we weren't taken in and booked, that amounted to my third arrest since the March on Washington.

We wanted to continue the sip-ins, but the novelty had worn off and too few supporters were willing to defy a TRO, so we no longer had enough sippers to make the tactic effective. We kept up some picketing and leafletting, but by now most of our days were spent in court and our evenings in fundraising to cover our bail and legal costs.

The second trial was for those of us who had been arrested on warrants stemming from April's Thrifty Mart shop-in. That trial began in mid-July. Our pro bono attorney was Luke McKissack, who later became famous for defending Sirhan Sirhan and members of the Black Panther Party and American Indian Movement. He put up a helluva fight trying to get at least one Afro-American on our jury. To no avail.

A source we had in the D.A.'s office told us that an edict had been handed down from on high that under no circumstances were any Blacks to be allowed on any jury trying any civil rights case — ever. In essence, it was a jury-stacking strategy not that much different from the all-white jury systems in Alabama and Mississippi, except that in California it was technically illegal and in the Deep South by explicit official policy Blacks weren't permitted to serve on *any* juries at all.

As I recall, McKissack mounted a "necessity defense." The point being that it's legally permissible to violate some minor law if doing so is necessary to prevent some greater harm or crime. In our case racial discrimination was the greater evil and we were justified in disturbing an unjust peace in order to call public attention to it — an argument that still seems valid to me. McKissack was a charmer, juries just loved him, but no matter how much the jury liked our lawyer they still convicted us of disturbing the peace. I guess we must have appealed that case and won, or maybe for some reason the D.A. later dropped charges, because I never served any time for that conviction. Or, for that matter, my sip-in contempt of court charges.

Our trial for the Van Nuys sit-in began in early August and it quickly turned into a *mano a mano* grudge match between Judge K.L. Holaday and Hugh Manes (pronounced "May-ness") our pro bono lawyer. Hugh later became famous fighting against police misconduct and abuse. Rather than a charmer he was a legal slugger, a sort of Churchillian character in both appearance and oratory. He took no shit from nobody, not even a judge, and he didn't know the meaning of "back down." My kind of lawyer.

It took almost three weeks to select a jury because Manes dug in and used every piece of legal ammo he had to get an Afro-American or Latino on the jury. The judge constantly and consistently overruled each and every one of Hugh's motions and objections. It got so that Holaday began to anticipate Hugh's points and sometimes overruled them before they were even made — just out of habit. We started keeping score, and in late August, Hugh was overruled a record 141 times in a single day. In the end, as usual, our Black and white group of civil rights protesters was judged by an all-white jury. A "jury of our peers" as they told us with straight faces.

Because it took so long to seat the jury we were on trial for almost all of August — all day in court except for a long lunch break. On most days we grabbed a quick bite at Philippe's on Alameda Street. Philippe's was one of those quirky L.A. traditions — they claimed to have invented the French Dip roast beef sandwich — and their clientele was a real (and rare) social cross-section ranging from hookers and pimps, through working stiffs, defense lawyers, prosecutors, and judges, to bankers and business executives. Afterwards, for the rest the break we'd picket the Van de Kamp's outlet in the nearby Grand Central Market until we had to return to court.

The actual trial took only a few days. Manes quickly demolished the disturbing the peace and trespass accusations and I believe he argued that blocking a fire exit was a ridiculous charge because the law was intended to prohibit stationary objects like furniture and crates, not people who could simply get up and leave along with everyone else if a fire broke out.

Apparently the jury had a hard time coming to a verdict, because it took them two days to finally decide we were guilty of violating the fire ordinance. What did they think? That if a fire broke out we'd just sit there are let ourselves be burned? Apparently so.

It's quite rare for anyone to be convicted of criminally blocking a fire exit — normally offenders are just told to unblock it — and rarer still to receive any punishment stiffer than a modest fine. Judge Holaday — by now we were publicly referring to him as "Hanging Judge Holaday" — sentenced us to 30 days. Longer for Woody. I guess we must have appealed (and eventually lost) because we didn't serve our sentences until a year later.

After the trials we continued to picket Van de Kamp's locations all through September and October, but we were worn out and no longer had enough new people to sustain nonviolent civil disobedience. Most of what energy we had was consumed raising money to pay off the $7,000 we owed Celes King for bail bonds (equal to over $55,000 in 2018), plus the amounts we owed various lawyers for legal expenses.

A year earlier we had formed N-VAC to test the limits of militant, nonviolent direct action. We hit those limits against Van de Kamp's, a corporation far too large for our small group to impact. Eventually, reluctantly — very reluctantly — we accepted defeat. Van de Kamp's continued to discriminate against nonwhites. N-VAC turned to other campaigns.

[Van de Kamp's went out of business in 1990. An unrelated company later bought their trademark and now sells frozen foods under the Van de Kamp's label.]

Pistol on the Table ~ 1936

Through her Party contacts, in the mid-1930s Mom found a better, higher-paid, job as a secretary in the Federal Theatre Project. Meanwhile, in her off hours, she continued working with and organizing the teenage bike messengers. By '36, the messenger group had become, in effect, a union local, though not officially recognized by anyone as such. Nevertheless, they were now large enough to start talking about a strike.

My mom was still meeting with Saturn and in her oral history recorded decades later she told me:

I got wonderful information from Saturn, really. He would say, "The company is saying this. Here's how they're going to respond to your leaflet. Here's what they're going to do." So we were a step ahead of them all the time.

So one night, we had a messengers meeting and just before I went to the front of the meeting room to start, there was flurry in the back and two guys came in. They had fedora hats pulled low over their foreheads, looked like gangsters — and they were gangsters. We said, "What do you want? Who are you?" They didn't tell us their names. They said, "We want to talk to you." So Abe Dubrowski, who was the president of the messengers group, and I sat down at the desk.[6]

Abe was 17, with a pimply face and thick glasses. My mom was an old lady of 22. As usual she was on her own, Office Workers Union president Dick Lewis and Party cadre "Laura" had important other matters to attend to. The union offices were in a long, narrow, second-floor loft on 14th Street near 8th Avenue. It had once been a garment "factory" like those my mom's father had owned before the Crash. Now it was rapidly filling up with close to 200 teenage boys in their blue messenger uniforms, and extra folding chairs were being brought in from union offices on other floors.

Looming over Abe and my mom, the two thugs claimed that they — not the Office Workers Union — were now organizing the messengers. One of them took a pistol out of his pocket and laid it on the desk. He pointed to the gun. "You kids better cancel this meeting and call it quits if you know what's good for you. We're warning you."

I don't think my mom had ever actually seen a gun, and she once told me she wasn't sure it was real. It looked like a toy to her. She also told me, "I was still too — we were too young and too stupid even to be really afraid." She remembered that Saturn had warned her the company was planning to start a competing union to confuse and divide the messengers. That infuriated her.

"I don't give a damn what union you're organizing," she told the hoods. "We have our own union and we're going to have a meeting in a few minutes. So just get out of here, we're too busy to talk to you now."

As they left they pointed out the window to a long black limousine parked across the street. "We'll be waiting for you."

"By this time we began to get a little nervous," Mom later told me. So she called the Workers Ex-Servicemen's League — World War I veterans and Party members who protected "Red" protesters from the increasingly aggressive fascist groups then sprouting up in America — organizations like the Silver Shirts, an anti-Semitic, white-supremacist outfit modeled on Hitler's Brown Shirt storm troopers, and the pro-Nazi

German-American Bund. "We'll send some fellows over right away," they told her.

Mom called the meeting to order — never easy with a group of rowdy teenage boys — and the various organizing teams reported that a majority of the messengers in Manhattan, Brooklyn, the Bronx, and Queens had signed up with the union and could be counted on. (As usual, Staten Island lagged.) Abe moved that a strike vote be taken and suddenly there was shouting and disruption from one corner of the room. Provocateurs had been sent by the company to break up the meeting.

"Don't let them get away with it," my mother shouted. "The only way to get what you need from the company is to strike — but we'll strike only when we're ready for it and when we know we can win." To cheers and applause from everyone but the disrupters, the vote authorizing a strike passed.

> So we voted for a strike. Some big guys from the Workers Ex-Servicemen's League came. They marched us down the back way out of the building, put us in cars and took us to the workers' cafeteria in the building where the Communist Party headquarters was. They got us in the back door, and we sat there, and we weren't followed, and they stayed with us until it was about two in the morning and they said, okay, you can go home. So we got in the subway, and we went home.[6]

A few days later, Saturn told her that while Western Union still refused to recognize or negotiate with a union, they would stave off the threatened messenger strike by giving the boys a 20% raise from 25 cents to 30 cents an hour plus $3 a month for cleaning their uniforms and maintenance of their bicycles. It was a significant victory. Thirty cents an hour in 1936 was equal to about $5.30 in 2018, not enough to live on even back then, but far more than most child laborers were paid. And as would later be the case in the Civil Rights Movement, the bold courage of "unimportant" youth inspired their elders. Clerks and teletype operators and even a few of the highly paid linemen began signing up as union members.

Cashing a Dead Chicken ~ 1964

In the spring of 1964, election fever was running high. Though everyone knew that Johnson would be nominated for reelection by the Democrats, he was being challenged from the right by Alabama Governor George Wallace who was running on a "white-backlash," states-rights platform explicitly appealing to whites outraged by the Black Freedom

Movement. Nine candidates were vying for the Republican nomination, but leading the pack was Arizona Senator Barry Goldwater, running on an ultraconservative, states-rights platform. In the mid-1960s, "states-rights" meant the right of states to impose unconstitutional racial restrictions, customs, and laws on nonwhite citizens.

LBJ was promising "Great Society" government programs such as Medicare, a "War on Poverty," and continued support for Black civil rights. Time and time again he swore he would never send us to war in Vietnam (even though there were already more than 20,000 Americans on the ground "advising" the Saigon military junta). For his part, Goldwater opposed the Civil Rights Act of 1964 that was then being debated in Congress and called for an aggressive expansion of military action to "halt the spread of Communism" in Vietnam — including the use of nuclear weapons.

UCLA had a strong cohort of Young Republicans and throughout the spring they were actively campaigning against each other for either Goldwater or Nelson Rockefeller, the "moderate" Republican.

Since Wallace had almost no support on campus there was little student interest in the Democratic primary. Nevertheless, we of N-VAC and Bruin CORE managed to stir up a little teacup-tempest within UCLA's small circle of progressives and leftists when we passed around a flyer with the slogan "Boycott Baby, Boycott," meaning don't vote for either of the establishment parties because both of them supported or accommodated segregation and both stood on the wrong side of the anti-colonial struggles wracking Africa and Asia.

No one on the UCLA campus or in L.A.'s Afro-American community paid the slightest attention to our radical provocation — except the Communist Party and their DuBois Club adherents who were horrified that not only were we refusing to support Johnson and the Democratic Party but we were urging others to do the same — heresy!

Loud arguments and bitter recriminations broke out around our tables in the student union commons.

"You idiots, Goldwater will kill the Civil Rights Movement and start a war in Vietnam!" they grimly warned us.

"So will Johnson!" we retorted.

As it turned out, both sides were half right. LBJ did take us into a devastating Vietnam War (and in fact was planning to do so even as he swore he wasn't), but on civil rights he did respond to our Freedom Movement demands, he did get strong and effective legislation through

Congress, and though we continually criticized him for not doing as much as he should to enforce the new laws and rulings, he did more than anyone ever had before him (or since). And he fulfilled his Medicare, Medicaid, and federal-funding-for-education promises too. So on the domestic side Johnson turned out to be one of our best presidents — though that's small comfort to the 60,000 or so Americans and more than a million Indo-Chinese who died in his war.

For us in N-VAC and Bruin CORE however, the election was largely irrelevant — a sideshow so far as we were concerned. All of our attention and work was focused on building the Freedom Movement. Whoever ended up in the White House, we were damned straight going to continue nonviolently fighting in the streets for justice and equality.

The four CORE chapters up in the Bay Area — 'Frisco, Oakland, Berkeley-City and Berkeley-Campus — were larger, more active, and noticeably more creative than our chapters in Southern California. When the new school year began in September of '63 they too switched focus from housing segregation to employment discrimination. That fall they and other civil rights groups launched a series of militant direct action campaigns against racist employment practices by Lucky Markets, Mel's Diners, the Sheraton-Palace Hotel, and the Auto Row car dealers, all of which led to mass arrests and eventually resulted in clear victories with signed fair hiring agreements.

Then in May of '64, the NorCal CORE chapters called for a statewide campaign against the San Francisco–based Bank of America (BofA).

With 900 branches and almost 30,000 employees, BofA was the largest bank in California and one of the largest in the country at a time when banks were not allowed to operate across state lines. It was estimated that less than 3% of their workers were nonwhite in a state where nonwhites were 16% of the total population (9% Latino, 6% Afro-American, 1% Asian). Almost all of BofA's nonwhite employees were in menial positions, with just a tiny token handful of Black and Latino tellers in ghetto and barrio branches. BofA's basic policy was clear — anyone who handled or managed money had to be white — tellers, desk officers, managers, and of course corporate officers.

As we expected, BofA executives fervently denied any racial discrimination on their part. Yet when they met with CORE negotiators they refused to supply race-related employment statistics and blamed the obvious absence of nonwhite tellers and desk officers on "lack of qualified applicants" — despite long lists of clearly qualified applicants they had rejected.

In mid-May, CORE called for consumers to boycott the bank and CORE chapters began leafletting and picketing branches around the state. With L.A. CORE still controlled by the action-averse moderates and most of the L.A. suburb chapters more or less moribund, Bruin CORE and its N-VAC ally, along with the small but feisty San Diego CORE chapter, ended up shouldering the brunt of the BofA campaign in SoCal.

Bruin CORE initially focused on the BofA branch in UCLA's Westwood neighborhood. We handed out boycott leaflets and mounted picket lines — some as large as 50 protesters. But finals began at the end of May and then the school semester ended in early June. Students went home for vacation or found summer jobs and the number of people we could mobilize sharply declined.

Meanwhile BofA continued to proclaim their corporate spin, "We don't discriminate... lack of qualified ..." They refused to sign any kind of enforceable agreement with CORE as other large employers had done, but in early June they did sign a memorandum of understanding with California's Fair Employment Practices Commission (FEPC) promising to *eventually* hire 400 new Black and Latino employees and to report their progress toward equal job opportunities.

This was far short of what CORE was demanding. It would only increase the percentage of nonwhites in their labor force from 3% to 4% and it was not a legally binding agreement — they could walk away from it whenever they wished. We were certain that absent an enforceable agreement they would return to their policy of racial discrimination as soon as the public pressure generated by our protests eased off. So we continued direct action.

BofA then announced to the media that they had hired some 300 new Black and Latino employees statewide, so we figured that the CORE actions were having some good effect, particularly the large late-May protests up in 'Frisco and Berkeley that had had hundreds of participants. It didn't occur to us, though, that school semesters up north had also ended and they were now facing the same summer doldrums problems we were.

By now Bruin CORE had absorbed some of N-VAC's mystique — or *'tude* as it might be called in today's jargon. Since our summer numbers were small we had to be more provocative to make an impact. With students no longer thronging Westwood we shifted our attention to Santa Monica and escalated to what we called "coin-ins."

Those BofA protests took place long before there were ATMs, bank credit cards, automatic payroll deposit, or "cash-back" at store checkout registers. To deposit your paycheck you had to go to your branch and line up at a cashier window. Ditto to cash a check or withdraw money. Since most people got paid on Friday and needed dough for the weekend, Friday afternoon was banking rush hour. Banks closed at five o'clock in those days, and from 3:00 to 5:00 people were normally lined up half a dozen deep at each teller window. Today if you go into an older branch office you can usually see a long line of unused teller windows that were originally put in place for those Friday rush hours.

Our first coin-in was on June 12, a Friday afternoon, in the BofA branch at Wilshire and 15th in Santa Monica. We set up our picket line of about 15 folk and waited until we were sure that all customers in the bank had seen our protest and chosen to cross our line. Then about half of us went inside and lined up, one at each of the six windows.

When I got up to the teller, I handed her a dollar and asked for change (all the tellers were women). She gave me the usual quarters, nickels, and dimes. "Oh, no, I'm sorry. I need pennies." She gave me two rolls of pennies. I slowly unwrapped the first roll and started to count them. "One .... two .... three ..." and so on. "Oh, there's only 49 here, you count them." She counted them and discovered 50. But, of course, I had to count them again to check her accuracy. Back and forth. Back and forth. Obviously we were trying to hold up the line and inconvenience the other customers for as long as we could so they'd take their business to some rival bank (there used to be lots of different banks competing with each other for customers — they even offered toasters and other bribes to people who transferred their accounts).

Some of the tellers reacted to our coin-in with outrage, as though we were committing sacrilege or some sort of obscene blasphemy. Others thought it was amusing, a welcome break in boring routine — an attitude we encouraged with as much humor as we could generate. I'd smile and try to entice them into accepting the prank — sometimes that worked, sometimes it didn't. At the risk seeming a braggart, I was quite good at "coining." I could keep a buck in play for more than 15 minutes, often longer.

Side by side with me at these Bruin CORE protests were N-VAC warriors Jerry Farber, Jay Frank, and Josh Gould. We four were nonviolent musketeers, one for all and all for one, always showing up where the action was hottest. Jay had gotten involved in CORE when he happened to encounter the picket line at Don Wilson's housing tract. He recently told me, "I was a pretty naive white kid back in '62 and had never seen such a thing, nor was I at all familiar with the Civil Rights Movement. All I knew was that the idea of segregated housing struck me as immensely stupid and unfair, so I joined the demonstration." He was around my age, maybe a little older, solidly built (I was usually referred to as "that skinny kid" — alas, no longer), and he was always cheerful and wore a friendly grin.

Josh Gould was a Bruin CORE mainstay, a Santa Monica College student, tall and muscular with a strong commitment and a rich baritone. And out on the picket line we knew we could count on Lynn Busch — the "Widow Busch" as she was fondly referred to. Her husband had been killed a year or so earlier in a car wreck leaving her with a toddler to raise, so she couldn't risk arrest, but she walked the line, sometimes pushing her daughter in a stroller, and she was the one we counted on to arrange bail for us when we were busted.

The first coin-in went well and so did a second one a week later. But in the N-VAC and Bruin CORE way, we began to get bored (or maybe it was just me as Bruin picket captain). I consulted a lawyer and confirmed that a check was simply a written message instructing the bank to transfer a certain sum of money from a particular account to a designated recipient and that so long as it had the proper names, amounts, and routing numbers it did not have to be written on the official printed forms everyone had in their checkbooks.

So I opened a small checking account at an out-of-the-way BofA branch we'd never leafletted or picketed, and then used a big marker to write out several one-dollar checks on the back of picket signs emblazoned with "Bank of America discriminates," "Boycott BofA," "Racism must go," and so on.

Normally, we never attached our signs to sticks because they could be snatched out of our hands by hostile adversaries and used to club us in the head or face. Instead, we always wore signs hanging by string from around our neck. Sometimes they'd be torn away and ripped up, but they were easily replaceable. In this case, however, we attached the picket-sign checks to broom handles so they'd stand out while we were waiting in the teller queues. Around 4 o'clock on June 26, half a dozen of us walked off the picket line and into the branch carrying our signs.

The manager immediately came bustling over. "You can't picket in here! This is private property! No picketing in here!"

"Oh, I'm not picketing, I'm here to cash a check. See —" I pointed to the $1 check I'd written on the back. It was made out to "Cash."

As a properly trained middle manager he immediately got on the phone for instructions. When I got up to the teller I slapped my sign down on the marble counter with an audible *Clack!* and endorsed it with a flourish. By now the manager was back. He instructed the teller to give me my dollar, and I promptly began going through the coin-in routine. We called this new tactic a "cash-in."

On Wednesday of the following week, I got a call from the branch where my little account had been set up. They told me they couldn't send my canceled picket signs through the mail. They offered to send me a receipt instead. Unless, of course, I wanted to come down and pick them up. Which I did. The guy I dealt with at that branch was clearly having a bit of fun himself because he'd written "Canceled" in a big bold hand across the check. (I kept those signs for years, but eventually as I moved from town to town they disappeared.)

Well, okay, good to know, we could cash a picket sign. *Hmmmm*, if we can cash a picket sign, what else could we cash? The next Friday, July 3rd, we showed up at the Wilshire branch with checks written on picket signs, and also on an old whitewall tire, a big tin washtub, and a wooden crate with a dead chicken inside. We'd actually had a long discussion about this at one of our meetings. The connection between our picket signs and the campaign against BofA job discrimination was pretty clear — not so much though for tire, tub, and crate. But we really wanted to do it, so we came up with some lame rationale about the junk representing poverty in the ghetto, or some such nonsense. I mean, who could resist cashing a dead chicken at a Bank of America? Certainly not I.

Sure enough, they cashed signs, tire, tub, and crate. But their patience was clearly running thin. This time I was not given the option of picking up our canceled junk and smelly carcass. Receipts were sent instead. A couple of days later we were informed by the Santa Monica chief of police that the manager was now under instructions to press charges against any protester who entered the bank regardless of reason. He asked us to come by his office to discuss how that would go down, because he'd never arrested protesters before — drunks and DUIs, yes, rowdy kids on the beach, potheads, the occasional "sexual deviant" (homosexuals), and the odd robber — all those he was familiar with, but not racial agitators. (In many ways Santa Monica was still a small suburban town in those days.)

So Jerry, Jay, and I went down to police headquarters to impress upon him that we were nonviolent and that we would not forcefully resist arrest in any way that might harm or endanger his officers. If arrested we might link arms and they would have to pull us apart, but then we would go limp and all they need do is carry us to the paddy wagon that was always stationed near protests in case it might be needed to haul us away. He assured us that he completely understood and that his men would be very professional (the few female officers in those days were restricted to desk duty so we never encountered them on protests).

Since we knew they were planning to arrest us we decided to stick with a plain old coin- in, no signs, no junk, no cash-in (sigh). After setting up the picket line about ten of us entered the Wilshire branch on July 10 and joined the queues at the teller windows.

Off to one side I noticed a little commotion. The manager and a couple of cops were ordering CORE activist Jon Tavasti to leave the premises. He asked why and they placed him under arrest. Well trained as he was, he immediately sat down and started to sing a freedom song. For a moment the other CORE kids looked at each other wondering what they were supposed to do. They didn't have to wonder long. N-VAC warrior Jay Frank asked me what was going on and I said, "Looks like they've arrested Jon." Three seconds later he was sitting next to Tavasti and they'd linked arms. Jerry Farber immediately followed suit and so did Josh Gould and the other CORE members. Within 20 seconds or so, everyone except me was sitting in a line on the lobby floor, arms linked, singing *We Shall Overcome.*

I could see Jerry and Jay looking at me, obviously wondering why I was just standing there. As picket captain, however, I had duties and responsibilities. I mean, someone had to act like an adult. And, of course, I also had a plan. I went out to make sure everyone on the line knew what was going down and that they should keep on picketing. I told Lynn to go to the pay phone and begin executing our arrest procedures. She was equipped with a couple rolls of coins for calling the bail bondsman, alerting the press, notifying the CORE office on Venice, arranging legal help, and so on — all the civil-disobedience details that need to be planned out and assigned in advance when arrests are likely to occur.

While I was taking care of business outside, a squad of cops had come in and brutally broken up the line of sit-ins, who were now being roughly dragged out and tossed in the waiting paddy wagon. I guess that took about 20 or 30 minutes. At which point, with Lynn on the job and the line holding well, I stepped in front of the van and shouted as loud as I could, "I protest unjust arrests!"

Then I dropped down, rolled underneath, and wrapped my arms around the front axle. I could hear the cops shouting and yelling. I guess the driver decided to scare me by starting up the engine (he succeeded). That caused even more shouting.

Then they started pulling on my legs and eventually managed to drag me out from under, at which point I went limp. I was carried to the rear and lifted up to be shoved through the wagon's double-doors. Jerry, Jay, and Josh had seen what I had done and decided to support my protest by sitting across the door opening so as to prevent me from being placed inside. I was, of course, quite limp, so the cops were trying to shove me through a human blockade which was working about as well as trying to push toothpaste back into the tube.

Eventually, of course, they finally managed to get me properly taken into custody. Battered and bruised, we were all taken to the station and placed in a holding cell. At which point the chief showed up with a big grin on his face asking us how did they do? He seemed quite surprised when we failed to compliment his officers on their professionalism. Looking back on it now, though, I don't think they were intentionally brutal like the LAPD tended to be when arresting protesters — they were just poorly trained, overexcited, and ineptly supervised by their sergeant. I considered offering to run a nonviolent training session for them but in the end decided it would be too confusing all around.

That, however, was our last militant action at BofA. I had now been arrested four times in less than a year, with trials and sentences on the horizon. Jay and Jerry had been busted even more than I. None of the Bruin CORE members wanted to go for two, so for the rest of July and August we just picketed and leafletted.

The Bay Area CORE chapters in NorCal were also running out of steam. Over the course of that school year, more than 600 people, mostly students, had been arrested for protesting job discrimination at several different firms and locations. But now most students were gone for the summer and as with N-VAC those previously arrested were tied up in a series of lengthy and costly trials leading to jail sentences. Where once Berkeley Campus CORE could mobilize hundreds of pickets for a BofA protest, now they were lucky to get 30. That was double what we could muster in SoCal, but it wasn't enough. Early in September CORE leaders in the Bay Area reluctantly conceded defeat and suspended the BofA campaign.

The previous Bay Area job actions had ended in clear-cut victories with signed, legally enforceable hiring agreements. That was not the case with Bank of America. Under their agreement with the FEPC they were supposed to report their progress towards becoming an equal opportunity employer, but their data did not have to be made public, and so far as I know, it never was. According to the bank's unverified statements, by the end of CORE's campaign BofA they had hired several hundred Afro-Americans and Latinos, which was far fewer than we had demanded though many more than they had before our protests began.

Of course, we feared those new hires would be fired once our pressure on BofA ended. So when the campaign petered out it felt like a defeat. We were wrong about that though. True, no one handed us any gold cup engraved with "VICTORY," but over the next few years our achievement became quite clear. By the end of the decade it had become commonplace to see people of color at teller windows and behind bank desks up and down the state — and not just in the ghetto. And back then, those were good jobs with decent pay for people without college degrees.

Nor was it only at BofA. When other financial institution saw that white customers did not flee in horror at the sight of a Black cashier they too signed equal employment agreements with the FEPC. Other large employers significantly altered their hiring practices as well, Pacific Telephone (PacBell), Pacific Gas and Electric (PG&E), and the western division of Greyhound bus lines all signed equal hiring agreements with the California Public Utilities Commission.

I and the others arrested in Santa Monica were charged with trespass, disturbing the peace, and resisting arrest. Since we had legally gone into the bank as customers, disturbed no one's peace until after we had been placed under arrest, and "resisted" only in the sense of holding on to someone else (or in my case, a truck axle) before going limp, the Santa Monica authorities (unlike those in Los Angeles) were smart enough to avoid tying up their court in a lengthy and embarrassing trial that might result in them hosting us with free room and board in a city or county jail. That December they dropped all charges against us.

Victories & Defeats ~ 1964

Simultaneous with our campaign against BofA, the Civil Rights Act of 1964 was being debated in Congress. Its eventual passage was a huge and hard-won victory for the Freedom Movement nationwide — achieved through courage and determination in sit-ins, Freedom Rides, and mass action in places like Albany, Georgia, Greenwood, Mississippi, Birmingham, Alabama, and St. Augustine, Florida.

In SoCal, of most immediate concern for us in N-VAC and CORE was Title VII of the Act, which addressed job discrimination and fair employment. Title VII was noticeably weaker and watered down from what the Freedom Movement originally demanded. The kinds of employers covered by the Act were reduced, the scope of coverage was narrowed, and the penalties and remedies were weakened. Nevertheless, *overt* discrimination on the basis of race, religion, gender, or national origin by employers covered under its jurisdiction was prohibited and the federal Equal Employment Opportunity Commission was established to oversee the Act's implementation.

With passage of the Act, explicit, overt race and gender employment discrimination was made illegal. More importantly, it became socially unacceptable. Help Wanted ads, for example, could no longer legally specify "white" or "male" as job requirements, nor would the public accept such flagrant unfairness. But *covert* employment bias did not, and has not, ended. Substantial inequity in employment continues to this day. Controversy and litigation over the meaning and scope of Title VII also continues, so much so that there are law firms whose entire practice is devoted to Title VII cases.

Nevertheless, in the two decades after passage of the Act, average income for nonwhites and women rose significantly as more, and better, jobs became available. As a result, many nonwhite Americans and a significant portion of white women and were able to climb out of poverty into the middle class.

But those gains went almost entirely to those with the education and skills to find jobs in the previously closed occupations. Nonwhites and women at the bottom of economic and educational ladders benefited little (if at all) because the wages paid for traditional "Colored work" and "women's work" — particularly in the agriculture, unskilled labor, and service sectors — remained stagnant or actually declined in purchasing power. And mechanization, technology, and the transfer of jobs to low-wage, non-union states and later to slave-wage foreign nations made that work scarcer and harder to find.

Since the Reagan administration in the 1980s, income and poverty gaps between men and women, whites and nonwhites, have not narrowed at all and in some respects have widened as economic policies and programs driven by conservative ideologies have increasingly been designed to favor the already wealthy at the expense of everyone else — particularly the working poor.

As for N-VAC and Bruin CORE, we were not able to sustain the level of militant direct action we had hoped for. People wearied of constant action and protest. Bail, trials, sentences, and their costs in time and money overwhelmed us. Nonviolent direct action was then, and still remains, a powerful weapon for social justice. But as we learned in the university of real life there are limits to how long it can be sustained.

During the Watts revolt in August of 1965, N-VAC members mobilized to provide food for hungry people trapped in the interdicted zone by cops and National Guard. Afterwards, led by Robert Hall and others, N-VAC more and more directed its energy away from direct action into a community organizing endeavor called "Operation Bootstrap." In part influenced by SNCC's work in the South, Bootstrap combined political empowerment, job training, community-based self-help, and an employment coop.

Most of the hardcore N-VAC members remained political activists in one form or another for the rest of their lives. Woodrow Coleman continued on with N-VAC, then Operation Bootstrap, became a founder of the California Peace and Freedom Party, organized for welfare rights, and worked with juvenile delinquents. Though he is in his 80s today, he is still active with the L.A. Bus Riders Union and the Labor Community Strategy Center. Danny Gray also continued a life of social and political activism with various organizations, causes, and careers. Mari Goldman put herself through law school, became a legislative aide to Congressman Merv Dymally, a champion for women's rights, and eventually an administrative law judge.

Jay Frank continued for some years as a political activist in the Bay Area and today lives with his family in the Midwest. Jerry Farber never ceased being a social commentator and gadfly. He recently retired from teaching at UC San Diego and San Diego State. Josh Gould later did voter registration work for SNCC in Alabama, ran an anti-war GI coffeehouse in Texas, served a year in prison for draft resistance, became a radical labor activist, and today is a Teamster truck driver in Atlanta. Sadly, Robert Hall died young, and Lynn Busch and Jon Tavasti are also no longer with us.

As for myself, I left Los Angeles that fall, never to return. First I headed north to support the Free Speech Movement at Berkeley and then went south to Alabama and Mississippi to carry on the freedom fight with the Southern Christian Leadership Conference (SCLC).

Free Speech Movement at Berkeley ~ 1964

When the UCLA school year ended in June of '64, I was placed on academic probation due to my abysmal grades. Grades which, in my opinion as a psychology major, failed to measure, or even take into account, all that I was learning about the influence of economics and politics on the psycho-sociology of racism, rage, and resistance. I was learning a huge amount, but just because it wasn't the psychology being taught at UCLA they didn't see it that way — perhaps because I failed to turn in any of my term papers, missed half the class sessions, and fell seriously short of "acing" my midterms and finals.

But back in the 1960s, students having academic difficulties were allowed to temporarily withdraw from the university with the assurance that they would be readmitted when they were ready to resume their studies. It was a common-sense method of helping young people who were having a hard time orienting and focusing themselves — as young'uns often do at that point in their lives. I filed the temporary withdrawal forms and told my parents I wasn't going to enroll for the fall semester.

My mom, of course, was distraught and voluble in trying to convince me otherwise. My dad, calmer and surely wiser, simply told me it's my life and my choice, but they weren't going to pay for my civil rights work. If that's what I wanted to do, I'd have to do it on my own without their $50-per-month stipend. Fine by me.

However, as a college dropout my "2S" student draft deferment was no longer valid. I expected to be reclassified "1A," which meant I would be available for immediate conscription into the Army. With an expanding war in Vietnam now looming ominously on the horizon that was no small concern. But Draft Board 102 of Los Angeles County — bless their hearts — bestowed upon me a welcome surprise gift. They informed me I was now classified "1Y." As it was explained in their little brochure, the "1Y" classification was for men who were "physically, mentally, or morally unfit for military service except in times of extreme national emergency."

In other words, until an armada of Vietcong rowboats appeared off the California coast I wasn't going to be drafted — *Hallelujah!*

Since they'd never given me any kind of pre-induction physical or mental evaluation my draft board must have concluded that I was *morally unfit* to fight in Vietnam. No doubt because of my civil rights arrests. This is not as surprising as it might first appear. Boys were assigned to draft boards based on the neighborhood they lived in. Since my family lived in a working-class, mixed-race area of inner-city Los Angeles where relatively few kids went to college, Draft Board 102 had no problem meeting their monthly quotas. So it was easy for them to reject me as a potential troublemaker who might lead innocent recruits astray. Had I hailed from a more middle-class area like Beverly Hills or the San Fernando Valley it would have been quite a different story.

University of California classes resumed in mid-September of 1964 but as a dropout, I couldn't have cared less — or so I thought. By then

CORE's campaign against BofA had been suspended, and while N-VAC was still doggedly leafleting and picketing Van de Kamp's, our numbers, energy, and enthusiasm were low. The truth is we were just going through the motions while we gradually accepted defeat. Maybe defeat is like what they say about dying, with five stages of acceptance, I don't know. But by November we had finally bowed to the inevitable.

I was sick of Los Angeles. I hated it. Actually, I'd always disliked L.A., now I actively loathed it. But I was still committed to the Freedom Movement. The heart, soul, and center of that Movement was in the South. My court trials had prevented me from participating in Mississippi Freedom Summer and now I was determined to "go South." There were just three little problems holding me back. First, I had no money. My old car had given up the ghost, my part time fry-cook job barely paid the rent, and I had no savings at all. Second, was simple inertia. And third — I was scared. I knew how dangerous it was to be a southern civil rights worker. Luckily for me, Republican Senator William F. Knowland and the UC Board of Regents broke me free.

People today cannot imagine how restricted and constrained college life was in the '50s and early '60s. Young women, known *co-eds*, were governed by *parietal rules* under the rationale of *in loco parentis* — the concept that it was the responsibility of the university to function as a parent — a socially-conservative parent — for female students. Parietal rules included dorm curfews, bed checks, and at many colleges so-called "character" requirements. Such rules were intended to control the personal and social lives of female students in the manner it was assumed their parents would do if she were still living at home. The clear purpose, of course, being to ensure that girls remained virgin until properly married — a goal neither university or parents had much hope of achieving in those halcyon years *after the pill and before the plague.*

Intellectually and academically, colleges and universities severely limited freedom of thought, speech, and association of *everyone* regardless of gender. Faculty at public universities like UCLA were officially subject to loyalty oaths and unofficially bound by the political dogmas of conservative regents and legislators. Courses were limited to those subjects approved by the powers-that-were and content was tailored to avoid the ire of Republican alumni. Throughout the University of California system, controversial speakers and ideas that might offend conservative politicians or upset right-wing newspaper editors were either forbidden outright or strictly regulated.

Speakers could not be invited to address classes, clubs, meetings, or any other on-campus events without prior administration approval.

Which they adamantly refused to grant for anyone deemed "too controversial." You could not hand out political literature that had not been vetted in advance by campus authorities — you literally had to have a university official stamp *approved* on a copy that you had to keep on file before you could post notices on campus bulletin boards. You could not recruit for participation in off-campus political activities such as a civil rights protest, nor could you raise funds for the Freedom Movement or other liberal social causes. Even the officially recognized Young Republicans and Young Democrats were not allowed to engage in, or mobilize support for, off-campus events.

During the civil rights protests of the previous '63–'64 academic year, Berkeley CORE activists had circumvented the no-political-activity rules by using a wide strip of sidewalk just outside the main campus entrance on Bancroft Way. Everyone, including UCB administrators, had assumed it was city property governed by the U.S. Constitution. So on that small piece of turf, groups were free to hand out flyers, set up literature tables, stage small rallies, and recruit for direct action protests against the Bank of America.

But during the summer of 1964 while school was out of session, CORE and other civil rights groups staged nonviolent protests at the Republican National Convention held in San Francisco's Cow Palace, and civil rights activists had begun picketing the *Oakland Tribune* over its discriminatory hiring practices. At that time, the *Trib* was owned by William F. Knowland, a former U.S. Senator. He was titular head of the California Republican Party and a staunch conservative. The protests outside his corporate office and what he regarded as *his* convention did not meet please him. He wielded enormous political power in the state and he had no intention of allowing his political party or his personal newspaper to become the target of mass student protest once classes resumed in the fall. He demanded that civil rights recruiting on the Bancroft strip be suppressed and his cronies on the UC Board of Regents acquiesced to his command.

On the first day of class in mid-September, Berkeley administrators announced that the university owned the Bancroft strip and that it was now under the control of the UC Board of Regents. Henceforth, they declared, all political activity on that sidewalk would be governed by campus regulations — in other words, banned. It's been said that "nothing is more powerful than an idea whose time has come," and I suppose the corollary must be that "nothing is more futile than trying to *stop* an idea whose time has come."

Among the students returning to school that September were veterans of Freedom Summer projects in Mississippi and Louisiana who had stood side by side with Afro-American sharecroppers and courageous Black schoolchildren daring to defy Klan violence and ferocious repression by state governments. Some of those Berkeley students had gone on to challenge Lyndon Baines Johnson, President of the United States, at *his* Democratic Convention in Atlantic City. These Freedom Movement veterans were not the kind of men and women who could be intimidated by the Dean of Bureaucratic Buffoonery or the Vice-Poobah of Alumni Appeasement.

The regents' political ban proved to be a spark in dry tinder that exploded into the Free Speech Movement (FSM). By mid-October newspapers in Los Angeles were filled with stories of student defiance at Berkeley, mass protests, and calls for action. I saw the FSM in terms of student support for a Civil Rights Movement that was challenging the Jim Crow status quo — South and North. The FSM was led by CORE and SNCC veterans. So for me, the Freedom Movement and the Free Speech Movement were one and the same.

Heeding the siren call of fife and drum, at the end of November I bummed a ride north, ending up in a shabby 'Frisco crash pad — an empty store on Buchanan Street that was awaiting demolition as part of an Urban Renewal project we referred to as "Negro Removal." Its ancient wooden floors were warped and splintery, the windows were grimy, and there was no heat at all. It was occupied by a shifting ménage of itinerant musicians and poets, political activists, strange drifters, and free spirits. I slept on the floor in my sleeping bag, shared communal meals of stews, brown rice, and thick soups, smoked some bodacious weed, went to beatnik coffee houses, and debated and argued the issues of the day long into the night. I loved every minute of it.

Like most newcomers, I was surprised at how much colder San Francisco was than the rest of California. From a local war surplus store I acquired a dark Navy peacoat and a blue wool watch cap. In the early years of the Freedom Movement, to show their respectability activists had dressed up in coats and ties, heels and hose, but by the end of '64, jeans, work shirts, and Army jackets were de rigueur for the serious protester.

My main expense was bus fare over the bridge to Berkeley where the Free Speech Movement was furiously engaged in a massive, and ultimately successful, struggle against the established order. I knew almost no one at Berkeley, had no roots there, and was no longer even a student, but I pitched in to help wherever I could.

Since I was on its periphery, the FSM story is not mine to tell. I was, however, immensely impressed by the sheer scale and power of a mass peoples' movement — so very, very different from our small N-VAC and Bruin CORE guerrilla-type protests in SoCal.

One day a speaker at one of the Sproul Plaza rallies asked for volunteers to help get out a fund-appeal mailing. I knew how to do that, we did it all the time in N-VAC. Four or five of us would sit around a kitchen table, folding, stuffing, and sealing, affixing mailing labels and stamps, and then sorting by city or zipcode.

So I showed up at an off-campus office and was astonished to see nearly 100 people working at long rows of tables set end to end, four or five rows, each an industrial-size mailing assembly line. At the end of each line, boxes and boxes of finished envelopes were being moved around on dollies. It wasn't just the scale of the mailing itself that amazed me, it was that they had such a huge list of potential supporters to make it necessary.

Looking back now, that memory of the mailing operation is as vivid to me as my memories of the truly impressive FSM protests on campus, which dwarfed anything I'd ever previously participated in. I suppose it may seem a bit strange that memories of a mailing remain with me all these years later, but by the fall of 1964 I had become a professional Freedom Movement activist — unpaid, true, but a professional in the sense that I saw it as my calling — and for professionals, methods and techniques can be as fascinating as the dramatic events are for amateurs.

And the FSM protests *were* filled with power and drama, thrilling and inspiring. And those too, I remember well. On Wednesday December 2nd, hundreds of students and supporters occupied Sproul Hall, the administration building, with a massive sit-in. The campus cops blocked the doors too late and they had neither the numbers, nor the training, nor the facilities to clear the building. After they started guarding the doors to prevent additional supporters from joining, we used a ladder up to a second story rear window to enter and exit.

Like a good CORE action, the sit-in was well disciplined and tightly organized. Only the hallways were occupied, no one entered the offices. Impromptu classes were being taught and films shown in the second-floor hallways, the third floor seemed to be where most of the passionate political arguments and debates were raging, and the fourth floor had been set aside as a silent area for those who wanted to study.

Late that night a swarm of 600 Oakland cops and Alameda sheriffs in riot gear began forming up to clear the building of the 800 or so people still sitting in. I was emotionally torn, I wanted to stay and be busted with all the others who were putting their bodies on the line. But if I was awaiting trial in Berkeley I couldn't go South. So I reluctantly left the building by the backside ladder just before the police seized it.

It took them almost 12 hours to clear the building, roughly dragging limp protesters down the stairs, kicking and punching them when the press wasn't looking. By mid-morning the cops were still hauling people away, and I phoned in live reports to a support rally at UCLA hastily organized by Bruin CORE and the DuBois Club.

The Berkeley campus was now occupied by an army of cops and in total turmoil. Students were spontaneously boycotting classes and forming protest rallies. By Friday the last of the arrestees had been bailed out and were back on campus, welcomed as heroes. A student strike was called and picket lines went up at entrances to class and lab buildings across the sprawling campus. I borrowed a bicycle and volunteered to ride a scout circuit, bringing reports back to Strike Central. At least two-thirds, perhaps as many as three-quarters of the student body were now boycotting classes, and graduate students were refusing to tend their laboratory experiments (though they continued to feed the lab-animals).

Over the weekend there were meetings — many, many meetings — students, activists, faculty, administrators. I attended one for outside supporters. None of the experienced FSM leaders were present, I suppose they must have been in some kind of strategy session. The room was filled with energy and passion, but there was also chaos and confusion. Students wanted labor unions to honor their strike. Regular industrial unions, that is, not unions of campus workers, because California public employees had no collective bargaining rights until the late 1970s.

I remember someone from the International Longshore and Warehouse Union (ILWU) — 'Frisco's feisty (and politically influential) longshore union — asking the students what their "beef" was. Not understanding that he was asking them to explain what the issues were, some of the students reacted as if it were a hostile question. I should have realized that someone needed to translate *laborese* into *studentese*, but in the excitement and hurly-burly of a disorganized meeting it didn't occur to me at the time. They kept shouting and demanding unions respect their picket lines and eventually the longshoreman threw up his hands and sarcastically told them, "Okay, fine, we won't unload any ships on your campus," and then he walked out. Such a valuable opportunity missed.

On Monday the 7th, the student strike continued to hold strong. University President Clark Kerr called a "convocation" of all students and faculty to meet in the open-air Greek Theater. Students and faculty overflowed the benches and aisles, occupied adjacent roofs, and climbed trees to see. Though the convocation had been called in response to an overwhelming student strike, not a single student was allowed to address the audience or even ask a single question. Not one. Not. One. The presidents, deans and department heads who did speak (at length) had only bland platitudes to share. No one was impressed.

When they finished lecturing us, FSM leader Mario Savio walked towards the microphone to announce that a student rally would immediately take place in front of Sproul Hall to consider and debate what the administrators had said. He was jumped by campus cops and manhandled off stage to a location unknown. Pandemonium erupted.

Eventually Mario was released, but for most of us the police suppression of his effort to make a simple announcement and the fact that no students had been deemed worthy of speaking clearly illuminated the contempt that those in authority had for students — all of whom were old enough to be drafted into the Army, some in fact were military veterans, and many of whom were registered voters. Yet as the self-defined "adults," they considered and treated us as unruly children.

By now, though, the faculty — long held in forced political conformity by Red Scare threats and loyalty oaths — had finally begun to bestir themselves. On Tuesday the 8th, the strike was suspended while the professors deliberated. That evening almost the entire tenured faculty gathered in Wheeler Auditorium. For an hour and a half they debated, their words broadcast by loudspeakers to a throng of students waiting outside in a dark and frigid December night. By an overwhelming vote of 824 to 115 the Academic Senate passed a campus free speech resolution that did away with University authority to restrict or regulate political activity and the content of ideas.

As the professors left Wheeler Hall, we spontaneously formed two applauding lines on either side so that they walked in a kind of procession through a cheering crowd of their students. I don't think anything like that had ever happened to them before and I could see that many of them were visibly moved — in some cases stunned. For me this was what victory felt like. For the next six months, all through Selma and the March to Montgomery, I wore my blue and white FSM button as a badge of pride and honor — a pin I still have and still treasure today.

Audacity & Humor

As must be obvious by now, I enjoyed protesting. I found saying "No!" to the bullies and bigshots empowering. But I always understood that protests and demonstrations were a means of social change, not ends in themselves.

What N-VAC's shop-ins and CORE's coin-ins taught me is that audacity and humor are far more effective tools for achieving social change than anger and rage. Gandhi said, "The role of a civil protester is to provoke a response, and to keep protesting until there is a response." Humor and unexpected social audacity are more likely to provoke a response than activities that are routine and expected — even if they're passionate. And they're far more likely to provoke a *positive* response than fury and violence.

Audacity and humor get talked about. Defiant sit-ins by Black students in the South and our audacious shop-ins, coin-ins, and sip-ins in SoCal generated social buzz because people talked about them.

Of course, not all of that talk was positive — we violated the social order of custom and courtesy and that deeply offended many people and frightened others. Businesses were disrupted by our actions, property was mishandled, cupcakes had been squished. "Innocent" shoppers and bank patrons had been inconvenienced, people were delayed in line, Sunday brunches were disrupted, afternoon teas delayed. Pundits and editorials denounced our "coercive" tactics. Commentators and community personages darkly warned of threatened "anarchy" and the collapse of "civility."

We who supported racial justice countered by raising the long-term economic devastation of systemic job discrimination. We called out Bank of America and Van de Kamp's role in perpetuating a system that was inherently unjust and socially destructive. Those two companies had hundreds of outlets across SoCal, and our little band of audacious protesters only visited a handful. But word of mouth and media coverage spread our issues far and wide and it was impossible to talk about shop-ins and coin-ins without also talking about racist hiring practices.

Though N-VAC failed to win against Van de Kamp's, CORE did change Bank of America's hiring practices — as anyone who visits a bank branch can see for themselves today.

In the American South of the 1960s, simply asking for a cup of coffee at a white-only lunch counter, attempting to register to vote, or carrying a freedom sign, were audacious enough to provoke a response —

in many cases a violent response — from those determined to maintain the Jim Crow system of racial apartheid. But in the North, and in later decades and other struggles, more sophisticated and powerful adversaries learned to ignore small protests. When actions produce no response they appear futile (though, in fact, they may not be).

When our protests were ignored we felt impotent and some participants reacted with anger. Rage might be an effective tactic in a social situation where expressed anger commands attention and disrupts a valued harmony. But against entrenched power defending its privilege, shouted fury is simply a loud form of futility. It may feel good for a moment and it may energize that fraction of the population who are thrilled by acting out in public. But power elites are impervious to militant slogans, and if anger erupts into violence the police are ready, willing, and able to quickly suppress it long before it poses any inconvenience to distant rulers safe and secure in their bastions of wealth and privilege.

As a matter of practical politics, humor is more effective than anger. Those whom we poke fun at we cease to fear. Laughter and ridicule undermine authority and diminish its ability to compel obedience. You can weaken, unbalance, and ultimately overthrow the king more effectively by laughing at him than by impotently screaming fury at him.

Humor appeals to observers and potential supporters where rage frightens and alienates them. Humor disarms and confuses adversaries, fury triggers ingrained patterns of defense and mobilizes opposition. Humor is more sustainable than anger. Anger is exhausting, most people cannot sustain intense rage over long periods of time. But humor is energizing, both in the short run of a single protest, and in the long run of an extended campaign.

I know that for some folks nonviolent audacity and humor appear less effective — and certainly less macho — than rage and violence. But consider this, stories of audacity and humor are told, retold, and remembered in ways that conventional protests and violent outbursts are not. To this day, most every child and adult in America can tell you the basic story of the Boston Tea Party — an audacious nonviolent protest from back in 1773. Yet the teacher and textbook that taught you the Tea Party also taught the Battle of Saratoga — a crucial (but conventional) military turning point in the Revolutionary War. Outside of some history buffs and professors, no one can recall anything about Saratoga — nor that the brilliant general who won the battle for the rebel colonists was a guy named Benedict Arnold (who later betrayed his fellow revolutionaries).

Certainly in my life as a protester and activist, most of the countless marches I've been on and the picket lines I've walked have blurred and disappeared into the musty attic of what's left of my memory. But I still recall in detail those coin-ins and cash-ins.

Contrary to the deeply held beliefs of some ideologists, there has never been any instruction manual for achieving political reform (let alone revolution). There's no easy how-to pamphlet, no 12-step program. What I've come to understand is that social struggle is like water flowing to the sea. If something dams the water it goes around. If it can't go around it goes over, if it can't go over it goes under, if it can't go around or over or under it eats away at the blockage until it dissolves. That's the "water theory" of social change.

All of which means that social change is a Darwinian process. You try something. If it works you do more of it until it stops working. If it fails you get creative and try something else. That which succeeds survives and thrives, that which fails dies. And in that context, humor and audacity provide far greater opportunities for new creative strategies and unexpected tactics than do rage and fury.

Over the Edmund Pettus Bridge

Selma, Lord, Selma ~ 1965

Shortly after the FSM victory I left San Francisco to visit my parents in New Haven, though I knew I'd someday return. 'Frisco felt like home to me in a way that L.A. never did. I rode the dog to Connecticut and my dad picked me up at the Greyhound depot. Through their contacts at Yale, I was able to pick up unskilled work assisting graduate students who hired me with funds from their research grants. Since I was living with my folks my expenses were minimal and I was able to save money for going South, which I was still determined to do.

From my Freedom Movement work in L.A., I had contacts and people who would vouch for me to both CORE and SNCC. And in late 1964 the Freedom Movement was still remarkably open to anyone willing to — as the saying went — "put their body on the line." Obviously, as a white man, I did not enjoy the same presumption of solidarity that was automatically offered to Black activists. But for the most part, whites willing to share the risks, treat Afro-Americans as equals, and respect Black leadership found a warm welcome in the Movement. Though I wasn't aware of it, the growing influence of Black nationalism and the increasingly poisonous effects of the FBI's COINTELPRO spying, sabotage, and disruption program were beginning to change that in SNCC and CORE — though due to King's influence not so much in SCLC.

I was therefore reasonably confident that if I showed up at the Atlanta SNCC or New Orleans CORE office and explained who I was I could find a place in the southern wing of the Freedom Movement — first as a volunteer and then, hopefully, as paid staff. That was my plan. By February of 1965, I'd saved around $300 (equal to about $2,400 in 2018), which I figured was enough to support me for half a year in the lavish lifestyle that southern civil rights workers were known to enjoy. If at the end of that time I hadn't been hired on to a freedom project, I'd return to California and figure out what to do with the rest of my life.

So why was I still in Connecticut?

When I was a kid and my parents took me to a swimming pool I was afraid to jump into the deep end. I'd stand there faltering, desperately wanting to jump — but I couldn't. I just couldn't. I loved and respected my mom. In many ways she was a great woman, but in regard to me and my brother she was burdened with obsessive anxieties that she had no clue how to handle. So she worried and fretted and verbalized, "Be careful, be careful," which helped me not at all. My dad, however, was calm and supportive. He gently encouraged me but he didn't push me. He let me solve it on my own. Eventually I jumped into the deep end.

I was scared to go South. On this matter my mom was vociferously clear — she did not want me to go. No way. No how. And she used all of her considerable verbal and — let's be honest here — manipulative talents to prevent me. But by then I'd lived with her for 21 years (I turned 21 in January of '65) and had become much better at minimizing the degree to which her anxieties constrained and influenced my life.

With my father the situation was more complex. Unlike my mom, Ken was not only a southerner by birth, he'd been a Communist union organizer in Georgia, Alabama, and Mississippi. He once mentioned to me that one time a gang of Klansmen threatened to kill him if he wasn't on the morning bus out of Tupelo, Mississippi. He really wanted to defy them, he hated the idea of cowardly running away, but he already had a ticket for that same bus because his attendance was required at a union meeting in New Orleans. (He didn't use his motorcycle while organizing in the South — too easily run off the road and too exposed to bushwhackers with rifles.)

Obviously he did the intelligent thing, but I completely understood his dilemma and how appearing to submit to their threats still rankled him 30 years later. I would have felt exactly the same — and hopefully I would have made the same smart decision. I do regret though that I was too full of myself and my own concerns to ask him for the full detailed story of that event (and many others).

So Ken's fears for my safety were solidly grounded in realities my mom, thankfully, had only theoretical conception of. Decades later when I posted on the Civil Rights Movement Veterans website some stories about my work in the South she told me that if she had known the truth of what I was involved in she would have come down herself and dragged me home whether I wanted to go or not. And she would have. Or rather, she would have tried. Which is why the stories I'll be getting around to in this memoir somehow never made it into any of my letters home. To his credit — and Mom's forcefully expressed displeasure — while my father did not actively encourage me, neither did he try to dissuade me from going South.

Meanwhile, news reports of the brutal voting rights battle in Selma and Dallas County Alabama had begun to percolate up into the North. SNCC had been working and organizing in Selma since January of 1963, engaging in voter registration efforts and courageously enduring ferocious repression. While little known to the general public, those stories were familiar to me as a CORE activist.

Among civil rights workers Selma had a reputation as one of the roughest hell-holes in the South, a violent stronghold of a white supremacy enforced by the four guardians of Jim Crow — Council, Klan, courts, and cops. Ruling over Dallas County was Judge James Hare, a self-proclaimed "expert" on racial eugenics, who firmly believed in Black genetic inferiority. Though 57% of the population were Afro-American, he ran Dallas County as if it were his personal political plantation.

Sheriff Jim Clark was Hare's porcine-looking, whip-cracking overseer and enforcer. In addition to his hired deputies, Clark was backed by an armed posse of more than 200 volunteers — all white, of course — many of them KKK members. The posse was originally formed in the 1940s after World War II to suppress labor organizers like my father, but by the 1960s their mission was to crush Black challenges to white supremacy. And not just in Dallas County. Clark sent his posse on missions far and wide — to beat Freedom Riders in Montgomery in 1961, to riot against the admission of James Meredith to Ole Miss in '62, and to crack the heads of Birmingham children in '63.

Supporting Hare and Clark was Selma's powerful White Citizens' Council, composed of bankers, landlords, politicians, clergy, and other pillars of the established community. They stood ever-vigilant against any attempt to undermine the "southern way of life," which they fiercely defended with economic terrorism — firings, evictions, foreclosures, blacklists, and boycotts. And if economic retaliation failed there were murderous Klan cells active throughout the state. Together, Hare, Clark, Council, and Klan maintained an interlocking reign of judicial, economic, and violent terror that held most Dallas County Afro-Americans in an iron grip.

Yet against all odds there was a gutsy local Freedom Movement in Selma. The Dallas County Voters League (DCVL) had been formed after the NAACP was outlawed in Alabama in the mid-1950s. It was small but courageous. Unfortunately, courage alone was insufficient, and against adamant white opposition they made little headway. Eight years after *Brown v. Board of Education* and the Montgomery Bus Boycott, Selma remained totally segregated with but a bare handful of Afro-Americans registered to vote. In 1961 less than 1% of the 15,000 adult Afro-Americans living in Dallas County could vote.

In January of 1963 two SNCC organizers, Bernard and Colia Lafayette, began helping the DCVL break that grip of fear. Soon other young SNCC freedom workers joined them. They organized house by house, block by block, holding meetings, staging protests, demanding that Blacks be allowed to vote in Selma, Alabama. During a "Freedom Day" in October of 1963, SNCC and DCVL encouraged 350 Afro-Americans to defy a century of Jim Crow by lining up at the courthouse on registration day. Almost none were registered — but some were arrested, and many were fired from their jobs or evicted from their homes for daring to assert that they were American citizens entitled to vote.

SNCC was so bold in thought and mighty in courage that most northern supporters didn't realize how few they actually were and how meager were their finances. In 1964 they had to concentrate almost their entire force in Mississippi for Freedom Summer and its follow-up campaigns — leaving behind just a skeleton staff in Selma.

In June of '64 the Civil Rights Act was enacted over the ferocious opposition of southern whites. SNCC members and Black students tried to implement the Act in Selma by patronizing a white-only drive-in and attempting to sit in the white section of the movie theater. They were beaten by white thugs and arrested for "trespass." Judge Hare then issued a sweeping, unconstitutional injunction that effectively outlawed all civil rights activity in Dallas County. Protests of any sort were forbidden, and so too were private meetings where people simply discussed voter registration.

Of course, the DCVL filed legal appeals against the injunction, but those motions were stalled in the Alabama state courts and neither DCVL nor SNCC had the human, financial, or legal resources to openly defy the injunction with large-scale civil disobedience. Unable to engage in public activities, the Selma Movement was driven underground and forced to meet clandestinely behind closed doors.

After five months of stagnation under the injunction, the DCVL asked Martin Luther King and SCLC for assistance. King and SCLC were seeking a battleground for a Birmingham-style mass protest movement powerful enough to force a voting rights act through Congress — as

Birmingham and St. Augustine had done for the Civil Rights Act. DCVL leaders told them that Selma was the place.

SNCC, of course, saw Selma as their territory, and as a matter of principle they opposed mass protest movements, which they considered detrimental to the kind of deep community organizing that was now their primary strategy. But the local DCVL leaders prevailed and King accepted their invitation.

On January 2nd, 1965, hundreds of Selma Blacks successfully defied the injunction by attending a mass meeting in Brown Chapel addressed by Dr. King. With the full glare of national media attention focused on Selma and powerful legal resources standing ready to take effective court action, Judge Hare and Sheriff Clark backed down — mass public defiance had nullified the no-civil-rights-activity-of-any-kind injunction.

Large-scale attempts to register to vote quickly followed, as did marches to the courthouse. Hare issued a new injunction forbidding protests near his courthouse, which became the legal pretext for beatings and mass arrests of protesting students, while adults who attempted to register continued to face economic reprisals. By February, Selma, Alabama had become a war zone occupied by hundreds of blue-helmeted state troopers, club-wielding sheriff's deputies, and armed possemen — all in confrontation with nonviolent Afro-American protesters, young and old, who were determined to become full citizens free of segregation, Jim Crow, and racial subservience.

The protests and registration attempts began to expand outward into adjacent counties like Wilcox and Perry, where Afro-Americans outnumbered whites three or four to one and no Blacks at all were registered. On February 18th, a small band of freedom marchers in Marion, the Perry County seat, were brutally attacked by troopers and some of Clark's possemen. These so-called lawmen first shot out the streetlights and broke news media cameras so no record could be made; then they attacked with flailing clubs and searing cattle prods. Jimmy Lee Jackson, a Black military veteran and church deacon, was shot point-blank by a trooper.

Perry County had no hospital, and the publicly-funded hospital in Selma refused to treat civil rights activists, so Jackson was taken to the small, Catholic-run, Good Samaritan infirmary. A few days later he died of his wounds. Thousands of mourners, mostly Black, a few white, attended his funeral and memorial.

On March 7 — "Bloody Sunday" — some 600 protesters attempted to march from Selma to the State Capitol in Montgomery seeking redress of their grievances from Governor Wallace. As they crossed over the Edmund Pettus Bridge a horde of deputies, troopers, and possemen savagely attacked them. They were clubbed, beaten, teargassed, and whipped by possemen on charging horses.

That Sunday night my parents and I were watching the movie *Judgment at Nuremburg* on ABC when it was suddenly interrupted by a breaking news flash showing film of atrocities in Selma, Alabama. My fears and hesitations were instantly burned away. I knew — and my parents knew — that next morning I'd be on my way to Selma.

Defying the Gravity Law ~ 1937

Don't ever confuse working for a nonprofit agency with being a freedom fighter or a justice warrior. Movement activism ain't a nine-to-five job, there's no stable routine, and it certainly isn't safe. If political activism came with a job description it would have to include a caution that you'll never know in advance what unexpected responsibilities might land on your shoulders with no warning and no preparation — suddenly you're the one on the spot.

Which reminds me of one of the few stories my mom did share with me when I was a kid, a story that has stuck with me all my life. Back in the 1930s, the volunteer union-organizing work she was doing with the bike messengers was transferred from the Office Workers Union to the new American Communications Association (ACA), which had recently affiliated with the Congress of Industrial Organizations (CIO). By signing up with the CIO, the ACA gained resources to hire full-time organizers.

"Saturn," my mom's clandestine information source, provided the union with valuable inside dope on the company. He also had influence with Communist Party leaders — he personally knew Earl Browder, the CP's General Secretary. No question Saturn was sweet on my mom and wanted their arrangement (whatever it was) to continue, so in 1937 he somehow got the Party to agree to hire her as a full-time, paid ACA organizer. She was assigned to the Midwest regional office in Chicago, with time off as needed to continue meeting with him.

Mom was thrilled to quit her secretary job with the Federal Theatre Project and become the only woman on the ACA organizing staff. But she resented obtaining the position because of her relationship with Saturn rather than as an award for her proven abilities.

At that time no more than a tiny handful of women were elected union officials — and only in unions where the great majority of the workers were female, such as textile, garment, and clerical. It's possible that a couple of those unions might have had a female organizer or two, though if so they were few and far between. But in predominantly male industries like communications, women leaders and organizers were unheard-of.

During the long railroad journey from New York to Chicago, Mom made plans for hitting the ground running — meeting with the organizers in each town, setting up training programs for shop stewards, creating an index-card file system of local leaders and activists, starting a series of themed leaflets on key shop issues, and so on.

New York was a "union town." Not so Chicago. Chicago was a labor battleground, fierce and violent. A week or so before she arrived, workers at Republic Steel on the city's South Side went on strike. When they tried to set up picket lines they were brutally beaten down and arrested by the cops.

Mom arrived in Chi-town around sunset on Memorial Day, May 30, 1937. Earlier that afternoon, Chicago area unions had organized a support march to the nearby Republic Steel plant from Sam's Place — a former bar, dance hall, sometime brothel, and now strike headquarters. As a thousand or more workers and their families, including children, neared the factory they were blocked by more than 250 police who assaulted them with clubs and tear gas. As the marchers fled the choking gas, the cops suddenly opened fire with shotguns and pistols. Ten protesters were killed and 30 wounded by gunfire, all but four of them shot in the back. An unknown number were brutally battered by clubs. Newsreel film of the massacre was suppressed by the news agencies because — as they put it — "it might cause mass hysteria." In the hidden history of labor this became known as the "Memorial Day Massacre."

Caravans of police cars with sirens screaming were then sent surging back and forth across the city in a political pogrom against the labor movement, as they raided and trashed union offices, threw files and typewriters out the windows, beat down union members, and rounded up and arrested every union leader they could find.

Mom stepped off the train at Chicago's Union Station into that maelstrom. She was 23 years old, reporting for work as a union organizer. Meeting her at the station was Art, the ACA regional director, who informed her that the union office had been smashed to shambles and set on fire by the cops. Sheriffs were prowling the streets looking for "commies," and he was on his way to a secret strategy meeting. There was no safe place where she could go, so he brought her along, down into a windowless basement near Printers Row, where an emergency gathering of those leftist union leaders not in jail was already underway. In addition to local leaders and organizers, national figures like Joe Curran of Maritime, Mike Quill of Transport, and Ben Gold of the Furriers were there.

Mom was the only woman present. When Art introduced her they all cracked wise, making jokes and laughing about ACA picking a "pretty girl" as an organizer. But given the urgency of their situation, that diversion didn't last long. The labor movement was reeling under police attack, strikers had been killed and wounded, leaders and organizers jailed, members were becoming discouraged and afraid. They needed to find some way to show that they were still in the fight, that they hadn't been beaten, that resistance and organizing would continue.

The Chicago City Council had recently passed a new ordinance making it illegal to hand out to the public anything "subject to the law of gravity" — like a union leaflet, for example. In those days leaflets were the lifeblood of organizing, the only way to communicate with workers *en masse*. Few factory workers could afford a telephone, and the commercial mass media — newspapers and radio — wouldn't carry pro-union advertisements or statements even if the unions had money to pay for them, which they didn't. In many industries, immigrant employees spoke only their native tongues, but flyers could be translated into Spanish, Yiddish, Italian, German, Polish, and so on. They could be handed to workers entering or leaving the workplace and clandestinely passed from hand to hand inside the plant gates. The "Gravity Law" was clearly aimed against union organizing.

As a show of resistance and to provide a legal test case for overturning an obviously unconstitutional ordinance, the men at the meeting decided that somebody had to go down to the Loop and publicly defy the Gravity Law by handing out union leaflets — and be arrested by the same cops who were currently beating and shooting union organizers.

"Well, it can't be me," said one of the big leaders. "I'll be arrested as soon as I'm spotted on the street." "Yeah," agreed another, "I'd never make it as far as the Loop. And we have to notify the press in advance so they can cover the story. That means the cops will be on the lookout for every single one of us." "Right," said a third man, "we need to find someone they won't know or recognize."

All eyes turned toward my mom.

"How would you like to put your fair, white body on the firing line?" smirked Art, her new boss.

When I was a kid hearing her story at the kitchen table she never mentioned that Saturn had gotten her the job and she didn't describe how she was treated as a woman. But 66 years later, when I recorded her oral history, she was still pissed off:

> I resented that terribly and I told them so. I told them, "You know, there may be a reason to send a woman, I won't get clubbed like you might get clubbed." But I didn't like the way they said it. It was outside the context of organization. It was like you can do what you want with a female. There was a disparaging sexist orientation that bothered me. It was like a game or a trick or something at the expense of females, I thought. I hated when they made sexist remarks in the context of organizing and they did that very frequently.[6]

Nevertheless, the next morning she strapped on her high heels, took a cab down to the big Postal Telegraph office in the Loop, and began handing out leaflets to the morning shift in defiance of the Gravity Law. The press had been alerted and a union lawyer was on hand to observe.

> The workers received the leaflets very happily. So, along comes the policeman. It was, like, choreographed. He says, "Young lady, you can't do that. There's a law against it." I said, "There shouldn't be a law against it. They have every right to receive reading material, and I have every right to give it to them." He said, "That's not the law. Pack it up and go away or there'll be trouble." I said, "I'm not going away. It's a wrong law and I'm not obeying it."
>
> Well, I was arrested. The workers were very startled to see all this as they were coming in and they started, you know — in groups — and they were whispering and showing support in a moderated way.
>
> So I'm brought in the police car to the court and the policeman tells [the judge] what this is all about. He looks at me, he says, "You knew you were violating the law, did you not?" I said, "Yes. It's a bad law and it shouldn't be in existence. You're denying me my rights. You're denying the workers their rights." He said, "Young lady, you're going to be in trouble." I said, "So be it." So anyhow I was bailed out and I won the case. It came up several months later and I won the case. It was ruled unconstitutional.[6]

First day on the job. Nine to Five routine? Not so much.

Selma Under Siege ~ 1965

I quickly cut myself loose from the odd jobs I was doing for the Yale grad students and converted my cash into American Express traveler's checks, which is what everyone used back in those dinosaur days before credit cards and ATM machines. I linked up with a guy who was driving down to Selma, and by evening I was rolling South. Scared — but determined.

We drove straight through, taking turns at the wheel and trying (with scant success) to sleep in the shotgun seat — New York — Philly — DC — Charlotte — Atlanta. While we were on the road Tuesday, Dr. King and several thousand marchers made a second attempt at reaching Montgomery. When troopers blocked them he peacefully led everyone back over the bridge to Brown Chapel rather than force a bloody confrontation. This sparked an intense controversy between SCLC and SNCC over what became known as "Turnaround Tuesday." That evening, four Klansmen in Selma brutally assaulted three Unitarian ministers with baseball bats, severely injuring Rev. James Reeb of Boston, who had answered King's call for people of conscience to come stand with the embattled Black community of Selma.

It was deep in the night when we finally reached Brown Chapel AME Church in Selma. Along with the nearby First Baptist Church, it served as Movement headquarters and rally point. Despite the hour it was open and welcoming. People from out of town were sleeping on the pews. Exhausted from the long drive, I joined them.

I awoke bleary-eyed to early morning hustle and bustle. Attached to the rear of the sanctuary was a kitchen and utility room that had been set up as a dining hall for outside supporters where we were fed strong coffee, hot bacon and sweet corn bread in the morning, and fried chicken and collard greens for the rest of the day. From dawn to midnight Black women — volunteers all — cooked with pride for the mostly white visitors who had come from across the nation to support them in their fight for freedom. They welcomed me with smiles and issued me a little meal card good at any of several similar church kitchens in Selma's Afro-American community.

Today Brown Chapel is a National Historic Landmark, but back then it was just a worn and shabby 60-year-old building of red brick, white stone, and aging wood with peeling paint. Though the sun had barely risen above the horizon, the church was already filled with activity as local Blacks and northern whites hurried in and out on errands and tasks. Pete Seeger with his banjo and Jimmy Collier with his guitar were sitting on the outside steps leading an impromptu songfest for a throng of kids who had no intention at all of going to school and missing all this excitement. Everywhere I looked, groups of people were talking, sharing rumors, and speculating on what was to come.

Brown Chapel with its two bell towers sat in the center of the totally segregated Carver public housing project — 30 or more two-story brick buildings, each with multiple apartments. Surrounding the project area like a feudal army besieging a rebellious village were swarms of hostile troopers, deputies, game wardens, possemen, and Klansmen. Racial hatred radiated off them like a foul stench. Hatred for defiant Afro-Americans, hatred for SNCC and SCLC, and hatred for white "race traitors" like me.

The local kids quickly clued me in: state troopers wore blue battle helmets and spiffy gray and blue uniforms, sheriff's deputies wore brown with white helmets, and the Selma city cops were in standard police uniforms. The state game wardens, who had been brought to reinforce the troopers, had green helmets. Clark's possemen wore khaki work clothes, cheap tin badges, and plastic construction helmets in various colors. They were armed with pistols on sagging belts and swaggered around carrying ax handles for "whupping burr-heads," as their racist vernacular expressed it. Klansmen had been mobilized from all over the state and as far away as Mississippi and Louisiana — the only way to distinguish them from the local posse was that the KKK didn't have badges or bother with "sissy" helmets.

Now please allow me a momentary pause for a brief language digression. A baton is a little stick that orchestra conductors wave to keep the musicians on the beat; a club is what cops use to beat people into submission. In the 1960s the mass media suddenly started referring to police clubs as "batons" to soften and disguise the brutal use of state violence against nonviolent demonstrators protesting racism, segregation, and systemic injustice. Media euphemisms notwithstanding, troopers with their clubs and possemen with their ax handles knew precisely what they were carrying and for what purpose — and so did we.

The Carver project siege was not airtight. While groups of protesters attempting to leave the project area would be immediately blocked and attacked, individuals could come and go by car or on foot. But outside the project area, anyone the Klan or posse identified as a civil rights activist risked a brutal beating if they were caught out of view of the press cameras. The Black community to the north and east of the project was more or less safe, but even there the Klan prowled in cars looking for "troublemakers," "shit-disturbers," and "nigger-lovers" to attack.

By now it was known that the Selma public hospital had refused to treat Rev. Reeb and the Catholic-run Good Samaritan infirmary was neither equipped nor staffed for massive head trauma. During the night he'd been transferred by hearse to a hospital in Birmingham. (Few white-owned ambulances would serve Afro-Americans, so hearses owned by Black funeral parlors were often used to transport the ill or injured.)

Around noon we gathered in Brown Chapel and were told that Reeb's condition was grave. Rev. Anderson of Tabernacle Baptist Church was one of the main local Movement leaders. He led us out for a march to the Dallas County Courthouse where we intended to pray for Rev. Reeb's recovery. Sylvan Street was the main road through the center of the project and like all roads in the Black community it was unpaved. Though in the summer it was dry an dusty at that time of year it was muddy, with water-filled potholes. Today Sylvan is well paved and named Martin Luther King Street.

As our march approached the project boundary we were blocked by a line of Selma police. Chief Baker announced that under an emergency decree just issued by the mayor all marches outside of the Carver project were banned — for our safety, he told us.

The cops strung a rope across Sylvan Street marking the limit of where we could march. Students — high school and college — were the heart and soul of mass protests in Selma as they were everywhere in the South. They instantly dubbed that rope the "Berlin Wall" and quickly made up a freedom song about it:

> *We've got a rope we call a Berlin Wall,*
> *Berlin Wall, Berlin Wall,*
>
> *We've got a rope we call a Berlin Wall,*
> *In Selma, Alabama.*
>
> *We're gonna stay here till it falls,*
> *till it falls, till it falls,*
>
> *We're gonna stay here till it falls,*
> *In Selma, Alabama.*

Rather than retreat back to the church we halted against the rope and began an around-the-clock vigil, face to face with the line of cops and deputies. All day, all night, we stood in the street waiting for the rope wall to fall, singing songs and making impromptu speeches about segregation and voting rights to the cops, the press, and each other. People would vigil until they got tired, then grab a bite to eat and some rest while others took their place.

Mass Meeting ~ 1965

As evening fell a group of the younger children — junior high and elementary students — began marching around the project buildings singing freedom songs. That signaled that the nightly mass meeting in Brown Chapel was about to begin.

I left the confrontation at the Berlin Wall and climbed the worn wooden stairs up to the balcony as a line of high school students and two little elementary school girls led the crowd in freedom songs. The church was packed with some five or six hundred people. In all my life I have never, ever, heard singing like that — never before, never since, not even in other Freedom Movement battlegrounds.

The emotional power of that singing was indescribable. It wasn't a performance. It wasn't poetry set to music. It was the rage of generations erupting forth in a passionate torrent of melody. It was the defiance of people determined to be free — sustained by the power of their mass singing. It was their declaration of pride, standing strong in the face of police beatings, gassings, arrests, evictions, firings, and murder.

In her remembrance, *Selma, Lord, Selma*, Sheyann Webb, who was nine at the time and one of the song leaders, would later describe the immediate aftermath of Bloody Sunday:

> When I had first gotten to the church ... my eyes were still swollen and burning from the tear gas. ... I sat with Rachel up toward the front. ... we were just sitting there crying, listening to the others cry; some were even moaning and wailing. It was an awful thing. It was like we were at our own funeral. But then later in the night, maybe nine-thirty or ten, I don't know for sure, all of a sudden somebody there started humming. I think they were moaning and it just went into the humming of a freedom song. It was real low, but some of us children began humming along, slow and soft.
>
> At first I didn't even know what it was, what song, I mean. It was like a funeral sound, a dirge. Then I recognized it — *Ain't Gonna Let Nobody Turn Me 'Round*. I'd never heard it or hummed it that way before. But it just started to catch on, and the people began to pick it up. It started to swell, the humming. Then we began singing the words. We sang, "Ain't gonna let George Wallace turn me 'round." And, "Ain't gonna let Jim Clark turn me 'round. "Ain't gonna let no state trooper turn me 'round."
>
> *Ain't gonna let no horses ... ain't gonna let no tear gas — ain't gonna let nobody turn me 'round. Nobody!*

We was singing and telling the world that we hadn't been whipped ... I think we all realized it at the same time, that we had won something that day, because people were standing up and singing like I'd never heard them before. ... But when that singing started, we grew stronger. Each one of us said to ourselves that we could go back out there and face the tear gas, face the horses, face whatever Jim Clark could throw at us.[7]

The speeches that night — freedom sermons really — were many, passionate, and deeply based in faith and Bible. At least 50 or so of those in the audience that night were northern whites like me. We were warmly welcomed, the famous called forth and honored by name, the rest of us thanked for our presence. I was not the only Jew in the audience, a visiting rabbi was asked to address the crowd. I did not feel at all out of place. Nor did I feel uncomfortable singing Christian hymns, because it was a Freedom Movement service, not a denominational event.

Rev. Hosea Williams called the collection. I was so moved by his oratory and by the entire experience of my first Freedom Movement mass meeting that I actually signed one of my $20 traveler's checks (equal to about $160 in 2018) and dropped it in the bucket that they were passing from hand to hand. That's not like me at all — then or now. I'm quite generous with my time — with money not so much.

During that time between Bloody Sunday and the March to Montgomery there was at least one mass meeting every day and sometimes more than one, and Brown Chapel was always packed to the rafters with local Selma folk, Afro-Americans from the surrounding counties, and Black and white Freedom Movement supporters from far and wide. Day after day, night after night, from that balcony bench I had the privilege of listening to some of the finest public speakers of the mid-20th century.

I loved hearing Martin Luther King speak. Schooled in the rhythm and cadence of the Black church, he is justly considered one of America's greatest orators. Deeply rooted in both biblical calls for justice and the unfulfilled promise of the American creed, his speeches were visions of compassion and brotherhood that still inspire me to this day. Most people have heard portions of his famous *I Have a Dream* speech, but to hear the full text of one of his freedom sermons was to be carried to a higher plane of existence. He not only sounded the call for justice and equality, he made it seem possible in a way no one else in my lifetime has ever been able to replicate.

Rev. Ralph Abernathy was King's closest friend, confidant, and collaborator. More than anyone else, Abernathy was the man King relied on. When King went to jail, so did Abernathy. He was also a skilled speaker and preacher, but his style was totally different from King's. Where King was lofty, eloquent, and cerebral, Abernathy was exuberant and earthy in the peoples' vernacular. One time, I was told, he was pounding the pulpit at a mass meeting and a hidden police microphone attached to a wire was knocked loose. He didn't miss a beat. Grabbing it and holding it up for all to see, he addressed it as *doohickey* and in no uncertain terms told off the police assumed to be listening at the other end — all to gales of tension-easing laughter from the crowd.

Rev. James Bevel — everyone called him "Bevel" or "Bevels" — was the fiery tactical genius behind the Birmingham and Selma campaigns. His use of language was so brilliant and his delivery so compelling as to be messianic. Not, "almost messianic" — *actually* messianic. He wove such a magic spell around us that had he told us to walk through fire we would have done so without hesitation so long as he led the way, which he might well have done, because there was at times an obvious touch of madness about him that only Dr. King seemed able to keep in check — most of the time. Usually.

I remember one afternoon sitting in the kitchen attached to Brown Chapel listening to Bevel rail against bombing attacks by U.S. warplanes against the river dikes in North Vietnam. He said we might have to go sit on those dikes as nonviolent defenders, and if he'd actually done it I might well have joined him. Maybe. He did have his dark side though, particularly his treatment of women, which was abusive and exploitative, though I only learned of that much later.

SCLC's command structure was hierarchical. Directly under King followed by Abernathy was the Executive Staff. Of all the Executive Staff members, Hosea Williams and Bevel were the fiercest rivals. Hosea was both an ordained minister and a chemist by profession and when it came to fiery freedom sermons few could match him. From Savannah, Georgia, he had something of the urgent energy of the urban street about him that resonated with me. When I later joined the SCLC field staff I was assigned to the department he headed, and while I respected and admired his legendary personal courage and willingness to defy white authority, I had trouble adapting to his mercurial temper and flamboyant egotism.

Rev. C.T. Vivian was the SCLC leader closest in age to young SNCC and CORE activists like me. He was also closest in outlook. Whenever I was in his presence he seemed to burn with a fierce anger — a rage that I shared. He had come out of the SCLC affiliate in Nashville and he too was a powerful speaker and fearless in defiance. He was well known in the Freedom Movement for boldly confronting Sheriff Clark face to face on the courthouse steps, shouting, *"You're a racist the same way Hitler was a racist!"* Every time Clark knocked him down, he rose again and got back in the sheriff's face.

I greatly admired and respected all of those fiery and passionate SCLC leaders, but it was Dr. King who I truly loved. I loved him for his compassion, the breadth of his vision, the power of his oratory, and what I can only describe as his *mahatma* — his great soul. We used to joke about being part of his "freedom army," and in the context of that metaphor he was the general and I was — at best — no more than a corporal, maybe eventually a sergeant. Generals and sergeants don't normally socialize, and I never spent any personal time with King. When he saw me in Selma, or later Grenada, Mississippi, he'd recognize me as someone who worked for SCLC and he occasionally asked me to run some errand, but I doubt he ever recalled my name. Yet though I knew him only at a distance, what impressed me most was that his public and private personas were identical. He was as caring, thoughtful, and compassionate toward others in day-to-day interactions as he appeared to be from stage and pulpit.

Later on in life, when I encountered other famous folks, I learned how rare that was.

On the Line at the "Berlin Wall" ~ 1965

My first mass meeting ended around 11pm and I returned to the Berlin Wall for a while before crashing on one of the wooden pews in Brown Chapel until the next morning. Thursday the 11th was more of the same, though a hard, cold rain began to fall, and those of us who didn't have real raincoats cut slits in green plastic garbage bags to use as makeshift ponchos. While vigiling we tried to shelter under plastic tarps held up on poles. That provided some protection — until they shifted and dumped a waterfall down the back of our necks.

The Carver housing project remained under siege, with deputies and troopers confining our ability to march and the posse and Klansmen prowling the perimeter looking for prey. The only place where white Movement supporters or Blacks wearing freedom pins could safely buy sodas, snacks, smokes, and other incidentals was the tiny candy shack near Brown Chapel. It was just a small wooden hut, no name, no sign, with a window for customers. A dozen or more people were always lined up in the muddy street from dawn to dark. Back in those days I was a hardcore Coke fiend (the drink not the drug) and on warm afternoons I'd be in that line a couple of times a day — sometimes just ahead of a visiting rabbi, other times behind a famous Afro-American entertainer, a local high school kid, or a Maryknoll nun.

Meanwhile at the vigil line we were still face to face with the cops and posse, though eventually Chief Baker removed the rope. He told a reporter he was tired of hearing us sing about it. We continued to sing about it anyway.

Though some in SNCC were turning away from nonviolence, that was not the case with SCLC. I met some of the SCLC staff, and when they found out I was CORE-trained they asked me to do what I could to encourage people to remain nonviolent on the vigil, where emotions were running high.

While most of the northern supporters who had come to Selma were white, quite a number were Afro-Americans, some of whom were super-militant Black nationalists who vehemently rejected nonviolence as either a strategy or tactic. Afro-Americans from Selma and the surrounding counties understood the necessity of Tactical nonviolence in relation to the cops. And for them, overtly expressing defiance in speech and song to white authorities armed with badge, pistol, and club was sufficiently defiant. Not so for some of the northern Blacks. So when we weren't singing or preaching freedom at stone-faced troopers and possemen we debated nonviolence.

It didn't take long, however, for me to realize that the is-ness of reality was far more compelling than any intellectual argument I could muster — CORE training notwithstanding. Local teenagers, Freedom Movement veterans all, would stand face to face with the troopers and possemen singing:

"We love everybody!
We love George Wallace!
We love state troopers!"

And it was completely clear to everyone present on both sides that none of them loved Wallace or the troopers. But singing that song was driving the cops crazy. It was a way of defying them that they had no way of countering and it was frustrating the hell out of them. They yearned and ached for an opportunity to whip heads with their clubs — you could see it plain as day, it was just obvious. When it was dark or no cameras were around they'd taunt us and poke us with their sticks and ax handles, trying to provoke us into some small act of violence that they could seize on as a pretext for beating the shit out of everyone and arresting all of us as violent "troublemakers."

Even northern super-militants could (eventually) see that violence on our part was precisely what our foes wanted. And if you wanted to effectively fight "The Man" in Selma, you didn't do what he wanted you to do, you did what he *didn't* want you to do — which was nonviolently defy white supremacy. So after a couple hours on the line I'd see those same northern militants I'd been arguing with to no avail singing at the top of their lungs, "*We love George Wallace! We love state troopers!*" So I stopped arguing theory in favor of allowing practical reality to take its inevitable course.

That night we learned that Rev. Reeb had died in a Birmingham hospital. In Selma's Black community there was great sorrow. Though the cold, heavy rain was coming down hard we kept the vigil going. Now we were determined to march to the courthouse for a memorial rather than a prayer for his recovery.

Somehow that night I ended up at the home of the West family in one of the two-story project buildings close to Brown Chapel. Alice and Alonzo West and their 12 children were well known in the Movement, the older ones marching and going to jail, eight year-old Rachel leading freedom songs with the high school kids, the family apartment a haven for out-of-town SNCC and SCLC activists. All their beds, their one couch, and every inch of floor space were already occupied by others, but I found a cozy sleeping spot on top of their side-by-side washing machine and dryer just off the kitchen (with a dozen kids you can't be running back and forth to the laundromat all day).

Among their semi-permanent Movement guests was Jonathan Daniels, an Episcopal seminary student from New Hampshire whom I got to know and came to like quite a bit. He was always cheerful and upbeat, calm and steadfast. A quiet rock in the Freedom Movement maelstrom.

For the next couple of weeks the West home became my home, their family my family. It was from the Wests, around their crowded formica table in the kitchen, that I learned the ins and outs of Selma and the local Movement. Who was who, where it was safe to go, where it wasn't, what they thought about all that was happening, and why it meant so much to them.

And they were curious about me as a Jew — "You mean you don't believe in Jesus?" It was hard for them to grasp. For them "religious differences" meant Catholic versus Baptist. There was a small Jewish community in Selma dating back generations, and some of the stores catering to the "colored trade" were run by Jews. Those that treated Afro-Americans decently were looked upon favorably by the Black community, those that didn't — weren't. But there was no social interaction at all. I was the first Jew the Wests could talk to, argue with, and relate to on a basis of assumed equality — which was far more important to them than religious doctrine. And, of course, I was no great proponent of religious doctrine myself.

Third-grader Rachel West and her next-door neighbor Sheyann "Shy" Webb were familiar figures in the Selma Movement. Dr. King called them his "littlest freedom fighters." Along with the teenagers, they led freedom songs in Brown Chapel. Shy had been on the bridge during Bloody Sunday. And Rachel had almost been trampled by possemen on horses when they charged into the housing project. They later wrote a wonderful memoir titled, *Selma, Lord, Selma* that Disney turned into a film of the same name.

I've heard folks scoff and claim that Rachel and Shy were too young to know what they were involved in and that King cynically and selfishly manipulated and used them. Bullshit, total bullshit. Too often grown-ups dismiss children as inconsequential or discount them because their breadth of understanding is less than that of adults. But how old do you have to be to see unfairness and resent injustice? I adored them both. They were frightened, yes, they knew the dangers better than I, but they marched precisely because they did know what they were doing — and *why* they were doing it.

It might seem odd to you that families would open up their homes and lives to complete strangers the way the Wests did for us. And it wasn't just the Wests, many families in the projects and the larger Afro-American community took in and cared for out-of-town supporters. As I was walking down the street, Blacks I have never met would often ask me to share a cool lemonade on the porch, or even invite me to join them for dinner.

Some of them called us "freedom fighters" others referred to us as "freedom riders." The first few times I was called a "freedom rider" I tried to explain that while I was a civil rights worker I had not been on the Freedom Rides of 1961. But I soon realized that those rides had so impressed Afro-Americans living under the yoke of segregation in the Deep South that "freedom rider" had for them become a generic term for anyone who came from outside the community to help them fight for freedom. So I accepted the title of freedom rider in the sense they intended.

By Friday the rain had temporarily halted. The vigil continued. The siege continued. The mass meetings and freedom songs continued. As on previous days, from time to time Selma students — by now highly experienced protesters — organized nonviolent guerrilla marches. Two or three hundred of them would secretly assemble in First Baptist Church or some other location and then make a dash, trying to evade the encircling cops and reach downtown. Caravans of state trooper cars with sirens screaming careened through the streets to head them off, the blue-helmeted lawmen leaping out with curses and flailing clubs to drive them back.

Only a few SNCC workers were left in Selma during this period, most of them had shifted to Montgomery where mass street protests were also underway involving Black students from Tuskegee and Alabama State College. We heard rumors that the SNCC-led marches in Montgomery were being ruthlessly attacked and savagely beaten by possemen on horses, but the local news was completely untrustworthy and utterly biased against us. The national TV networks only broadcast one 15-minute evening news show per night and copies of northern newspapers were few and far between. So we often knew less than people in New York about what was happening 50 miles away. Mostly we existed and operated on rumor and hearsay.

We did hear, though, that prominent Americans, Senators and Congressmen, religious leaders, and other notables were sending telegrams of condolence to Rev. Reeb's home in Boston. Pundits were commenting, analyzing, and moralizing at length on his murder. President Johnson had Mrs. Reeb flown to Birmingham on an Air Force jet to retrieve her husband's body and return with it to Massachusetts for his funeral.

We in Selma, however, were acutely conscious that there had been no such reaction at all when Jimmy Lee Jackson was shot to death by a state trooper. No note from the White House, no phone calls from anyone in Congress. Other than few lines in the national press, little attention or notice. For Afro-Americans the contrast between white public reaction to the two killings was stark and bitter — utter indifference to the police murder of a Black man, enormous compassion and concern over the death of a white man. Most galling of all was that most whites, even liberal ones, didn't even notice the discrepancy. But the anger in Selma was not directed against Rev. Reeb. Selma Blacks knew he risked his life to stand with them, and they honored, respected, and mourned him.

During those days when we were holding the line at the Berlin Wall, I met three nonviolent warriors who are indelibly painted on the walls of my memory: Annell Ponder, Septima Clark, and Dorothy Cotton. Three Afro-American women who though almost completely unknown to the general public and the mass media were key members of SCLC's bedrock leadership. The organization's visible leaders were all ministers, all male, and except for Dr. King, all competitive and self-promoting. Not so Septima, Dorothy, and Annell, who labored quietly behind the scenes doing much of the grassroots organizing work that sustained SCLC's local affiliates and built a cadre of local activists and leaders across the South. While some in SNCC condemned SCLC for its seeming lack of interest in local community organizing, no one in SNCC who actually knew those three ever included *them* in that criticism.

Mrs. Clark, 66 years old at the time, had been born in 1898, the daughter of a former slave. She, Dorothy and Annell were the main leaders of the Citizenship Schools, which I had never heard of but was soon enormously impressed by. Originally a project of the Highlander Center in Tennessee, SCLC had rescued the program in 1961 when Highlander had come under ruthless legal attack by the state.

Under the innocuous cover of adult literacy classes, at a time when government repression and KKK terrorism were smothering other forms of Black resistance, the Citizenship Schools taught democracy and civil rights, community leadership and organizing, practical politics, and the strategies and tactics of nonviolent resistance and struggle. Eventually almost 10,000 citizenship teachers, most of them unpaid volunteers, were conducting classes across the South in churches, kitchens, and beauty parlors, on front porches and beneath shady trees in the summertime and around wood-burning stoves in the wintertime. Those classes and SCLC's teacher training program developed many of the local Freedom Movement leaders who became the backbone of the struggle — people like Fannie Lou Hamer, Hollis Watkins, Victoria Gray, and Marie Foster — folks who may not have been well known to the public at large, but who were giants within their own communities.

Howard Zinn once described Annell as "tall, black-skinned and beautiful," and certainly I found her so. For me she epitomized the steadfast essence of a true Freedom Movement organizer. The truth is, I had a crush on her but was too shy to say anything.

Day after day the vigil continued. In cold rain and blazing sun we held the line at Selma's Berlin Wall across the middle of Sylvan Street. Rachel West later wrote:

> During that time it seemed each day and each night was like the one before it; nothing changed. The rope stayed there, we stayed there, the troopers stayed there; we'd sing hour after hour until our throats became hoarse. The rain fell, fell almost constantly. The sun would come out briefly, then it would start raining again. We'd be soaked to the skin. It would turn warm; it would turn cold.[7]

And while the vigil continued without pause, the Carver projects seethed with life and energy. More supporters from the North were showing up — mostly white, some Afro- American — as were Freedom Movement activists from across the South — mostly Black, a few white. SNCC folk showed up from Mississippi, Georgia, and Arkansas, so did CORE members from Louisiana and Florida, as well as NAACP and SCEF folk from all over.

Out on the line it was the young Selma students who were the soul of the community's resistance. They were the ones who bore the brunt of direct action protests and marches. Throughout the South, youth who were too young to vote themselves played a vital role in the struggle for voting rights. Not that I was all that far from them in age, they were 15, 16, 17, and 18 and I was an "old man" just turned 21 and not yet registered to vote myself because I had no fixed state of residence.

Two of Selma's student leaders remain vivid in my memory more than 50 years later. Charles Bonner, "Chuck" to everyone who knew him, was tall, very dark, and thin as a rail. He had graduated from Selma's segregated R.B. Hudson high school the year before and had recently been expelled from the private, Baptist-run Selma University for leading student marches to the courthouse. By virtue of his courage, skill, and experience, when he was on the line he was the students' picket captain and recognized as such by any SCLC and SNCC field secretaries or local movement leaders who might also be present.

Former Hudson High student Bettie Mae Fikes was the daughter of gospel singers. Her voice rang with the clarity of crystal, soaring over all others as she led the teenage song leaders in Brown Chapel mass meetings, belting out the verses, leading the call, guiding the response. She later became a professional blues singer.

Gray-haired Nannie Washburn was at the other end of the age spectrum. White, Georgia-born, child of sharecroppers, a textile worker from age seven, a union organizer in the 1930s like my parents, and a life-long Red, she was a stalwart opponent of racism and exploitation. After Bloody Sunday she answered Dr. King's call along with her blind son and her daughter Nellie. When you're 65 no one thinks of you as a "child," but if they did she would have been the poster child for the concept of "feisty." Some years later, in reference to the Brown Chapel kitchen she told reporter Howell Raines:

> Well, ... my daughter, son, and I we refused to eat the Jim Crow food, because there wasn't anybody in the kitchen a cookin' except black women that was older than ... as old as I was, and I was sixty-five. ... I went to Rev. Hollis and asked him. I said, "We not gonna eat ya Jim

Crow food." And he says, "Why?" I said, ... "My daughter has droved us, my son and I, down here, and I didn't think I'd come to a Jim Crow kitchen." And he said, "You a guest." I said, "No, I'm not. I just one of 'em." And he said then, "I don't know nothin' we could do about it." I says, "Well, don't you think the black women's been in the kitchen too long cookin' for the white people?" And he commenced studyin', and he said, "The only thing I can do is to let yo'r daughter go in the kitchen. I wouldn't let you." You know, I was sixty-five.[8]

She later marched the entire distance from Selma to Montgomery and then volunteered as a Freedom Movement nurse in Marengo County to the west of Selma, where she was arrested on vague charges. The authorities concluded that as a southern white woman she was obviously insane for associating with and supporting Blacks, so without trial they incarcerated her in the state mental institution for 21 days before Movement lawyers could finally locate and free her.

Finally, on Monday March 15, after six days of confrontation and tension came victory. The Wall was struck down! A federal judge had issued an injunction permitting a march to the courthouse and a memorial service for Rev. Reeb. We surged out of Brown Chapel into Sylvan Street and immediately began forming a march column three abreast behind those still holding the vigil line. Deputies, possemen and troopers gripped their billy clubs with white knuckles. Angrily, grudgingly, they stepped aside, their faces a mask of hate, frustration, and defeat.

Singing *Ain't Gonna Let Nobody Turn Us 'Round*, a thousand or so Afro-Americans and two or three dozen white supporters marched forward. As we passed the spot where they had blocked us for so long I was filled enormous satisfaction and pride. Under the terms of the injunction we were not allowed to gather in a group at the courthouse steps or otherwise block street traffic, so only those at the front of the column were actually able to hear Dr. King's brief memorial tribute and prayer. But we all marched by the steps singing *We Shall Overcome*, and tasted the sweetness of triumph.

Then that evening, a hush fell over the projects. Everyone, and I mean *everyone*, was inside, gathered around a TV or radio to listen as President Johnson addressed Congress on the issue of voting rights. The Wests' living room was packed with their entire family and at least a dozen Movement people — SNCC and SCLC organizers, Jonathan Daniels, other northern supporters, and myself. The kids were on the floor watching, chin in hand, adults were perched on every stick of furniture and the stairs leading up to the second floor. No one spoke. The intensity of our attention was palpable.

To this day, my feelings about LBJ remain deeply conflicted between respect for his civil rights accomplishments and rage at his obscene war on Vietnam. But that night he spoke as a true American statesman. He called for strong, effective, and immediate voting rights legislation. Then he echoed our signature slogan, "We shall overcome." There were tears, and cheers, and smiles a mile wide. Rachel West later wrote:

> I remember lying on the living room floor in front of the set, watching, listening. It seemed he was speaking directly to me.
>
> "The effort of American Negroes to secure for themselves the full blessing of American life must be our cause, too. Because it is not just Negroes, but really, it is all of us who must overcome the crippling legacy of bigotry and injustice.
>
> "And we shall overcome."
>
> When he said that all the people in the room, my sisters, my parents, the ministers, all cried out and applauded. I just lay there watching, listening. Somebody had heard us. ...
>
> Except for that one time, we just listened quietly. Once in a while I'd hear my mother or father agree with an, "Um-hmm," but that was all. I remember after his speech going over to Sheyann's, and she was just sitting there in the living room, thinking about it.
>
> And I said, "You hear that speech?"
>
> And she says, "I heard it." Then after a long time she said, "But he's there in Washington, and we be down here by ourselves."[6]

Voter Registration March ~ 1965

After the memorial march to the courthouse, the siege that had kept us confined in the Carver project dissolved. Troopers and deputies remained, but the number of roving Klansmen began to dwindle. It still wasn't safe for identifiable Movement supporters to wander around white neighborhoods or the white section of downtown, but if we were careful, and willing to endure being cursed, heckled, and harassed by possemen, we could venture into the Black business district just east of Broad Street.

I don't remember if the mayor's emergency decree banning marches was overturned, or withdrawn, or simply evaporated into irrelevance, but at some point during the next few days several hundred of us marched to the courthouse to resume demanding that they register Black voters. Unlike the student-led protests, this was mainly a march of Afro-

American adults defying white supremacy. By attempting to add their names to the voting rolls, they were risking their jobs, their homes, and their lives. Some of them had applied and been denied multiple times.

Under an order from a federal court, previous applicants were allowed to be listed in an "appearance book" and queue up for admission to the registrar's office according to numbers they had been issued. Sheriff Clark and his deputies herded us all into an alley behind the courthouse. Then he ordered the Black applicants with numbers to line up on the steps at the back-door service entrance (using the public front entrance was a privilege reserved for whites).

Those of us who were supporters waited in the alley while the line of voter applicants slowly crept forward as they were allowed to enter the courthouse one person at a time to fill out the registration forms, which were four pages long.

While we waited in the alley we were surrounded by deputies and troopers gripping their clubs in both hands — obviously itching to start swinging at our heads. We waited. We waited. Inside, the registrar clerks processed the applications and administered the tests as slowly as humanly possible. Over the course of hours, only a handful completed the process and most of the applicants never made it inside the door. It would be weeks before those who completed the complex procedures learned if this time they had been added to the voting rolls — or had once again been denied.

Jerome and the Orchard Strikers ~ 1953

Childhood memories are so strange, the oddest little things remain vivid for decades while far more important events are lost in the memory mist. I suppose if I'd paid more attention to my UCLA psych courses I'd understand how and why that works, but I didn't, and I don't.

Sometimes my father would go on work or Party-related trips and on rare occasions I would accompany him, most likely because there wasn't day care available or they couldn't afford it. One time in the early 1950s, when I was seven or eight I guess, I was in a car with him and we were driving somewhere in Northern California. Orchard workers were on strike and they were picketing by the road.

Ken pulled off the road to chat with them. They frightened me. They were different. Their clothes were worn and dirty, their faces darkened by harsh sun. They looked so grim and tired and desperate. Even though my father greeted them and they responded to him as a friend, I was still scared of them though there was absolutely no reason to be. I suppose my dad and I must have talked about it afterwards, I have no recollection of that at all. But the memory of my fear remains with me to this day.

As I've mentioned, Ken loved camping trips, and since that was all we could afford we took a lot of them. One summer we were in Arizona, no doubt going to or from the Grand Canyon, which was one of our favorite destinations. Somewhere along the way we drove through this strange, eerie town. It was perched — hanging really — on the steep side of a mountain. I had no idea where we were, but it was clearly an old mining town, mostly abandoned, gray, forbidding, half falling to ruin, and in some sense deeply foreboding.

This must have been a few years after encountering the orchard strikers because by then I had begun to absorb fragments of labor history and struggle in the way that children half understand things they half hear from adults. There was a big water tank with "Phelps Dodge" painted in square black letters on the side and I associated that name with others that evoked a similar sense of evil, cruelty, and corporate greed — names like Homestead, Ludlow, Flint, and Pullman. Somehow I sensed that this town, whatever its name was, had a dire and bloody past filled with ghosts, violence, and tragedy. So much so that I was actually frightened as we passed through it — though of course I said nothing to my parents. But it too lodged in my memory.

Like my dad, to this day my favorite vacation is still driving around the backroads of the American West — I don't camp, though, I prefer a good motel and a decent restaurant to sleeping on the hard ground and cooking beans over a Coleman stove. One day in the 1990s, I was taking the scenic route from Prescott to Sedona and suddenly I was in that town. The second I saw it, I recognized it immediately. It's Jerome, Arizona. And yes, it had seen its share of labor struggle, though probably nowhere near as terrible and tragic as in my child's imagination. Now, however, it was bustling, occupied by artists, bikers, and tourists, with lively, thriving bars and art galleries in a strangely eclectic cultural mix. It had become so much a tourist destination that parking was quite scarce. What a contrast between my childhood terror and the reality of the present day.

Like a Runaway Slave ~ 1965

Federal Judge Frank Johnson was famous in liberal circles as a "racial moderate," one of the few such judges in the South. So after

Bloody Sunday everyone assumed he would quickly rule that American citizens had a constitutional right to march from Selma to Montgomery to petition for redress of grievances. But that didn't happen.

To the amazement of legal experts, it took SCLC lawyers *nine* days of hearings and testimony to win that ruling in what everyone had assumed would be an obvious, open-and-shut, slam-dunk case of First Amendment rights. There was a lot of speculation as to why it took him so long to issue his ruling. Some of the more cynical activists (like me, for example) suspected that he was deliberately delaying and stalling until his political ally LBJ announced his proposed voting rights bill. That way, his political patrons in Washington could then spin the march as a pro-Johnson demonstration in *support* of the administration rather than a protest *against* federal inaction in regard to Afro-American voting rights. In any case, on Wednesday, March 17 he finally ruled in our favor.

SCLC and the volunteers like me who were working with them immediately shifted our efforts from courthouse marches to organizing and preparing for a five-day road trek to the Alabama Capitol in Montgomery.

One morning I was sent on some errand to the First Baptist Church, a block down Sylvan Street from Brown Chapel. First Baptist was one of the three main Movement churches in Selma and after Bloody Sunday the Medical Committee for Human Rights (MCHR) set up an emergency aid station in its basement staffed with volunteer doctors and nurses.

When they weren't treating injured protesters they provided free care to anyone who needed it — though they had to be careful, since the state medical establishment refused to honor their out-of-state licenses, so they were limited in the services they could legally provide. Nevertheless, Black folk quickly started coming to them for medical problems that Alabama's system of segregated healthcare ignored, refused to address, or priced out of their reach.

While I was down in the basement I noticed young Black woman creeping down the stairs, cautiously, almost furtively. She was carrying an infant maybe a week or so old. Even I could see it was bad sick. Clearly frightened, she kept her eyes cast down as she spoke softly to these white strangers. She was a sharecropper living on a rural plantation out in the county somewhere. Her newborn was dying, but the landowner refused to let her bring it to a doctor.

That was no surprise. In Alabama's Black Belt, plantations were still run like it was 1865 not 1965. Dallas County field hands were supposedly paid $1.25 for a 12-hour summer day — sometimes not even in cash but rather in credit at a crooked company commissary. That's about 11¢ an hour for hot, backbreaking labor (equal to 88¢ an hour in 2018). Plantation owners didn't want to pay medical expenses for their "pickaninnies," and they were not about to risk their "help" being contaminated with the kind of radical ideas they might encounter in a town where "Martin Luther Coon" was preaching sedition against the southern way of life.

But like slavemasters of old, that plantation owner couldn't entirely suppress the grapevine, that secret rumor line that ran like an invisible network beneath the notice of the white power structure. Somehow she heard about doctors at First Baptist who would treat Afro-Americans for free. In the dead of night, like a runaway slave, she had snuck away carrying her child all the way to Selma on foot through miles of fields and bogs.

She was clearly frightened of what the owner would do when he discovered her escape. She knew she could never return to what had been her home. The MCHR nurse kept reassuring her that she wouldn't be sent back, but she was terrified. They say on TV that "what happens in Vegas stays in Vegas." I don't know if that's true, but I do know that what happened on those feudal Alabama plantations in the 1950s and '60s was buried there, never to be spoken of or revealed to outsiders. And I know that Sheriff Clark and his deputies would have dragged her back to that plantation in a heartbeat — no one the wiser and no questions asked. After all, she couldn't vote, she was no one.

I was just there on some errand when she came in. My assignment was elsewhere and I had to leave without knowing what happened to her or her child. I have no doubt that MCHR did what was needed regardless of license technicalities. And they wouldn't have forced her back to the plantation or turned her over to the sheriff so I don't know what happened to her and her child — though over the years and decades since I've often wondered. Recently, though, I came across the following paragraph in a letter I wrote a couple of weeks later quoting Dr. Herbert Krohn of the MCHR:

> "Most people are malnourished. Especially with vitamin deficiency. I have seen some babies with starvation diarrhea. One baby was brought to me at the point of death. I saw a child with a classical case of malnutrition such as you read about in concentration camps. It is very common to see malnutrition masquerading as obesity because of the high starch and low protein diet."[9]

Marching to Montgomery ~ 1965

The march from Selma to Montgomery would take four days. On the fifth day we would march from the city outskirts to the Alabama Capitol Building where we were determined to speak our truth to the power of Governor Wallace. The logistic challenges were enormous. Food — where and by whom would it be obtained and cooked? How would it be kept more or less hot and delivered to the marchers out on the road? Clean drinking water. Portable toilets. Jackets and rain gear. Tents and sleeping bags. Garbage and trash pickup. Trucks and transport. Radio communications. Portable generators at campsites to provide security lights at night. And so on, and on, and on.

With an adequate budget, a professional staff of paid event organizers could have easily pulled it together in no more than a month or two. We had three days and hardly any money at all. And other than a few military veterans of WWII and Korea, no experience whatsoever in multi-day road marches. So everyone pitched in as best they could. Precision and coordination ranged from haphazard to nonexistent, but enthusiasm and energy were high.

The route from Selma to Montgomery followed U.S. Highway 80, a stretch of road that in Alabama was (and still is) known as the "Jefferson Davis Highway" — the largest Confederate monument in the nation. It was four lanes wide leaving Selma, narrowed to two lanes across Lowndes County, and then widened to four lanes again in Montgomery County. Under the rules issued by Judge Johnson, an unlimited number of people could march on the four-lane segments but for traffic safety reasons no more than 300 could march across Lowndes County on the two-lane blacktop.

Of course, everyone wanted to be among the 300 who would "go all the way." Well, everyone but me. I was a true Angeleno, I loved to drive — hiking was not my thing. Those chosen to be among the 300 included 250 Black Freedom Movement veterans from Selma and the surrounding counties plus 50 out-of-town notables and special honorees, most of them Afro-American, a few white. Those not chosen to "go all the way" were asked to volunteer for one of the logistic committees — food, transportation, etc.

Protection from hostile whites, particularly the Ku Klux Klan, was our biggest concern. Under the judge's order, the county sheriff's departments and state troopers were required to facilitate and protect the march, and the federal government was ordered to send in Army and National Guard troops for the same purpose. We knew that many deputies, troopers, and Alabama guardsmen were dedicated racists and some were actual KKK members themselves. The Guard's shoulder patch was the Confederate battle flag — the same "stars and bars" that adorned Klan pickup trucks and that hostile whites screaming "the South shall rise again!" and "niggers go home!" waved at us.

So we knew we had to form our own security teams. I volunteered for the campsite night watch which was led by Morris Samuel, an Episcopal minister whom I had known through L.A. CORE. He had been one of the moderates that N-VAC rebelled against, but neither he nor I carried that contention into Alabama where we worked well together.

As soon as the march date was set, Freedom Movement supporters from all over America began flowing into Montgomery and Selma by plane, bus, and car. Some came from as far away as Hawaii — they made themselves known by handing out beautiful flower leis. Contingents also arrived from voting rights battlegrounds across the South, bringing with them memories of their own struggles and suffering.

On Saturday afternoon, March 20th, olive drab jeeps and trucks of the United States Army began appearing on Selma streets, rolling through town to the county armory. Rifle-armed GIs with fixed bayonets — Black and white both — were soon standing sentry on street corners, replacing the hated troopers and possemen. When President Kennedy had sent troops to Oxford Mississippi in 1962 to quell rioting whites enraged about the admission of James Meredith to the University of Mississippi, Afro-American soldiers had been disarmed and shunted aside so as not to offend the white racists. To his credit, President Johnson did nothing of the kind, and seeing Afro-American fighting men in uniform standing guard over them was a huge point of pride for Selma Blacks who welcomed them as brothers.

The Army troops were followed by sullen members of the now-federalized Alabama National Guard — all white, of course — who resentfully reported to their military commanders. Some of them didn't have to travel far, they lived in Selma, Montgomery, and adjacent counties. Among them, I was told, were some of the possemen who had beaten freedom marchers on the bridge during Bloody Sunday.

The March to Montgomery was scheduled to start from Brown Chapel at 10am on Sunday morning. By 11am, Dr. King and most of the dignitaries had finally arrived to commence the pre-march mass meeting. The church was so jammed I didn't even try to squeeze in. It was well after noon before the 3,000 or more marchers begin lining up on Sylvan Street, filling its entire width. Afro-Americans, mostly from Selma and the surrounding counties, made up the bulk of the marchers, but there were hundreds of Movement activists of all races from both South and North. We stepped off just before 1pm, a mere three hours behind schedule.

The Edmund Pettus Bridge over the Alabama River humps up out of Broad Street like an ugly hill of steel and asphalt. It was named after a Confederate general who later went on to become a Grand Dragon of the Ku Klux Klan. It felt good striding up the middle of the road to the bridge crest with thousands of like-minded people all around me, it was like I was walking over his defeated and discredited memory. I believe in nonviolence as an effective strategy and tactic, but while I deeply admired Dr. King, I was not one to love my enemies.

Sheyann Webb later expressed some of what I felt so much better than I ever could:

> What I remember so much about that day was the happiness of the people. I had never seen them like that before. When we finished singing *We Shall Overcome* we started off and went to the bridge and there were soldiers with rifles and bayonets everywhere, protecting us. Well, when we crossed that bridge and started on down the road for Montgomery, the people just seemed like something had been lifted from their shoulders. They were so proud, but it was a pride that was dignified. We had always maintained that dignity.[6]

A furious crowd of hostile whites had gathered on the flatland across the bridge where the troopers had attacked the original march on Bloody Sunday. They had cars with "I hate niggers" and "Yankee trash go home" painted on their sides, and they jeered, and cursed, and waved Confederate battle flags as we strode past singing. We held them in utter contempt and no one deigned to respond to their obscene and racist taunts. I could tell, though, that their vitriolic hate and almost hysterical verbal violence shocked and frightened some of the white northern supporters who had never personally encountered that form of traditional southern gentility. Nor were they prepared for the local newspaper stories claiming that the nuns and white women who had come to support the march were only there for sexual orgies with Black men.

Army soldiers in jeeps escorted us past the shouting whites while two military helicopters circled above us. As we marched down the Jefferson Davis Highway toward Montgomery I noticed that soldiers were checking under every bridge and culvert for explosives. Earlier that morning, five dynamite bombs had been discovered before they exploded at Afro-American churches, schools, and homes in Birmingham.

That day the march covered only seven miles to a campsite on land owned by David Hall, an Afro-American farmer. Seven miles doesn't sound like much, but it was a hard trek for people like me, used to driving everywhere and just walking from the parking lot to the checkout counter. A lot of the marchers, and not just northerners, were weary and footsore by the end of the day.

Advance teams had set up four large tents. Two were sleeping tents for the 300 who would go all the way — one for men, the other for women. The third was for supplies and equipment, and the fourth tent was the MCHR emergency first aid station. Almost 100 volunteer doctors and nurses from around the country had responded to the call, arriving in Selma with their canvas first aid satchels ready to treat injured and wounded if there was another attack like Bloody Sunday. A fully equipped mobile field hospital had been provided by the International Ladies Garment Workers Union (ILGWU) and local Black funeral parlors loaned hearses to act as ambulances if necessary. As it turned out, none of those preparations were needed. The medical teams mostly dealt with blisters, sunburn, insect bites, indigestion, and exhaustion.

Since only the chosen 300 would be camping overnight, the other 3,000 marchers had to be taken back to Selma. Carpools had been arranged, but by now night had fallen and the crowd of hostile whites by the bridge had turned into an ugly mob — bigger, angrier, and more violent than before. Cars driven by Blacks and autos with northern license plates were being hit by rocks and threatened with assault despite the presence of soldiers and cops. It was clearly too dangerous to ferry people back to town by automobile. Some were taken by hastily assembled buses using a roundabout route to avoid attack. The remainder were ferried to a nearby railroad stop where a special nine-car train chartered by the Justice Department returned them to Selma.

Food for the 300 marchers and those of us overnighting at the campsite in support roles finally arrived in a rented truck. Cooked by Black women laboring in the kitchen at Green Street Baptist Church, the lukewarm spaghetti, pork & beans, and coffee were ladled out from brand-new steel garbage cans. Squares of corn bread were cut from large rectangular baking pans. Gourmet it wasn't, but we devoured it quickly and regretted that there wasn't more.

The day had been pleasantly warm, but the night turned so cold we could see our breath. The 300 marchers bedded down in their sleeping bags while I and others of the night watch patrolled the perimeter. The Alabama National Guard — the "Dixie Division" — was supposed to be guarding our camp from Klan raiders. But most of them were facing inward with their loaded rifles obviously ready to protect the "southern way of life" from us. We trusted them not at all, so our team of unarmed

Freedom Movement veterans patrolled the perimeter on the alert for Klan attackers and warily watching the guardsmen to make sure that none of them were "cleaning their rifle" in our direction. If we saw any danger our orders were to raise a shout and a warning. Unstated, but well understood, was our duty to nonviolently stand between the threat and the sleeping marchers. Fortunately, that did not become necessary.

By sunrise the temperature was down to 28 degrees. Sparkling white frost crusted the leaves, and the water buckets had a skin of ice. The marchers woke stiff, cold, and grouchy from sleeping on hard ground. A *New York Times* reporter wrote:

> At dawn the encampment resembled a cross between a *Grapes of Wrath* migrant labor camp and the Continental Army bivouac at Valley Forge. The marchers, bundled to the ears with blankets and quilts, huddled around the fires...[10]

Though we didn't know it at the time, this would be the most comfortable — or, rather, the least uncomfortable — campsite of the entire march. After a more or less warm breakfast of oatmeal, toast, and coffee delivered in the metal trash cans, the 300 marchers formed up and headed down the highway into Lowndes County.

Known as "Bloody Lowndes," KKK terror ruled the county with an iron fist. Just driving through it on US 80 was so scary that we often sang freedom songs in the car to keep our spirits up. The brutal history of Bloody Lowndes was a tale of exploitation, land seizures, evictions, arson, beatings, murders, and frameups on false charges. Over 80% of the county's population were Afro-American and not a single one had been allowed to vote since the turn of the century. Zero. Zip. Nada. None. As Carl Golson, the Registrar of Voters, explained to a reporter, "I don't know of any Negro registrations here, but there is a better relationship between the whites and the niggers here than any place I know of."

A carload of us from the night watch accompanied the marchers into Lowndes. We'd drive ahead and pull off the road, wait for them to pass, then leapfrog forward. The first sign of the approaching march was the loud *thwop-thwop-thwop* of helicopters circling above. A state trooper car then appeared on the two-lane blacktop moving slowly at footstep pace with its blue warning lights flashing. It was followed by Army jeeps containing rifle-armed soldiers. Then came the lead marchers with American and United Nations flags waving in the wind and behind them the marching 300 — men and women, some old, some young, most in the prime of life. They were singing and talking and walking proud. Behind them came the vans and cars of the news media with their cameras clicking and whirring. Then the MCHR medical van and finally the support truck with port-a-potties and other equipment followed by more soldiers and state trooper cars.

That portion of Lowndes was mostly pasture, cotton and corn fields, alternating with stretches of swamp where gloomy trees trailed long veils of Spanish moss and the dark water was slimy with algae. Charles "Chuck" Fager, an SCLC staff member later wrote, "The dead trees seemed like the stumps of burned crosses, and it was easy to imagine mutilated black bodies, the victims of the county's quiet methods of social control, bloated and rising suddenly out of the mud ..."

At first the few isolated Afro-Americans living in dilapidated, "shotgun shacks" along the highway watched the march go by in silent astonishment. No one in Lowndes had ever seen such a public display of Black pride, Black assertiveness, and Black opposition to white racism and white power. Equally astounding was the sight of Black and white, men and women, marching together as friends and allies. Then as word began spreading through the grapevine, Blacks began to gather along the road to wave and cheer. If you look at photos of those who dared come out to show support for the march you can see such enormous joy in their faces.

One of the places where we waited in our car for the march to catch up was across the road from a White Citizens' Council billboard claiming to show "Martin Luther King at a Communist Training School" (the photo was actually from a speech about the Montgomery Bus Boycott that he gave at the Highlander Folk School). The marchers passed it by with laughter and derisive comments. We also passed other billboards like "Help get the U.S. out of the U.N," and a round sign with crossed American and Confederate flags saying, "Citizens Council, States Rights, and Racial Integrity."

By mid-morning the sun had turned hot and bright and on the open stretches sunburn was becoming a problem. MCHR nurses distributed white sunscreen ointment and some of the young marchers used it to write "Vote" on their foreheads.

By now, we of the night watch were exhausted and bleary-eyed, so our car finally headed back to Selma, where we hoped to catch a few winks of sleep before resuming guard over the second campsite, which was in the center of Lowndes County on land owned by Mrs. Rosie Steele, a Black woman 78 years old who told a reporter:

> At first I didn't think it amounted to much, I guess I've lived too long and just didn't think things would change — until I heard the president's speech the other night. ... When they come and asked me if they could use my land I felt I couldn't afford to turn them down. If the president

can take a stand, I guess I can too. ... I don't know, I almost feel like I might live long enough to vote myself.[11]

It took great courage for her to defy the Lowndes County Klan and Citizens Council power structure by offering her land for our use and we were grateful to her. Unfortunately, however, her field was infested with swarms of red ants that bedeviled and stung us wherever we sat to eat or lay down to sleep. Selma was by now 20 miles distant, and when the trash cans of spaghetti finally arrived the food was cold and congealing.

That night as we stood guard it began to rain, a light drizzle at first that by mid-morning the next day had turned into a downpour. The marchers hit the road early after lukewarm coffee and a breakfast gone cold in the cans. At first they tried to stay dry with make-do ponchos made from plastic garbage bags and improvised hats from flattened cornflakes boxes, but between the hard blowing wind and spray kicked up by passing cars, the marchers were soon drenched to the bone. Though they didn't know it, their bedrolls loaded on a stake-bed truck were also getting soaked through beneath a leaky tarp.

It was raw spirit, grit, and determination that kept them going. Chanting *"Freedom! Free- Dom! Free-Dom!"* they crossed over Big Swamp in a driving rain on a long causeway raised above the dark foreboding water. For some marchers, cheap fake-leather shoes were all they owned, and now they were beginning to fall apart. One young woman taped cellophane around her feet to keep on marching. Legs and feet were sore, soaking wet garments chafed and rubbed, blisters ached and burned with every step. *"Free-Dom! Free-Dom! Free-Dom!"*

The third campsite, just before the Montgomery County line, was on the Robert Gardner farm owned by A.G. Gaston of Birmingham. Though by afternoon the rain had dwindled to an intermittent drizzle, the site was soggy and dotted with standing puddles. The dark soil had turned to thick sticky mud that oozed over shoes and glued down feet. Unless you stepped carefully your shoe remained stuck and your sock-clad foot plopped down into the wet goo.

The advance crew had spread hay on the ground, but that just thickened the quagmire. We had to slog through mud, stand in mud, sit in mud, eat in mud, and sleep in mud. Dinner of BBQ chicken, peas, and carrots was provided by Tuskegee students. It had to be eaten either standing on exhausted feet or sitting in cold wet mud. Cheap air mattresses had been obtained from somewhere and people tried to sleep on them but many deflated in the night and marchers awoke in clammy ooze.

Breakfast the next morning came from Selma, now more than 40 miles distant. It was cold coffee, cold toast, and cold oatmeal choked down in cold mud. Few of the marchers had managed a good night's sleep in their wet, clammy sleeping bags and by now those of us on the night watch were running on adrenaline fumes. Everyone was caked with mud, exhausted, sullen, and gritty-eyed.

But the day dawned warm and bright. As the 300 marchers slogged down the road they began shedding their jackets and ponchos and piling them into the supply truck. Then everyone was abruptly soaked by a sudden spring shower.

When we reached the Montgomery County line where the road widened to four lanes and the 300-marcher limitation ended, we of the night watch jumped out of the pickup truck we were riding in and merged into the marching column. Another rain shower was pouring down. Suddenly this incredible frision of energy ran through the entire line and we all started singing like crazy. It felt like Louis Armstrong blowing "When the Saints Go Marching In" at his most passionate.

Trucks, and cars, and a couple of chartered buses started pulling up with people jumping out to join the march, the vehicles rushing back to Montgomery and Selma to pick up more marchers. The column grew longer and longer — 400, 500, 600 — everyone singing, singing as loud as we could against the rain.

By the time we reached the Montgomery city limits the shower had tapered off and we were now a thousand strong. We came up on motel row, just the Ramada and Holiday Inns back then. The room maids — all Black of course — were out in front with their mops and pails and linen carts and they were just staring, just looking, smiles as wide as the sky. Standing right behind them were their white managers and they were staring too but with completely different expressions. A couple of the maids looked back at their boss, looked again at us, threw down whatever it was they had in their hands, and ran out to join the march — still in their uniforms. I couldn't believe it. But I saw it happen.

The line continued to swell as we passed through the outskirts and into the city proper — 1500 — 2000 — 3000. By the time we reached the final campground at St. Jude, we were 5000 strong. Thousands more were on hand to cheer us in through the brick gateposts and tears were flowing down my face. And I tell you true, tears flow again today as I write this remembrance.

The City of St. Jude's was a Roman Catholic institution providing education, health, and social services to Afro-Americans. Dr. King's two eldest children had been born there. Here too the ground was soaked from days of rain, though the mud wasn't as deep as at the Gardner farm.

By evening there must have been 10,000 people milling around. The logistic operation that had been performing miracles on a shoestring for four days was swamped, the volunteers exhausted. One of the old generators began to fail, plunging portions of the campground into periods of partial darkness. The food truck couldn't get through the crush or find the 300 road-marchers to deliver dinner. A tentpole broke and the canvas partly collapsed. Trucks and cars became mired in the mud.

Nobody cared — we had made it! We had marched from Selma to Montgomery in the face of Wallace, in defiance of the cops and troopers, in the teeth of the Klan.

For me, the march from Selma had been a study in contrasts. The contrast between the magnificent beauty of the march as a political and social concept and the daily discomfort and petty misery of actually being part of it. The stark contrast between the smiling happy faces of the cheering Black supporters along the way and the sullen, hate-filled faces of white lawmen, guardsmen, and grim-faced onlookers. The marchers were odiferous and ill-clad, dirty, disheveled, with blankets and knapsacks on their backs and sometimes barefoot. The soldiers, many with Confederate patches sewn on their uniforms, were well-equipped, neat and clean. Most intense of all was the contrast between the marchers' determined "We'll never turn back" spirit and the frustrated, angry, and yet somehow impressed-in-spite-of-themselves attitude of white Alabamians.

Long-time Movement supporter and dedicated social justice activist Harry Belafonte organized a free "Stars for Freedom" show for a huge crowd at St. Jude. From an improvised outdoor stage laid atop coffins loaned by Black funeral homes, Mahalia Jackson, Dick Gregory, Joan Baez, Leonard Bernstein, Nina Simone, Nipsey Russell, Pete Seeger, Sammy Davis, Odetta, Ossie Davis, Ruby Dee, Peter Paul and Mary, Ella Fitzgerald, and scores of others entertained the throng.

I was told the next day that it had been a fabulous show, but I neither saw nor heard any of it. I had been up all night for three nights straight on security duty with no more than a few hours sleep and then had marched all day into Montgomery. I was utterly exhausted and just fell out. I lay down in an empty tent to rest for "just a moment" before going to see the show. I could hear Peter, Paul and Mary singing something in the distance. The next thing I knew, some kid was kicking me awake next morning because they had to start taking down the tent. I missed the whole thing. But everyone sympathetically assured me it had been absolutely amazing.

That Thursday morning, the 25th day of March 1965, there was bustle and confusion everywhere. The ground was still soggy, there was light morning drizzle, and cars were spinning their tires in the mud. Like a tide coming in, inevitable and relentless, a river of Movement supporters from South and North were pouring onto the grounds for the final leg of the march through the heart of Montgomery to the State Capitol.

Singing their hearts out, some 200 Tuskegee, Alabama State, and Montgomery high school students who had been arrested on SNCC-led protests in the city proudly marched into the swelling throng, having just been released after enduring incarceration in Kilby prison. A mass of Tuskegee and Tougaloo students and adult contingents from Birmingham and Bessemer, Gadsden, Anniston, and Tuscaloosa joined the multitude. From Jackson and Meridian, Mississippi; Atlanta, Albany, and Savannah, Georgia; Northern Florida and the Carolinas; and from other embattled communities across the South came carloads of civil rights activists to participate in what we all knew by then was going to be the climactic march of the decades-long campaign for voting rights — a battle that some were now referring to as the "Second Reconstruction."

Rumors were rife that KKK assassins were stalking Dr. King and security was tight — so tight that Army sentries refused to let his car enter the St. Jude gate. Andrew Young, then Ralph Bunche of the United Nations, and finally King himself tried to talk their way past the young sergeant dutifully manning his post. To no avail. Finally a Montgomery motorcycle cop recognized King and yelled at the GI, "You danged fool. This is the man! Let him through!"

Those of us who had been part of the night watch were issued armbands and designated march marshals, as were other volunteers. Big James Orange, an SCLC field organizer, explained the plan, which was for King, selected Freedom Movement leaders, and special guests to join the 300 and together lead the march to the Capitol. Fluorescent highway-worker safety-vests were being handed out to identify those who were to have the vanguard honor.

That was the plan. But all sorts of other people were trying to snatch the vests so they'd have the pride of "leading" the march with King. Some heads of major organizations, out-of-town preachers, and those simply filled with their own self-importance insisted that they were entitled to march side by side with King. They resented having to follow behind "kids" — meaning the 300.

But the young protesters who had marched all the way were having none of that. Selma student Profit Barlow, age 17, shouted back at them, "All you dignitaries got to get behind me. I didn't see any of you fellows in Selma, and I didn't see you on the way to Montgomery. Ain't nobody going to get in front of me but Dr. King!"

As King tried to reach the head of the column to start the march he was intercepted by Montgomery County sheriff's deputies who served him and other Movement leaders with multiple lawsuits and summonses for a variety of nonsensical offenses and phony court claims. Just one more petty, mean-spirited act on the part of Alabama officialdom.

We marshals tried to help Dr. King reach his place, but we were overwhelmed by a surge of the vainglorious eager to be seen and photographed next to him. Rosa Parks was supposed to accompany King as a special honoree. I remember she was wearing rimless granny glasses, and her long hair, now beginning to turn gray, was wrapped in a neat bun. She was rudely shoved aside by dignitaries in fine suits. Mahalia Jackson tried to hold a place for her (nobody was able to push Mahalia Jackson around), but I later saw that Mrs. Parks had found a spot farther back among the rank and file. She didn't seem to mind, but she knew who she was and she was proud of it. "You know," she told me, "some folks call me the mother of all this." I assured her I was one of those who considered her to be so.

There was no way short of violence that those self-important bigshots were going to allow themselves to be separated from King or prevented from getting as close to him as they could shove themselves. So the SCLC field staff quickly adapted, placing the 300 in their orange vests ahead of King as a kind of honor vanguard, leaving behind them an open space for reporters to photograph the march "leaders" — both actual and self-appointed.

With all this *mishegas* going on, the march was almost two hours late getting started — not that unusual for Freedom Movement events, as I was coming to learn. Singing strong, with American flags waving in the breeze, more than 12,000 of us strode out of St. Jude's. An equal number were impatiently waiting to join the column at various staging areas along the four-mile route to the Capitol.

As we marched through Afro-American neighborhoods the column grew bigger and bigger as the assembly point groups merged in. Other folks simply stepped off their porches to join. All along the way Black folk waved and cheered us on with huge smiles and grins. This was a Thursday, supposedly a school day, and we passed a Colored elementary school where kids were jumping out the windows to join the march — the Negro principal futilely standing in the door trying to stop them.

When we entered the downtown business district the streets suddenly became eerily quiet. Governor Wallace had proclaimed a "danger holiday" for female employees (whites only, of course) and urged all whites to stay away. Most had complied, but a few knots of hostile white men jeered and taunted us with racist slogans and chants. Lines of troopers guarded every foot of state property from our odious presence. Plywood panels had been placed over the bronze plaque on the plaza at the Capitol to prevent any Black feet from "desecrating" the spot where Jefferson Davis had been sworn in as president of the Confederate States of America in 1861.

Ever since I was a kid I've had a passion for history — not the doings of kings and generals but the history that was forged up from below by people struggling for justice and freedom. We passed Holt Street Baptist Church, where in 1955 a very young Dr. King had addressed the first mass meeting of the Montgomery Bus Boycott. He had been just 26 that day, five years older than I was on that March day in 1965.

Our route took us not far from the Greyhound Bus station where the Freedom Riders were so brutally beaten by a white mob in 1961. And as we turned up Dexter Avenue we went by the bus stop where on a dank, dreary December night less than ten years earlier, Mrs. Rosa Parks had refused to move to the back of the bus and endured the humiliation and terror of a lonely arrest. By now I'd lost track of her in the huge throng, but I knew that today she was no longer alone. Today she was proudly walking with 25,000 fellow freedom warriors — Black and white.

Tears were again flowing down my face and I was not alone in that as we surged up the gentle rise of Dexter Avenue toward the looming Capitol edifice. The march column was by now so long it took over an hour for all of the marchers to finally fill the full eight-lane width of Dexter, from the foot of the Capitol steps back for blocks. Law enforcement authorities — no friends of the Freedom Movement — estimated a total number of 25,000. The media and historians to this day accept and repeat that figure without question. Movement organizers and participants thought the number to be higher, but there was no general consensus as to the actual total, so 25,000 is what everyone says.

In the final analysis though, what defined this march was not numbers, but rather *who* the marchers were. Almost all of them were hard-working southern Blacks — farmers, maids, sharecroppers, laborers, and a smattering of teachers and business owners — all determined to end both white supremacy and the "southern way of life." Though the overwhelming majority of the marchers were Afro-American and poor, the media, as usual, focused its coverage on the white and the notable.

The speakers' platform was just a flatbed truck equipped with microphones and loudspeakers. The rally began with songs by Odetta, Oscar Brand, Joan Baez, Len Chandler, Peter, Paul and Mary, and Leon Bibb. I could see big tripod-mounted TV cameras recording the event, and I later learned that it had been broadcast live until Mary Travers — young, blond, and beautiful — joyfully kissed Harry Belafonte on the cheek. At which point so many outraged whites around the nation swamped studio phone lines that CBS switched to their regular soap operas until a counter-flood of equally angry viewers on the other side of the issue forced them to restore coverage.

Dr. King gave the main address. Today it's known as the *Our God is Marching On* speech. It was powerful and moving. By now I'd heard him speak several times in mass meetings and, of course, I was present for his *I Have a Dream* speech at the March on Washington. But if *Dream* was a call to conscience and hope, on this day, standing on a makeshift platform at the foot of the Alabama State Capitol with the hated Confederate flag flying from atop the dome and surrounded by state troopers in blue battle helmets gripping their clubs and scowling in anger, he delivered a declaration of truth to power, articulating what Afro-Americans across the South wanted to say — directly and unambiguously — to a white-supremacist power structure whose oppression they were no longer willing to endure or tolerate.

From his truck-bed podium, Dr. King could easily see Dexter Avenue Baptist Church, where just ten years earlier he had begun his ministry as a small-town pastor and then risen to fame as leader of the Montgomery Bus Boycott. While I listened to him I wondered if that personal journey was in his thoughts as he ended his speech with a declaration of faith that still rings across the decades:

> I know you are asking today, "How long will it take?"
> I come to say to you this afternoon, however difficult the moment, however frustrating the
> hour, it will not be long, because, "truth crushed to earth will rise again."
> How long? Not long, because "No lie can live forever."
> How long? Not long, because "You shall reap what you sow."
> How long? Not long, because the arc of the moral universe is long, but it bends toward justice.
> How long? Not long, because:
> Mine eyes have seen the glory of the coming of the Lord;
> He is trampling out the vintage where the grapes of wrath are stored;

He has loosed the fateful lightning of his terrible swift sword;
Our God is marching on.
Glory, hallelujah!
Glory, hallelujah!
Glory, hallelujah!

Glory, hallelujah!
His truth is marching on.[12]

The Murder of Viola Liuzzo ~ 1965

As was so often the case with Dr. King's great speeches, a surge of hope, pride, and commitment uplifted us all and the throng responded with fervent cheers and applause. For mass movements to be sustained over time, anger alone is not enough, there must also be hope, optimism and a long-term vision, which King provided in a manner and degree never replicated since.

By the time the rally ended it was late afternoon and now confusion reigned as the marchers in their thousands began dispersing. Hundreds of supporters who had come directly to the city from distant locales needed help finding the homes and churches where their luggage was waiting and then transportation to airports and bus depots. The Black-owned taxis were overwhelmed, and white taxis wanted nothing to do with "agitators" and "race-mixers" of any color.

Thousands of Afro-Americans had to return to Selma, Wilcox, Perry, and other Alabama communities and counties. With what little funds they had left, SCLC had chartered some buses — but not nearly enough. Most of the Alabama marchers had to be ferried back along US 80 in hastily organized carpools. I managed to catch a ride back to Selma with some SCLC folk I had become friendly with. All of us were exhausted and hyper with the emotion of the day and the success of the march.

From the moment we left Brown Chapel in Selma five days earlier to the end of the program in Montgomery the U.S. Army and federal law enforcement agencies had kept us all safe. Now that elaborate protection system began to rapidly wind down just as thousands of people were headed home through Klan country. It was a premature withdrawal that cost Mrs. Viola Liuzzo her life when a KKK "action team" gunned her down on the US 80.

I don't recall seeing her shot-up car by the side of the road so I assume I must have reached Selma before the killers chased her down. It's probable that we had passed her going the other way as she drove back to Montgomery to pick up more marchers. I don't remember how I learned of her murder, probably at Brown Chapel or the SCLC office later that night.

Leroy Moton, a local student active with the Movement whom I had met several times, had been in the car with her. Covered in her blood, he had feigned death when the Klan killers came back to check on their work. When he managed to catch a ride back to Selma with others returning from the March, he reported the assassination to the police, who immediately arrested *him* — apparently on the assumption that if a Black man was riding with a murdered white woman he *had* to be the culprit. We knew he was a witness the KKK would try to silence. Fortunately, Movement lawyers were able to get him out before he was murdered in jail. He was spirited away to safety in the North.

I hadn't known Mrs. Liuzzo but I felt her murder deeply with a seething mixture of rage, sorrow, despair, and fear. Which, of course, was exactly what her killers wanted. A couple of days later I joined a small memorial service by the side of the road in Lowndes County where she had been shot, and later at a nearby Afro-American church. We prayed, listened to eulogies, and stood in a circle holding hands while we sang "We Shall Overcome." It all felt totally inadequate.

I also remember the campaign of character-assassination and racist, sexual, and political slander that FBI Director J. Edgar Hoover later waged against her memory — no doubt to divert media attention from the fact that a long-time, well-paid FBI informant was in the Klan car with the killers and did nothing to halt the murder or dissuade the killers. And whom some believe was himself one of the shooters.

"We the People," and the Right to Vote

That battle for the ballot — which to this day I am enormously proud to have been part of — can only be understood within the historical context out of which it grew.

The struggle for voting rights neither began nor ended in Selma. Nor did it spontaneously spring into existence. Nor was it an isolated event. Rather it was built on a foundation of voting struggles going back to the founding of our nation. It was pushed forward in the early 1960s by hard and dangerous campaigns throughout all the southern states. Yet it was the battle for the vote in the Alabama Black Belt — based on, and building from, all that came before — that finally, finally, forced passage of the Voting Rights Act of 1965, perhaps the most politically-significant victory of the entire Civil Rights Movement.

Back then we used to talk in terms of "first- and second-class citizens." Today, Bob Moses of SNCC analyzes our voting rights campaigns in the framework of *"We the People."* The very first words of the American Constitution are: "We the people ... do ordain and establish this Constitution for the United States of America."

It does not say: *"We the rich and powerful"*
It does not say: *"We the politicians"*
It says: **"We the People."**

But who *are "We the People?"*

Abstract political debates aside, as a matter of practical politics those who are eligible to vote — and who actually DO vote — are members of *"We the People."* They are the recognized stakeholders of our society. Those who are barred from voting, or choose not to vote, are not part of "We the People" and their social and political treatment by society and government reflect that inferior position.

When the U.S. Constitution was being debated and drafted in 1789 a fierce political battle erupted over who would have the vote. Women? Slaves? Indians? Indentured servants? Catholics? Apprentices? Rich? Poor? Renters? Laborers? In essence it was a fight over who was included in "We the People." We have been fighting that political war ever since. We continue fighting it to this day because those who are well served by the way things are want to limit the voting power of those whom they justly fear have good reason to be dissatisfied with the status quo.

It is estimated that in the presidential election of 1800 no more than 10% of the adult population were eligible to vote. The other 90% were barred from voting, they were not included in "We the People."

Who were those 90% who were not part of "We the People?"

Women — half the population — could not vote. For 151 years, women fought to become part of, "We the People." For their temerity they were beaten, jailed, brutalized, and demeaned. But they carried their battle to every city, town, and rural hamlet in the nation.

In the election of 1800, Native Americans could not vote. Indians did not win legal voting rights until 1927 — 140 years after the Constitution was adopted.

In most states in 1800, only white males who owned property could vote. Renters, apprentices, tenant farmers, laborers, sailors, and hired hands could not vote. In New York City in 1800, roughly three-quarters of white men were denied the vote because they did not own property. The struggle to end *explicit* property qualifications was fierce and often violent. North Carolina was the last state to end property requirements in 1856 — North Carolina, last in so many respects to this day. But *implicit* income restrictions were not ended until poll taxes were finally outlawed in 1964.

In 1848, the treaty of Guadalupe Hidalgo ended the war against Mexico. It promised that Mexicans living in the conquered lands would be free American citizens with full voting rights. That did not happen. In Arizona and New Mexico, Mexican-Americans were legally denied the vote until 1912. During those 64 years, their lands and water rights were confiscated by judges and legislators elected only by Anglo voters. In Texas and California, Anglo terrorism, legal tricks, and official fraud prevented all but a few from actually casting ballots. The Voting Rights Act of 1965 also won voting rights for Latino citizens — rights that are today under attack by those who see people of color as somehow less than "real" Americans.

After the Immigration Act of 1870 and then the Chinese Exclusion Acts that followed, Asian immigrants were denied the vote. Asian immigrants did not finally win full citizenship and voting rights until 1952. One of the reasons that Japanese-Americans could so easily be rounded up and sent to concentration camps during World War II was that most of them could not vote — they were not considered part of "We the People."

As originally adopted, the Constitution defined slaves as property rather than citizens. And in most states free men of color were denied the vote through legal barriers and intimidation. Despite what the passionate defenders of "southern heritage" may now claim, the Civil War was a war against slavery. But in a broader sense it was part of the long — and still ongoing — fight to include those of African descent as part of "We the People."

After the Civil War, the 13th Amendment abolished slavery (though Mississippi didn't ratify it until 1995). The 14th Amendment established that anyone born in the United States was an American citizen. When you hear conservative politicians railing against "anchor babies," they are attacking the 14th Amendment. The 15th Amendment granted the vote to citizens regardless of "race, color, or previous condition of servitude." When states adopt restrictive "Voter ID" laws today, those laws are designed to subvert the 15th Amendment.

I was recently asked, "Are you surprised that 50 years after passage of the Voting Rights Act we're still fighting over race-related efforts to limit voting?"

A good question. My answer was, "No, I'm not. For those sitting on top of the heap more than enough is never enough. They relentlessly scheme to protect and expand their wealth, power, and privilege. They will always attempt to limit the voting power of those below them."

When I arrived in Selma, Alabama in early 1965 I had only an abstract, intellectual understanding of the importance of voting rights. I knew it in my head — but not in my gut. That profoundly changed for me when that terrified young women brought her dying baby to the MCHR doctors in the basement of First Baptist Church. She knew she could never return to her home on that plantation because she had defied her master's edict. She knew that no matter what he did to her, he would face no sanction or consequences from any elected official or court. He could brutalize her, rape her, even kill her with no fear of punishment.

She had no vote. She was not part of "We the People." She knew with dead certainty that not only would white officialdom fail to protect her, they would turn her over to the plantation master. I don't know what happened to her or her baby, I never even knew her name, but I owe her a debt of gratitude because without realizing it, without even noticing my presence, she taught me the real meaning of voting rights.

The Southern Way of Life

Green Clouds and Klan Trucks ~ 1965

On a warm spring day in early April a week or two after the march, I was driving some folk from Montgomery to Selma in an old Volkswagen minibus we used for Movement work. Shortly after we crossed into Lowndes County on the two-lane blacktop of U.S. 80, a pickup truck with a Confederate flag license plate on the front bumper came up fast behind us. It was driven by a pair of white men. We were trained to prevent anyone from pulling up alongside us on the open road — that's how they shot Mrs. Luizzo — and so far as I was concerned, any car with a Confederate plate was presumed Klan. But a VW minivan with a load of passengers couldn't outrun an old jalopy, much less a modern pickup. I told my passengers to lie down on the floor.

Up ahead of us was a Trailways bus which we didn't have the speed to pass. By flooring it, I managed to pull up close behind in the hope that if the men on our tail had evil intent the possibility of witnesses might deter them. Maybe. I hoped.

Then local Selma kid who was riding in the shotgun seat muttered, "Uh-oh."

"What?"

"Look up ahead."

As the road swerved left and right, I could from time to time see around the bus. A thick band of dark black clouds stretched across the horizon in front of us. It was a springtime squall line — a bad one — moving fast in our direction, and the highway to Selma was taking us right into it. We began passing cars that had pulled off the road to hunker down in open areas away from any trees. The pickup was now only a few feet behind us, practically riding our bumper, and with Klan on our tail, we didn't dare halt.

As the squall line came closer I could see that the lower portion of the clouds were not black but green from leaves and branches stripped from trees by the gale-force winds. Winds that were already beginning to rise around us as the first fat drops of rain began splattering against the windshield. This was the kind of weather front that spawned tornados and it had everything except an actual twister-funnel. The Klan truck behind us was no longer my main concern.

Suddenly the minibus was buffeted by a gust so powerful it tilted us over on our left side wheels with the right side off the pavement. I swung the wheel hard left to bring us down. The wind lashed at us. The van shimmied and shook as I fought the wheel to keep us upright. Lighting flashed like rock-concert strobe lights. The continuous roll of thunder was deafening. Rain flooded against the windshield like it was being pumped from a fire hose. Blowing leaves and branches were smacking into our windows. Suddenly a flying something smashed into a side window, cracking it into a maze of shatter lines. We were terrified.

So I did what we always did when we were scared.

"Wade in the water,
Wade in the Water children,
Wade in the Water,
God's gonna trouble the Water!"

As I've mentioned before, I can't sing for shit, but everyone else joined in as I fought the wheel to keep us upright and moving.

"Who's that yonder dressed in red,
Wade in the Water,
Must be the Children that Moses led,
God's gonna trouble the Water!"

The Trailways bus had slowed to 10mph and I tucked in as close behind as I could, almost touching its bumper, for whatever shelter it might provide. The rain was now so heavy I couldn't see if the pickup was still behind us. All I could see were my slapping windshield wipers and the blurry red tail lights of that big bus a couple of feet in front of us.

"Who's that yonder dressed in black,
Wade in the Water,
Must be the hypocrites turning back,
God's gonna trouble the Water!"

Somehow, someway, we made it though. After a while the wind began to drop and the rain tapered off. The Trailways bus picked up speed and I let the gap between us widen. There was no sign of the pickup truck with Confederate plates. Though the highway was littered with tree branches and leaves and there were wide pools of standing water on the pavement and shoulders, it was still open to slow traffic. As we approached Selma I saw that the "Martin Luther King at a Communist Training Camp" billboard set up by the White Citizens' Council had been blown over.

God's gonna trouble the waters indeed.

Boots on the Ground ~ 1965

In Hollywoodland, good triumphs over evil in the epic battle, the lovers are always reunited, the credits roll, and everyone happily goes home. In real life — not so much.

After the March to Montgomery, SCLC staff member Charles Fager later wrote:

> To most [Alabama Blacks] the march had been nothing less than a kind of miracle, with wonders piled on wonders: the president's address, the coming of troops to protect them from Wallace, Lingo and Clark, the influx of whites ready to stand, suffer, and even die with them in their struggle, and soon enough a voting law which would open up the voting booths to them. They had made more history in three weeks than most of them had ever studied in their lives. Throughout the rest of the spring they were still trying to comprehend it all, savoring the memories it left, and basking in its lingering euphoria. They were also a little exhausted, especially the people in the counties around Selma who had been most actively involved. Thus they were by no means ready to put on their marching shoes again on cue and go right back out to repeat or even surpass the march's accomplishments. [11]

Selma after the march, however, still remained largely segregated. Sheriff Clark's reign of police terror had been somewhat weakened and was now to a degree constrained by public pressure and the threat of federal action. But he, his posse, the courts, and the powerful White Citizens' Council were still committed to maintaining the traditional Jim Crow "southern way of life." As a visible symbol of that determination, Clark wore a prominent "Never" button on his chest.

Within Selma's Afro-American community, however, the old habits of subservience and fear were dying a well-deserved death. With a united community behind it, the Black boycott of Selma's white merchants had taken hold in support of demands to end job discrimination and the daily humiliations of Jim Crow segregation. Political organization was flourishing, with a strong cadre of local leaders, an empowered Dallas County Voters League (DCVL), and local ward groups with elected leaders developing neighborhood programs.

By April, most of the outside supporters had returned to their homes, but in addition to a small cadre of SCLC and SNCC field staff a fluid group of around a dozen or more unaffiliated civil rights activists — like me — remained to lend support to community organizing, voter registration efforts, and the mass meetings which were now being held two or three times a week rather than daily.

I was still living off the money I had saved working for the Yale grad students. That was not difficult because many of my meals were provided by local Movement supporters and for a while I was still sleeping on top of the Wests' washing machine, though by the end of April I had graduated to a spare bed in the home of a local activist on Green Street.

In the rural South at that time, male freedom fighters of all races were quite attractive to many of the local Afro-American girls. We had a kind of macho glamour and our connection to, and familiarity with, the great world outside of small-town Selma was alluring. Teenage girls and young women flirted with us a lot — yes, even with me. Nella, Alice, and Charlene were the oldest of the West girls, all in high school and so beautiful they put me in mind of that line from the Song of Songs, "Dark am I, yet lovely, daughters of Jerusalem." Living in their home as I did for almost two months, the West girls came to trust me enough to flirt, even when their mom, Alice, was present.

As a randy young man recently turned 21, I must confess that I was flattered and quite tempted. Yet if there was one thing I had learned from overhearing my parents when they thought I wasn't listening, it's that nothing divides and destroys social movements quicker than messing around with wives and daughters. So I was determined to treat the West girls as if they were younger sisters. Somehow I managed to hold to that resolve — but, oh, it was difficult. So very, very difficult.

The March to Montgomery and the dramatic events leading up to it had been a once-in-a-lifetime event — not in any way typical of day-to-day civil rights work in the Deep South. Once the march ended and the hoopla subsided, I had to learn how to be an effective, full-time southern freedom activist with all that entailed. SCLC and SNCC were continuing their work in Selma and the surrounding Black Belt counties and there was intense rivalry between them — I knew I would have to choose one or the other. Before going South I had assumed I would join the staff of either SNCC in Alabama or Mississippi or CORE in Louisiana, but that's not the way it turned out.

I never saw myself as any kind of community leader, and though SNCC exalted the role of "organizer," I didn't see myself as that either. I was a young, inexperienced, northern white guy — what did I know about organizing a Black community? Nothing. Planning and coordinating protests, yes, that I knew. The scut work of operating and maintaining a political action organization, that too I could handle. So my role, as I understood it, was to be an ally, to assist local Movement leaders however I could. To perform whatever staff work they needed, and to make available to them what limited skills I might possess.

I also understood that an important aspect of my role was to simply endure and, in defiance of Klan, Citizens Council, cops, and courts, survive as an advocate for racial justice — and by so doing show that it could be done by others. I also came to see that I was living witness and political proof to both Blacks and whites alike that the Freedom Movement was a struggle between right and wrong, not a race war of Black against white. The local Afro-American leaders and SCLC staff I worked with clearly understood that if the conflict was framed as Black versus white they would inevitably be outnumbered and overpowered politically. The presence of white allies at their side helped define issues in right-against-wrong ways that gave them at least a fighting chance of winning.

Many of the Black SNCC workers, however, were moving away from that view towards a more nationalist stance that saw no role for white civil rights activists in Afro-American communities. So I found myself more and more in the company of SCLC folk. While some of the SNCC staff I encountered in Selma were warm and friendly, others were antagonistic and even deliberately hateful towards white activists like me.

SNCC was also increasingly hostile towards nonviolent direct action protests which they felt disrupted and set back their strategy of deep community organizing. As I saw it, though, organizing and protests were complementary, each one strengthening the other, and that to achieve substantive reforms both were necessary — an opinion that became firmer the longer I worked in Alabama and Mississippi and an opinion I continue to hold to this day.

So despite the fact that SCLC did not maintain as large a field staff as did SNCC or CORE — and therefore my chances of being added to their staff were poor — somewhat to my surprise I found myself gravitating towards the SCLC folk who were engaged in the traditional kind of "Black and white together" organizing and nonviolent protesting that had been my political world since that first Torrance picket line two years earlier in 1963.

Not long after the March to Montgomery I accompanied James Orange and Andrew Marrisett, two longtime members of SCLC's field staff, to a local freedom march in Marion, where a month earlier Jimmie Lee Jackson had been shot to death by state troopers. Marion was a tiny hamlet, the classic southern seat of rural Perry county. An imposing courthouse painted entirely in pure white with six stately columns occupied the central square. Lining the four streets surrounding and facing the square were the post office, jail, bank, a couple of churches and funeral homes, and brick stores some with second stories where the doctor, dentist, and other professionals conducted their less than bustling businesses.

About 50 people rallied in the little Zion Methodist church on the edge of the miniscule "downtown" district, mostly Afro-American locals with some SCLC organizers and a couple of white activists like me. Then we marched by the square to encourage a Black boycott of the white-owned stores. Since we were violating anti-boycott and anti-picketing laws we expected to be arrested, but the police and troopers just fingered their cattle prods and glared or smacked billy clubs against their gloved hands — what a difference the Freedom Movement had wrought from a month earlier, when those same cops had reacted with savage violence to a similar freedom march.

A few days later I rode down to Camden, the seat of Wilcox County, with Charles Bonner and a carload of other young Selma activists. After an afternoon mass meeting in a rural roadside church, maybe 75 of us started marching two by two along the side of the highway towards the courthouse where we intended to hold a voter registration rally. Suddenly, out of nowhere, white men on galloping horses charged into our line, cursing, yelling, and flailing at us with long clubs, walking canes, and bullwhips.

"It's Clark's posse!" shouted one of the Selma kids.

A blow across my back knocked me down and I rolled into a roadside drainage ditch with grass growing in an inch or two of stagnant water. I heard the clatter of horse hooves on the pavement as the posse pulled back and then, *Pop! Pop!* A cloud of acrid, eye-burning teargas enveloped me. I felt like I couldn't breathe. Gasping, choking, and coughing, somehow I managed to get out of the ditch and retreat back towards the church along with everyone else.

By the time we got inside, the cloud of gas had dissipated but our clothes and skin were covered in the residue, and our sweat reactivated the fumes. My clothes were so drenched with the toxic chemicals that when I put them in the washing machine the next day, eye-stinging vapor drove everyone out of the West family's kitchen.

A number of people in the church were battered and bruised and some were being tended to by MCHR volunteers. SCLC leader Dorothy Cotton, who had been one of the march leaders, rose to the church podium. Proud and defiant, she spoke not at all but rather sang the most emotional and memorable rendition of "Why Was the Darkie Born" that I've ever heard. To this day, the memory still haunts me and sends shivers down my spine.

> *"Mommy, why was the Darkie born?*
> *Mommy, why was the Darkie born?*
>
> *Somebody had to pick the cotton,*
> *Somebody had to pull the corn,*
> *Somebody had to build a great nation,*
> *That's why the Darkie was born.*
> *That's why the Darkie was born.*
>
> *Somebody had to cry at midnight,*
> *Somebody had to weep and moan,*
> *Somebody had to love everybody,*
> *That's why the Darkie was born.*
>
> *Somebody had to go to jail,*
> *Somebody had to walk a picket line,*
> *Somebody had to fight for freedom,*
> *That's why the Darkie was born."*

Shotguns, Cockroaches & Old Jim Crow ~ 1965

The social insanity and petty humiliations of segregation never failed to both shock and infuriate me.

To make it difficult for Klan assassins to target Dr. King, his addresses to Selma mass meetings were always held on short notice with little advance publicity. Some of the more affluent Afro-Americans had telephones, and while kids passed out "King will speak tonight" flyers in the poorer neighborhoods, we made calls to alert people and encourage them to attend. The Selma phone directory made it easy for us to distinguish whites from Blacks. If the name was preceded by "Mr." or "Mrs." we knew the number belonged to a white person. If there was just a name — "Marie Foster" or "Alonzo West," for instance — we knew the number was that of an Afro-American. While it proved very helpful to us, I was astonished at the bigoted, small-minded lengths segregationists — even those working for major companies like "Ma Bell" — would go to reinforce their sense of white superiority.

That April we did a lot of door-to-door canvassing in Black neighborhoods to encourage people to honor the boycott, continue trying to register if they hadn't already done so, and attend the next mass meeting. Unlike Los Angeles or other residentially segregated northern cities, Selma was divided into a patchwork quilt of Black and white areas, some large, others quite small. And while whites in general were much better off economically than Afro-Americans, there were plenty of poor whites living in shacks no different from those of Blacks. Yet in Selma it was easy to tell which race lived where. If the street was paved it had white residents, if it was dusty dirt or gooey mud Afro-Americans lived there. Some streets alternated back and forth, paved and dirt, white and Black. Like the absence of courtesy titles in the phone book, the dirt streets showed us which homes we could safely approach.

Canvassing was hot and tiring. It was also frustrating and depressing. Two things struck me again and again — the constant, all-pervasive fear we encountered and the wretched poverty. Like many other northerners, my most intense memories of being a southern freedom worker were not of Klan violence, mass protests, inspiring oratory, or filthy jail cells, but rather images of devastating, systemic poverty — remembrances of tumbledown sharecropper shacks, children thin to the point of emaciation, and babies so comatose from malnutrition that they had not the energy to brush away the flies drinking the moisture from their suppurating eyes.

After the passage of four decades, I thought I had buried those mental images until TV reports of hurricane Katrina's aftermath in 2005 forcefully reawakened them, reminding me once again that beneath America's celebrated affluence are rural and urban wastelands of human suffering and soul-destroying poverty. And that poverty and economic inequality know no color, there are poor whites just as there are poor nonwhites.

By late April I saw myself as — and was seen by others as — an SCLC volunteer. Not yet a member of the SCLC staff or invited to attend staff meetings, but someone who worked with and took direction from SCLC leaders and organizers like Albert Turner, Dorothy Cotton, Big James Orange, Annell Ponder, and Septima Clark. Turner was Alabama field director for SCLC but unlike most SCLC leaders he was a farmer rather than a preacher. He had built and led the local Freedom Movement in Perry County and was one of the finest leaders I have ever worked with — the kind of guy that people refer to as "salt of the earth," and that Jews like me call a "mensch."

The common practice in Selma at that time was for SCLC and SNCC workers to pair off in two-person teams for canvassing so that each organization was represented and able to share the organizing data we collected. But with so few staff members from either organization left in Selma a lot of that work was being done by volunteers like me. Since I was seen as an SCLC volunteer I was often paired with one of the SNCC workers. One day a Black SNCC guy and I were crossing the railroad tracks at Jefferson Davis Avenue (today it's J.L. Chestnut Boulevard, named after the local civil rights leader and attorney). A car with young white men suddenly pulled up and blocked us. One of them aimed a double-barreled shotgun out the window and shouted, "We're going to kill you niggers!" Without a moment's hesitation the SNCC guy snarled back, "If you're going to do it go ahead and shoot, motherfucker!"

The whites laughed and drove off. Not exactly the kind of nonviolent response I'd been trained to use by CORE and N-VAC — but it worked. We were both a little shaky, though, as we reported back to our respective organizational offices to add the incident to the long list of similar encounters by others.

With spring came warm humid weather — and cockroaches. Apartments all over the Carver Project were infested. They'd crawl on the table while we were eating and over our skin while we were resting. Some were so big you could actually hear the clicking of their legs as they wandered the floor at night. If you turned on the light, you'd see hordes of them scurrying for their hiding places.

Though it was a federal housing project, Carver was totally (and illegally) segregated. All the residents were Black. All the bureaucrats who ran it were white, and they ran it for the benefit of themselves and their white business cronies rather than the residents. The roach infestation was a typical example. They contracted with a pest control company — white-owned, of course, and probably politically connected. But instead of spraying all the apartments in one building to exterminate all the bugs at the same time, they would only treat one apartment and then move on to an apartment in another of the 30 buildings. That way they just drove the roaches back and forth from one set of rooms to the next.

After each spraying there'd be hundreds of dead bugs on the floor in the treated apartment. We'd sweep them up in a mound three or four inches high and dump them in the trash, but within a day or two they'd be back as plentiful as before. The exterminator company had crews working the project full time, five days a week — paid for by tenant rents — but with no noticeable long-term effect.

And no matter how many times the Black residents complained and argued for killing all the roaches in a building at once, the white managers refused to alter their one-apartment-per-building-at-a-time schedule because it was so profitable for the exterminator company. They knew that if all roaches in an entire building were exterminated at the same time they wouldn't repopulate so fast and the need for exterminator services would noticeably drop. Profits would go down.

When Afro-American residents complained they were ignored. When Movement organizers asked a white reporter inquire, I was told that the managers responded with, "You know how dirty those coloreds are, they don't mind roaches — they like 'em."

In May, word came down from SCLC headquarters in Atlanta that their next big effort would be a multi-state, summer-long, voter registration project called Summer Community Organization & Political Education (SCOPE). In some ways it would be similar to the Mississippi Freedom Summer of the previous year that had been organized by SNCC and CORE. But since the Johnson administration had promised that the Voting Rights Act would be passed by June, it was expected that SCLC's project would actually be able to register large numbers of Afro-American voters in six southern states — enough, perhaps, to influence the 1966 mid-term elections.

SCLC leaders working on that project asked me to join the SCOPE staff and travel to northern campuses to recruit student volunteers. I thanked them but declined. In conversations with other civil rights workers over the years, I've noticed that most of us, particularly those from the North, sort of fell in love with the first southern community we worked in for any length of time. Certainly that was true for me and Selma — I didn't want to leave and return to the North. I was committed to staying in the South, on staff if possible, as a volunteer if not.

Between a Rock and a Hard Place ~ 1965

After the March to Montgomery, SCLC leaders returned to Atlanta, only occasionally showing up to speak at mass meetings, SNCC's focus and attention shifted to Lowndes County, and most of the field staff of the two organizations were now working the surrounding Black Belt counties rather than Selma. Which meant that the Dallas County Voters League (DCVL) was left to fend for itself just at a time when it needed experienced, national-level support to address a new and unanticipated crisis.

Large amounts of food and clothing had been sent to Selma by Movement supporters in the North — a generous impulse that could have strengthened the Movement and solidified the local organization. But no structure or a plan was in place for how to handle and distribute the unexpected windfall. Neither SCLC nor SNCC were paying much attention to Selma, nor were they providing insight or offering advice learned from similar situations in Greenwood, Birmingham, St. Augustine, and elsewhere.

After the March to Montgomery ended, the Medical Committee for Human Rights dismantled their aid station in the basement of First Baptist Church, which was then used to store the goods arriving from the North. The cartons and boxes filling the basement looked like a huge trove, but compared to the needs and hopes of tens of thousands of impoverished Afro-Americans it didn't amount to even a drop in a bucket. What appeared to be a horn of plenty was actually a form of scarcity, because almost everyone, regardless of income level, wanted a share of the bounty. Yet there was nowhere near enough to go around — not even close.

Those who had been most active in the struggle, the men and women who had been beaten and gassed, those who had gone to jail and risked their homes and livelihoods, argued that they deserved the rewards their courage and sacrifice had sowed. On the other hand, those who were most impoverished felt that the bulk of the largesse should go to them because their need was greatest. But precisely because their economic situation was most precarious — and for the most part they were the least educated — they had been less active than others in the protests and few had dared white retaliation by trying to register to vote.

And some Afro-American ministers — including some who had not participated at all in the struggle — asserted that they were the acknowledged community leaders with a long tradition of providing aid and assistance to those in need, so distribution of the windfall goods should be placed in their hands. Their assertion was not met with universal agreement. Many people were convinced that the preachers would skim the cream for themselves and use the remainder to reward favored parishioners who supported them in their church's internal politics, leaving both Movement activists *and* the poorest of the poor out in the cold.

By early May the March to Montgomery unity that had bound together Selma's Afro-American community was being torn apart by bitter acrimony over who was getting what from the donated food and clothing and who controlled its distribution. Angry accusations that the best items were disappearing into the hands of persons unknown began to be hurled — everyone had their suspicions and many had little hesitation about pointing fingers.

Thankfully I was not personally involved in any of that, but I heard disheartening tales of furious arguments, fist fights, and even people being threatened with guns over the supposed treasure in the church basement. Even worse, rumors were spreading that donated funds were unaccounted for or misappropriated. Eventually legal charges were brought against some community leaders and activists for embezzlement and malfeasance. A sad and tragic denouement to what had been one of the widest, deepest, and most courageous local movements of the entire freedom struggle.

Around this time I received a letter from Los Angeles informing me that Michael Robinson had been killed. Mike, a Black man about my age, had been an N-VAC stalwart one of the group's key members. He had always been at the forefront of our sit-ins, shop-ins, and picket lines, and had then gone South to work with CORE in northern Louisiana at around the time I came to Selma.

His death was never fully explained nor adequately investigated. All that CORE could learn was that he had been driving at night on a rural highway, something happened, there was supposedly an "accident," and he was dead. No other cars were reported involved, and I was told that the passenger riding with him was completely unharmed but wouldn't talk about it. She refused to say anything to anybody. We all figured the most likely explanation was that Mike had been run off the road by the Klan and beaten to death, and that the killers had terrorized his passenger into remaining silent by threatening her or her family.

Mike's death shook me. As with Mrs. Liuzzo's murder, I was filled with rage, sadness, and loss. Frustration — from the certain knowledge that here was yet another murder that the racists were going to get away with — etched deep into my soul. And, of course, it intensified my own fear, because I knew that the same thing could happen to me — any time, any where, so long as I was a civil rights worker in the Deep South.

On the Streets of Selma ~ 1965

During that time, Freedom Movement offices were in an old shabby three-story brick building on the corner of Alabama and Franklin streets. On the ground floor was an Afro-American funeral home, on the second floor the SCLC office, and on the third the SNCC office. Directly across the street was a newer three-story structure of yellow brick and white stone. On its street level were City Hall and the police station, above were the Selma and Dallas County jails. You could look from the windows of the Movement offices into those of law enforcement and vice versa. We were literally across the street from each other — though hardly friendly neighbors.

With Selma's Black community dividing against itself over the donated food and clothing, the boycott of white-owned stores was beginning to weaken. Support for the boycott was urged in mass meetings, Sunday sermons, and door-to-door canvassing, but that was no longer enough to sustain it. Boycotting sounds easy — just don't shop somewhere — but Afro-Americans had been shut out of the merchant economy for so long that there were few Black-owned alternatives. A handful of small mom-and-pop stores in the Afro-American community tried to carry the load, but they were systematically overcharged for their goods by the white wholesalers who supplied them, which meant they had to set their prices higher than the larger and better-stocked white-owned stores. As a practical matter, supporting the boycott meant either paying higher prices or traveling 55 miles to Montgomery for supplies and necessities. Few Dallas County Blacks owned cars, and gas was expensive for people living below the poverty line, so honoring the boycott was hard.

Early in May we began passing out leaflets and small-scale picketing to reinforce the boycott. Regardless of what the U.S. Constitution might say about freedom of speech, in Alabama asking people to boycott a store was illegal. In Selma, handing out flyers or picketing were grounds for immediate arrest on spurious changes of "disturbing the peace," or some other trumped-up excuse. Yet though it meant certain arrest, direct action was the best way to publicize and strengthen the boycott. Not only did it get people's attention, the presence of cops and the inevitable disruption and turmoil in the street deterred both Afro-Americans *and* whites from coming downtown to shop.

On Friday May 7th, I and a local kid were handed a small stack of boycott leaflets and told to give them to customers entering the liquor store next door to the SCLC/SNCC offices. This was a state-owned "ABC" outlet run by the Alabama Beverage Control department. I was surprised to learn that socially conservative Alabama was (and still is) in the retail booze business, but as the old saying goes, "Money talks, bullshit walks."

Of course, we knew we would be arrested as soon as we were spotted, and since the store was across the street from the police station, that wouldn't take long. It was also, I assumed, a kind of test by SCLC to see if I was willing to face arrest and how I would handle it.

Sure enough, a minute or two after we started handing out our flyers, Lieutenant "Cotton" Nichols, second in command of the Selma police force, strode across the street and placed me under arrest on charges of disorderly conduct, disturbing the peace, and conspiracy to encourage a boycott. Off to jail I went. The local kid managed to escape around the corner while Nichols focused his attention on me.

Like all white freedom riders, I greatly feared being placed in a cell with hostile white prisoners eager to curry favor with the guards by beating the crap out of me. So I was relieved to be thrown into the large holding tank for "Colored" men which already contained others arrested on various protesting and boycotting charges. It was a big, dimly lit cell. I don't recall any windows at all and only a few feeble lights. The bars were painted red and the walls some kind of cream color but they were so dark and grimy it was hard to tell. The steel beds had been stripped of their mattresses, the toilet was overflowing, and the stench was overwhelming. Our spirits, however, were high. We sang freedom songs, talked, and welcomed in other fresh-caught "fish" as they were captured and incarcerated.

SCLC was still flush with cash from all the donations that had poured in after Bloody Sunday, and rather than go through a trial and appeal process before white judges and all-white juries, they simply paid my $17 fine (equal to about $130 in 2018). I was released the next day.

Meanwhile dissension and conflict over the donated food and clothing was getting worse. Community solidarity was fracturing and the boycott faltering. DCVL leader Rev. Reese was often out of town speaking and raising funds, the main SCLC leaders were usually elsewhere, and SNCC's attention was focused on Lowndes County. It was clear that something dramatic had to be done to prevent the boycott from completely falling apart, so the local leaders called for a large-scale picketing effort. Saturday was the big shopping day. That's when rural Afro-Americans came into town, some in cars or pickups, a few in horse-drawn wagons or on foot. (All Selma stores, of course, were closed on Sunday for the Sabbath.)

Albert Turner was SCLC's field director for Alabama and he knew about my CORE background. I later learned he had written to L.A. CORE to check me out. With most of the SCLC field staff either working in the outlying counties or recruiting for SCOPE up North, he asked me to organize and coordinate the picketing. Okay, that I knew how to do.

I wasn't responsible for mobilizing and recruiting the protesters. The local student leaders handled that, yet it wasn't easy even for them. Most of the high school and college-age students who had been the backbone of the mass protests in January and February were awaiting trial on multiple arrests, and some had been told by their parents not to get busted again until they saw what the outcome was on the previous charges. There were, however, junior high kids who had been kept out of the February marches by their parents because of the danger. Now that it was a little safer their parents were less opposed, and the younger kids were eager to finally protest and show their defiance of segregation and Sheriff Clark.

My job was getting the boycott flyers printed in Montgomery (there were no Black printers in Selma), conducting nonviolent training sessions for the those who were not already experienced protesters, planning strategy and tactics, and coordinating the action.

Using the same approach and format as with the N-VAC training sessions I had run for Bruin CORE, I held my first nonviolent training session in the Movement offices at Alabama and Franklin. There was a large room up on the third floor with an old, warped wooden floor. About a dozen Afro-American kids attended, mostly between 13 and 16 years old, two-thirds of them girls. All went well until we got to the part where I demonstrated how to handle being hit. While the other kids watched, I asked Margaret Griffen to slug me. She was maybe 14 or 15, stood about five foot three, and weighed less than 100 pounds. It had always been quite hard to get the UCLA students to actually strike me (or each other) with any real strength, so as I was in the habit of doing I urged Margaret to "hit me hard."

She looked puzzled. "Are you sure?"

"Yes, yes, don't hold back. And keep on hitting me."

A huge grin lit up her face. She hauled off and slugged me so hard in the chest I was knocked on my butt and slid across the rough wooden boards, scraping my back and leaving a small scar that I bear to this day. I quickly curled up in the nonviolent protection position while she kicked and pummeled me with great enthusiasm. By now, everyone was laughing — including me. Except for that scrape and a bruise or two, I wasn't hurt. Then they all practiced on each other. In subsequent training sessions afterwards, however, I never made such a big deal about urging the students to "hit me hard."

To be seen on a Selma street carrying a protest sign — even if under your arm or with the lettering concealed — was grounds for instant arrest. We wanted all the arrests and turmoil to take place in the downtown shopping district rather than on the way from Brown Chapel, so well after dark on Friday night we stashed our supply of picket signs in the back of Walkers Cafe on Washington Street and in the empty coffins of the funeral home on the ground floor of the Movement offices at Alabama and Franklin.

On Saturday morning about 50 or 60 protesters gathered in the church. I formed them into teams of half a dozen or so, each led by an experienced captain. The first team was led by a 16-year old girl. They left at mid-morning, casually sauntering into the downtown area in twos and threes, then picking up their signs at the funeral home. When they were all assembled they stepped out on Franklin together with their signs held high. They got almost the full block to Water Avenue before being busted. Every half hour or 45 minutes thereafter, a new team would leave the funeral home or Walkers Cafe and picket as far as they could get before being arrested. The cops scurried around trying to figure out where the pickets were coming from so they could seize the signs. They finally found the stash at Walkers, but though they checked the funeral home it didn't occur to them to look in the empty coffins.

By early afternoon we were down to the last few protesters and almost out of signs. I joined the last team from the funeral home. Only a couple of us had signs, so the rest of us just clapped and sang freedom songs. I guess the cops were tired because we got almost to Broad Street before we were arrested. The cops marched us down the middle of Alabama Street back past the funeral home to the jail.

Close to 75 of us had been arrested over the course of the day. Almost half were under 16 and two-thirds were girls. Their courage was inspiring. When the booking sergeant asked a girl what her name was she insisted on using "Miss" before her name in utter defiance of Jim Crow custom. The cops hit her with their fists and kicked her when she fell to the floor, but she refused to give in, insisting on using her courtesy title. She couldn't have been older than 15. All the kids booked after her also referred to themselves as "Miss," and "Mister" to the obvious frustrated fury of the cops.

Again I was put in the Colored holding tank, which was way too small for the 30 or so male protesters plus the regular prisoners, most of whom had been arrested on Friday night for possession of moonshine or being drunk in public. We were singing our freedom songs, preaching to each other, and defiantly celebrating our protest and arrest with humor and wisecracks. We could hear the girls singing in a nearby cell but we couldn't see them.

One of our favorite jokes was that sooner or later someone newly arrested for the first time would be shoved into the crowded cell and would inevitably ask, "How long do you think we'll be in here?"

A veteran of the cage would reply, "Well, what did you say your name was, again?"

When the new fish answered, the old hand nodded wisely and said, "Oh, yeah, you're on the B-list."

"The B-list? What's the B-list?"

And then everyone would shout, "You're going to beeeeee here for a looooong time!" We all thought that was hilariously funny.

Three middle-aged Black women were in an adjacent cell and we could speak with them through the bars. They were from Bogue Chitto, a little district way out in the deep rural of Dallas County. I don't recall if they had been arrested on the voter registration line at the courthouse on Friday or in a boycott action that morning, but I remember them telling me that to participate in the Freedom Movement they'd walked almost 20 miles to Selma. They weren't boastful, but they showed a kind of quiet and serene pride in having done their part for freedom.

By the next day we had all been released on bond. I never heard how that arrest was resolved, whether SCLC paid a fine or if the case was removed to federal court under the Civil Rights Act of 1957 and eventually dropped, as happened with many other southern civil rights cases.

[While the Civil Rights Act of 1957 was largely a toothless sham, it did contain an important provision allowing the Justice Department to block state and local prosecution of people who were arrested for activities connected to voting rights. Under that provision, arrests of civil rights activists on minor charges by local police could be transferred to federal court and eventually dismissed if the federal judge determined that the arrest was part of a pattern of police conduct intended to suppress voting rights and interfere with voter registration. Because the boycott was an aspect of the Selma voting right campaign, arrests for leafletting and picketing might have been set aside by federal court without our having to stand trial.]

I coordinated three more Saturday picket actions, though Turner ordered me not to get arrested myself. Despite our efforts though, by early June the boycott had essentially collapsed, largely because of dissension and conflict over the donated food. So far as I know, it was never formally called off, but as fewer and fewer people honored it, it ceased having any economic effect on the white merchants.

Behind the 8-Ball ~ 1954

I was ten years old in 1954 and that must have been a hard year for my parents — in part I suppose because of me, though not, I maintain, through any fault of my own.

That year my father was subpoenaed to appear before one of the Red Scare witch hunt committees, and both he and my mother resigned (or were expelled) from the Communist Party. Two events which had to have been traumatic for them. Not only were they under attack by the state and a hostile mass media, but the political organization they had devoted their lives to had turned against them (or they against it).

To the extent they could, my parents shielded my brother and me from the full impact and danger of that subpoena, committee hearing, and media attack. And they entirely concealed their traumatic break with the CP. I could sense, though, that something terrible was happening, but I didn't know what it was — and yet I did know I wasn't supposed to ask. Later, after I was grown, my parents were still reticent about Party matters, so I've had to piece this story together from little bits and snippets. As such, I can't vouch for its detailed accuracy, but in general it echoes experiences relayed to me by other red diaper babies of my era.

My mother and father joined the CP in the 1930s and it quickly became the center of their working and social lives. The political work they cared so passionately about was shaped and commanded by the Party and all their friends were fellow CP members. Party activities filled every hour of every day. Of all the luxuries they sacrificed on the Party altar, free time that could have been spent with family was surely the most precious.

The Party was rigidly hierarchal. It functioned like a military unit, with obedience to authority and orders the prime directive. The political and social behavior of members were guided, judged, and, if the Party felt it necessary, corrected by those in power over them. In many ways — far more than most members would care to admit — it was like being in an authoritarian cult.

My parents voluntarily submitted themselves to Party discipline because they believed in social justice and were determined to fight for it however they could. All around them were the ravages of the Great Depression of the 1930s: a quarter of the workforce unemployed, eating in breadlines or begging for scraps. Those lucky enough to keep their jobs were ruthlessly exploited, their wages cut and then cut again. Relief and reforms of any kind were furiously opposed and blocked by the nation's corporate elite — those who Roosevelt referred to as "economic royalists."

Government at all levels deferred to and defended the interests of wealth and property and ruthlessly suppressed anyone who dared call for change. My mom and dad were convinced that only through the absolute unity and fierce discipline of the Communist Party could progressive changes be achieved against the adamant and often violent opposition of the rich and the powerful.

They believed they were revolutionaries dedicated to overthrowing capitalism and *bourgeois democracy,* and replacing them with socialism and true *proletarian democracy.* But in actual fact, their work was entirely reformist — building trade unions, fighting for unemployment insurance and social security, opposing segregation and lynching, and campaigning to elect candidates to office in the established government — "revolutionary" in rhetoric, but reformist in reality.

Yet in a broader sense, they truly were *revolutionaries* insofar as the reforms they fought for amounted to a *social* revolution against laissez-faire, Darwinian capitalism. In that same sense, our ending Jim Crow segregation and overthrowing the southern way of life in the 1960s was also a social revolution — though not a political or economic one. As was woman's suffrage in its time and women's liberation later in our time. There's a huge difference, of course, between political revolutions that violently overthrow governments and economic systems and reforms that achieve social revolutions in how people live, behave, and treat each other. My parents thought they were engaged in the former, when in fact they were successfully achieving the latter.

My dad and mom were also passionate American patriots and true-believers in *We hold these truths to be self-evident...* and *Government of the people, by the people, for the people.* They were deeply committed to the premise that in a democracy citizens had not only a right but a duty to stand up and criticize government officials when they were wrong, and to speak truth to power regardless of personal consequences — would that we had more such heroes today.

Like my parents, most of the other CP members I encountered as a child and later as an activist myself were good and decent people who sought peace, justice and equality. Sadly, the Party to which they dedicated their lives proved unworthy of them. It was rigid, bureaucratic, and riddled with hacks, careerists, FBI provocateurs, and paid disrupters. And from all I've read and studied, those who charged that the Party leadership's overriding commitment and loyalty was to the national interests of the Soviet Union rather than to American working people were essentially correct. Though it took my parents a long time to see those faults, by the 1950s it was getting harder and harder for them to ignore painful realities.

Many years later I was talking to one of our close family friends from that era — the "Bruce" after whom I am named — and I asked him why *he* had left the Party. Like my parents, he too was reticent. All he said was, "I got tired of being brought up on charges by people who later turned out to be FBI agents and stool pigeons." ("Stool pigeon" was lefty slang for snitches and provocateurs.)

The Party had its own internal discipline process and it was not uncommon for members to be *brought up on charges* for violating rules, policies, or political directives. Since they had no jail cells or execution chambers, and members were already tithing all the dough they could spare, the only real punishment the CP could impose was suspension or expulsion. But from their point of view that was counterproductive because they wanted to make it *hard* for members to leave, not easy. So what they did was criticize and harangue and inflict painful mental manipulations until the penitent member admitted guilt, abjectly groveled in shame, and vowed to correct whatever crime or error it was. Such *criticism self-criticism* sessions were always unpleasant and often psychologically brutal.

As a white Southerner in an organization dedicated to combating racial discrimination, my father was particularly vulnerable to suspicion on phony charges of "racism." One time he was brought up on charges for using the phrase *behind the eight ball* to criticize some tactical ploy put forward by someone higher up in the Party. *Behind the eight ball* was a common pool hall phrase for a bad tactical position, but he was charged with racism because the eight ball is black and somehow the CP boss managed to construe his comment as disparaging to Afro-Americans. Another time he brought a watermelon to a workers picnic in Arroyo Seco Park and was charged with racism for *insulting our Negro comrades*. Both times he had to publicly confess his guilt, humbly apologize, and vow never to repeat his reprehensible behavior.

Though I didn't know it at the time and didn't learn of it till years later, as it turned out I was the cause of my parents leaving (or being expelled from) the Party. As I mentioned before, I was a loner, preferring to read in my room rather than play with the hostile neighbor kids. For all of her charisma and political leadership skills, my mom was a world-class worrywart (my dad's term) and my lack of a "normal" social life caused her great anxiety. She feared that my social withdrawal was caused by the Red-baiting being inflicted on our family, which to some degree was true. So she was wracked with guilt. (Had there been a University of Jewish Motherhood, she would have taught the masters class in self-blame and guilt.)

So she decided that I needed professional help from a child psychologist. It was, however, against CP rules for members *or their children* to seek any form of psychiatric help. The Party prided itself on its modern thinking, so the "no-shrink" edict wasn't from any ideological opposition to psychotherapy. It was rather a security measure, because what was told to a therapist might be reported to the FBI. And given the anti-Red hysteria of the witch hunt era, that fear was not far-fetched.

As it happened though, Dr. "K" was one of the best child psychologists in L.A., and he was not only a CP member but he belonged to the same Party unit as my parents. They often met in our living room and any secret that I might have inadvertently acquired he already knew about in specific detail. So obviously there was no security risk in him treating me.

But I didn't want to go to no psychologist. Not out of any loyalty to a Party policy of which I was wholly ignorant, I just thought it was stupid, insulting, and demeaning — I liked reading in my room and I didn't consider it either "abnormal" or a "problem." Neither did my dad, but Mom's anxieties and guilt could not be assuaged. So to gain my acquiescence she bribed me. The shrink agreed that during each session he'd walk with me to the corner drugstore and buy me a comic book (by that time my interests had evolved beyond Donald Duck and Batman to the *Classics Illustrated* series). All right, granted, I sold out for a pretty low price, but how much can you get for betraying your principles when you're just 10 years old?

When the Party discovered I was being treated by Dr. "K," my mother's district leader called her to account for violating the "no psychology" edict. That the therapist in question was already privy to CP secrets was irrelevant — a rule was a rule. I'll give my mom her due, she didn't flinch. As she later wrote, she told them, "I think this policy is outrageous but if that's the way the Party thinks, then I am no longer a member." When she told my dad, he didn't hesitate a second. Between the Party and Mom there was no contest.

In the CP's self-contained world, however, no one was ever allowed to resign, they were *always* "expelled" for ideological heresy, disruption, indiscipline or some other face-saving charge that the apparatchiks ginned up. What other Party members were told about my parents' abrupt separation I never knew, but many of those who had been family friends before remained so afterwards, so I guess that by the mid-50s resignations were so common that few members believed the "expulsion" bullshit.

Still, it was a wrenching and agonizing experience for both of them. For two decades the Party had been the center of their lives, they'd fought for it, endured persecution because of it, and sacrificed the best years of their lives in its name — and now they were out. Out! Out! Out! Looking back on it now, I realize that while my father took leaving the Party more or less in stride, my mother became quite depressed and bitter. She once likened it to a Catholic being excommunicated from the church, saying that at times she felt "so drained I couldn't even cry."

The thing is, though, I've come to believe that they didn't really leave because of me — or at least not entirely so. The CP's idiocy around my unwanted child psychologist was just the final straw. For years my parents had been reluctantly adhering to and rationalizing political positions they disagreed with, obeying commands that made little practical sense or were actively repugnant, and pretending they didn't see the organization's increasing isolation, dysfunction, and irrelevance. So they were ready to leave, even if they didn't know it until the Party in its bureaucratic stupidity gave them the push they needed.

As for me, other than increasing my collection of comic books the child psychologist had no effect whatsoever, at least so far as I could see. To Mom's continued distress (though not mine), I remained a loner with a limited social life — which is pretty much still the case today, though now I write as well as read.

Jim Clark and the Commie Kike ~ 1965

On Monday, May 17, the juveniles arrested the previous Saturday were appearing in court. Since I had sent them out to picket, I thought I should be there to support them. As soon as I entered the courtroom the judge furiously ordered me out and the bailiff shoved me into the hall.

I didn't know what to do. Go back inside as a defiant protest or wait outside in the hallway while the kids who had been arrested on the action I coordinated were berated and, for all I knew, sentenced to juvenile jail?

Being young, brash, and not too bright, I went back in. Before I could even sit down, the judge ordered me arrested on charges of contributing to the delinquency of minors — a serious felony.

The courthouse was three blocks from the county jail and Sheriff Clark was pleased to haul me off. As he shoved me into the back seat of his car he called me a "communist."

Still operating in brash and stupid mode, I answered, "Communist? What do you mean? What's a communist?"

Clark wasn't stumped at all, he knew the answer right off. "A communist is any God Damned New York kike that wants our nigrahs to vote!"

Well, except for the fact that I was from Los Angeles he had me dead to rights. If he wanted to define "communist" as someone who thought that American citizens had a right to vote, who was I to argue? I thought he was giving communists more credit than they deserved, since by that time I was pretty down on the Communist Party. I considered them nothing more than a bunch of liberal do-nothings. And I still resented the way they had treated my parents. But even in brash and stupid mode I knew that wasn't a discussion I wanted to have with Sheriff Jim Clark of Selma, Alabama.

I was booked and incarcerated in the Dallas County Jail, which was bigger, brighter, and cleaner than the Selma city jail. On the downside, though, Clark threw me into a 9x9-foot cell with a white prisoner, saying, "Here's one of them race-mixing nigger-lovers. Why don't you two get acquainted?"

Well, that made the agenda clear. The other prisoner was a big husky guy, taller than me and in good physical shape. As soon as Clark walked away and before I had time to feel much fear he clobbered me. I curled up in my nonviolent defensive ball, making sure to get my back up against the bars so he couldn't kick me in the kidneys. He proceeded to kick me in the shins and my arms, which were protecting my head, to stomp on my ribs, and to punch me wherever he could reach.

After a while, though, he got tired and stopped. I had never quite realized it before, but beating up on someone is hard work. That's probably one reason why professional boxers only fight for three minutes before they get a rest break. I was hurting and bruised, my ribs were sore, and I had some bloody scrapes on my bare arms, but I wasn't really injured in any serious way.

I remained sitting on the floor with my back against the bars in case he decided to go a second round, but instead he sat down next to me. I offered him a smoke. He was out of cigs, so he thanked me and lit up.

As it happened, I didn't smoke tobacco. I never cared for it. And, of course, I never touched pot while I was in the South because it was way too dangerous — if I'd been caught it would have meant a long prison sentence for sure. But like most southern civil rights workers I was in the habit of always being ready for an unexpected arrest, which meant hiding some notepaper and the flexible cartridge of a ballpoint pen in the lining of my jacket and always carrying a pack of Camels or Lucky Strikes to offer other inmates in case I ended up in the slammer — as had just happened.

Another reason even us non-smokers carried cigs was that while driving around the rural areas we would often come across chain gangs of Black prisoners doing roadwork. It was considered a mark of activist professionalism to drop a few smokes out the car window — out of sight of the white guards — as we slowed down to pass them by.

Anyway, there we were, two guys in the same jail cell. He didn't like me or what I stood for — and vice versa — but he'd clearly been in jail for some time and I guess he was lonely. Since we had nothing else to do, we started to talk. He asked me was I really a "nigger-lover" and all the usual crap. Though I was circumspect in my answers and careful not to allow any anger-feedback dynamic to get started, I didn't deny who I was, why I was in Selma, or who I worked for.

He asked me if I had marched in Camden. I told him I had, and out of the blue he asked, "Did you see me?"

"What do you mean?"

"I was in the posse, I was there on my horse." He left unsaid the *beating the shit out of you* part, but we both understood his subtext. He went on to explain that he was a member of Clark's posse.

"But Clark's posse is for Dallas County, what were you doing in Wilcox County?" "Oh, when Sheriff Clark tells you to go, you gotta go."

Yes, I thought to myself — but didn't say — like a feudal baron's armed retainer you're sent to suppress rebellious peons wherever they might be.

"Well, if you're a posseman, why are you in jail?"

So he had this long involved story, the details of which I don't remember. He thought he had been arrested for some crime — burglary or robbery or some such — but he didn't actually know what the charges against him were. He assured me, though, that he hadn't done whatever it was, and that he was being framed.

"You don't know the charges against you?"

He didn't. He'd been in jail for more than a week without, he claimed, anyone officially telling him what crimes he was being held for.

"Well, what does your lawyer say?"

He told me he hadn't been allowed to talk a lawyer or, for that matter, to his family, though they knew he was in jail because they had sent him some smokes a few days earlier.

He had a theory though. He had done something that pissed off Clark — he wouldn't tell me what — and that was why he was being held.

What amazed me was that he didn't seem to feel there was anything unusual about his treatment. He took it as the normal course of events — he'd pissed off Clark and Clark had thrown him in jail out of pique. He didn't like being incarcerated, but he didn't seem to resent being held incommunicado without charges and no bail. His attitude was that eventually Clark would get over being mad at him for whatever it was and he'd be let out. Just another aspect of the southern way of life. A classic case of a feudal thinking, I concluded (but didn't mention to him).

So we sat there talking until sometime in the late afternoon this kid came walking down the aisle between the rows of cells. He was maybe 10 or 11 and obese like Porky Pig. I mean corpulent, his eyes were like raisons set deep in a doughy face. He saw us in the cell and started taunting us. "Nyaaa, nyaaa you're in jail. Jailbirds, jailbirds." And then he began throwing stuff at us, cigarette butts and wadded up toilet paper and whatever he could find. After a minute or two, a pudgy little girl joined him. She was maybe 7 or 8, and they both taunted us.

"Who are they?" I asked posse guy.

"Oh, they're Sheriff Clark's kids. He knows the niggers are out to get him — and his kids too — so they live in a cell down the hall."

I kid you not. Clark was literally raising his kids in the county jail. They had a cell of their own and though their door obviously wasn't locked they were, in a sense, prisoners too. After dinner we could hear them watching TV, squabbling, and playing. Clark was so paranoid he wouldn't let them go outside unless they were accompanied by an armed deputy to guard them at all times. Their playground was the aisle between the cell rows. I don't know where their mother was, I never saw her or heard a woman's voice.

Normally I like kids, but those two were something else. Years later, I read the *Harry Potter* novels, and the obnoxious cousin he had to live with during the summer brought those two brats back to mind.

Speaking of dinner, the food was utterly vile. Half-cooked lima beans crusted with what seemed to be some kind of chemical, bitter coffee, and slices of white Wonder Bread. I couldn't eat it that first night, nor breakfast the next morning, though eventually hunger compelled me to choke down lunch.

Later, I learned that the common practice was for the state and county to provide the sheriff a small amount of money for each inmate's food. He could spend it as he saw fit to feed his prisoners, and whatever was left over went into his pocket — the less he spent on feeding us, the more he made for himself.

And in many counties the sheriff was actually paid like a for-profit business rather than a public official. In addition to any salary he might receive, he was paid a fee for every arrest, for each court document served, prisoner transferred, and so on. Even better, he was entitled to a share of all criminal and traffic fines. The more people he or his deputies arrested or issued tickets to, the more money he made. Of course, if he was too aggressive he might be voted out of office. But since Afro-Americans weren't allowed to vote, they were easy prey and his personal cash cow. Which helped to explain why Clark and other southern sheriffs were so ferociously opposed to Afro-Americans getting the vote.

Using the pen cartridge and notepaper hidden in my denim jacket I wrote a note to the SCLC office across the street, letting them know where I was being held. One of the Black prisoners was a trustee allowed to go outside on errands for the guards and deputies. I snuck the note to him when posse guy wasn't looking and he passed it on and relayed a response back for me. For some reason it took SCLC a couple of days to arrange my release. I guess the judge, or maybe Sheriff Clark, were delaying matters. After I was released, I never heard anything more about that arrest either, so I suppose charges were eventually dismissed through federal intervention.

A University Without Books ~ 1965

There were two tiny private Black colleges in Selma: Concordia College of Alabama, run by the Lutheran Church, and the Baptist-run Selma University. Neither had more than a few hundred Afro-American students. In 1965, Selma University (SU) was a "university" in name only, it was not accredited, offered no degrees recognized by the general academic establishment, and its educational program was focused on "Christian training" for a pre-*Brown* social milieu of accommodation to Jim Crow. SU students sarcastically described its academic level as roughly equivalent to that of a white junior high school. Its social structure was autocratic, manipulative, and rigidly controlling — with an intense focus on ensuring that female students remained virgin until suitably married to a "proper" husband.

Beholden to white patrons for its funding, SU's Afro-American administrators and faculty publicly opposed the Selma Freedom Movement and the voting rights campaign as "un-Christian." Students who participated in protests or who worked with civil rights organizations were first disciplined and then if they persisted were expelled on phony pretexts. Despite the risk, some students and ex-students were active in protests, and after the March to Montgomery they began clandestinely circulating petitions and newsletters criticizing the SU administration and advocating reforms. Those who were caught were suspended or dismissed.

In addition to the food and clothing donated by Movement supporters in the North after "Bloody Sunday," thousands of books ranging from college texts to modern best-sellers were also sent. But Selma had no Afro-American community center to make use of them and despite the Civil Rights Act the public library was still, for all practical purposes, white-only. Chuck Bonner, a Selma student leader, SNCC worker, and former SU student who had been expelled for participating in the protests, proposed that the books be given to SU, which had recently constructed a new library building for which they had practically no books — 90% of the shelves were empty. In a sense, the new library could be seen as a metaphor for SU itself, an impressive building without content.

Fearing that accepting the books might be interpreted by whites as support for the Civil Rights Movement, the Black president of SU rejected Chuck's offer. SU students appealed his decision to the Board of Trustees. In late April, Chuck, I, and several others snuck in to eavesdrop on the trustee discussion — the door to the room where they were meeting had been left open and we quietly lurked just out of sight in the hallway.

Almost all of the trustees were opposed to adding the donated materials to their empty library, partly for fear of antagonizing whites, but even more so because they felt it their duty to protect their students from whatever dangerous notions and radical un-Christian ideas might lurk in northern textbooks and reading materials.

Since the trustees didn't know we were listening, they had no idea they were teaching me an important lesson that I needed to understand if I was to be an effective civil rights worker in the South. White activists like me existed in a kind of political bubble because Afro-Americans who opposed the Freedom Movement — either out of fear or sincere belief — carefully avoided contact with us. So we rarely encountered Black opponents of the Freedom Movement and most of the time we interacted only with Afro-American supporters. Today, everyone automatically assumes that back in the '60s *all* Afro-Americans enthusiastically supported Dr. King and the freedom struggle as a matter of course — but in reality that was not the case, which the SU trustees unwittingly made plain to me.

The donated books rejected by SU were later used to establish the Selma Freedom Library, which eventually grew to around 18,000 volumes. For a while, it was one of the largest libraries in western Alabama.

Yale University, Meet My Dad ~ 1962

Speaking of universities, in late 1962 my father was hired as the business manager of Yale University's Biology Department.

The '50s had been rough for my parents, both politically and economically. Unions purged their ranks of "Reds" and both my father and mother were fired from the organizing jobs they'd held since the 1930s. Ken found work as the manager of the Community Medical Center (CMC), a nonprofit health plan for union members. Back then group health plans were a radical idea, and the American Medical Association launched a crusade against "socialized medicine" which forced CMC to shut down.

Even after my parents left the Party in 1954, in its anti-communist zeal the FBI pursued them from job to job, informing employers they were harboring *known subversives*. The business association where my mom worked demanded she sign an *Are you now or have you ever been...* loyalty oath, which she could not do without perjuring herself. The toy store she later worked at as a secretary quickly fired her after a visit from the feebs. And so it went, sooner or later the FBI would show up to have a word with whomever hired them and they would be out on the street. Nevertheless, no matter how tight our finances were, both Dad and Mom regularly sent $25 a month (equal to $230 in 2018) to their own mothers to eke out their small social security benefits.

So Mom set herself up as a freelance bookkeeper operating out of a little home office in our den. She also found occasional acting work in film and TV under the stage name Lori Ford. The entertainment unions were still strong in the '50s so even work as a non-speaking "extra" paid a minimum of $32 a day (equal to $300 in 2018). And you got a lot more if you landed even a tiny speaking part. My brother and I also began working as child actors and that also brought in some much-needed dough. I loved those movie jobs, I got to skip school and being on the set was endlessly fascinating. Being around movie stars held no interest for me at all, but I loved exploring the sets and back lots. Once I reached my mid-teens, however, it all dried up because experienced adult actors in their 20s could play 16- and 17-year-olds, so they didn't need child actors and all the additional health and safety regulations that applied to us.

When finding a job proved impossible for my father, he tried to earn a living by remodeling and modernizing homes under the name NuMode Kitchens. He was a skilled carpenter, mechanic, and handyman, and he did great work, but his years as a socialist radical and nonprofit foundation manager left him ill-prepared for profit-making. Nor did the experience and skills that made him a successful organizer serve him well in the business world. Ken viewed his clients as potential friends rather than lucrative prey, so he didn't charge enough and he didn't cut corners. So as a family we barely limped along on an economic shoestring.

Then in 1962 an old friend who had known my parents in California offered Ken the job at Yale. The salary was good, way higher than anything he'd ever earned, but with the FBI dogging them at every step, pulling up stakes and moving across the country from L.A. to New Haven was a huge risk. So my dad went to check it out and make sure that Yale knew in advance about his background before they hired him. He returned and assured us (particularly Mom) that the offer was solid. I expressed skepticism. "Come on, are you kidding? Yale? Do they even allow Democrats, let alone ex-Reds?"

Ken grinned and told us the following story. Sometime earlier, the student-run *Yale Daily News* (known as the "*Yalie Daily*") had run stories revealing that the head of Yale's security department — a retired FBI agent named Powell — was diligently building a *subversives file* of dossiers on known or suspected dissidents among university faculty, employees, and students. A huge uproar over academic freedom, civil rights, privacy, and matters of conscience erupted. So much so that Kingman Brewster, Yale's Lord High Provost, decisively stepped in to halt such endeavors. He ordered that the subversive file be destroyed, and as reported in the *Yalie Daily* he instructed Powell:

> You are not authorized to engage in the investigation of student or
> faculty political activities or views. You are not authorized to respond to
> any outside inquiry with regard to student or faculty political activities
> or views. No record or information concerning Yale students, faculty or
> staff shall be divulged to non-university people except when requested in
> the course of a legitimate legal investigation or enforcement action. [13]

I still wasn't convinced. As far as I was concerned, Yale was a bulwark of white Anglo-Saxon Protestant Republicanism. My dad chuckled at my youthful naiveté. It turned out to be a class thing. From Yale's lofty point of view, the FBI was its servant, not its master. As the alma mater of presidents and corporate tycoons, Yale looked down its patrician nose at impertinent, badge-wearing bumpkins who at their best might presume some status equal to that of lower middle management. In the same vein, Yale held HUAC in utter contempt — along with most of the other grubby, upstart strivers squabbling in the halls of Congress.

So Ken, Mom, and my brother Dan moved to Connecticut in the summer of '63. I stayed in L.A. and continued to work with CORE. I was 19 and way beyond ready to be out on my own and free of parental influence. Make no mistake, I loved and deeply respected both my parents, but I chafed at and resented their restrictions and guidance — loving and for my own benefit as later in life I finally understood it to be. Mine was a stubborn, dig-in-your-heels–type rebellion against parental authority. I didn't boost cars, do drugs, or act out violently (though there was the occasional flat-out, raging, shouting argument with my mom).

After we separated, I'd visit them from time to time, and I loved teasing Mom by mentioning, tongue-in-cheek, to her friends that my parents had "abandoned" me. She always rose to the bait to protest, but my father just laughed.

Ken did very well at Yale. He hadn't had much success in the business of making a profit, but he was a wiz at running a nonprofit. His innate people skills and experience as a union leader stood him in good stead with the staff he supervised, and they soon came to respect, trust, and like him. In part, I think, because he brought to the work a sense of mission similar to that which had carried him though his union days. So much so that when the Yale Health Plan was established to provide medical services for faculty, students, and staff, he was hired to manage it.

I was immensely proud of him. He was so self-educated that he could hold his own in meetings and social events with the most erudite of professors, and he was totally at ease discussing culture, philosophy, politics, and history at receptions, symposiums, and seminars. So much so that none of those Ivy League intellectuals had a clue that his formal education had ended with the sixth grade in a Kentucky elementary school. I do wonder, though, what myths he spun on his résumé and what they assumed his background was. Sadly, I never thought to ask him.

And, as it turns out, old habits die hard. My dad quickly caught on that as a mere *business* drone his status was clearly inferior to that of the professors, department heads, and deans. Not so low as the bottle-washers, clerks, and janitors, but enough so that it made a difference when advocating for budget increases, program changes, and improved personnel policies for the staff he supervised. So he did what he knew how to do. He organized.

He saw that academics, coaches, technicians, accountants, and other "professionals" garnered prestige and a kind of bureaucratic power through membership in their occupational associations. More than that, Yale respected and acknowledged those groups, paid travel expenses for meetings and conventions, and allowed members to include association work as a component of their job.

In 1966 (while I was marching for freedom in Mississippi) he organized the other Yale lab and department managers into a group to meet with university administrators. A year later he gathered 100 colleagues from schools and commercial labs across the country and they formed the Society of Research Administrators. Today they're known as SRA International and they modestly describe themselves as follows:

> The Society of Research Administrators International is the premier
> global research management society providing education, professional
> development and the latest comprehensive information about research
> management to over 5,000 members from over 40 countries. In this
> time of increasing international research collaborations, SRA
> International maintains the largest network of research managers in the
> world. [14]

I do wonder, though, if they knew they were being organized by a former commie into what was essentially a kind of managerial union? In any case, way to go Dad!

Once an organizer always an organizer.

The Wrong Question

When Freedom Movement veterans participate in panel discussions and educational programs we're frequently asked, "Why did you join the Civil Rights Movement?" It's a fair and reasonable question but it always makes me uncomfortable. For one thing, it's impossible to provide a short concise answer to a very complex set of motivations. The truth is, nobody does the big things in their life for simple reasons that can be easily summarized in a brief sound bite.

But beyond that there are deeper problems. To begin with, as a white activist what I'm often being asked, either implicitly or explicitly, is why was I as a *white* person involved in fighting for racial justice? And I suspect that lurking behind that question are two invalid assumptions.

First, there may be an assumption that racism and discrimination were (are) Black problems and therefore Afro-Americans have to solve them. But racism wasn't (and isn't) a Black problem — it's a white problem. Afro-Americans didn't deny themselves the right to vote or limit themselves to the back of the bus, nor did they create separate and unequal school systems, or white-only jobs, or segregated housing, or racially-motivated police shootings. They didn't lynch themselves either. So since whites were (are) the root of the problem, whites therefore have to be part of the solution.

Second, there may be an assumption that it's self-evident why Blacks were involved in the Movement, so only whites need to be asked. But the truth is that while most (though not all) Afro-Americans approved of and voiced support for the Movement (unlike most whites), only a small fraction of Blacks actually attended a mass meeting, joined protests, attempted to register to vote when it was a dangerous act of courage, or even just signed a petition, helped with office work, or contributed money to an organization. The great majority of Afro-Americans in the 1960s did not actively participate in any way in the Freedom Movement other than offering passive support.

Social scientists tell us that social movements rarely involve more than 5–10% of the affected population in active participation. I recall reading some historian who estimated that no more than 7% of the American colonists actively participated in the War of Independence, and that figure included folks who just attended a meeting, signed a petition, or donated supplies to the colonial armies. So it's not surprising that no more than a small fraction of Blacks were actively involved in the Freedom Movement. Which means that it's not obvious at all why those who *did* put their lives and livelihoods on the line did what they did, which brings us back to that *Why did you?* question, which is just as applicable to Afro-Americans as it is to white activists like me.

Okay, so it's fair and reasonable to ask both white *and* Black activists, "Why did you?" But for me it's still the *wrong* question. For me the more important — and certainly the more interesting — question is to ask those people who didn't support freedom and equality, *why not?*

I'm not referring to our active opponents. Back then, the explicit overt racists loudly and boldly defended their beliefs in white supremacy with their traditional lies, clichés, and stereotypes. That's old news, though they haven't gone away and remain with us to this day, actively spreading their poisonous hate — and recently electing one of their own to the White House.

No, who I'm talking about are the people who either didn't care about, or were simply oblivious to, the *concept* of racial justice. Someday I'd like to be in the audience and ask a panel of that so-called *silent majority* who did nothing, said nothing, noticed nothing: "What part of 'With liberty and justice for all' do you not understand? Was there something in 'We hold these truths to be self-evident, that all men are created equal' that you disagreed with?"

I'd also like to ask a question of those who rejected (and still reject) any thought that they themselves were (are) in any way racist, yet vocally expressed their deep concern over *social turmoil, breakdown of civility,* and *disruption of order* while saying nothing about segregated lunch counters, literacy tests and racial lynchings. Then (and now) they fervently avowed their love of American freedoms, so I'd like to ask them, "Why did you remain silent as those freedoms you profess to love were (and are) denied to people of color — and, for that matter, protesters of all races?"

And I'd also like to ask those flag-waving patriots who throw hysterical fits whenever someone dares criticize the United States in any way, "How do you justify your utter failure to defend the liberties you proclaim to love so passionately — including the liberty to freely speak up and criticize the actions and inactions of our political leaders?"

When are those questions going to be asked?

And while we're on the subject, the media closely interrogates political candidates about their military service (or lack thereof) during the Vietnam War and later conflicts, but how come candidates of a certain age are never asked what they did do to defend freedom here at home during the Civil Rights era?

Just asking.

Summertime in Crenshaw County

Secret Mistress of the French Premier ~ 1937

When you're an activist engaged in real-world struggles (as opposed to the armchair discussions of intellectuals) you can be dead certain of one thing — you're never going to know in advance what unexpected challenges might suddenly confront you. Which brings me another of those stories I heard from my mom about being a union organizer in the late 1930s.

Mom's first husband, Ben Iceland, volunteered to fight fascism in the Spanish Civil War as a member of the Lincoln Brigade. The Spanish people had democratically elected a leftist government which right-wing army generals then rebelled against. Mussolini and Hitler actively supported the generals with money, arms, and troops. But instead of supporting the elected Spanish government, France, Britain, and America were pressured by their own right-wing conservatives to enact "neutrality" laws that denied aid to *both* sides. Since Germany and Italy were actively supporting General Franco with bombers, tanks, and soldiers, the "neutrality" of the democracies was really nothing of the sort, because it crippled the Spanish resistance while doing nothing to slow the flow of weapons to the fascists.

Under the U.S. Neutrality Acts, it was *illegal* for Americans like Ben to fight for democracy in Spain, so my mother had to keep secret where her husband was. Meanwhile, she was working as Midwest organizer for the American Communications Association (ACA). Young and beautiful as she was, a lot of men were attracted to her. And with a husband she mentioned but no one ever saw, women were also curious. Nothing piques interest like an air of mystery.

Labor organizing in the '30s was hard. People feared being fired if they joined a union, and with the country still mired in the Depression jobs were hard to come by. The telegraph companies fought the union with fierce determination, using spies to report the names of those who had secretly joined and thugs to disrupt meetings. Nevertheless, despite the company's opposition, by 1937 the ACA had made enough progress to begin holding membership meetings where they discussed what the union should demand in contract negotiations. Some of those meetings drew more than a hundred workers.

Though the European democracies were unwilling to support a left-leaning government, the Soviet Union and communist parties around the world were doing all they could to aid the anti-fascist side. My parents were active members of the Communist Party (CP), and the Party ordered my mom to raise the issue of Spain in her organizing work. They told her to get the fledgling union to adopt a resolution supporting the Spanish Republic and opposing the U.S. Neutrality Acts.

But except for a small number of committed leftists, American workers at that time paid scant attention to foreign affairs. The telegraph operators my mother and father were organizing knew nothing about the Spanish Civil War and cared less. She knew that trying to get them to pass a resolution that had nothing to do with their working conditions would be divisive, and ultimately futile — they wouldn't do it.

Caught between the rock of reality and the hard place of Party orders, Mom tried to meet both needs by writing a letter to President Roosevelt and sending a personal telegram to Léon Blum, the French premier, urging them to lift the arms embargo. "Of course," as she told me years later, "stupid me, I didn't realize that if I sent a telegram with my name on it, you know, everybody in the operating room was going to know about it."

Suddenly, all hell broke loose. Company stool pigeons spread a rumor that she was Blum's secret mistress — and a French spy sent to America to sabotage the communications industry. Within hours not just the operators, but workers in other departments, and within the union leadership too, were in an uproar. Members were calling union officers with questions, and rumors were flying that she was carrying Blum's love child, that she was this, that, or some other thing. Instead of discussing issues like wages, working conditions, and contract demands, all anyone wanted to talk about was my mom's sex life. *Oy veh!*

Well, of course she immediately turned to her Party leaders for advice and help. After thoroughly criticizing her for failing to obtain a union resolution on Spain as she'd been ordered to do and for allowing her personal life to disrupt the organizing campaign, they told her she'd have to call a membership meeting to confront the secret-mistress issue head-on. And she'd have to do it on her own — they had important work to do, they didn't have time to waste on trivial female imbroglios.

Two days later, close to 300 workers showed up at a membership meeting to find out if my mother was the secret mistress of the premier of France. That was three times the number who had ever turned out to talk about working conditions or union organizing. Almost everyone present was older than her and three quarters of them were men — some of whom were drunk (as usual).

My mom normally spoke next to the podium rather than behind it because even in her high heels (which she always wore) she was too short to be seen over the lectern. So she stood there on the stage, put her hands on her hips and glared at them (take it from me, she was a world-class glarer).

"I don't know whether to be flattered or furious at the purpose of this meeting. If I were the French premier's lover what the hell am I doing here trying to organize a union and knocking myself out to win improvements for ordinary workers? I'd be riding around in a chauffeur-driven limousine, wearing diamonds and furs, being waited on by maids and butlers. What's even more to the point, do you really think I'd be with a man who's 70 years old?"

A few in the audience laughed — with her, not at her.

"You know, I'm flattered at being considered a French spy. Ooo la la, when I don't know a word of French, and have never been in that country."

By now, more people were laughing.

Then she told them off. "Isn't it absurd that such a rumor could spread and that enough of you believed it to make this meeting necessary? What's serious about all this nonsense is that it was so easy for the stool pigeons and company spies to spread rumors that could disrupt the solidarity of our union."

From there she went on to explain about the Spanish Civil War, the German Nazis and Italian Fascists, what it meant for working people in Chicago, and why she sent that telegram. All to cheers and applause. Rank and file members stood up to condemn the rumormongers and union disrupters, and it turned out to be one of the best meetings they'd ever had.

Decades later, she and I discussed the incident and I pointed out that she'd actually accomplished what the Party had ordered her to do, she'd succeeded in bringing the Spanish Civil War into her union work — though not exactly in the way the Party (or she) had expected. She conceded that might be true, but it still irked her that the Party had failed to stand behind her when carrying out their edict blew up in her face.

And she quite clearly viewed their trivialization of her situation in the context of male discomfort with female sexuality. "Male chauvinism" was the term she used, and I could tell by the way she said it that 66 years later she was still pissed off (though, of course, she never used words like "pissed" — that kind of language I got from my dad).

"I'm Gonna Blow Your God Damn Brains Out!" ~ 1965

By June of 1965, the SCOPE project had become the focus of SCLC's attention. The original idea had been for 2000 northern volunteers — mostly white, mostly college students — to implement the new Voting Rights Act in 120 counties across Virginia, the Carolinas, Georgia, Florida, and Alabama.

There were obvious similarities between SCLC's SCOPE project and the Mississippi, Louisiana, and Florida summer projects organized by COFO, SNCC, and CORE the previous year. But the 1964 projects had had half a year to recruit the thousand or more volunteers who participated, and their recruitment had relied on the active assistance of CORE and SNCC groups across the North. SCLC had only a couple of months to pull SCOPE together without any comparable northern base. Yet despite those handicaps, SCLC still managed to field roughly 500 northern volunteers working in some 80 counties.

Compared to SNCC and CORE, the SCLC field staff was small, perhaps a dozen or so. For the SCOPE project it had to be rapidly expanded. Along with others in Alabama, I was hired by Albert Turner as an SCLC "subsistence" worker to direct a county SCOPE project in that state. Unlike the more egalitarian SNCC and CORE, SCLC's staff structure was hierarchical and "subsistence" staff members were the lowest level, paid $25 a week (equal to about $200 in 2018).

I was immensely proud to be hired as a member of the SCLC field staff. It affirmed me as a real and acknowledged full-time freedom fighter. At the same time, though, I was daunted and (frankly) terrified by my assignment to direct the SCOPE project in Crenshaw County, Alabama. Yes, I'd been active in the Freedom Movement for two and a half years, but I'd only been in the South for a bit less than three months — and that almost entirely in one town — Selma. Hardly adequate preparation for directing a voter registration project in a rural Black Belt county.

When he assigned me to Crenshaw, Turner told me that the team of SCOPE volunteers would arrive in the county fully trained and ready to roll. Based on my (assumed) knowledge of Alabama realities, which I was supposed to have absorbed from a few months and three arrests in Selma, my job was to coordinate with the local Crenshaw leaders, oversee the SCOPE volunteers, and keep them safe and out of trouble while they got on with the work they were trained to do. (Gulp.)

The truth was, though, that I probably had as much — or more — experience as many of the others who suddenly found themselves directing SCOPE projects. That was the way the Freedom Movement worked, you were thrown unprepared into the deep end. Or as one SNCC member once put it, "leaping off a cliff and learning to fly on the way down."

Crenshaw County was immediately south of Montgomery and had never been worked by Freedom Movement field organizers. It was a late addition to the SCOPE list, largely because the two local leaders, Havard Richburg and James Kolb, lobbied Turner and national SCOPE director Hosea Williams for it. Unlike some SCOPE counties where the local leadership was lukewarm at best, they really wanted us. The local Movement organization was the Crenshaw County Civic Association (CCCA), which at that time consisted of Mr. Kolb, Mr. Richburg, and a small handful of courageous others.

SCLC provided a small amount of money to reimburse the families who had agreed to house and feed us outsiders and also for stipends to four local youth who would work with the project full time. It was clearly understood that Richburg and Kolb were in charge, they would tell me what they wanted done and I would coordinate the volunteers in carrying it out. In essence, we would be CCCA's field staff. For a project pulled together at the last minute with little on-the-ground preparation, it actually worked out surprisingly well.

Because Crenshaw was a last-minute addition and I was one of the last of the new staff hires, I wasn't sent to Atlanta to participate in the week-long SCOPE orientation and training. Instead, Turner took me to Luverne, the Crenshaw County seat, so I could get to know the local leaders and activists, learn the lay of the land, and orient myself before the SCOPE volunteers arrived. Luverne was a small village on Highway 331 between Montgomery and the Florida panhandle. It had a total population of around 2200 or so, of whom maybe 800 were Afro-Americans.

As proclaimed by the all-white Chamber of Commerce, the town motto was "The Friendliest City in the South." An exaggeration, as I was soon to discover. Racism and Jim Crow segregation were deeply embedded in the culture of both town and county. Many Blacks still recalled the lynching of Jesse Thornton 25 years earlier. Thornton, a 26-year-old Afro-American man had committed the crime of addressing a white cop by just his name without the honorific of "Mister." For this transgression against the southern way of life he was beaten, arrested, held in jail while a mob formed. The mob then attacked him with bricks, bats, dumped him in a truck, took him to an out-of-the-way spot where they shot him dead, and then disposed of his corpse in a swamp. His decomposing corpse eventually turned up in a stream near Tuskegee Institute more than 60 miles away.

Mr. Kolb was usually working his rural farm, so Havard was the leader I directly worked with the most. He was a part-time teacher, part-time college professor, part-time barber, and part-time proprietor of a little store in Luverne's Afro-American community. His combination store and open-air barbershop was set off from the dirt street and up a little rise. Turner dropped me off around noon one day in mid-June and I started getting to know Havard and several other Black men who appeared to be just casually hanging around the shop (but who in reality had gathered to meet and assess me).

As was true with most other southern Black communities, Luverne had an efficient network of neighborhood snitches who reported everything Movement-related to the cops and white power structure. So no more than ten minutes after I arrived a cop car pulled up. From the driver's seat, the officer waved me over to his car and I went down the dirt steps cut into the embankment. He introduced himself as Harry Raupach, Chief of Luverne's tiny police force, which consisted of him and two or three others. He asked me to identify myself, which I did.

He had a shoebox on the seat beside him filled with alphabetized 5x7 cards. He riffed through them and pulled out one with my name, photo, arrest record, and other details of my nefarious existence. The Alabama authorities — ever vigilant they — had compiled dossiers on all known civil rights activists and distributed them to every police agency in the state, even minuscule, out-of-the-way ones like Luverne's tiny constabulary. Since I had been in the state for less than three months, I was impressed by their bureaucratic diligence.

Raupach showed me the card. "Is this you?"

I confirmed that it was.

He asked me what I was doing in Luverne and I explained about SCOPE, emphasizing that we were only there to register voters, not protest or sit in or integrate anything. That was SCLC's official policy for that summer — voter registration and political education only. He was polite and completely professional. After he drove off and I returned to the barbershop, the local men told me that Raupach was actually a northerner who had married a local girl and that he had a fair amount of respect in the Afro-American community as a fair and even-handed lawman (a rarity in rural Alabama in 1965).

Twenty minutes later another car pulled up. Not an official car, no markings. A white guy in civilian clothes got out, waved some kind of tinplate badge, and ordered me down to speak with him. I went to see what he wanted and he immediately started shouting all sorts of racist hate at me. Then he pulled out a leather blackjack. Waving it around my head like he was going to bash in my skull, he ordered me to get out of Crenshaw County. "Or else!"

Without conscious thought, I automatically fell back on my nonviolent training. Keeping my voice calm and casually conversational, I told him I was there to do a job, to register voters, and so on. While carefully not reflecting back any of his hostility or escalating the tension, I made clear I was not going to run away or obey orders to leave. I asked him who he was. He told me it was none of my God damned business.

We went around and around on this for a bit, him threatening me with his lead sap if I didn't agree to leave and me being quietly, courteously, obstinate. Then he shoved the blackjack into his pocket and pulled out a .38 revolver, jammed the muzzle against the side of my head and screamed, "I'm gonna blow your God damned brains out right now!"

I responded in a calm conversational voice — though, of course, on the inside I wasn't calm at all. I explained that if he did that, yes I'd be dead. But then what? Martin Luther King would come to lead mass protests, sit-ins, and freedom rides. The news media would be all over the place poking around and asking questions. So would local, state, and federal police agencies. He'd be investigated by the Department of Justice, and he'd go through the hassle of a trial (we both knew that no white jury in Alabama would ever convict him of killing a civil rights worker, so I didn't imply he'd end up in jail). He clearly hated the federal government and the news media as much, or more, than he hated Afro-Americans — or me.

This went on for what seemed like quite a while, but was probably no more than 10 or 15 minutes, him cursing and threatening me, raving about "niggers this," and "coons that." It was (and still is) my habit to carry a pen and blank 3x5 cards in my shirt pocket in case I need to note something down. So I waited until he momentarily moved his pistol away from my head and then, slowly, unthreateningly, I stepped to the rear of his car so that I could write down his license plate number. Again I asked him his name, which he still wouldn't tell me.

So there he was, yelling and ranting and doing his anger-intimidation thing, and there I was, replying calmly and doing my writing-down-notes thing, and in a weird sense it was like we were in two different conversations, not interrelating at all. Eventually, his rage ran down, he issued some final death threats about me being gone by tomorrow, and then drove off.

All the while, Mr. Richburg and the other men in the barbershop were watching this confrontation. And I suspect quite a few other Afro-Americans were peeking out from behind their curtains. When I rejoined Havard in the barbershop, he identified the guy as head of the Crenshaw County Ku Klux Klan and a member of the sheriff's posse, which was what his tin badge had signified. He owned a diner out on the highway — a racist, white-only hangout openly defying the Civil Rights Act. Richburg was one of the very few Blacks in Crenshaw who had ever stood up to him and defied his threats — which was why he was one the two local Movement leaders.

Looking back on it now, it seems likely to me that Mr. Richburg must have had guns in his shop. That was the common practice in the South, particularly for a Black man who had defied the KKK. With a .38 held to my head, he couldn't have prevented the Klansman from murdering me. But I've often wondered whether he or one of the other men would have shot in retaliation if the Klan guy had killed me. Realities being what they were, I think they probably would not have — nor would I have expected or wanted them to.

When Turner had dropped me off an hour earlier, I'm sure Havard and the other men must have had some serious doubts about this young white guy presented to them as an SCLC freedom worker, though, of course, they were far too courteous to indicate any such thing. But after nonviolently standing up to that KKK leader, refusing to be intimidated by him — and somehow not getting killed or hurt in the process — I think I gained some measure of respect from them and others in the Afro-American community as someone who really might be one of "Dr. King's men."

Of course, I didn't let on to them how little I actually knew about what I was doing, and how completely unsure I felt about myself and my abilities to lead a voter registration project. I guess I was a living example of that old saying, "Fake it till you make it."

There is, however, no question in my mind that my training in nonviolent tactics saved me that afternoon from serious injury or death. Training — and luck. You can count on training, but never on luck. Later that summer, on August 21st, my friend Jonathan Daniels, and had stayed with the West family in Selma at the same time I did, was shot to death by a Klansman in Lowndes County, which abuts the northwest corner of Crenshaw.

I later learned that Jonathan had been ambushed by Tom Coleman, a racist killer determined to murder civil rights activists. Like the Crenshaw Klan leader who had threatened me, Coleman was also a member of the sheriff's posse. Jonathan was well trained in nonviolence, but that day his luck ran out. When Coleman stepped out of a doorway with a shotgun and opened fire on an integrated group of four, Jonathan had no time to use his de-escalation training. All he could do was pull Ruby Sales aside and step in front of her, shielding her and taking the full blast himself. Though it occurred only 45 miles from Luverne, I heard about it from news reports. I hadn't even known he was in Lowndes working with SNCC.

As with the mysterious death of Mike Robinson, after Jonathan's murder I experienced anger, loss, sadness, and intense frustration because I and everyone else knew there was not a snowball's chance in hell that an all-white jury in Alabama would convict the killer. It was bitter and infuriating — and frightening because now I too was a KKK target.

From time to time over the years I've told this story about my welcome to Crenshaw County and the later assassination of Jonathan Daniels, and folks sometimes ask me whether I was scared. Yes, of course, I was — a crazed racist holding a pistol to your head is good reason to be scared. But I was concentrating so hard on applying my nonviolent training that I really didn't have much time or attention for experiencing terror.

I think what they're really asking, though, is why, with that immediate and unambiguous death threat and the recent murder of my friend Mike Robinson, did I stay in Crenshaw? Why the hell didn't I get on the first bus out of town? And I believe the answer is that I had worked through those fears in the weeks (well, months) before I left the North. Unlike many summer volunteers, I knew the real dangers of being a freedom worker in the South, so I had had to face and master those fears before I ever got in that car headed for Selma.

The SCOPE Project ~ 1965

That first night I slept in Havard Richburg's snug brick home. The next day he took me to an old, abandoned shack that we would use as our "freedom house" and where I would sleep.

Empty homes were not hard to find in Alabama's Black Belt. In the 20 years between 1940 and 1960, close to 41% of Crenshaw County's Afro-American population had migrated out, riding the dog north or west from Montgomery's Greyhound depot in search of jobs and an escape from segregation. Mostly it was the young adults who left, so the county's Black population was skewed towards children and elders, many of whom were raising their grandkids away from the crime and urban poverty of the northern ghettos where their parents were struggling to eke out a living. Stark and brutal as rural poverty was for Afro-Americans in Alabama, there was at least a sense of shared community and mutual support that was largely missing from the packed urban slums of the North.

Like Richburg's combination store & barbershop, our freedom house was in Luverne's small Afro-American community. It had holes in the floor, and the cracks between the warped wooden slats of the siding were covered over by flattened cans and old license plates nailed to the boards. There was no running water of any kind, just an outhouse. Taking a shower meant standing in the dirt yard in a swimsuit and pouring water over your head from a bucket or washbasin. The shack — excuse me, I mean the "freedom house" — was furnished with an old iron bed and an equally ancient feather mattress. I placed the legs of the bed in tin pie-pans that I kept filled with water to discourage roaches and other local vermin from joining me in bed as I slept. Some of the local bugs were so big they made audible clicking sounds as they skittered across the floor at night.

To the enormous envy of SCLC field staff like me, SNCC workers had the Sojourner Motor Fleet of new Plymouth Furies, fast as a getaway and equipped with citizens-band, two-way radios. SCLC had some hand-me-down clunkers donated by northern churches. But there weren't enough of those to go around and I hadn't been issued one. Turner had promised that the SCOPE team would have at least one car, but until they arrived I was on foot. Mr. Richburg drove me around the county, showing me who and what was where, teaching me the road network, and introducing me to those local folk who weren't terrified of being seen speaking to a civil rights worker.

In Crenshaw County at that time there weren't all that many Afro-Americans willing to publicly identify themselves with the Freedom

Movement. The Klan was strong in that part of the state and Black folk were justifiably afraid. Not a single church was willing to allow us to hold a civil rights meeting or voter registration class on their premises. Not one. Not one. We ended up using the local pool hall as our headquarters and meeting space. Unlike the wood-frame churches, the pool parlor was made of fireproof concrete blocks.

The SCOPE team arrived around noon on June 21st following their week-long orientation in Atlanta. Personally, I think Crenshaw was blessed with one of the better teams (though perhaps I'm biased). Arriving along with the volunteers was Elbert Thomas, a Black SCLC subsistence-staff member who Turner had assigned to co-direct the project with me. Not long after, however, he was shifted to another county. Paula Ferrari, a young woman from San Francisco, was also later transferred to another project, leaving Crenshaw SCOPE with four volunteers from outside the state, four local teenage activists who received a small SCLC stipend — and me.

Jerome and Willa Mae Ware, Charles Jackson, and Beverly Street were the young activists. I say "young," but at 21 I was only a couple years older than they. The four local teens teamed with us outsiders in canvassing and organizing so that whenever possible our work was done on an integrated Black-white basis. With Mr. Kolb and Mr. Richburg working full-time at their jobs, the young activists also provided the essential day-to-day local knowledge that the project had to have.

The out-of-state SCOPE volunteers were also all in their early to mid-20s. Two of the them arrived in their own automobiles. David Sookne, a math major at the University of Chicago, had previously done some voting rights work in Fayette County, Tennessee and participated in protests in the North. He had a fairly new Volkswagen bug that could seat four (five in a squeezed pinch). It wasn't fast, but it was reliable and it became our precious project car. Dunbar Reed III, an Afro-American college student from Atlanta, had a shiny, red, two-seat, sports car convertible. A sweet ride indeed. Unfortunately it provoked local whites to chase him at high speed, so I reluctantly had to ask him to take it back home and park it for the duration of the project.

Carroll Richardson was a former student and CORE activist at the University of Florida. An Air Force veteran, he had participated in part of the Selma to Montgomery March with others from Gainesville. Richard (Dick) Klausner was from Grinnell, both the town and the college. He had participated in the March on Washington and had been arrested a couple of times at protests in the North.

SCOPE had been organized out of the Atlanta office and those of us who had been working in Alabama really didn't know much about it. We'd had a couple of very general orientation meetings that were long on vision but short on details. "Don't worry about it," they had assured the Alabama staff. "The volunteers are going to be thoroughly trained. You're the veterans, all you have to do is be the liaison with the local leaders, keep the SCOPE volunteers out of trouble, and keep them safe. They'll know the whole SCOPE program."

So that afternoon we had our first meeting of the Crenshaw County SCOPE project in the freedom house — Me and Elbert from SCLC, four local SCOPE volunteers, and five volunteers from outside the state. After everyone introduced themselves, I asked, "So, what are we supposed to do?"

The out-of-state volunteers looked surprised and one replied, "What do you mean? You're the county director, you're supposed to tell us."

That's when I learned that while they had received intensive training in southern racial realities, cross-cultural relations, history of the Freedom Movement, and so on, their practical training had all been oriented around how to implement the Voting Rights Act (VRA). But the Act had not yet passed. It was still being filibustered by South Carolina Senator Strom Thurmond with no end in sight. Absent the VRA, we were back to the traditional voter registration methods of the Deep South. Which they had *not* been trained in. *Oy veh!*

For Afro-Americans in Crenshaw County before the VRA, registering to vote was a complicated ordeal. You had to go down to the courthouse on one of the few days the registration office was open, which meant you had to take off from work — with or without your employer's permission — and risk being fired. The sheriff, his deputies, and the white courthouse loafers who hung around the building made it their business to discourage "undesirables," so you had to run their gauntlet of intimidation, insults, threats, and sometimes arrest on phony charges just to get to the registration office.

Once at the right window, you faced harassment and humiliation from the clerks and officials and then the application and the literacy test. The Alabama Voter Application Form was four pages long and deliberately designed to intimidate. You had to swear a legally binding oath under penalty of perjury that your answers to every single question were true — including those about your family, landlord, and employer. Yet, as you well knew, your answers would be passed on to the White Citizens' Council (and probably the KKK) for appropriate action on their part. So if you told the truth you endangered family members and risked being fired or evicted, if you lied you risked being jailed for perjury.

After completing the application and swearing the oaths, you then had to pass the so-called "literacy test," which was in no way a fair or objective test. It was merely a pretext allowing registrars to "pass" or "fail" applicants according to their personal whim. By long custom, registrars had the power to exempt white applicants from taking the test if in their opinion the whites were of "good character." Afro-Americans, however, were always required to take the "test."

In "Part A" of the test, the registrar chose a section of the Alabama Constitution for you to read aloud. He could select an easy section or a long one full of legal double-talk. He judged whether in his opinion you read and pronounced all the words correctly. Then you had to verbally interpret that section to his satisfaction. His judgements were final and could not be appealed. After that, you had to either copy out by hand another section of the Constitution or write it down from dictation as he mumbled it. Again, he and he alone determined if you did that correctly.

Then came Parts "B" and "C" of the test which were two sets of four questions each that you had to answer correctly in order to prove that you had sufficient knowledge of government to vote wisely. Questions like:

> Who pays members of Congress for their services, their home states or the United States?
>
> If a person charged with treason denies his guilt, how many persons must testify against him before he can be convicted?
>
> At what time of day on January 20 each four years does the term of the president of the United States end?
>
> Can the state coin money with the consent of Congress?
>
> In what year did the Congress gain the right to prohibit the migration of persons to the states?
>
> The president is forbidden to exercise his authority of pardon in cases of
>
> ———————. [15]

Based on his opinion of your responses the registrar then determined whether you were sufficiently "literate" to become a voter. (Of course, even if he judged you insufficiently literate to vote, you still had to obey all the laws and pay all the taxes enacted by the public officials you weren't allowed to vote for or against.) [*]

According to the 1960 Census, there were 2200 Afro-Americans old enough to vote in Crenshaw County. Less than 500 of them, roughly 22%, were registered. Compared to most other Black Belt counties that was actually a high percentage, but since whites in Crenshaw outnumbered Blacks by two to one and 98% of them were registered, Afro-Americans made up just 7% of the total electorate. Not enough to even influence, let alone win an election. Not enough to gain even minimal courtesy from elected officials. So our goal that summer was to register enough Afro-Americans to give them a political foothold in the county.

In Selma I had begun to learn that civil rights work differed considerably between North and South, and Crenshaw furthered my education. In northern cities, political work generally revolved around organizational meetings, the written word, and speeches. But in the rural South, community organizing and voter registration were almost entirely about conversations. Not slogans, not chants, not oratory, not exhortations, but extended personal interactions with *individuals* on their porches or in their homes and with small clusters at little country stores, barbershops, beauty parlors, and even out in the fields.

For northerners like me and the SCOPE team, that took some getting used to. And part of that was learning how to deeply listen to what people were *saying*, what they were actually *meaning*, and what they weren't *explicitly* saying but still trying to tell us. Not so easy as it might sound.

And just as difficult as adapting to conversational politics was the slow pace and heavy accent of spoken language in rural Alabama. To a degree, I had already encountered that in Selma. The first few days I was there I often found it hard to understand people, and when I did grasp their meaning I was sorely tempted to finish their sentences to hurry them along — not a good idea as even an ignoramus like me understood. On their part they found me equally difficult to comprehend, my California accent and slang was foreign to them, and my speech was way too rapid.

I was soon getting on fairly well in Selma, but Crenshaw took some additional getting used to. For SCOPE volunteers fresh from the North it was harder, though after a week or so they managed. Eventually I came to understand that in the North we put a premium on clear and rapid exchanges of necessary information because everyone had somewhere else they had to be or something else they needed to do. But in the rural South, particularly impoverished Afro-American communities, conversation was the main pastime and often the only available diversion

---

* For detailed information on pre-VRA voter-registration systems and sample literacy tests in the Deep South see www.crmvet.org/lithome.htm.

from the drudgery of routine tasks. It was, therefore, a highly valued social art, not to be rushed.

From stories in the mass media (and, to be honest, our fund-appeals), Movement supporters in the North assumed that civil rights work in the Deep South was an action-packed series of dramatic protests, police violence and intimidation, inspiring mass meetings, confrontations with the Klan, and stoic suffering in brutal jail cells. The reality, however, was far more prosaic. Mostly what we did all day was canvass door-to-door in pairs. Our goal was to have conversations about voting, or attending a meeting, or the meaning of "freedom," or how to respond to some local problem. If we were lucky and did our work well, a small evening house meeting in someone's home with two or three of us and hopefully half a dozen or so local participants might result.

Maybe two or three times a month there might occur a "mass meeting" with one or two dozen people. And on registration days, between 50 and 75 courageous people would show up at the courthouse to face the sheriff and attempt to register.

Luverne, and Crenshaw's other little towns and villages, replicated Selma's model of dirt streets indicating Afro-American homes and the local SCOPE volunteers knew who was who and who was living where. But out in the rural, South whites and Blacks were scattered randomly and only the main highways were paved. The country lanes and byways were just dirt roads, regardless of the race of those who lived where.

Most white-owned properties were obviously upscale and easily recognized as such. But the shacks of poor whites with sagging porches and outhouses in the back were often indistinguishable from those of Black sharecroppers. Which posed significant dangers for us because whites at the bottom of the economic pyramid were often the most virulently racist and violent, and they fiercely resented freedom riders thinking their home was that of an Afro-American — an unforgivable insult.

So unless whoever was living there was visible, we had to carefully assess each rundown, tin-roof shanty for signs of who dwelled within. A Confederate battle flag was an obvious sign, but most of the time it wasn't that easy. So if we saw a little blond-headed kid playing in the dirt yard we'd usually pass that house by. But not always, because more often than you'd think, the local person canvassing with us would casually tell us, "Oh, they're Negro."

Meaning, in the unspoken but deeply ingrained code of southern race relations, that the child's Afro-American mother, who might or might not be married to a Black husband, had experienced what was sardonically referred to as "midnight integration" with a white man. In some cases that might have been consensual, but often it was rape — either brutal and violent or coerced through economic power or some other form of threat. Genteel whites actually had a term for white men coercing sex from Black women, it was referred to as "paramour rights."

Poverty among Crenshaw's Afro-American community was endemic and their fear palpable. Fear of their bossman, fear of their landlord, fear of the sheriff, fear of the Klan. Fears that were well-founded and based on long experience. Sometimes they'd just tell us right out, "Can't talk to you." So we'd briefly say what we could, then walk on to the next house. As everyone knew, we were under constant observation by both the law and snitches and some folks just didn't want to risk being thought of as friendly with us "outside agitators." So often no one would come to the door though we could hear someone inside.

I'd seen fear in Selma, but nothing like Crenshaw. By the time I arrived in Selma, the Freedom Movement had been active there for more than two years and had wrought great and liberating changes. So I took encouragement from knowing that when Bernard and Colia Lafayette of SNCC arrived in Selma at the beginning of 1963, they faced, and eventually overcame, the same level of fear we were seeing now in Crenshaw.

For me, the saddest, and most troubling encounters were with Black men and women caught in double fear, fear of local whites suspecting them of dangerous sympathies and fear of offending these strange white folk standing on their doorstep. Sometimes the people we spoke to were afraid to make eye contact with us and when they told us, "Yas suh, I'll go register, suh," we knew they were just saying whatever they needed to say to get us to go away. We'd pretend to believe them, leave them our flyers, and promise to come back another day.

Not everyone, of course, was paralyzed with fear. Some Afro-Americans in Crenshaw were willing to risk everything by taking a stand — that's why there was a small but growing movement. That's why they asked SCLC to send in a SCOPE team. When we knocked on the door of those homes we'd be greeted with smiles of welcome, offers of cold lemonade, invitations to sit a spell on the porch and rest our feet. Some folk were ready, even eager to come to meetings, offer us rides, talk to their neighbors, and try to register. And feed us. Among some Black families in Luverne there was actual competition for the honor of hosting civil rights workers at their table.

As I canvassed door-to-door all over Crenshaw County, every once in a while someone would ask me if I was that guy the Klan leader had threatened. Which confirmed something I had learned in Selma, that civil rights workers lived in a fishbowl, that everything we did and said was carefully noted, discussed, and evaluated by both Afro-Americans and whites. If we drank whiskey, it was noted, if we took up with local girls it was gossiped about. How we carried ourselves, how we behaved, how we interacted with the community and each other, had as much, *or more*, influence and effect on our work than the explicit political content of our conversations, speeches, and protests.

By mid-July, we were having several house-meetings every week. And each Sunday members of different congregations invited us to attend services. Most of the time we were introduced and allowed to say a few words after the sermon. But no church was willing to risk being bombed by allowing us to hold a voter registration meeting on their premises, so we continued to use the pool hall as our base.

Yet even among those willing to be identified as Movement supporters — including those who might have tried to register in the past or had been willing to attempt it before the March to Montgomery — there was now reluctance to go down to the courthouse, because they knew the VRA was going to be enacted. Why expose themselves to humiliation and degradation and *not* get registered, when in a few days or at most a few weeks, the Act would pass and they could actually register in safety?

I understood the logic of that. Our counter argument was that going to the courthouse now was an act of defiance, a stand for freedom, a statement against segregation and the southern way of life. And that by showing up at the courthouse they kept the pressure on Congress to pass the bill. From a movement-building, social-change perspective I think what we said was valid, but I understood why some folks wanted to wait.

The SCOPE team had arrived in Crenshaw County on June 21st and the project was scheduled to end the last week of August, when the outside volunteers returned home before colleges reopened for the fall semester. During that July and August, the voter registration office was only open on seven days.

On each those seven days 50 or more Afro-Americans attempted to register, and the racial atmosphere at the courthouse was tense. The furious hostility of Sheriff Horn, his deputies, and the white courthouse loafers boiled off them like the stench of hate. Richburg and Kolb feared that the visible presence of "white race traitors" might trigger violence. So on registration days, they and SCOPE volunteer Dunbar Reed handled matters at the courthouse while I and the white SCOPE volunteers concentrated on encouraging folk in Luverne to make the attempt and transporting rural applicants to the courthouse and back.

On the two registration days in June prior to my arrival, the Crenshaw County Civic Association — mainly Mr. Kolb and Mr. Richburg — had brought 31 Afro-Americans to the courthouse, all of whom completed the application process but only 7 of whom were registered. In July and August, the first six registration days of the SCOPE project were conducted under the old traditional Alabama literacy test rules. With our encouragement and logistic support, 287 Afro-Americans attempted to register over the course of those six days for an average of 48 on each day.

The registrar delayed as much as he could, so only 101 managed to complete the application process before he closed the office each afternoon. In an attempt to prevent passage of the VRA, word had come down from the governor's office that at least some Blacks had to be allowed to register to "prove" that the new law was not needed. So out of those 101 about half "passed" the test and became registered voters. But even so, that was just 17% of those who courageously defied the Jim Crow system by showing up at the courthouse to register.

The VRA was finally enacted into law on August 6th and the only August registration day after that was August 16th. With the VRA now the law of the land, the registrar could no longer force people to take the literacy test. But he could still delay, obstruct, confuse, and impede. On that day some 175 Afro-Americans lined up to register. Only 50 were processed before he closed at 4pm. No one who arrived at the courthouse after 10am managed to complete the procedure. The last applicant allowed to apply had had to wait six hours in the sweltering August sun. All of those 50 who managed to apply became registered voters as the VRA required, which was in itself a significant victory, but the registrar's continued delaying tactics were so bitterly resented by us that we reacted with discouragement.

Over the two months of the SCOPE project, 462 Blacks attempted to register, 261 completed the process, and 101 were registered. Looking back on it now, I understand that encouraging and facilitating roughly 20% of the 2200 voting-age Blacks in Crenshaw County to defy generations of Jim Crow intimidation by attempting to register in a short two-month period was actually a significant achievement. But compared to the high hopes we'd had of registering much larger numbers under the VRA, I felt like a failure. As a passionate young activist, what I didn't understand back then was that no social struggle *ever* succeeds as much as the participants want or hope, but that doing the best you can in the situation you face is how progress is made — however slow and frustrating it might be.

A week after that last registration day on August 16th, the SCOPE project began to wind down. After we departed, Kolb and Richburg continued the struggle, encouraging people to register and pestering the U.S. Department of Justice to enforce the Voting Rights Act against the delaying tactics of the registrar. And eventually the act did take hold. Today, it is arguably the most effective and important civil rights legislation of the 20th century — which is why racists and right-wing conservatives in the Republican Party are determined to weaken and gut it.

In 2016, the percentage of both Blacks and whites registered to vote in Crenshaw County was high and more or less equal. But because of population differences white voters outnumbered Afro-Americans 6800 to 2300 (74% to 25%). The 2016 presidential vote split almost exactly on racial lines with Trump receiving 72% of the vote and Clinton receiving 27%. Which indicates that no more than 2% or 3% of whites voted for a Democrat. Nevertheless, though outnumbered three to one, Afro-American voters are today numerous enough to insure courtesy and respect from elected officials — their streets are now paved, and the chairman of the five-person commission that governs the county is Afro-American. Discrimination, poverty, and exploitation still continue, but Blacks in Crenshaw are now at least treated as citizens.

To some small degree, SCOPE played a role in that achievement.

License to Drive ~ 1965

Driving in the Deep South was always tense and sometimes downright terrifying. Cops and Klan knew our cars on sight and threats of arrest, ambush, and chase were ever present. What had happened to Viola Liuzzo and other freedom workers could happen to us at any time. Sometimes we were so scared going through particularly dangerous areas that we'd sing freedom songs just to keep our courage up.

Police frequently pulled us over for imaginary traffic offenses or other pretexts. Such stops might end up with anything from bogus tickets and fines, to physical attacks, to arrests on a variety of trumped-up charges. Like Ivanhoe Donaldson of SNCC who was delivering a truckload of donated food and medical supplies to the Movement in Clarksdale, Mississippi when he was arrested for transporting "narcotics" (aspirin). Or another SNCC worker who was stopped for a "dim taillight" and then busted for carrying a "concealed weapon" in the vehicle — the "weapon" being an empty Coke bottle. Sometimes not only the car's driver but the passengers as well would be jailed for some phony infraction that in the rest of America would result at worst in a citation. Chaney, Schwerner, and Goodman had been stopped for "speeding" by deputies working hand-in-glove with the Klan, then held in jail on that excuse until the KKK assembled a lynch mob to murder them.

Most of us in the Movement had two different driving modes. In towns or other places where cops were plentiful we drove slow, cautious, and careful like the legendary "little old lady from Pasadena." We ostentatiously obeyed the letter of every regulation. In rural areas, particularly Klan country, we drove like the proverbial "bat out of hell" as fast as we could.

According to Alabama law, if you lived in the state for 90 days you had to obtain a 'Bama license. I knew there was no chance of getting a license in Selma or Crenshaw County where I was well known to law enforcement, so a Black friend from Luverne drove me up to Birmingham and let me use his car for the driving test. As owner of the vehicle, however, he had to appear with me before the examiner, and there was no place in Alabama where "Black and white together" wouldn't be taken note of.

After successfully completing the written portion it was time for the driving test. The examiner told me to pull out into traffic, which I did. At the first intersection he said, "Turn left." At the next intersection, he again told me to take a left. At the third corner it was yet another left. Finally a fourth left and we were back at the starting place. He told me to pull over, stepped out of the car, and without a word stamped, "FAILED" on my test sheet.

My friend from Luverne — and later other Afro-Americans back in Crenshaw — all thought this was hilariously funny. "Now you know what it's like to be Black in Alabama," they told me with big grins. Of course, we knew that was a gross exaggeration. In no way did I really experience Black life under Jim Crow segregation. What they meant was that for Blacks, it was a common humiliation of daily existence to be harassed, degraded, and denigrated by whites in authority who used their power for no reason other than to express their white superiority. Just as I had been "failed" for being a civil rights worker, Blacks would often be "failed" at the whim of the examiner simply because they were Afro-American.

A few days later, Dave Sookne and I took his VW up to Montgomery and since we were two white guys together I had no problem obtaining my Alabama license.

Luverne Sit-In ~ 1965

By the end of July we were worn down from intense 14-hour days, unremitting danger, constant tension, and the enervating heat of an Alabama summer. When you're exhausted you do dumb things out of sheer weariness. One evening in Luverne I was walking back to the freedom house after a house meeting. The dome light of a car parked on the street up ahead of me briefly came on when someone inside opened the door for a moment and I saw it was occupied by white teenagers.

Since there were no streetlights in Afro-American neighborhoods, white kids parked there in the dark to drink and neck where they knew neither their parents nor any nosy (white) neighbors would catch them. Local Black folk resented that custom because it evinced a contempt for them and their community — as if it were a place of no decency, where morals were nonexistent and "sin" socially acceptable. Of course there was nothing they could do about it, it was just another one of the many social humiliations of white supremacy they had to endure.

The direct route back to the freedom house took me right past that car. To avoid it I would have to go some blocks around. I knew it was dangerous, they were white and they were drinking, but I was just too exhausted to give a damn. So I walked right past them. They called me "nigger lover," and threw a half-empty beer can that hit me in the forehead, raising a bruise and causing a cut that ran blood into my left eye. I was lucky they didn't pile out of the car and beat the crap out of me. Dumb. Dumb. Dumb.

Meanwhile, the Voting Rights Act (VRA) was still hung up in the Senate by a southern filibuster. After more than a month's hard, sweltering, frustrating work, we'd gotten more than 200 Afro-Americans down to the Crenshaw County courthouse to try registering under the old Alabama rules. But only 42 had succeeded in being added to the voting rolls, which, compared to our initial high hopes, was disappointing and discouraging. Wiser in the ways of both Alabama and political reality, Mr. Kolb and Mr. Richburg, were pleased and satisfied with 220 applicants and 42 new Afro-American voters. They understood the difficulties far better than I did.

We of the younger generation, however, were frustrated. The local teenage SCOPE volunteers working with us were even more bored and disgruntled than us outsiders. When they had agreed to join SCOPE for the summer it had seemed a bold and glamorous opportunity to challenge racism and defy white supremacy. A chance for them to strike a blow for freedom like the marchers and freedom riders they'd been watching on TV for years. Instead, all they'd done day after day was the hot, weary drudgery of door-to-door canvassing. So they came to me and said they wanted to integrate Luverne. It had been over a year since the Civil Rights Act of 1964 had become law, yet everything in town was still segregated, still white-only.

From the get-go, SCOPE Director Hosea Williams had decreed, "No protesting. Voter registration and political education only." But that, I concluded, had been based on the assumption that the VRA would be in effect and we could actually get large numbers on the voting rolls. It seemed to me now that direct action would not only add pressure to pass the bill but encourage more people to come out and attempt to register. I explained the situation to Richburg and Kolb and proposed that on August 2nd, the next registration day, the young activists would test compliance with the Civil Rights Act while the adults were at the courthouse attempting to register. They agreed and told me to go ahead.

Deciding that it was better to beg for forgiveness afterwards than attempt to obtain permission beforehand, I didn't check with either Albert Turner, my direct SCLC supervisor, or SCOPE headquarters in Atlanta. I was pretty sure that Turner would have agreed, he was that kind of guy. But I didn't know Hosea or what he would say. Anyway, I figured no one in Atlanta would notice what happened in little podunk Luverne — a tiny flyspeck behind the back of way beyond. And since lunch counter segregation had been illegal for more than a year I really didn't expect any trouble if some young folk implemented the Civil Rights Act — Wrong!

Thank God for CORE and N-VAC though, because due to the habits they had drilled into me I insisted that everyone taking part in the integration testing go through a real N-VAC style nonviolent training session on the Sunday beforehand. One of those screaming, in-your-face, how-to-survive-a-beating type trainings. And, of course, in proper CORE fashion, I informed the mayor and Police Chief Raupach of our intentions.

On Monday, August 2nd, we gathered at the pool hall. Our integration team was made up of our four local volunteers and half a dozen other local youth, Dunbar Reed, Carroll Richardson, David Sookne, and me. We formed two groups, a first team led by me and Dunbar and a reserve, led by Carroll and Dave, which would form the second wave if the first team was arrested. (Dick Klausner was on voter registration duty that day, transporting people to and from the courthouse.)

At that time there were only three public eating establishments in "downtown" Luverne, a dime store lunch counter and two small cafes. Our little group of eight or nine integrators arrived at the first cafe around 11:30am. It was closed, locked up tight to prevent any Afro-Americans from drinking a Coke in a "white" establishment. The dime store was open but their lunch counter wasn't. The stool tops had been removed, leaving just the bare pipes sticking up so that we couldn't sit in. No Black customers were going to defile that white-only lunch counter on that day — no siree, Bob!

The third joint was Lowe's Cafe, which did double-duty as Luverne's tiny bus stop. I assume they had a contract with Greyhound and they must have been under integration orders from the Interstate Commerce Commission ever since the Freedom Rides of 1961 — though so far as we knew no Afro-Americans had ever dared test them. Anyway, they were open. We walked in around noon and the two or three other customers (white, of course) quickly left. We ordered Cokes and were served, though not graciously.

A gang of white men began gathering outside. It was lunch hour at the peanut plant, which is what passed for "industry" in Luverne. A deputy sheriff came in and hauled Dunbar out of the cafe. He didn't say why, perhaps it was for the crime of "drinking a Coke while Black." We paid our bill and followed them out. A pair of Afro-American girls too young for sitting-in were standing by as messenger-runners. I didn't like the look of the crowd, so I told them to run back to the pool hall and tell the reserve group to stay where they were and *not* to come up. But before I could make sure they had the message straight, a dozen or more white men suddenly flashed over into a mob.

They attacked with fists and feet and our team was scattered by the sudden violence. I was knocked to the ground on the pavement of an adjacent Chevron station where I curled up in the nonviolent defensive posture. I had fallen on top of a cross-shaped lug wrench. So while one jerk was kicking my legs and back and another one was jumping up and down on me, that damn wrench was digging into my ribs. Not that I noticed it very much, I was singing (well, screaming, really) "We Shall Overcome" at the top of my voice and I could hear the others doing the same as they too were attacked. But I couldn't see anything because the thugs were all over me and I was curled up in a tight ball.

After a few minutes (it seemed like much longer) they stopped kicking and hitting me. Chief Raupach — he of the shoebox dossiers — had come up. He told the mob that *we* (not they) were under arrest. That seemed to placate them (and besides, they were getting tired). With the violence halted we got up off the ground. I was relieved to see everyone on the integration team appeared okay other than some minor cuts and bruises, which was pretty much my state as well.

As we started to follow the Chief off to jail, I was surprised to see the reserve group from the pool hall arriving. The messenger girls had gotten it wrong and told them to come up. The mob immediately jumped them, hitting, kicking, cursing, screaming epithets and insults. I watched as everyone on the team instantly dropped to the ground and curled up as I'd trained them to do just like pros. They weren't under attack for long, Raupach quickly went over and rounded them up too and we all walked a block or two over to the little Luverne police station where Dunbar had been deposited by the deputy sheriff.

We were now more or less out of sight of the mob — which was no doubt going back to work after doing their civic duty defending the southern way of life. Raupach simply told the local kids to go home. The outsiders, Dunbar, Carroll, Dave and me, he held. He was not pleased. He quickly made it clear that he thought trying to integrate Luverne was a really stupid stunt, and that doing it during the peanut plant's lunch hour was even dumber. Though I didn't say anything, I knew he was right about the timing. I hadn't even considered that and I certainly should have.

He also made it clear that since we hadn't done anything illegal he wasn't going to arrest us. He was, however, going to hold us in the station until he was certain the mob had dissolved and it was safe for us to be back on the streets. He also asked us not to go back to Lowe's Cafe. Having made our point about the Civil Rights Act we agreed — at least for that day.

For myself, the adrenaline was wearing off, my cuts and bruises were beginning to make themselves known in no uncertain terms, and I was depressed and worried. Well, all right, to put it in those technical psychological terms I had studied as a UCLA psych major, I was freaked out. Not about the attack as such but over how Mr. Kolb, Mr. Richburg, and the Afro-American community were going to react. I mean, I'd been sent to Crenshaw to help adults register to vote but now I'd gotten their children beaten up by racist thugs. I was utterly despondent. I knew I had royally screwed up — Wrong!

When we finally got back to the pool hall it looked like at least half of Luverne's Afro-American community was there. They were ecstatic. They were so proud of their kids they could bust. For years they'd been seeing demonstrations on TV, lunch counter sit-ins, white mobs, protesters curling up in nonviolent defense, youngsters defying white racists. But that was city stuff, Birmingham, Montgomery, Selma, not rural Alabama. Not little Crenshaw County deep in Klan country. But now *their* kids had done it! *Their* kids were civil rights heroes!

Parents kept coming up to me: "Did my boy do it right? They did it right, didn't they?"

"Yes, they did it just right. They were champs. When Dr. King hears about it, he'll be proud of them."

It was like everyone was walking on air. Their children had confronted white supremacy, integrated Luverne (or at least forced them to shut down their white-only lunch counters), and done it right as rain. And safely. No one had been hurt bad at all. Just bruises, cuts, and scrapes. So everyone was celebrating. It felt really, really good. Of course, I realized that if any of the kids had gotten seriously injured the reaction might not have been so positive. But "sufficient unto the day are the evils thereof," as they say.

Both Albert Turner and Hosea Williams also had positive reactions, largely, I assume, because that's the feedback they got from Richburg and Kolb. And as I later learned, other SCOPE projects throughout the South were facing the same issues and coming to the same conclusions. A number of SCOPE projects had already turned to direct action, including mass marches and arrests in Americus Georgia that Hosea himself had led. So all in all our Luverne sit-in had been a great success and Crenshaw County's Afro-American community was pleased, proud, and noticeably more inclined to go down to the courthouse next registration day.

As it turned out, though, I later learned that our action did result in one significant casualty. Not long after I and the SCOPE team left Crenshaw at the end of August, Chief Raupach was abruptly fired for his failure to actually arrest and prosecute us and his obvious unwillingness to use his office as a weapon of white supremacy. Someone later told me that he and his family had been forced to leave the county, but I don't know if that was true.

Dave's Driving Lesson ~ 1965

Later that evening we were still at the pool hall celebrating the sit-in when the phone rang. The local leader from Brantley's Black community was on the line. He was a Korean War vet and I believe his name was Mr. Greene, though I may not be remembering that correctly. He was calling to say that the local youth in Brantley had heard what the kids in Luverne had done and they wanted to do the same thing. (The rumor line in those rural counties was as efficient as today's Internet.) He asked me to come down to teach them how to sit in and test compliance with the Civil Rights Act.

Now anyone with the sense that God gave a goat would think that having just dodged a bullet maybe we should think twice about this. Not me, of course. We agreed that on the following Saturday we'd hold a training session for the Brantley kids and proceed from there.

Brantley was ten miles south of Luverne down Highway 331 and the second largest town— well, "village" would be more accurate — in the county. It had perhaps 1,000 people, maybe 350 of whom were Black. Luverne had a single traffic light which they didn't really need but were quite proud of. Brantley at less than half the size only had a stop sign or two. The first time I saw Brantley was when Mr. Richburg was driving me around on my second day in Crenshaw. As we drove through its minuscule business district I noticed several white men wearing pistols on their hips — civilians, not cops.

This was long before the National Rifle Association and the Republican Party made "open carry" a conservative political cause and seeing armed citizens on the streets was quite unusual. I asked Havard about it and he told me that white men in Brantley liked to have their guns handy in case they needed to shoot someone. In the slang I heard later from my Vietnam-veteran friends, Brantley was "one hardcore 'ville."

The next Saturday, Dave Sookne, Dunbar Reed, Dick Klausner, and I drove down to Brantley in Dave's VW bug for the nonviolent training session, which was supposed to take place on a little make-do softball field in the town's tiny Afro-American community. What we didn't know (but should have) was that almost all of Brantley's Black men had gone over to adjacent Butler County that day for a softball match. Leaving mostly women and kids back home.

About seven or eight Afro-American kids were waiting for us. We'd hardly begun to introduce ourselves when suddenly half a dozen cars loaded with white guys came roaring in, skidding to a halt on the dirt infield in a cloud of dust. Yelling, cursing, and shouting racist epithets, they leapt out carrying bats, ax handles, and chains, and charged right at us with no hesitation at all. It was obvious that they'd been tipped off in advance — either by a snitch or a tap on our phone — and had been waiting in ambush for us to arrive. I guess there were about two dozen of 'em — I didn't take a formal count — and so far as I was concerned they were all Klan.

"Run!" I yelled to the local kids and they scattered immediately knowing exactly where to take cover. I figured the Klan would chase us rather than them, so we bailed too, darting into a nearby shack. An old Afro-American woman ran out on the porch swinging her broom at the Klansmen and yelling at them to stay out of her house. That gave us just enough time to get out the back door, dash around to our VW, and boogie out of Dodge.

The white guys immediately ran back to their cars, leaving the old woman and the Afro-American community unharmed. They had big powerful cars — a Trans Am, a Pontiac GTO, a pickup truck with Klansmen clambering into the bed, and three or four other vehicles bringing up the rear. We had four people squeezed into a VW bug with a little four-banger engine. Not the recommended vehicle for a desperate car chase.

Dave was driving and I was in the shotgun seat. As I've mentioned, Dave was a graduate student in mathematics at the University of Chicago. Now as a disciple of Dr. King, I was, of course, opposed to racism and all other forms of stereotyping. But the truth of the matter was that in many ways Dave matched the classic mathematician stereotype. Very precise, very meticulous, very orderly. Earlier that month his VW had come due for its 12,000 mile service, so at exactly 12,000 miles he took it up to the dealer in Montgomery, even though we needed it that day (well, we needed it every day). He never drove over the speed limit, he always came to a complete halt at every stop sign, and ... well, you get the idea. Steve McQueen, he was not.

As we drove out of the Black neighborhood towards the paved highway we passed three cars parked side by side on a little patch of grass: the state trooper's car, the sheriff's car, and a new Cadillac. Sitting on the hood of each were: the state trooper assigned to Crenshaw County, the county sheriff, and the Mayor of Brantley. They had big shit-eating grins on their faces and as we passed by they waved at us. Duh, no need to guess how that mob got formed.

Immediately beyond where they were parked was Brantley's stop sign. Dave came to a full stop. So in a manner I'm sure you can imagine, I gently inquired as to why he was stopping with the Klan coming after us? He replied, "Well, they might try and arrest us." Which, granted, in other circumstances would have been a valid point.

I told him (again, in the manner you can imagine) that getting busted looked like our best chance of surviving because if they arrested us they might have to protect us. Then I jammed my left hand down on his knee so his foot couldn't move from the gas pedal to the brake and shouted, "You better steer, cause you ain't touching that brake till we reach Luverne!"

So we start boogying north on two-lane Highway 331, hell hounds on our tail (to paraphrase bluesman Robert Johnson). Now Dave was getting into what was going down. When the Klan cars behind us tried to pull up alongside — to either run us off the road or open fire on us — he swung left and right to block them. He had this grim look on his face, teeth set, eyes wild. It was obvious that he'd slipped the bounds of space and time and was now in some savage alternate universe — he was actually going over the speed limit!

The road was hilly and curved. I'd eased my hand up off his knee but I still wasn't about to let him touch the brake, so when we came up behind someone he had to pass right then and there. We passed cars on hills. We passed cars on curves. I looked back and the Klan was still behind us, but they were passing more cautiously, which is how we managed to stay a bit ahead of them. Their lead car — the Trans Am — sported a Confederate battle flag license plate and I could see the thugs in the pickup truck behind it leaning out, waving their ax handles and bats as they shouted at their driver to "Get 'em! Get 'em!" For some reason they weren't shooting, I don't know why.

We came up behind a station wagon with Minnesota plates — Land of 10,000 Lakes. The back window was filled with beach toys and suitcases — obviously Ma and Pa and the kids coming back from summer vacation on the Gulf. Dave passed them up a hill and around a curve — a suicide pass. The driver's jaw just dropped in amazement as we went by. I always wondered what he thought as the Klan cars then started to flash by him. Guys waving Confederate flags and ax handles, whopping it up like mad. I imagined him saying to his wife, "Oh my God, Martha! People down here are crazy! We ain't stopping till we reach the Ohio River!"

So by now Dave's got our little VW up to 70, 75 miles per hour, even faster on the downhill. The road was poorly paved and the bug was shaking and shimmying. The Klan cars were swinging back and forth trying to get in position to run us off the road, but Dave kept blocking 'em. Three miles on, five miles on, somehow we managed to stay ahead of them. Six miles. Seven. At eight miles the highway widened to four lanes just outside of Luverne. No way in hell could we block them on four lanes.

The Trans Am and the GTO hit their accelerators and got ahead of us, then came to a tire-burning stop skewed across the highway as a barricade, the pickup truck was coming in right behind us. But they had blocked the road just beyond a turn-off. Dave wrenched the wheel left and we skidded into a dirt lane.

Years later he told me, "Dick pointed it out to me. I said that I thought it was a dead end, but he was sure that it cut across to another road leading into Luverne. And it did. As I prepared to turn, I had to remind myself mentally, 'Don't signal left, don't signal left,' and I did not."

So there we were bumping along on a narrow dirt road. Our Klan pursuers regrouped and came back on our tail but the rutted lane was just one car wide so they couldn't pass. They fell back a bit, either because our VW was better on the dirt or the dust we were kicking up partly blinded them.

A few minutes later we reached another road leading into town. It was also four lanes. We turned into it and headed north towards Luverne, flat out flying as fast as that bug could go. We'd managed to pull ahead of them a bit on the dirt lane, but now that we were all back on hard-top they were catching up. If they passed us they would blockade us again.

Suddenly we saw three cars speeding towards us from Luverne — full force, pedal-to-the-metal. As we flashed by each other I saw they were filled with Black men armed with shotguns and rifles. They slammed their brakes and came skidding to a halt, tires smoking, spun around and dodged in behind us — between us and the Klan.

What had happened was that Brantley people had called up to the pool hall, "They're being chased, they're trying to make Luverne." The community immediately mobilized. Cars of armed men had gone out on both roads to escort us back into Luverne.

The Klan cars charged up on the three cars of Afro-American men who were driving side by side across the width of all four lanes to block them. The Black men thrust their rifles out the windows in a clear and unmistakable warning. The Klan cars abruptly slowed, fell behind, and then turned around. They were up for a beating or a lynching — not a battle with armed men ready to fight back.

One time, after hearing that story, someone asked me, "But I thought you were supposed to be nonviolent?"

A fair question indeed. As practitioners of Tactical nonviolence none of us on the SCOPE project carried or used weapons, and we made clear that when they were doing Movement work with us — canvassing, sitting-in, registering to vote — local folk were expected to also be nonviolent. And as a practical matter, in most dangerous situations nonviolence was still the safest and most effective tactic, which is why I used nonviolence when the local Klan leader put a pistol to my head rather than trying to violently wrestle it away from him. Had that mob caught us we would have tried to survive using nonviolent tactics — not out of ideology but because we were unarmed and heavily outnumbered.

But we respected and honored the principle that Afro-Americans had the moral and constitutional right to protect their community and the people in it from terrorist violence. And had it come down to cases those three carloads of armed and determined Black men could have stood off that mob and I for one was grateful to them. Afterwards, we all slept better at night knowing that Luverne Blacks were armed and ready if the need arose. The Klan knew it too.

Showdown in Brantley ~ 1965

With our guardians behind us we tore at high speed through Luverne's Afro-American community until we reached the safety of our pool hall headquarters. There we profusely thanked the men who had risked themselves to protect us. After I'd calmed down a bit and my pounding heart had slowed, I phoned Albert Turner to report. He said he'd come right over — a two-hour drive from his home in Marion.

While we waited for him we described to the others what had occurred and speculated on what would have happened if they had caught us. From the aggressive way they drove up in Brantley, leapt out of their cars, and charged in without a word, we had no doubt they intended to beat the living crap out of us. But since they didn't come in shooting my guess is that lynching us might not have been their initial intent.

Yet once violence breaks out, emotion and adrenaline spike and there's no way to know how far a mob will go or what they might do. Psychologists and social scientists use terms like "the madness of crowds" because it's impossible to predict what people will do in the heat of the moment. And once the car chase was underway it created a predator-prey emotional dynamic. Had they caught us on the road — with fewer witnesses than in Brantley's Afro-American community — there's no way to know how it might have turned out.

Turner arrived and as we were describing what happened, the phone rang. It was Mr. Greene, the local leader from Brantley, now home from the softball game. He was furious, livid with rage. Angry at the whites because we were his guests and they had attacked us, and pissed off at us for fleeing.

"Are you going to come back?" he asked Turner.

"Yes, we're comin' back," Turner responded quietly.

"Are you gonna let them run you out again?"

"No, we're not going to be run out."

I later learned that when Brantley's Afro-American men returned from the game in Butler County and found out what had happened, an emotional wave of rage at those who had attacked their community and threatened their kids swept over them. Brantley's white mayor showed up, no doubt to put them in their proper place, and to his shock it didn't go as he expected. Blacks were shouting fury at him face to face. Some of them were carrying weapons. "I'm a Korean War veteran!" Mr. Greene shouted at him. "You can't do this to us!"

They jawed him up one side and down the other, so much so that he retreated. And I suspect that defiance, that speaking truth to power, felt empowering. Which is why, I assume, Mr. Greene called to invite us back, in essence throwing down a challenge to white supremacy in Brantley.

After he hung up, Turner told us what Mr. Greene had said, and asked, "You all ready to go back?"

We looked at each other (gulp) and in small voices replied, "If you say so." The next day was Sunday — everyone-go-to-church day — so our return to Brantley was set for Monday.

Albert Turner had a big, Detroit-type car large enough to seat six. So on Monday morning the four of us from Saturday plus Turner and Carroll Richardson returned to Brantley's Afro-American community.

Based on Saturday's phone call from Mr. Greene, I expected to see supporters in evidence when we arrived at his home because they knew when we were coming. Not the case. The dirt streets were empty. No one was sitting out on their porches. No one. All the windows had their blinds drawn.

The bold, righteous anger of Saturday evening had been replaced by fear. "Oh Lord, what did we do? We cursed at the mayor!" Whites in Brantley outnumbered Blacks two to one, and in the local lingo they were "mean as rattlesnakes." The community's fear of white retaliation was rooted in long, hard experience.

Not Mr. Greene though. "You guys gonna stay?" he challenged us.

"We won't be run off," Albert Turner assured him quietly.

So we sat out on Mr. Greene's porch with him and his two sons, who were in their late teens or early twenties. Now, of course, we're Dr. King's people. And since this was, in effect, similar to a protest situation, we were pledged to nonviolence. Not Mr. Greene though, he had a right to protect his home and his community — a right we respected and supported, as I believe Dr. King would have. Mr. Greene was armed and so were his sons. They had rifles and shotguns close to hand on the porch — but not visible from the street, not out threatening or challenging anyone. Not displayed in macho bravado. But ready if needed.

The Black neighborhood was eerily empty. No one was visible at all, it was like we were in a ghost town. But up the slope of a little hill, in the bushes, we sensed that Black folk were watching. From behind the windows with the curtains closed, people were peeking out. What's gonna happen? What's gonna happen? Greene's neighbors were afraid to stand with us, but everybody was waiting to see what would happen.

No more than ten minutes after we arrived a car drove up and an Afro-American woman jumped out. She was the mayor's maid and she was in a state. "Oh! The mayor sent me to tell you to get out of town. He's gonna call his mob!"

As the guest of honor — so to speak — Turner was in the rocking chair on the porch and he was slowly rocking back and forth. "Well," he told her, "you can let the mayor know we're not leaving."

"Oh! He's serious! He's gonna call the mob! He told me to warn you off!"

Turner just rocked back and forth. "Well, we have a right to be here. We're guests of Mr. Greene. We're not leaving."

She got in her car and drove off. Maybe 20 minutes later, a car filled with white men drove by. They gave us hard looks and we looked right back at them. They looked at us and we looked at them. Nobody said nothing. Our faces were set like stone. We didn't make any threatening gestures, just tracked them with our eyes. Another carload drove by. They looked at us and we looked at them. They looked at us and we looked at them. A third carload drove by. Then the first carload came around again. Then a fourth carload. Them looking at us we looking at them. They came around again. And again. And then after a while, they stopped driving by.

The people who had been hunkered down and hiding realized that the mob wasn't coming back. Not that day. Not when we were ready for them. We had stared 'em down. They were up for ambushing someone by surprise — that was the Klan way. But against people standing ready for them it was they who weren't ready.

Suddenly the whole Afro-American community came pouring out into the street. Abruptly, without planning or preparation, there was a party going on. Women were there with food, people had beer, everyone was talking fast and grinning — exuberant with relief. The next registration day, August 16th, some 35 people from Brantley went up to the courthouse to register. The biggest single group we'd ever had from that section of the county.

As it happened, August 16th was the last registration day for our SCOPE project. Over the next week we began winding things down and the volunteers, both local and northern, began leaving for college. I too left the South at the end of that month, returning to Los Angeles for yet another N-VAC trial.

57.110.11c ~ 1965

Not long after leaving Luverne I was once again spending day after day in Los Angeles County Superior Court for yet another sit-in trial. Our convictions for sitting in at the Van de Kamp's restaurant in Van Nays had been reversed on appeal, probably because of the obvious bias shown against us by Judge Holaday. The district attorney, however, was determined to uphold "law and order" so I and the other N-VAC protesters were being retried, this time in front of a fair judge. Most of those days were occupied in a futile attempt to get at least one Afro-American or Latino juror impaneled on the "jury of our peers" that would try our integrated gang of nonviolent protesters for offenses against "the people of California."

Again we had an all-white jury and again they convicted us but this time without solid grounds for appeal. For the heinous crime of sitting on a restaurant floor and singing freedom songs I and the others were sentenced to 30 days in county jail.

L.A. is the land of euphemisms and make-believe, so the county prison farm was called the "Wayside Honor Ranch" — no doubt because being granted access to its posh accommodations was such a sought-after honor. It was located in the rugged northern portion of Los Angeles County near the tiny village of Castaic, right off Highway 99 (today, I-5). At that time the area was completely rural, mostly sagebrush and scrub with occasional patches of farmland. Today, Wayside has become the "Pitchess Honor Rancho" and it's no longer a farm, just a regular prison surrounded by typical suburban SoCal strip malls and housing tracts where an average home sells for a cool half million. One of those housing tracts right across the freeway from the prison includes a Hartford Avenue — sadly, though, I doubt it's named after me.

I began serving my sentence in early February of 1966. Robert Hall and I had the same 30-day sentence and we both went in together. But he was such a smooth operator that he managed to serve his entire bid in the relative comfort of the prison hospital. For an "infected boil," as I recall. Alas, I was not so slick.

For the first couple of days they kept me in the maximum security building, fondly known as "Max" or "Maxi," which was your traditional bars-and-guards slammer like the ones you've seen in so many movies. It was intentionally made miserable. Then I was transferred to the farm.

Instead of barred cells we were housed in barracks with rows of cots, open showers we could use whenever we wished, meals cafeteria-style in a mess hall, vending machines for those with coin, and a commissary if someone on the outside had paid in to give you store credit. When we weren't working, we could wander around within the fence among the various buildings. Basically it was like a World War II Army base but with guards — excuse me, I mean "correctional officers." In other words, it was much better than Maxi. And, of course, that was the deal. Be a good, obedient prisoner and you remained on the farm, act up and it was back to Maxi for the remainder of your sentence.

Of course I was nervous about prison, having never served a sentence before and having heard all the frightening stories — none of which proved true for me. No one tried to rape me or make me his "bitch," or shiv me in the shower, or force me into a gang, or ply me with smack. I would have welcomed a little pot but since this was before Nixon's "War on Drugs," no one had any for sale.

Before I went in, I was the beneficiary of much advice and cautions from people who had never themselves been in jail. I was told that asking other prisoners what they were in for was a terrible social faux pas. Which for all I know might be true in other jails, but it wasn't the case at Wayside, where everyone asked everyone else. The custom was though that you never named your crime, instead you gave the state penal code number. So if you were in for disturbing the peace, you'd say "415," or "602" for trespass, and so on. Everyone knew all the three-digit numbers for the common misdemeanors and minor felonies associated with inmates serving "county time."

I, however, had been found guilty of violating a fire ordinance prohibiting blocking an exit, so when asked, I replied, "*57.110.11C.*" Which sounded very impressive. "Wow! You must be some heavy dude, man! All them numbers!"

Every morning we all lined up in front of our barracks in the cold for "count," so they could see if anyone had managed to escape (no one did while I was there). Then it was breakfast and off to work. I was assigned to the nursery crew, which so far as I could tell mainly manicured the grass and hedges of the warden's home.

On weekends, families were able to visit together at wooden picnic tables. That first weekend I immediately noticed there were way more prisoners around than during the regular workweek. Back then, before all the hills and scrub land was built-up with housing tracts, L.A. had a huge brushfire problem. To contain the inevitable fires, they had to maintain all these dirt access roads and build firebreaks running down the ridges. And they had to have guys ready to hit a fire line at a moment's notice at any time of the year.

Fighting fires in an urban area requires a lot of training and skill. It's also highly dangerous. But containing rural brushfires was just grunt work with ax, rake, and shovel while the pros drove the bulldozers. And prisoners were cheap labor. Real cheap.

In fact, the county had come up with a really slick system. Under the law at that time a hungry or homeless family was not eligible for welfare unless the father had "abandoned" them — which was a felony. If dad lost his job or was laid off the mother had to swear out a "child abandonment" arrest warrant against him in order to get welfare or public assistance to feed the kids. Since he hadn't really abandoned his family it was easy for the cops to bust him by simply pounding on the door late at night. He would then be arrested on the warrant and routinely sentenced to a year in jail — yes, a full year for, in essence, being hungry and poor.

But instead of serving their sentences in the Wayside barracks those guys were put in fire camps, where they worked as penal labor for the county for maybe a quarter an hour or a dollar a day or something like that. Very "cost-effective" in the lingo of the bureaucrats. Those guys weren't criminals in the normal sense of the word, and since they were only in jail because that's what the system required so their families wouldn't starve or become homeless, they weren't high escape risks. Most of them were Latino or Black, and the attitude of the politicians, judges, and guards was, "They're just a bunch of spics and coons. It's good for them — three squares a day and healthy exercise. We're doing them a favor." And, of course, saving the tax-paying white public a pretty penny to boot.

I didn't enjoy barracks life and confinement was unpleasant, but what I hated most about Wayside was the way the guards harassed everyone. I'm not talking about the high-drama kind of abuse you see on TV shows, but rather constant petty humiliations on a daily basis. They enjoyed asserting their power over the inmates in trivial matters that clearly had nothing to do with penology, security, or rehabilitation but were merely to inflate their own egos and sense of importance. I suppose prison guard is the kind of occupation that attracts the kind of personality that hungers for such gratification.

A week or so after I started working on the nursery crew I came down with the flu. It was a cold winter that year and a mini-epidemic was raging through the camp. Rather than overload the camp's sickbay, they'd set up an infirmary ward in one of the barracks to isolate those infected while we recuperated with bed rest. One day the guard sergeant came through on inspection and he ordered me to shave off my mustache. Prison regulations permitted well-trimmed 'staches, which mine was, but he felt like exerting his authority. I trimmed it back some more, but didn't shave it off.

When he saw that I hadn't bowed to his authority he threw the sort of screaming tantrum that military drill sergeants use to intimidate their recruits, and he made me shave it off while he watched. Then he reassigned me from the nursery crew to the "punishment squad." I forget what its formal name was, but informally we were known as the "shit-shovelers" or other less savory sobriquets. Wayside had a dairy, and our job was to shovel up the cow manure, wheel it in wheelbarrows to open-air cesspools, and dump it in. We also got to put on tall rubber boots and wade into the slimy shit-pool and muck it out with buckets. It was tiring work and the stench was pervasive — but it was just work.

The guard in charge of that punishment squad was a tall, thin, Afro-American guy named Latimore who was tough as nails. But unlike the other guards, he wasn't into petty bullshit. He told me that if I gave him any trouble I'd deeply regret it but so long as I did my work he wouldn't mess with me. Hey, fine by me.

The first day I was on his crew I overheard him tell another guard that I was one of those "Vietnam protesters." Later I made sure he knew I was in for a civil rights arrest. Maybe he cut me some slack because of that, maybe he didn't, I don't know. As it turned out, though, I didn't mind being on his punishment crew because of his policy that he, and only he, would discipline his men. He made it very clear to the other guards that none of them were to mess with us in any way. I guess he must have had them intimidated because once I became a shit-shoveler for Latimore none of the other guards ever bothered me at all.

I spent the rest of my bid shoveling cow shit until I had served my debt to society. Then — no doubt thoroughly rehabilitated — I was deemed safe to release back into civil society

Hale County Primary ~ 1966

Shortly after being released from the Wayside Honor Ranch, I road Greyhound back to Alabama and resumed work as one of the few whites on SCLC's Alabama field staff. Albert Turner assigned me to Hale County, which is about an hour northwest of Selma. My job was to prepare for the May 1966 primary election.

The Alabama elections of 1966 were the first real test of the Voting Rights Act (VRA). All across the Alabama Black Belt Afro-American candidates were running for office. SCLC mobilized almost its entire southern staff to support those who were campaigning in the May 3rd Democratic primaries. SNCC, meanwhile, was supporting independent Black candidates and parties who would run in the November general election. Statewide, an estimated 180,000 Black voters cast ballots that May, and even more voted in November, a huge increase in the number of Afro-American voters.

Yet despite that increase, out of close to one hundred Black candidates only five were elected to public office. All the others, both in the primaries and the general election, were defeated by fraud, white intimidation, economic retaliation, and crooked counts. The 1966 Alabama elections were the first real test of the VRA, which had allowed nonwhites to become registered voters but failed to protect their right to fair, free, and honest elections. The VRA failed to prevent election fraud because the federal officials responsible for enforcing it chose not to do so. Hale County was no exception.

In Hale County, 70% of the population were Afro-American. The Rev. Henry McCaskill, a Black man, entered the race for sheriff. Prior to the VRA, less than 3% of eligible Blacks were registered in Hale and few, if any, dared show up at a polling place. Shortly before the 1966 primary — seven months after the VRA went into effect — the local paper published a list of registered voters: 4605 white and 4057 Black. The local people we were working with told us that almost 1,000 of the whites on that list were either dead or had long since moved out of the county. If those whites returned to Hale or somehow rose from the grave to cast their ballots (a common occurrence in Alabama elections) whites would have a majority and McCaskill would certainly lose. But if federal election monitors enforced a fair election and an honest count, potential Afro-American voters would outnumber whites by about 450 and McCaskill had a decent chance of victory.

Initially I was working Hale County alone, but soon a small SCLC team led by Leon Hall, a more experienced staff member, arrived to take command. We set up an office in Greensboro, the Hale county seat. Along with some local volunteers, the half dozen of us from SCLC were McCaskill's campaign staff. During April and into May we canvassed, held mass meetings and small house gatherings, recruited and trained poll watchers, distributed flyers, put up posters, and prepared for getting our supporters to the 16 polling places scattered around the county, one for each of the 16 beats (voting districts were called "beats" rather than precincts). We also tried with limited success to form permanent beat committees. It was intense and exhausting work lasting from dawn to well into the night but we were energized by hope that the VRA would be enforced and we'd be able to elect a Black sheriff for the first time in living memory.

While we were running our political campaign, white plantation owners were evicting Black tenants and sharecroppers to force them out of the county before they could cast their ballots, and white employers and landlords were engaged in economic retaliation and intimidation towards similar ends. And white residents were urging distant friends and relatives to return from wherever they currently lived to vote on election day. Federal election monitors ignored our reports and complaints about voter intimidation (a federal crime) and voter fraud (also a crime).

May 3rd was voting day. Officials misdirected many Black voters to the wrong polling places where they were barred from voting. And a number of Afro-American voters who did reach the right place were blocked from voting on one flimsy pretext or another. Our poll watchers were harassed both by election officials and white thugs who lurked in the vicinity. Observers from the Justice Department kept themselves busy noting down everything in their little books — with no discernible result.

After the polls closed, the counts were posted outside each beat's election station. That night our SCLC team drove from one to the other to tally the results. Like many other rural counties in the South it was the custom in Hale for a crowd of white men to gather at the courthouse on election night to drink whiskey and hear the returns announced. The courthouse, of course, was also a polling place and someone from SCLC had to walk through that throng, find the bulletin board, and record the tally for that beat. I was the only white person on the Hale County SCLC team so that honor fell to me, on the theory that I would be less noticeable and my presence less provocative than a Black civil rights worker. Personally, I didn't find that reasoning persuasive, but it was Leon's call.

Once again my nonviolent training served me well. The courthouse was our last stop. It was full dark and the area wasn't well lit but from what I could see there were at least a hundred or more white men hanging around on the lawn. They weren't densely packed, mostly they were standing in loose groups, smoking, talking, and discreetly sharing hip flasks and bottles in brown paper bags. While the other SCLC workers waited in the car with the motor running, I strode briskly through the crowd as if I had every right to be there while projecting a demeanor of placid calm. I was also careful to avoid all eye contact, a skill I had honed on the New York City subway system during visits to Manhattan.

When I got up to the bulletin board by the courthouse door and began noting down the tally I could hear some surprised muttering behind me, but since we were only interested in a few races I completed my task and was on my way out before they had a chance to recover from their surprise and mobilize their hate against me. I reached the car and we sped away — to my great relief.

McCaskill got 2,651 votes on May 3rd, which was enough to make the May 30th runoff. But he was 900 votes shy of the total won by his multiple white opponents.

The runoff at the end of the month was a repeat of the first balloting — harassment, intimidation, economic retaliation, and federal indifference. With only a single white candidate for each office receiving the entire white vote plus a small portion of the Black vote, all of our Afro-American candidates lost. Our hopes going in had been high, our disappointment at the outcome was deep and bitter. The pattern of intimidation, deceit, and fraud that we encountered in Hale was repeated in county after county across the state, as was the utter failure on the part of the federal government to enforce the law.

Poverty and Power

You may find this strange, but the Freedom Movement memories that haunt me to this day are not of pistols to my head, mob beatings, desperate chases, or dank jail cells, but rather remembrances of the abject poverty and human suffering that was so common and pervasive that most people simply accepted it as a normal aspect of the southern way of life. As I had canvassed door-to-door in Selma's Afro-American neighborhoods, the privation and suffering I saw shocked me. What I later encountered in Crenshaw County and other rural areas was worse. At that time in the mid-1960s, Movement activists were reading and debating *The Wretched of the Earth* by Frantz Fanon — a book title that certainly spoke to what I encountered.

America's dominant culture presents with two opposing views of poverty's root causes — one conservative, one liberal.

To oversimplify, the view from the political right is that there are two types of poor folk. The "deserving poor" — orphans, accident victims, those with debilitating illness, and so on — for whom society should provide some ameliorative charity. And a much greater number of "undeserving poor" who live in poverty because they are lazy, shiftless, alcoholics, junkies, or sexually promiscuous women who engage in serial pregnancies. In the conservative view, funding programs that aid the "undeserving poor" simply enable their lifestyle choices and encourage them to remain permanent social parasites feeding off the hard work and taxes of "productive" citizens.

To again oversimplify, the liberal view is that in most cases the root cause of long-term poverty is lack of opportunity. Insufficient education, lack of job training, child care not available, public transportation inadequate, no jobs to be had, or jobs denied because of race, gender, or some other form of discrimination. And therefore the corresponding solution is to supply opportunity by ending discrimination, providing education, training, child care, and transportation, and investing public and private funds to create new jobs.

Like most civil rights workers, I initially held the liberal view. But on the streets of Selma and the country roads of rural Alabama and Mississippi I soon came to see that while discrimination and lack of opportunity are indeed important factors, lack of political power is a deeper and more fundamental cause of systemic poverty. By "political power" in this context, I mean the ability to change (or maintain) some economic or social aspect of society. Despite libertarian fantasies, none of us exist as independent islands isolated from society at large. The laws, priorities, policies, rules, regulations, social customs, and court decisions of society all profoundly impact our economic situation.

Over decades, anti-union laws, regulations, and court rulings have steadily crippled the ability of workers to collectively bargain for living wages. Pro-business legislation and a myriad of government policies encouraged and subsidized "outsourcing" and "offshoring" of jobs in a race to the bottom of lower and lower labor costs. Housing and urban renewal policies have resulted in the poor paying a greater portion of their income for substandard housing than the affluent do for luxury accommodations, while the public transportation that the poor need has been starved and cut back. Reducing extremes of wealth and poverty was once a goal of tax policy, but today tax laws are written to transfer money from the many into the pockets of the richest few.

Political disinvestment in education, public works, transportation, and public health disproportionately impacted the poor to their detriment. And despite oft-repeated rhetoric about the sanctity of "family farms," federal agriculture policies and subsidies systematically enriched corporate agribusiness and impoverished small farmers. At the same time, business and consumer laws were — and continue to be — written to favor corporate profits at the expense of customers.

The result is that today most poor people have productive jobs — often multiple jobs — and they are working longer and longer hours yet remain mired in permanent poverty. That's not caused by lack of opportunity alone, it's caused by lack of power to change the systems, policies, and practices that create, and continually re-create, poverty.

Consider for a moment that young woman with the dying infant I encountered in Selma. There was no famine in Alabama, why were babies and children suffering malnutrition and starvation? It wasn't lack of employment or laziness, sharecroppers worked from *can see to can't see,* and that Dallas County soil was some of the richest and most fertile on the planet — that's why they put their cotton plantations there. But she had not a shred of political power, not even the vote, and that made her vulnerable to abuse and exploitation without justice or mercy.

The liberal "lack-of-opportunity" assumption was the intellectual foundation underlying President Johnson's "War on Poverty" programs of the 1960s. Despite LBJ's rhetoric, empowering poor people was not included in those programs and when people in the field made efforts in that direction they were immediately reined in by both local and national power elites. In state after state, the few War on Poverty projects that encouraged those at the bottom of the economic pyramid to take on decision-making roles and demand a voice in broader community affairs quickly came under immediate and intense political attack from local politicians and business leaders who fiercely opposed empowering poor people to exert influence and control over their own lives.

The same kind of political backlash occurred when poverty programs tried to hire actual poor people to staff centers and projects, as opposed to hiring middle-class college graduates. Similarly, efforts to form worker-owned coops that competed with local and corporate businesses were starved of resources and sabotaged by local power structures. Washington's War on Poverty quickly became a form of liberal charity where corporations were paid and middle-class professionals hired to provide services to the poor, who were expected to consume and accept what was given to them as passive clients.

During the Freedom Movement, our voting rights campaigns were, in essence, efforts to empower the disempowered. In the words of SNCC leader Courtland Cox, what we learned is that "the vote is necessary, but not sufficient."

Dr. King clearly understood the relationship between poverty and political power. In a lecture shortly before he was murdered he said:

> The dispossessed of this nation — the poor, both white and Negro — live in a cruelly unjust society. They must organize a revolution against that injustice, not against the lives of the persons who are their fellow citizens, but against the structures through which the society is refusing to take means which have been called for, and which are at hand, to lift the load of poverty. [16]

That was the underlying vision of his Poor People's Campaign. He sought to build a national multiracial alliance of poor people to fight on their own behalf. Not to plead for more charity or welfare, but to demand and win economic justice and government policies that leveled the playing field instead of tilting it in favor of the already rich and powerful. But the midst of that effort he was assassinated in Memphis, Tennessee while supporting garbage workers on strike for union recognition and a living wage.

Marching Through Mississippi

My Dad, the "Red Menace" ~ 1954

In Hollywood's version of history, the entertainment industry was the primary victim of "McCarthyism" — the Red-scare political witch hunts of the 1950s. And it's true that movie stars and screenwriters were targeted. Yet though attacks on entertainment celebrities generated huge windfalls of publicity for self-serving politicians, the main purpose of the right-wing hunt for "subversives" was to gut FDR's New Deal, control U.S. foreign policy, shape the political orientation of public education, and most important of all, destroy the American labor movement as a political and social force.

There had been a time in the 1930s and '40s when at least some unions led broad political struggles around social causes that went far beyond the immediate day-to-day workplace issues of their members such as fights for social security, unemployment benefits, racial justice and anti-lynching, tuition-free higher education, a peace-oriented foreign policy (as opposed to one that was pro-colonialist and anti-communist), and affordable healthcare.

Then in the 1950s, the "economic royalists" (Roosevelt's term) who hated unions as a matter of principle, changed their tactics. They agreed to allow labor to survive (though not necessarily thrive) if in return the unions expelled leftist leaders, echoed the approved anti-communist political cant, and entirely restricted their activities to wages and working conditions within their plant gates.

Unions that tried to continue fighting for broader social concerns came under savage attack by the red-baiters. Ten of the strongest industrial unions in the country were specifically targeted. Eight of them were destroyed. Only the International Longshore and Warehouse Union and United Electrical Workers Union managed to survive. One of the "red unions" destroyed by McCarthyism was the American Communications Association that my parents had devoted almost two decades of their lives to building.

For a time afterwards, my Mom worked as a union organizer in the Los Angeles garment industry and my dad was labor representative for the nonprofit Community Chest (today known as the United Way). But eventually the anti-communist zealots drove them out of those jobs too.

My father then became business manager of a small, racially integrated, nonprofit healthcare center. In the late '40s a group of left-leaning doctors had formed the Community Medical Foundation and Community Medical Center (CMC), which were dedicated to offering low-cost healthcare to working families regardless of race. Through union health plans, employers contracted with CMC to provide healthcare for their employees. The CMC was one of several early forerunners for what eventually evolved into the Health Maintenance Organizations (HMO) we have today. But — unlike most of today's HMOs — the CMC was run as a nonprofit, providing high-quality care and paying doctors reasonable but not extravagant salaries.

At that time in the 1950s, most MDs were in private practice, operating as independent professionals charging whatever the market would bear. Which, in the opinion of the American Medical Association, was the proper way for doctors to do business. In their view, other approaches, such as union-contract, prepaid health insurance using providers like the CMC plan, were "subversive," "un-American," and an invidious ploy to wickedly impose "socialized medicine" on an innocent public.

For the Los Angeles County Medical Association (LACMA), opposing nonprofit healthcare was a sacred duty, and they waged their crusade against "socialized medicine" on many fronts. They did their best to choke off growth of Kaiser Permanente, the huge prepaid medical plan that had come into existence during the war. Kaiser, however, was only half "socialized" — the Kaiser hospital and foundation were nonprofit, but the Permanente Medical Group (the doctors) was very much for profit — big profits — as it still is to this day.

Compared to Kaiser Permanente, the tiny CMC was a much easier target. Many of those employed by the center or on its board were either current or former Communists or non-Party leftists of some kind. And the CMC was racially integrated — Black and white medical professionals worked together as equals and the treatment given to patients did not vary according to race (as it often did elsewhere in Southern California).

The first CMC clinic was on Western Avenue, which at that time was on the edge of the South Central ghetto. I don't remember exactly why they had to move, it may have been too many burglaries, though I believe that one of the reasons was a LACMA complaint that their hallway did not meet the width required for hospitals. Why an outpatient clinic with no overnight patients had to be built like a hospital was not explained. Anyway, by the early '50s CMC had moved to Lake Street near Pico & Hoover, just outside the Afro-American ghetto. By that time they were caring for around 18,000 patients a year (compared to the half-million or so Kaiser Permanente members).

I was ten years old in 1954 when the LACMA asked the California Senate Committee on Un-American Activities to investigate the "red menace" lurking within the SoCal medical community. Commonly referred to as the "Burns Committee" after its chairman, a right-wing Senator from Fresno, the committee was the state version of the infamous House Un-American Activities Committee. They were happy — eager in fact — to oblige the Medical Association and, of course, garner a load of free publicity for themselves.

Subpoenas for CMC doctors and employees to testify before the committee arrived in late November of '54, and a bill was introduced in Sacramento authorizing the state to revoke the medical licenses of any healthcare professional who refused to "cooperate" with the committee.

To give their spectacle maximum local impact they held their hearing in Los Angeles rather than Sacramento. And, yes, "spectacle" is the correct word. Though presented as legislative hearings, McCarthyite "investigations" into "un-American" activities were a brutal form of political theater — public shamings and degradings, incitements of hostility, and direct assaults on freedom of speech, thought, assembly, and association.

The local media, of course, grabbed the story and ran with it in breathless headlines:

"Docs Here Check on Red Infiltration" — *Daily News*
"Doctors Defy Questions at Red Hearings" — *Los Angeles Times*
"Quiz Told Patients Acted as Red Links to Doctors" — *Los Angeles Examiner*

As intended, the media hue and cry prompted civic-minded do-gooders in the community to bestir themselves and take action against the "red menace" on Arlington Avenue. At the age of ten I enjoyed answering the phone on behalf of my parents (in the 1950s kids didn't own or even much use phones, so hardly anyone ever called *me*). But threatening hate-calls became so common that I was told not to pick up anymore. A red hammer and sickle was painted on our driveway and our car splattered with red paint.

My fifth-grade school teacher helpfully taught my class an hour-long lesson comparing the benefits of American freedom and democracy with the cruel dictatorships tormenting the suffering people of Communist Russia and Red China. Then, as a living example of American openness, she offered me the opportunity to address the other kids and explain why I favored red tyranny and oppression. Not knowing what to say, I hung my head, slouched down in my seat, and said nothing.

I did know, though, that I was going to get the crap beat out of me by the school bullies as soon as school was over for the day — after all, as our teacher had just made so plain, it was their patriotic duty. When class let out I was jumped and pounded and then managed to escape with a trio of bullyboys chasing me home yelling, "Red, red, wish you were dead."

Under the Burns Committee rules they could jail you for "contempt" if you refused to cooperate. This meant that you would be sent to prison if you refused to answer their invasive political questions on free speech grounds or told the interrogators that your political beliefs, the meetings you attended, and who your friends were, were none of their damn business. Only by invoking the Constitution's Fifth Amendment protection against self-incrimination could you thwart them without being jailed. But by "taking the Fifth" — as the saying goes — you were put in the position of implying there was something criminal or evil about whatever it was you were refusing to answer questions about. Which is just what they wanted for their political morality play.

They also had another rule: If you answered one question about a topic you then had to answer *all* questions about that topic — or it was off to the slammer for you. So when they asked my dad, "Where are you employed?" He couldn't forthrightly answer, "I'm proud to work for the Community Medical Center," because if he did so they could then force him to name (and publicly expose) every single person who worked there, describe what their political beliefs and affiliations were, and inform the committee whether they read leftist magazines, had Marxist books on their shelves, ever signed a peace petition, picketed for civil rights, voted Socialist, and so on. Instead he had to answer:

Hartford: "While I am very proud of the organization with whom I may work, I feel somewhat like Alice in Wonderland: everything is upside down.

Interrogator: "You don't look like Alice in Wonderland."

> Hartford: "You don't have to look like someone to feel like they do. Senator Burns doesn't look like the Queen of Hearts, but I would put him in that category."

> Chairman Burns: "Thank you." (Laughter from the audience.) [17]

Apparently Senator Burns was unfamiliar with the Queen of Hearts from *Alice in Wonderland*, whose approach to justice was "Punishment first, trial and verdict afterwards," and whose favored solution to just about any problem was "Off with their heads!" To the amusement of many in the audience, he seemed to think that my father was complimenting him.

But the Burns Committee interrogator continued to press my father for an answer, and eventually he was forced to reply.

> Hartford: "I decline to answer on the grounds that the Fifth Amendment of the United States Constitution, which was written to protect the innocent; the grounds of the First Amendment of the Constitution, which gives me the free right of association and belief; the grounds of Article I, Section 13, which gives me the same rights as being a witness against myself."

> Chairman Burns: "You imply that you may suffer incrimination."

> The Witness: "I may suffer incrimination, but that incrimination may be completely unfounded, unjustified, and come under the head of persecution, but not legitimate incrimination."

> Chairman Burns: "This is a duly constituted government agency seeking information. We want to know something about various organizations existing in Southern California. If you think it will incriminate you to tell us about them, that is one thing. ... Let's not have any more speeches. Let's get along with the hearing." [17]

When asked directly about the Community Medical Center (which he had not admitted he worked for), Ken answered:

> "The Community Medical Center, as I have heard of it, is an organization which is promoting prepaid plans, low-cost medical care. I know from the press that this is one of the organizations which the county medical association hierarchy, the 'Cadillac clique,' wants to 'get,' and which this committee is acting as hatchet man to help 'get.' I will not assist this committee in trying to destroy an interracial health center, one of the few health centers in the city that is interracial, that is trying to do a job of providing low-cost medical care to people in the lower income brackets. I therefore decline to answer this question." [17]

And so it went:

"Did you sign this booklet?" (opposing racial discrimination in hospitals).

"I decline to answer..."

"Have you ever been affiliated with an organization known as the Civil Rights Congress?"

"I decline to answer..." [17]

And on and on. And each question had to be rebuffed on grounds of self-incrimination. In a written statement that was totally ignored by the mainstream mass media, my dad wrote:

> Wittingly or unwittingly, the committee is lending itself to a selfseeking endeavor by those [LACMA] leaders to more firmly establish a lucrative medical business monopoly over the alleviation of pain and suffering due to illness. If the aims of this group are successful, those who are providing better and lower cost medical care through group practices, through service-type health plans and other methods to meet the complexity and high cost of medical care, will be deprived of their license or cowed into submission.

> It is not easy to be an "unfriendly" witness, with the personal stigma which currently attaches thereto, and subjects one's wife and children to the cruelty of hate groups and vindictiveness. However, I will not be an informer, a stool pigeon, or a tool of any vested interest, medical or otherwise. Therefore, I must choose to be an "unfriendly" witness in this investigation and to safeguard myself by claiming the protection of the First and Fifth Amendments to the U.S. Constitution.

Of course, every piece of political theater has to have heroes as well as villains. My father and the other "hostile" witnesses were cast by the Burns Committee as the bad guys. The good guys were the "friendly" witnesses — in our family, we referred to them as "stool pigeons," "finks," and "liars" — who out of either fear, belief, or self-interest named names, accused others of being leftists and commies, and echoed the Committee's mantra of subversion and political menace.

The Community Medical Center did not survive the Burns Committee attacks, nor those of LACMA and the *Los Angeles Times*. Patients became afraid to come in for medical care, most of the unions with health plans canceled their contracts, and some of the doctors resigned. Overwhelmed by political and economic pressure, CMC soon succumbed. I don't remember the details — or more probably I never really knew them — but not long after the hearing, the clinic shut down and my dad was once again unemployed. Though, thankfully, not headed to prison.

The American Medical Association won their war against nonprofit "socialized" medicine. Eventually though, HMOs did largely take over the healthcare marketplace, but as extremely lucrative, very profit-oriented corporate enterprises. In 1971, President Nixon's aide John Ehrlichman was caught on the once-secret White House Tapes explaining to "Tricky Dick" the HMO business plan. "All the incentives are toward less medical care, because the less care they give [patients], the more money they make." A strategy that proved so popular with patients that when the word "HMO" was mentioned in a movie, audiences spontaneously hissed and booed — or at least they did in my neighborhood.

Welcome to Mississippi ~ 1966

After the primaries in May, SCLC staff who had been temporarily brought in from other states returned to their regular assignments, leaving only a handful working in Alabama under SCLC State Director Albert Turner. Once again I was based in Selma and staying with the same family on Green Street who had cared for me before.

Turner assigned me responsibility for Hale, Perry, and Marengo Counties. In the weeks immediately after the election we had no clear SCLC program, so my role was simply keeping in touch with Movement activists and county organizations — letting them know that SCLC hadn't forgotten them and encouraging them to continue registering voters — while reporting back to Turner and through him up the chain of command to Hosea Williams in Atlanta. Given our total defeat in the May primaries, SCLC's lack of direction wasn't surprising. It would take a while to regroup and plan a new campaign or organizing strategy.

SCLC's orientation had always been direct action campaigns and supporting the activities of their local affiliates as opposed to SNCC's orientation towards deep community organizing. But by mid-1966 the protest fires had run their course in the Alabama Black Belt which had seen fierce, dramatic, and violent struggles in 1965. What was needed now was community organizing, but a lone activist responsible for three entire counties couldn't possibly do that effectively.

Though I wasn't aware of it at the time, while I was staying in touch with local activists in my assigned district and other SCLC field staff were doing the same elsewhere, Turner was doing some deep thinking.

Thinking and planning that eventually led to organizing the Southwest Alabama Farmers Cooperative Association (SAFCA), an economic empowerment coop that eventually covered ten Black Belt counties — a kind of deep-rooted community organizing and a sign that SCLC was slowly changing its focus from protesting segregation to addressing poverty and economics.

Few Afro-Americans in rural Alabama could afford a phone, so maintaining contact with local leaders and groups across three counties required a car. The other SCLC staff members in the state also had responsibility for multiple counties and they too needed transportation. An Afro-American church in Hartford, Connecticut offered to donate four used cars to SCLC and I was sent with three others to drive them down to Selma. I went up by bus a few days early to spend some time with my parents in New Haven, and on the morning we were to pick up the cars, my dad drove me up to Hartford, a city I knew nothing about and had never visited despite its possible connection to my family name.

We found the church easily enough. I was eager to go and connect with the other SCLC guys and carry on my Movement activities. I could tell that my father wanted to meet them too. And that made me really uncomfortable. As a young man of 22, filled with a sense of my own independence, I didn't want my Movement peers to think I was still dependent on my parents. The thought of the other guys seeing me arrive in the company of my dad embarrassed me, so I fobbed him off with some excuse. I realize now, of course, that he understood me far better than I knew myself. He acquiesced with good grace, though I suspect he did so with inner sadness.

What a stupid jerk I was! Thinking only of myself. I realize now that he wasn't trying to control or limit me, but rather he must have been remembering his own decade of hard, dangerous, work as a union organizer in Georgia, Alabama, and Mississippi. How he must have wanted to meet young activists and organizers now engaged in similar work a generation later, taste once again the kind of comradeship he shared with my mom and the other young CIO organizers of his day, maybe swap some stories and reminisces comparing the two struggles.

And I know now that rather than thinking of me as less-than-adult, they would have been impressed by this Kentucky white man of their parent's generation who had confronted the Klan and endured the same kind of dangers that we were experiencing. To this day, I deeply regret not taking that opportunity to share my Movement work with my father — and perhaps learn more of his own experiences as a union organizer in the

South. What's that old saying? — "The saddest words in the English language are 'if only'."

While I was driving back to Alabama on June 8 in one of those donated cars, the radio reported that James Meredith had been shot and wounded while trekking through Mississippi on his "March Against Fear" to encourage Afro-American voter registration. When I reached Selma and reconnected with SCLC I was told that the local police and Mississippi State Troopers who were accompanying Meredith's small band of protesters had made no move to protect him from a white racist with a shotgun.

SCLC, SNCC, and CORE, the main organizations of the Freedom Movement's direct action wing, quickly came together to continue the 200 mile march, which became known as the "Meredith Mississippi March." They sent in staff and mobilized resources, and their organizational heads — Dr. King, Stokely Carmichael, and Floyd McKissick — became the march leaders. The Medical Committee for Human Rights (MCHR) provided medical teams, and lawyers from the ACLU and Lawyers Guild gave legal support.

The Deacons for Defense and Justice from Louisiana accompanied the March to protect it from Klan assassins and violent white racists. The marchers themselves did not carry weapons (or at least they weren't supposed to), but everyone — white and Black — understood that armed Deacon guards were in the vicinity watching over the campsites at night and protecting the march from snipers and assassins while on the road.

For some reason, Turner's western Alabama staff was one of the last SCLC teams dispatched to support the march. On June 21st, Dr. King led a side march of several hundred people in Neshoba County, Mississippi to memorialize the lynching there of James Chaney, Mickey Schwerner, and Andy Goodman two years earlier during Freedom Summer. They were savagely attacked by a white mob in Philadelphia, the county seat. The next morning, June 22, six of us headed for Mississippi with Turner at the wheel.

It was about an hour and a half from Selma to the Mississippi line and we were all uncharacteristically quiet. The truth is we were scared. Other than Annell Ponder and the Citizenship School teachers, SCLC had never had much presence in Mississippi and we knew it only by reputation. We were familiar with Alabama and its dangers and we were confident in our ability to handle them. But Mississippi frightened us. There's another old saying, "the grass is always greener on the other side of the fence," which I guess is also true in reverse — distant dangers seem scarier than those you face every day. What I didn't know then was that while Blacks in Alabama were telling each other that bad as Alabama was, Mississippi was worse, Blacks in Mississippi were saying, "It's really bad here, but thank God we don't live in Alabama."

About the time we crossed over into Mississippi we found ourselves driving along a stretch of I-20 which had recently been completed. As we were approaching Meridian we saw that the lanes ahead of us were blocked off by Mississippi State Highway Patrol cars slewed across the freeway with their lights flashing. All traffic was being directed into a highway rest stop.

"Oh shit," I thought. "They must be looking for people coming to join the march." I could see that Turner and the other guys in the car had come to the same conclusion.

Yet when we entered the rest stop parking lot, instead of a posse of grim-faced cops with billy clubs and paddy wagons we discovered a temporary pavilion decorated with red, white, and blue bunting and state flags waving in the breeze. Beautiful, blonde, Miss Mississippi was there greeting visitors in her white gown with a sparkly tiara on her head. Pretty girls in cheerleader-type outfits and straw boater hats were going from car to car handing out free Cokes and "Welcome to Mississippi" buttons — I kid you not.

Mississippi Governor Paul Johnson was caught between a rock and a hard place. He had run for office on a platform of both preserving segregation and the "southern way of life," which appealed to hardline racist voters, *and also* attracting new business opportunities into the state's pathetic economy, which appealed to business-oriented "racial moderates."

Some of those white moderates were affluent businessmen who wanted lucrative national franchise opportunities like Burger King, Holiday Inn, 7-11, and the like. But those chains now insisted on full compliance with the Civil Rights Act because they'd face consumer boycotts in the North if they tolerated segregation in the South. Yet any consumer-oriented business that tried to operate on an integrated, desegregated basis in Mississippi faced economic boycotts by the White Citizens' Council and the threat of KKK violence. For those businessmen focused on their personal bottom line rather than the ideology of white supremacy, the old Jim Crow system of racial violence and segregation was now a hindrance.

And because of mechanization, cotton planters no longer needed large numbers of impoverished field hands to chop, weed, and pick for starvation wages. Now the South's wealthy power brokers — the men Dr.

King referred to as "Bourbons" — were eager to attract large-scale investment in new industries, but the region's reputation for racial strife, lawless violence, corrupt courts, and crooked politics stood in the way. The previous year, for example, Hammermill Paper had canceled plans to build a huge multi-million-dollar factory in Selma because they didn't want to be associated with Selma's image.

Of course, with one of the worst education systems in the nation, few mineral resources, poor roads, and an impoverished and stunted domestic market, what made Mississippi attractive to northern industry were mainly its low wages, anti-union laws, and low taxes. Policies that could only be maintained by suppressing progressive political and social movements.

Which meant that many of the moderates who were putting pressure on Governor Johnson to curb Citizen Council opposition to integration of public facilities and consumer-oriented businesses and to clean up the state's image by halting the kind of dramatic KKK violence that made headlines in the North essentially wanted to maintain the state's basic socioeconomic structure without the bad publicity. In essence, both the segregationist hardliners and the racial moderates wanted to keep Afro-Americans "in their proper place." The difference being that the hardliners saw that place as a kind of slave-like social inferiority, while the moderates saw the proper place of Blacks as dollar-spending customers and low-wage workers for white-owned businesses.

Yet while Mississippi business leaders were putting pressure on Governor Johnson to clean up the state's image and crack down on the kind of overt, violent racism that made headlines in the North, the majority of the state's white voters still adamantly opposed civil rights and any sort of social advancement for Afro-Americans. Politicians who failed to keep the "nigrahs" in line were doomed to electoral defeat. So Governor Johnson was trying to do the impossible. He was trying to enforce segregation with police clubs and arrests to appease white voters while simultaneously trying to improve how northern investors viewed the state. Hence the state troopers forcing us off the freeway for a heavy-handed "Welcome to Mississippi."

A couple of the cheery cheerleader girls, all smiles and pearly teeth, came over to our car. They saw me, "white as rice," sitting in the front seat next to Albert Turner, "black as coal," along with four other Afro-American men, and there was no mistaking who we were. For a moment their faces kind of dropped, but I give 'em their due props, they recovered. They had their job to do and they did it well. They gave us our free Cokes with a smile and a friendly "Welcome to Mississippi, y'all."

Once we realized this wasn't an ambush and we weren't about to be beaten down or arrested on some phony charges, we enthusiastically played into the game with gusto, laughing and grinning like crazy, and taking their Cokes and buttons and whatnot. I still have the "Honorary Citizen of Meridian" pin one of them gave me.

Weird shit, weird shit indeed

The Meredith March and Black Power ~ 1966

After escaping the siren allure of Miss Mississippi and her court of cheery cheerleaders, we drove across the state looking for the Meredith March. We knew the march was somewhere near Yazoo City — a small town of about 10,000 people on the southern edge of the Delta. The great majority of its inhabitants were Afro-American but all economic and political power was in white hands (today the mayor is a Black woman and three of the four aldermen are also Afro-American). As we drove down its main street Turner took one look at the Black folk on the sidewalk and knew that the march had already passed through. He could literally see it in their faces and the way they carried themselves. So we turned around and caught up with the march a few miles short of the tiny, unincorporated hamlet of Benton.

While Turner drove on ahead, the rest of us got out and started marching in the muggy heat. I guess there were maybe 100 marchers, about 15 of them white, the rest Afro-American. The great majority were local Mississippi Blacks, the rest were staff and volunteers from organizations like SCLC, CORE, SNCC, MCHR, MFDP, Delta Ministry, and other groups, or supporters from the North.

We had to walk on the poor footing of the muddy soft shoulder, the awkward down-slope of the roadside drainage ditches, and the thin curbs of bridges and culverts because the cops refused to let us step on the pavement. This because the free flow of traffic must never under any circumstances be impeded (except, of course, for state-sponsored welcome ceremonies that force everyone off the freeway into a rest stop).

Despite Miss Mississippi's welcoming smile, I was scared. This was the Mississippi Delta, stronghold of the KKK and birthplace of the White Citizens' Council. The whites who passed us in their cars or stood by the side of the road glowered and shouted their hate. Some cars swerved as if to run us down so we had to be in a state of constant alertness, ready to dodge aside at any instant. The cops and state troopers — themselves all white, of course — were no less hostile than the bystanders.

Our fellow marchers were also seething with anger over the white mob that had viciously attacked the Chaney-Schwerner-Goodman memorial the day before in Philadelphia. Along with Dr. King, a contingent from the Meredith March had driven over to Neshoba County to participate and some of those now marching had barely escaped serious injury — others had not been so lucky and were off the line still healing up.

From time to time someone would start a freedom song and everyone would join in, but mostly we talked as we walked — the march line was a moving agora of debate over the Deacons for Defense and nonviolence, the role of whites in the Freedom Movement, and Black Power. Discussions that expanded and intensified when we reached the Benton campsite that evening, and continued the next day on the march from Benton to Canton.

I was 22 in 1966, and utterly certain of all of my many, many convictions. What's that Dylan line? "I was so much older then, I'm younger than that now." Most of the CORE, SNCC, and SCLC field staff were also in their twenties and all of them equally sure of their own beliefs. Which meant we had some lively discussions and arguments because there was no agreement or consensus on those three issues — not even close.

Given all the media hype about gun-toting Deacons, I had expected Afro-American desperadoes armed with rifles and pistols stalking about like angry panthers. No one I saw fit that description. No one was aggressively waving weapons around or swaggering about in any kind of hostile or threatening manner. Not along the march nor at the camp. There were some Black men driving by or sitting in cars — some of them might have been Deacons but most of them were simply local folk come out to see the spectacle. Those who actually were Deacons no doubt had pistols concealed on their person or in their car and probably some hidden shotguns and rifles for use if need be, but so did most of the locals, because carrying heat was a normal way of life for Mississippi Black folk living in Klan country.

Scared of Mississippi as I was, I was glad to know the Deacons were somewhere nearby, even if I couldn't identify who they were. Yet as we marched through Mississippi the debates around the Deacons and nonviolence were endless and complex. Some marchers — mostly but not entirely northern whites — were arguing against the presence of the Deacons on grounds of Gandhian Philosophical nonviolence. At the other end of the spectrum, some super-militants — mostly but not exclusively Black northerners — were proclaiming their allegiance to "eye-for-eye" retaliatory violence and lauding the Watts explosion of the previous year as a model that should be widely emulated. Most marchers, both Afro-American and white, fell somewhere between those extremes.

My attitude was that Tactical nonviolence was necessary on protests. In the South of the 1960s demonstrations that turned violent would have been quickly and ruthlessly suppressed by overwhelming police power. And the resulting lengthy prison terms for participants would have killed any hope of a sustained political activity. Yet allowing Klan assassins to kill activists and leaders would have the same effect, so self-defense against white terrorism outside of protests was not only morally justifiable but politically essential.

The only way to achieve progressive reform in America against the status quo's money-power and violence-power is through "people-power" — mass movements of people demanding social change. By definition, "mass movements" have to include a wide range of people far beyond dedicated social activists. Activists are few in number and they are the crucial catalyst, but they succeed only when they win support from the many. And the truth is that while our modern culture glorifies and glamorizes violence as entertainment, the overwhelming majority of Americans are frightened and repulsed by actual violence — even verbal violence. Only a small fringe element will participate in or support aggressive violence. Violent rhetoric and violent deeds may appeal to young macho males, but they alienate almost everyone else. Which is why nonviolent direct action has been successful in building mass social movements but violent street action and violent rhetoric have generally had the opposite effect.

Details and nuances of nonviolence were topics of intense debate and discussion, particularly among the SCLC, SNCC, and CORE field staffs. One ongoing argument I recall was around the premise, *I'd rather be caught with it than without it,* regarding whether or not activists should carry weapons while *not* on protests. Should we keep pistols in our pockets? Should we drive with guns in the glove compartment? Should weapons be kept in freedom houses for defense against Klan attacks?

We all knew that if cops caught us with a gun they could and would charge us with concealed weapons felonies or other gun-related charges. And if there were no witnesses about they could, and very well might, shoot us down in cold blood and then claim "self-defense," citing the gun as evidence. On the other hand, if caught in a Klan ambush without weapons there was no way to fight back, and by 1966 a lot of civil rights workers, particularly in SNCC and CORE, had decided they wouldn't go the way of Chaney, Schwerner, and Goodman — not without a fight.

For me as a white civil rights worker, my daily presence was in some ways a permanent ongoing protest. Without question I was more likely to draw police scrutiny while going about my daily business or driving on the back roads than were Black organizers. Since I was so often stopped and singled out for harassment by cops I usually chose to go unarmed. But not always. There were some short periods later on when threats from the Klan were so immediate and so intense that I carried a pistol in an attaché case that I kept on the car seat beside me and by my bed at night. Fortunately, I never had to use it. But had the occasion required, I would have.

Some of the Black SNCC and CORE marchers, and some of the Black northerners who had come down to support the march, fiercely opposed the presence of white marchers and white participation in the Freedom Movement in general. A sentiment that had been growing ever since the Freedom Summer campaigns of 1964. A few of them were overtly hostile and quite hateful, accusing white civil rights workers of consciously trying to usurp Black leadership and deliberately subverting and sabotaging the Movement — either from ingrained habits of white supremacy or from deliberate nefarious intent. On a personal level, it was bitterly hurtful to be slapped with enmity, antagonism, and accusations from people I had thought of as fellow freedom fighters.

But opposition to white participation was far from unanimous — not even close. Many Black marchers, including the majority of the local folk, retained their firm commitments to integration and interracial solidarity. Beliefs that had formed the foundation of the Freedom Movement for years. Most of local folk went out of their way to make outsiders standing with them as allies welcome — regardless of race. A reality I took comfort from.

These were complex and emotionally charged debates. Compared to Afro-Americans, most (though not all) white activists did in fact come from backgrounds of relative affluence that gave them a kind of self-confidence that often resulted in paternalistic or "missionary" attitudes that justifiably infuriated Black freedom workers. And most (though not all) white civil rights workers tried to overcome such conditioning with varying degrees of success.

As I saw it, racism was so inherent in our society and culture that all Americans of *all* races were (and still are) infected from childhood with varying aspects and degrees of it. It's incumbent on socially conscious people of all races to oppose and resist racism, bigotry, and stereotyping as it manifests in themselves. Obviously, whites who derive social and economic benefits from racism face a more difficult internal struggle than do nonwhites. But no one is automatically immune from racism because of their skin color, class background, ethnic history, political ideology, or moral fervor.

As a deeply involved white man, I obviously supported white participation in the Freedom Movement. My argument was that racism is a white problem, not a Black problem. It wasn't Afro-Americans who created segregation and white-only lunch counters, it wasn't Blacks who forced themselves to ride at the back of the bus, it wasn't people of color who denied themselves the vote or perpetrated racial lynchings. But if racism is a white problem then at least some whites have to be involved in solving it — under Black leadership.

The SNCC and CORE workers who opposed white participation in the freedom struggle also viewed racism as a white problem. They argued that whites should address it by organizing in white communities, not working in Black communities. But in the violent and racially-polarized South of that time, anti-racist organizing among southern whites was at best ineffective and at worst impossible. Less effective, in my opinion, than the political value of providing visible interracial support for Black-led struggles.

Furthermore, I believed that white racism could only be confronted on an interracial basis. A model of Blacks organizing Blacks might very well build Black pride and confidence, but a segregated strategy of whites alone trying to organize other whites would end up perpetuating rather than challenging ingrained white racism. As I saw time after time, without direct confrontations by Afro-Americans, discussions about white racism among whites by themselves became abstract, theoretical, and devoid of transformative power.

Another factor that needed to be taken into account was that the presence of white activists made it impossible for racists and segregationists to frame the issue in exclusively racial terms or simply define it as "Blacks against whites" — a formulation that would leave Afro-Americans outnumbered, outgunned, and out-monied. The presence of white allies forced people North and South to confront questions of "right versus wrong" rather than "white versus Black."

Many Black staff members opposed white involvement in the Movement because they believed that Afro-Americans needed to rely on their own skills and resources. A valid point, I thought. Many white activists did have skills and experience not available to southern Afro-Americans and that did sometimes result in local Blacks deferring to them. But not always. Furthermore, that argument about deferring to outside skills could also be made on the basis of class rather than race.

Some of the college-educated Blacks had the same advantages as northern whites, and less-educated locals often deferred to them on a class basis — race notwithstanding. A reality that some Afro-American activists such as Andrew Young of SCLC were willing to acknowledge:

> The role of white people on the march began to be discussed. There was a decision on the part of some of the blacks in SNCC that we don't just want to get people free, we want to develop indigenous black leadership. And one of the ways to force the development of indigenous black leadership is to get rid of all this paternalism. Now, they and we were paternalists ourselves in many ways, because we were outsiders just as whites were. That's the reason SCLC never went along with that. We felt yes, we have to develop local leadership, but you don't want to blame the frustrations of local leadership development on whites alone. We were also partially responsible for usurping some of the leadership. [18]

By virtue of their backgrounds, white allies brought access to outside economic and political resources that the Freedom Movement desperately needed, particularly at the grassroots level where the ability to bail some kids out of jail, obtain food for evicted families, or scrounge up a typewriter, made a significant difference.

Black activists who were opposed to white participation argued that Afro-Americans had to see that they could build a political movement on their own without relying on whites. A position I agreed with. But I didn't buy the argument that the presence of a few white supporters was inherently detrimental to the development of Afro-American leadership. Blacks had been building and leading such movements for years and were continuing to do so. Local movements like Albany, Birmingham, Greenwood, Nashville, Durham, Orangeburg, Selma, and so on were built and led by Afro-Americans. Some of those movements had some white participation, others didn't, but they were all Black-led.

Much of the passion over this issue came from Afro-American SNCC and CORE activists who resented white activists who, they felt, challenged or threatened their status and position within their organizations. Yet SNCC and CORE's southern wing had always had some white participation, yet so far as I could see they were, and clearly remained, Black-led.

In SCLC, white allies like me were generally welcome without the arguments that were roiling SNCC and CORE because unlike the other two groups SCLC was a hierarchical organization with leadership clearly, firmly, and permanently in the hands of Black ministers. There was no possibility of whites pushing Afro-American leaders aside. If you wanted to rise in SCLC's ranks you pretty much had to be Black, male, and a minister — or at least an Afro-American landowner or professional. (A few Afro-American women managed to transcend the gender barrier, but they were rare exceptions to a general rule.) White activists like me were simply seen as foot soldiers. Which didn't bother me at in the least because I never saw myself as any kind of leader in the Black Freedom Movement.

And for me it is telling that while this issue of usurpation of leadership was raised by some CORE and SNCC staff members, I rarely heard any local leaders or local activists expressing any concern that their roles were being usurped or threatened by white activists. Quite the contrary. By and large, local Black leaders almost always welcomed the participation of white allies (though some arrogant and ill-behaved white *individuals* were on occasion told to leave).

Nor did local Afro-American leaders see whites as *political* threats. They knew white supporters were not going to stay and put down long-term roots in their communities. In some cases, however, local leaders *did* fear competition from Black activists who they thought were trying to usurp their position in the community — an issue rarely acknowledged by those arguing the anti-white position.

Those two issues of nonviolence and race were now caught up in, and had become inseparable from, intense debates over the "Black Power" slogan, that had burst into public consciousness just a week earlier when Stokely Carmichael of SNCC publicly called for it during a tense and passionate rally in Greenwood.

As a slogan, "Black Power" had immense impact. But it was difficult to discuss and analyze because there was no specific program associated with it, nor any common understanding or interpretation of its meaning, neither among its supporters nor its detractors. Since there was no consensus on what the slogan meant there was even less agreement on whether it was good or bad. In a sense, the phrase "Black Power" could mean anything to anyone, which made it hugely popular (or fearfully scary) — but elusive. So as it turned out, in some discussions I was a Black Power advocate and in others an opponent, depending on how the people I was talking with defined its meaning.

For the most part, my views on Black Power were shaped by Dr. King, Albert Turner, fellow members of the SCLC field staff, and Black Power proponents such as CORE leader Floyd McKissick who argued that "Black Power is a movement dedicated to the exercise of American democracy in its highest tradition; it is a drive to mobilize the Black communities of this country in a monumental effort to remove the basic causes of alienation, frustration, despair, low self-esteem and hopelessness."

As McKissick defined it, Black Power focused on economic justice, use of consumer boycotts, fostering self-reliance and Afro-American businesses, opposing police repression and brutality, engaging in independent electoral politics without subservience to the Democratic Party, enforcement of federal civil rights laws, Black pride, and Black leadership of Black organizations and struggles — but not automatic enmity or antagonism to white allies.

Dr. King supported some Black Power concepts, but considered its use as a slogan tactically counter-productive:

> Black Power, in its broad and positive meaning, is a call to black people to amass the political and economic strength to achieve their legitimate goals. ... We must use every constructive means to amass economic and political power. This is the kind of legitimate power we need. We must work to build racial pride and refute the notion that black is evil and ugly. But this must come through a program, not merely though a slogan... I had reservations about its use. I had the deep feeling that it was an unfortunate choice of words for a slogan. [19]

As I saw it, the Freedom Movement of the 1960s and the Afro-American movements that had gone before us were fighting to win a fair share of political power for nonwhite people and economic justice for those at the bottom of the economic pyramid regardless of race. For me, that's what the call for "Black Power" meant — and I supported it.

Others interpreted it quite differently. As you might expect, I opposed those who argued that Black Power meant repudiating tactical nonviolence and embracing retaliatory violence and race war as a political strategy for social change — as some proponents did. I may not be a political genius, but I can certainly spot a suicidal strategy doomed to quick suppression and utter defeat when I hear one.

As a matter of both principle and practicality I also disagreed with those who interpreted Black Power as a call for racial separatism and race hatred. I argued for both the moral and the practical necessity of interracial struggles for freedom, equality, and economic justice. I had no problem accepting Black leadership of the Black Freedom Movement and Afro-American organizations, I had always assumed that Afro-Americans were and should be the leaders of the struggle for Black freedom. But as an ally of that struggle I did feel that I deserved to be respected as such, treated as my actions rather than the color of my skin warranted, and have my voice and opinions at least heard and considered.

Looking back now with the benefit of hindsight, one aspect that I think we all gave too little consideration to was the danger that "Black Power" rhetoric would reduce the criteria for leadership in the Afro-American community to simply being Black and expressing passionate affirmations of "blackness." In the years that followed it seemed to me that in some instances opportunists seized personal political power on the basis of posturing — asserting Black pride and anti-white anger rather than demonstrating any real accomplishments on their part against entrenched white supremacy or achieving actual changes in people's lives. The result was that in some places the courageous pioneers who built the Freedom Movement in the hard and dangerous early years were later shoved aside by loudmouth blowhards grabbing the spoils under cover of militant-sounding bombast.

While we were on the Meredith March we had no access to TV or northern newspapers so we were largely isolated from the national hysteria over Black Power that was being hyped in the national press. It was only after the march ended that I discovered how overwhelmingly negative and alarmist the media's interpretation and description of the "Black Power" slogan had become. I know that fearmongering and exaggeration draws viewers and sells papers, but their sensationalized distortions made it very difficult to rationally develop constructive Black Power strategies and programs or even assess the tactical and strategic advantages and disadvantages of "Black Power" as a slogan.

Media distortion and disparagement of Black Power, however, was part of a broader context. Today, the liberal press pats itself on the back for the supportive and transformative role they feel they played in winning the battle for Afro-American civil rights (a struggle that many of us believe has not yet been won and still continues). But the period of mostly positive media coverage of the Freedom Movement was actually quite short — basically just the two years between the Birmingham "Children's Crusade" in the Spring of 1963 and the end of the March to Montgomery in the Spring of '65.

Before Birmingham, the northern media did provide sympathetic coverage of visually dramatic incidents like courageous nonviolent lunch counter sit-ins, the terrorist attacks on Freedom Riders, the white rioters trying to prevent James Meredith from integrating Ole Miss, church-bombings, Klan assassinations and so forth. But at the same time they simultaneously paired those supportive stories with cautions and fears about "communist infiltration and subversion." They warned that freedom protests were potentially aiding America's Cold War enemies in the global battle for influence between the "Free World" led by the United States and the dark forces of "Red totalitarianism." And they consistently harped on the perceived risk that our use of nonviolent civil disobedience might lead to "social anarchy" or some other form of dangerous social disruption. So at best, before Birmingham they were ambivalent.

After passage of the Voting Rights Act in August of 1965, the Freedom Movement increasingly began to address issues of economic injustice and northern-style segregation. As soon as we started raising those issues, the sympathetic coverage in northern media rapidly cooled. And after the Watts explosion in the summer of 1965 inflamed racial fears among northern whites — particularly northern liberals — the tone of mass media coverage shifted markedly.

By 1966, stories praising the hope and courage of nonviolent protesters in the face of southern bigotry and injustice had largely been supplanted by cautions regarding hate-filled "Black racism," "kill whitey" scare stories, and imaginary threats of race-based urban guerrilla warfare. Pundits, commentators, and editorial writers who had called for racial justice in '63 and '64 now seemed far more concerned with "law and order." Seen in that context, the northern mass media's almost universal condemnation of Black Power was no surprise at all.

Tear Gas and Rifle Butts ~ 1966

After weary, sweltering hours marching in the torrid heat, we camped next to a church on the edge of the unincorporated Benton community in Yazoo County, and local Black women brought food for us hungry marchers. Deep into the night we continued discussing and arguing issues, after which I slept the sleep of exhaustion.

When I awoke the next morning, June 23rd, my mind wasn't "stayed on freedom" (as the song went). I was still scared of Mississippi. So frightened, in fact, that I had not been able to urinate since crossing into the state before noon the day before. As the march slogged down Route 16 from Benton towards Canton, the heavy heat beat down on me and sweat soaked my blue work shirt — and I still couldn't pee. It was too dangerous for anyone to leave the line to use a restroom or convenient bush, so following along behind us at walking pace was a stake-bed truck with a couple of portable toilets. Twice I climbed up the little ladder at the rear of the truck, waited my turn, and entered a port-a-potty to pee — which I really needed to do despite all my sweating — but I couldn't. I was clenched so tight with fear I just couldn't.

This summer solstice had been the day before, so the sun rose around 6am and didn't set till after 8pm and the heavy, muggy heat beat down on us for 14 solid hours. During the lunchtime rest break I explained my situation to an MCHR medic and asked him for some kind of pill to help me urinate. I wasn't aware that except in "emergencies" Mississippi didn't allow out-of-state doctors or nurses to practice medicine without a state license — which they refused to issue to Freedom Movement medical professionals. He told me he'd rather not give me any medication and not to worry about it, I would piss when I was ready to piss. It turned out he was right, all it took was a massive dose of tear gas and a few good whacks from the butt of a police shotgun and I had no further problem.

Welcome to Mississippi, indeed.

My bladder problem aside, the march that day was in some ways quite surreal, a world unto itself. For a car-oriented person like me, time, space, and the walking pace of the march all seemed distorted and diminished. Time in the sense of clocks, deadlines, and appointments had little meaning. We woke in the morning when someone woke us, ate what was provided when it arrived, and then hit the road. There was no way to really mark time — or any reason to — other than the noon lunch stop when we could rest (though there was little shade from the merciless sun), and then the evening campsite as the shadows finally lengthened.

While we were marching, the outside world was little noticed and far away. Vehicles flowed past us, sometimes with Afro-Americans who honked and waved in support and other times with whites who yelled obscenities and occasionally tried to swerve into us with their cars. The rural countryside of cotton patches and shotgun shacks slowly unrolled to either side like a painted background except for occasional clots of supporters or opponents gathered by the side of the road to greet or jeer.

North, south, east, and west had no meaning. Instead we had right and left, front and rear, which formed the boundaries of our perception. We could observe to our left and right, but danger from hostile whites prevented us from leaving the line. "Front" was the press truck with their cameras clicking and whirring, moving at walking speed ahead of the march leaders. "Rear" was the trailing toilet and supply trucks. Preceding the press truck and trailing behind our supply truck were carloads of cops who we interacted with not at all.

What we did pay attention to was the tight little world of the march itself. Conversation, debate, argument, and of course putting one tired foot ahead of the other beneath a blistering sun. People moved forward and back along the line, nurses from MCHR passed out salt tablets, teenage boys with canteens shared water. Some folk pushed their way to the front to have their picture taken from the press truck with Dr. King,

Stokely Carmichael, or Floyd McKissick, while others drifted to the rear to use the port-a-potties on the toilet truck or simply ride for a few minutes to rest their feet.

The Big Black River — actually it was a muddy brown — was the boundary between Yazoo and Madison counties. As soon as we crossed over the narrow two-lane bridge our march line began to lengthen as more and more local folk joined. Afro-Americans made up some 70% of Madison's population and though it was a violent stronghold of white supremacy, over the years CORE organizers had built a solid base of Movement support. By evening local Blacks had swelled our numbers to several hundred.

By the time we reached Canton, a town of around 10,000 and the county seat, I was drenched in sweat and utterly exhausted from walking 20 miles in the muggy heat. And I still hadn't been able to pee.

We marched into Canton singing. Over a thousand Afro-American supporters were waiting in the downtown square to greet us on the courthouse lawn. I was so tired I wasn't paying all that much attention, but I knew the plan was to set up our tents that night on the playground of a nearby Colored school. On previous days, marchers had been allowed by local officials to camp overnight at schools and parks, but the authorities in Canton were refusing permission. There was a short, fiery rally and SNCC's Stokely Carmichael told us, "They said we couldn't pitch our tents on our Black school. Well, we're going to do it now!"

We resumed marching through Canton's streets to the McNeal Elementary School, and as we passed through the Afro-American neighborhood folk came off their porches to join us until we numbered several thousand. The cops weren't blocking our entrance to the unfenced dirt schoolyard, so we marched right in. Off to one side was a big posse of lawmen from different jurisdictions in various uniforms. All of them were wearing helmets and those who weren't carrying rifles and shotguns gripped long billy clubs in their gloved hands.

Our large truck drove onto the yard and we were told to surround it so the cops couldn't seize them. It was one of those big box types, and march leaders climbed up on the roof to address the crowd while a work crew began unloading and unrolling the canvas tents and others began to lay out the poles. A caravan of Mississippi Highway Patrol cars pulled up and disgorged almost 100 state troopers in full riot gear. They began lining up in attack formation. So did the local cops.

CORE leader Floyd McKissick had a bullhorn and from the top of the truck he was shouting that we had a right to use a Black school paid for by Afro-American taxes. He called on us to remain nonviolent if the police tried to arrest us on charges of trespass or disturbing the peace — which is what we all assumed was about to occur. Stokely and other SNCC folk were weaving through the crowd leading a chant of "Pitch the tents! Pitch the tents!" Dr. King then spoke, urging us to stick together and if necessary fill the jails in the state until they didn't have enough room to hold us all.

Then the cops and troopers began donning gas masks and pulling tear gas canisters out of satchels. At that point, most of the local folk in the crowd around the truck intelligently began to drift back and ease on out of the area, but there must have been well over a thousand of us still on the schoolyard. Retreat wasn't an option for me, of course, I was emotionally committed to stand with the Freedom Movement come hell or high water, and as an SCLC staff member my duty was clear. And by now the adrenaline of danger, conflict, and fear was filling me with renewed energy.

It was maybe half an hour before sunset and I remember the sun was low in the sky, casting long shadows. Without any warning at all or any order from the police to disperse, there came the loud sounds of *Pop! Pop! Pop!* Burning, stinging gas was everywhere. A white cloud enveloped me, blinding me with tears. My lungs burned with searing pain. I couldn't breathe. I thought I was going to die. Everyone was running, choking, gasping, fleeing in all directions, bumping into each other in the blinding miasma. A gas canister fired from a shotgun hit a woman near me and exploded — she screamed in agony but I couldn't see where she was.

Some kind of hideous monster with a long black snout — a cop in a gas mask, I realized — abruptly materialized out of the fumes and smashed the butt of his rifle into my shoulder, knocking me to the ground. Someone tripped over me before I managed to get up and continue trying to escape. Every gasping breath was agony. My chest burned, my eyes gushed tears.

More cops appeared and disappeared in the acrid, stinking smoke, flailing with their clubs at anyone and everyone. I could hear the sickening thuds of wood striking flesh, and I must have been hit several more times because the next day I had long, dark, aching bruises on my body. At the time, though, I didn't feel the blows at all. An adrenaline rush can often block out pain — for a short while.

Finally, I managed to make it across a street into the someone's yard and collapsed half-hidden by a big bush. All around me people were screaming and vomiting and sobbing. Some were thrashing around on the ground like they were having a seizure. By now it was twilight and the gas clouds were dissipating, though the invisible fumes lingered on. The skin on my bare arms and face burned as if on fire. Someone found a garden hose and we took turns flushing out our eyes, rinsing our mouths, and washing down our flesh with cool water. The water felt good, but my lungs still ached and my eyes were still seared.

Someone near me muttered something sarcastic about the Deacons for Defense failing to protect us from police assault. But I knew that wasn't their job. Their role was to guard us from Klan and other white terrorists like the guy who had shot Meredith in the first place, not engage in armed warfare with the state of Mississippi. They were far too smart to seek a battle with lawmen they couldn't possibly win — lawmen who had the full force of the American judicial system behind them.

To be honest, I was thankful for and relieved by the Deacons' self-discipline. Many of the troopers were carrying rifles and shotguns and all the cops had pistols they were eager to use. Had some fool started shooting there would have been bloody carnage, dozens killed and many more wounded. And all the blame would have landed on "militant black extremists" and the Freedom Movement as a whole.

In the dusky twilight, I followed others who seemed to know where they were going and by the time it was full dark I arrived at Asbury Methodist Church where people were gathering.

The church had a restroom and I finally urinated without any trouble at all.

I found Albert Turner, who was sending SCLC staff out to comb the area. Our orders were to tell people that the wounded should be brought to the adjacent Holy Child Jesus Mission where MCHR was setting up their emergency aid station and that those able to do so should gather at Asbury. Of course, never having been in Canton before, once I had gone a block or two on the now dark streets (no streetlights, of course) I no longer knew where those churches were or how to get back to them. But there were plenty of local folk around who did.

When I got back to the church a mass meeting had started and people were singing. Sandwiches and coffee were being handed out to the marchers, who had been on the road all day. I wolfed mine down while Turner briefed us. We would march that night through Canton's Black neighborhoods to express our defiance and provide a nonviolent channel for the community's rage.

Of all the Movement's nonviolent protest tactics, night marches in the South were the most dangerous. On the upside, they allowed adults with day jobs to participate. But on the downside, under cover of darkness Klansmen could ambush people with thrown rocks, flaming Molotov cocktails — or sniper fire from pistols and rifles. Most TV cameras of that era couldn't effectively film in the dark and flash-equipped still cameras had limited range, so the cops could attack with little fear of being photographed or filmed by the press and they could claim self-defense from imaginary violence on our part.

Along with the other SCLC staff, I was given a colored armband and assigned to act as a march marshal, keeping people moving, defusing trouble, and maintaining nonviolence. Five or six hundred of us marched out of the church into the unpaved and unlit roads of Canton's Afro-American community. This wasn't a lawful, on-the-sidewalk, avoid-blocking-traffic march. Instead we filled the streets singing and calling bystanders to come join us. Block by block our numbers grew as people joined us, but in the dark it was impossible to estimate or count how many were marching.

Seething with anger, for an hour or more we surged through the dark streets, defiantly singing our freedom songs and chanting "Black Power!" and "Freedom Now!" Some of the ultra-militants and the more strident Black Power advocates called for people to go downtown and "get whitey," others shouted that we should challenge the cops who were still guarding the disputed schoolyard. Fortunately, they had little support. Marshals like me urged the marchers to hold together and maintain nonviolent discipline, and since most of them were local folk with a solid grasp of Canton's tactical realities they heeded our call.

I was stationed about halfway down the line, so I never saw who was leading the march or heard what, if anything, was being discussed by the leaders at the front. After a time my adrenaline energy began to flag, as did that of others, and people started dropping away to return home. We ended up at the Holy Child Jesus Mission's gymnasium where those of us from out of town bedded down on the floor, some with a blanket or bedroll, others without. Utterly exhausted, I slept the sleep of the dead.

By the time the turbulent 1960s were over I had become quite the connoisseur of violent police assaults and tear gas attacks on nonviolent protesters. Looking back now 50 years later, Canton was, without question, the worst and most violent single attack I ever experienced.

On the Streets of Canton ~ 1966

After a few short hours of sleep on the hard floor of the basketball court, I woke the next morning to sore muscles and aching bruises. My eyes immediately began stinging and tearing from the gas chemicals still on my clothing. I couldn't move my shoulder without shooting pain, and my ribs hurt if I drew a deep breath.

Oh, yeah, most definitely welcome to Mississippi.

Again local people provided us with hot coffee, bacon, grits, and biscuits covered in delicious thick gravy. While we ate, Turner briefed the SCLC staff. Our tactical situation was complex. The overall strategic plan called for the last stage of the Meredith March to be from Tougaloo College on the outskirts of Jackson through the city to the Capitol for a mass rally. For maximum political effect the rally had to be as large as possible. If 10,000 Mississippi Afro-Americans assembled in protest at the Capitol building it would be a major political milestone — the first Black protest ever allowed at the Capitol, the largest civil rights demonstration in the state's history, and visible proof positive against segregationist lies about "outside agitators" and "just a few malcontents."

To achieve maximum participation by local Blacks, the rally was scheduled for after church on Sunday the 26th, two days hence and out-of-state supporters had made travel plans accordingly. So the rally date could not be changed. Therefore, in order to ensure that the march was symbolically continuous from Memphis to Jackson a contingent had to reach the Tougaloo campus no later than Saturday evening which meant that at least some of us on this Friday morning had to march out of Canton headed south on Highway 51.

Yet after the Chaney-Schwerner-Goodman memorial had been so viciously attacked in Neshoba County on the previous Tuesday, Dr. King had promised to lead a return protest in the county seat of Philadelphia to express the anger and defiance of local Blacks and to show the world that the Freedom Movement would not be stopped by mob violence. The date for that return had been set for this same Friday.

Movement supporters from Mississippi, Alabama, and elsewhere were already on the road, as were car caravans from Afro-American communities in Meridian, Hattiesburg and Jackson. And in Neshoba County itself, Black folk were mobilizing. If King didn't show up it would appear as if he had surrendered to fear of white violence and the courageous Neshoba community would feel abandoned and betrayed — no way in hell that was going to happen. So King, accompanied by a portion of the SCLC staff and a contingent of marchers from Canton, had to leave within the hour and drive east to join the Philadelphia march.

Meanwhile, local Afro-Americans and the Meredith Marchers in Canton were still enraged over the savage gas attack and beatings of the evening before. Many had been injured, a number of the wounded rushed to Jackson hospitals, and just as we couldn't let white violence in Neshoba deter the Movement neither could we allow police repression to do so in Canton. So that meant that in addition to marching south towards Jackson and resuming the protest in Neshoba we also had to take to the streets of Canton.

But the cops in Canton, particularly the state troopers who had been reinforced overnight, were now even more heavily armed and clearly eager for any excuse to again whip heads and stomp us troublemakers into the ground — Black and white both. So the plan was for a day of disciplined nonviolent protest in Canton as a show of determination and defiance. Since more injuries and arrests — or worse, wounds or deaths from police gunfire — would not strengthen the Freedom Movement and might derail the mass rally in Jackson, it was essential that the protest be as loud and militant as possible without edging over into violence on our part that the cops could use as an excuse for a second brutal attack.

Turner divided the SCLC staff into three teams. He led one south on Highway 51 towards Tougaloo with about 50 marchers. A second accompanied Dr. King back to Neshoba County. I was assigned to the third team, which would march through Canton.

The road contingent made an 18-mile forced march all the way to Tougaloo in just one day without incident. The Neshoba County group led by Dr. King was again met with mob violence. As on the previous Tuesday, they marched into the little downtown area from Mount Nebo Baptist Church in the Afro-American neighborhood. A throng of angry whites — Klansmen, teenagers, and local farmers — were waiting for them. A force of Highway Patrol officers provided protection from physical assault but not from not thrown bottles and rocks. Some of troopers "guarding" the protest were the same ones who the evening before had gassed and beaten us in Canton.

To segregationist fury, local Black leader Rev. Clint Collier, Stokely Carmichael, and Dr. King all addressed a protest rally from the courthouse steps. For many of the enraged whites, allowing Blacks to demonstrate at the courthouse and actually stand on the steps to speak against white supremacy was a kind of social desecration. "Go to hell!" they screamed. "Nigger, nigger, nigger! Wait till tonight, you black bastards, we'll find you then! We're gonna kill King! Kill King! Kill King!"

Back in Canton where I was, the Afro-American community was still seething with fury and boiling with energy. Local leaders were urging a general strike and a "Blackout for Black Power," meaning a boycott of white-owned businesses. By mid-morning, members of the Madison

County Movement were already picketing downtown and deliberately tying up traffic. Simultaneously, there was a voter registration march to the courthouse and almost 50 people were registered by federal registrars under authority of the Voting Rights Act.

While all that was going on, more than 500 singing and chanting marchers were snaking through the streets of Canton. In the Black neighborhoods we walked two by two on the side of the dirt roads next to the drainage ditches. In the white neighborhoods we strode on their well-kept sidewalks. Marching into white areas was a bold move, a decisive declaration that defiantly rejected the deferential subservience of the past. It also risked spontaneous violence from furious whites.

I was once again acting as one of the march marshals and I remember nervous rumors passing up and down the line — that a parked car we were about to pass concealed a dynamite bomb, that in the next block they had a pack of dogs waiting to attack us, that that old white woman scowling at us from her porch had a big pistol hidden under her apron as she rocked back and forth on her rocker and that she'd sworn to shoot anyone who stepped on her lawn.

Since I had never been in Canton before, I had no idea where the leaders at the front of the march were taking us, except that we were deliberately avoiding the McNeal Elementary schoolyard where a swarm of heavily armed state troopers were guarding that disputed turf like rabid dogs. Not only were they patrolling the perimeter, they had snipers with rifles on the roof and they were setting up spotlights for the coming night so the riflemen could see their targets in the dark.

Black Power advocates and other militants were stridently calling for returning to the school and pitching a tent in defiance of cops and officials. I agreed with them. I wanted to publicly defeat those who had beaten and gassed us. I wanted to force our tent down their throats. Of course, that risked another bloody confrontation and more people injured. And people would certainly be killed if some fool started shooting. But I didn't care. I was angry, and pumped up with battle adrenaline. I wanted to win regardless of potential cost. Fortunately, older and wiser heads were in charge rather than me. And as a march marshal, I accepted my assignment to maintain discipline and nonviolence even though I personally agreed with the hotheads.

Years later, I learned that while we were marching through the streets of Canton, fierce political battles were raging among Black leaders and also within the white power structure. The downtown (white) merchants didn't want to go through another Afro-American boycott — they'd been there and done that in previous years and they didn't want to endure another one. Boycotts were particularly effective in Canton because local merchants were in competition with the larger, better-stocked stores of Jackson just 30 minutes down the road.

And at both the local and state level, members of the power elite were urging some compromise that would avoid a renewed outbreak of violence which might trigger federal intervention which they greatly feared. They also wanted to avoid yet more negative publicity for Canton and Mississippi both of which were trying to attract northern investment. Investment like the huge Nissan auto plant that today is Canton's largest employer. Hard-line white voters, however, stood adamant against any concessions that might be interpreted as "rewarding" defiant Blacks.

On the Afro-American side, local leaders like C.O. Chinn and national figures like Stokely Carmichael argued for challenging the police state by finding a tent (the cops still had the ones they had seized the night before) and defiantly pitching it on the playground, come what may. But led by Mrs. Annie Devine, most of the community's Black leaders feared the long-term consequences of renewed violence that might easily spin out of control. Consequences that would be borne by the Afro-American residents of Canton, not us outsiders. There was a real and legitimate fear that if someone lost their head and assaulted a cop an avalanche of legal repression for "inciting violence" might come crashing down on local Black leaders and crush the Madison County Movement with lengthy felony trials and long prison sentences. Dr. King agreed with Mrs. Devine, seeing no advantage and substantial risk in another violent confrontation.

Local leaders also sensed an opportunity. They wanted to use the tent crisis to force open lines of communication with white authorities. For years, white politicians and power brokers had consistently refused to meet with Afro-American movement leaders. They had met with so-called "Negro leaders" who they themselves had handpicked, but never with spokespeople chosen by the Afro-American community itself — real leaders who might force them to acknowledge that Blacks had interests that white elected officials were obligated to address.

In Canton, in Mississippi, and throughout the Deep South the prevailing attitude of most white officials was, *You don't sit down with your mule and negotiate. You point it in the direction you want it to go, and if it balks, you beat it till it obeys.* That's why forming a biracial committee of the real leaders from both communities was usually one of the first demands a local Freedom Movement made and why it was bitterly resisted by white officials.

On that Friday though, the tent crisis forced Canton's white power structure to open negotiations with Afro-Americans who spoke for the

Black majority. They offered an alternate campsite and a promise of an ongoing dialogue as concessions, but Black leaders knew that their community needed some kind of return to the disputed McNeal schoolyard. Though we who were protesting in the streets knew nothing about any of this, just before the evening mass meeting a stormy summit of local and national Freedom Movement leaders agreed to a compromise with white officials.

The mass meeting in the gymnasium that night was packed. Between local folk and a couple of hundred Meredith marchers from outside the area there were close to a thousand of us in the sweltering heat. Local leader Annie Devine stood up and announced, "We're going to the schoolyard." Before she could say anything more, everyone erupted in cheers and applause and began surging out of the church to form up for a march.

Like me, most people were spoiling for another confrontation. I soaked my blue bandana in water to be as ready as possible for more tear gas. Others were doing the same with rags and towels. With militant pride we strode through the Afro-American neighborhood, singing and calling on bystanders to join us — and a large number did.

By the time we reached McNeal there were probably more than 1,500 of us. The state troopers were formed up nearby, but they weren't blocking our entrance. The spotlights had been removed and we didn't see any snipers up on the roof. But there was no truck and no tents. And the cops had flooded the field with water from fire hydrants so it was now ankle-deep in gooey mud.

A stepladder was set up, and while someone held it steady Mrs. Devine climbed up a few rungs to address us. She explained the compromise — we could hold a rally but not erect a tent. In return, white leaders had agreed to open up dialogue and communication with the Afro-American community and a meeting was scheduled with the mayor and city attorney.

We were all taken by surprise. I felt angry and betrayed. Someone yelled, "We been sold out!" Many shouted their agreement. King and McKissick were absent. Stokely didn't speak, but anyone looking at him could see he disagreed with the decision. SCLC was represented by Rev. Ralph Abernathy who tried with little success to portray the compromise as a victory. As did John Lewis, who had recently been replaced as SNCC Chairman by Stokely. But none of us marchers felt victorious.

"Get the tents!" people shouted. But there were no tents, the state troopers had them. A few SNCC and northern militants shouted that we should somehow set up a symbolic tent and force a confrontation in the name of "Black Power." But they were few, with scant support among local Afro-Americans, and what support they did have was mostly from high school boys and young men in their twenties. Though I was disappointed too, I did not join or support them in their call to disregard the local leaders. This was a decision for Canton's Afro-Americans to make, not outsiders like me who would soon be marching on to Jackson and then returning to wherever we came from.

Our march back to the church had none of the earlier spirit and exuberance. Again we gathered in on the basketball court, this time with reporters barred from attending. Local leader C.O. Chinn, Stokely, and other militants roundly condemned the compromise. Mrs. Devine and others defended it as an important step forward and the only alternative to another round of savage violence from the cops, which would help no one.

I could see that most of the local adults with families were relieved by the compromise, but many of Canton's young Black men were disappointed and disgruntled. Yet they respected Mrs. Devine and the other local leaders who had been in the forefront of the struggle for years at great personal risk. Most crucially, almost everyone understood the need for unity and discipline in the face of white hostility. They knew that if they split against each other over the compromise, whites in power would divide and conquer as they had so many times in the past.

The arguments continued long into the night. Over the course of that long discussion, I came to understand and accept the reasoning behind the compromise, though it still didn't sit well with me emotionally and I felt no sense of victory. The meeting finally came to an end well after midnight, and we marchers again slept for a couple of hours on the floor.

From my personal knowledge and observation, I believed then — as I still do — that all, or almost all, of those most stridently pushing for another confrontation were sincere. Back then in 1966, none of us knew about the FBI's COINTELPRO campaign of targeting the Freedom Movement with disruption and sabotage. But my leftist upbringing caused me to wonder if there might not be among them a few deliberate provocateurs sent in to create internal dissension and foment violence that could be used as a pretext for cracking down on the Civil Rights Movement with arrests, prison sentences and mass media scare stories. Now that the true scope of the FBI's tricks has come to light, it's reasonable to ask if the Meredith March and Canton had been targeted by COINTELPRO provocateurs. I don't know the answer. But I do know that if provocateurs *were* active that night they failed to break the Movement's discipline and goad it into self-destructive acts of aggressive violence.

Marching on the Capitol ~ 1966

On Sunday morning, June 26th, the Meredith March assembled on the grounds of Tougaloo College for the final leg to the Capitol building. Tougaloo was one of the rare Black colleges in the South where both administration and faculty fully supported the Freedom Movement. Students who had been expelled from other Black schools because of their civil rights activities were welcomed by Tougaloo. For years it had been a crucial Movement base and a steadfast sanctuary for activists — one of very few in Mississippi. And for that reason it had been forced to endure legal harassment, legislative hostility, and terrorist violence. Now its tree-shaded campus sheltered marchers arriving from all over Mississippi and around the nation — mostly Afro-American, some white.

The day was sweltering hot and so muggy it felt like a sauna. Salt tablets handed out by MCHR medics didn't seem to help much. An hour or so before noon several thousand of us marched out through the Tougaloo gate and started down North State Street — Highway 51 — towards the Mississippi State Capitol in the center of the city. No longer were we marching on the edge of the road, now we had a permit and filled the lanes. I was a marshal again, working the middle of the line as usual.

At first we marched through Afro-American neighborhoods where local Black folk waved, cheered, and handed out glasses of cool water and cold lemonade. Many of them joined the column.

The hot sun beat down on us out of a cloudless sky. Thermometers read mid-90s, but it felt so much hotter. At every gas station we passed the soda pop machine was already sold out by the time my section of the column passed by and the heat was making me woozy. I'd endured hot days in Alabama, but this was worse — maybe because of lack of sleep and tension or perhaps residual effects of the tear gas. I felt like I might pass out.

In a parking lot by the side of the road I spied a shed housing a coin-operated ice machine. I inserted a quarter and with a loud *thunk!* out came a five-pound block of ice. I lifted it up over my head and smashed it down on the pavement, breaking it into pieces, then wrapped a cold chunk in my blue bandana and pressed it against the back of my neck. What a blessed relief! For all I know, that might have saved me from the heatstroke that other marchers were already succumbing to. Folk saw what I had done and rushed over to grab up pieces of ice for themselves. As I continued down Highway 51, people were feeding their own quarters into the machine.

By now it was past noon. As local Afro-American churches ended their services, people formed up at eight designated assembly points to join the column moving down State Street. The number of marchers steadily swelled — 5000 — 7000 — 9000. As *Village Voice* journalist Jack Newfield later described it:

> The ragged band that had begun as one mystical prophet in Memphis, that became 100 in Hernando, that became 1,000 after the baptism of spite in Philadelphia and tear gas in Canton, had become 15,000 on Sunday afternoon. [20]

By now we knew for certain that we were part of the largest civil rights protest in Mississippi history, something only dreamed of by Freedom Movement pioneers in the hard, lonely, dangerous days of the early '60s. The Highway Patrol estimated 10,000 marchers, the U.S. Justice Department reported 15,000, Movement supporters claimed 25,000. From my assigned position in the middle of the march I could see neither its front nor rear so I had no idea how many of us there really were, just that it was a huge turnout that decisively countered Mississippi's claim that the Civil Rights Movement was nothing more than a few outside agitators and local malcontents seeking publicity in the northern media.

Overwhelmingly the marchers were Black Mississippians — students, maids, farm hands, laborers, and sharecroppers, with a leavening of preachers, teachers, and business owners. And the obvious reality that almost all of the marchers were local Blacks gave the lie to segregationist's self-serving myth that their "nigrahs" were contented and happy.

Some 500 local cops from a variety of jurisdictions and almost the entire force of state troopers had been mobilized to guard us — or more was it to protect the southern way of life *from* us? Judging by the way they scowled and fingered their clubs it was clear how they felt — except for the dozen or so Afro-Americans who had only recently (and very reluctantly) been hired by Jackson in response to a court order and intense political pressure.

As we approached downtown we began passing through a poor white neighborhood. Now instead of smiles and lemonade we were met with snarls of hate and white teenagers waving Confederate battle flags. In a marked shift from the nonviolent discipline of previous years, some marchers shouted their own insults back. Others chanted, "Black Power!" and "Freedom!" in defiant counterpoint. And I guess some of the Confederate flags must have been grabbed from the whites because later at the Capitol militants set one on fire.

My job as marshal was to prevent brawls from breaking out by keeping the line moving past the hecklers. "Keep moving, keep marching, keep marching." When the next marshal behind me arrived to relieve me, I trotted (it was too hot to run) forward to regain my assigned position until I had to halt at the next potential trouble spot.

As afternoon shadows began to lengthen we entered the downtown business district, still singing freedom songs, still chanting "Freedom!" and "Black Power!"

A block or two from the Capitol building someone handed out small American flags for marchers to carry. Most people took them eagerly — disregarding the passionate denunciations of a few Black Power militants. Personally, I didn't feel like waving the "Stars and Stripes," I was too angry and bitter at the complicity and failures of Washington in regard to voting rights and segregation, to say nothing of LBJ's expanding war in Vietnam. But I understood why Afro-Americans who had been excluded from full citizenship for generations and had just marched past hate-filled whites waving the "Stars and Bars" of the Confederacy would see carrying a U.S. flag through the streets of Jackson as both a powerful affirmation and a defiant protest. And it was obvious that white segregationist onlookers were as enraged at Blacks protesting with the American flag as they were at my "race traitor" presence among the Afro-American marchers.

Police presence became more pronounced as we approached the Capitol building. Even more so than county courthouses, the Capitol was holy ground for Mississippi whites. It was a symbol of their supremacy, never to be profaned by Black protesters. Governors were inaugurated on its front steps, ceremonies of white pride and power took place in its halls, and on the expansive tree-shaded plaza was a monument to women of the Confederacy, dedicated to "Our Mothers, Our Wives, Our Sisters, Our Daughters." For whites, it was unthinkable that Afro-Americans would be allowed to "defile" this monument to sacred white womanhood.

Just a year earlier, in June of 1965, demonstrators had tried to march towards the Capitol to protest actions being taken by the legislature to subvert the Voting Rights Act. Almost 1000 had been arrested and held in cattle barns at the state fairgrounds under brutal conditions. More recently, a clearly unconstitutional law had been enacted prohibiting political demonstrations of any kind on the Capitol grounds.

Yet now the all-white state government was in a bind. Their white constituents wanted the Capitol "protected" from the presence of defiant Blacks, but if the state arrested thousands of peaceful marchers for violating an unconstitutional law in the glare of national publicity, they'd be exposed as the racist bigots that they were. More importantly, as a practical matter they didn't have any place to hold so many prisoners — not even the fairground buildings were big enough — nor did they have the funds to feed us.

If they used tear gas and billy clubs to violently drive us off the Capitol grounds — as they'd done to our vastly smaller number in Canton — we'd be dispersed into the downtown business district, the state's premier shopping mecca jammed with white-owned stores, plate-glass windows, and buildings filled with expensive flammable merchandise. A Watts-type spasm of urban arson and looting could easily result — to the great displeasure of important white business leaders. And either mass arrests or mass violence would be a huge black eye for the state, the kind of investment-discouraging publicity they were trying to counter with ploys like the "Welcome to Mississippi" roadblock we had encountered outside of Meridian.

There was also a new factor just beginning to be felt in the halls of power. When SNCC had started trying to register Afro-American voters back in 1961, fewer than 4,000 of the 36,000 eligible Blacks in Hinds County were registered, and little progress had been made until passage of the Voting Rights Act in 1965. But by mid-1966, the number of Afro-American voters had quadrupled to some 16,000, representing roughly 20% of the county's total electorate. That was not yet enough to elect Afro-Americans to office, but it was sufficient to swing an election between rival white candidates and therefore enough to cause at least a few white politicians to begin adjusting their rhetoric, policies, and behavior to the new political realities now looming on the horizon.

Freedom Movement leaders, however, were also in a bind. We marchers were determined to protest at the Capitol, which had been the goal and focus of the entire trek from Memphis. We had a constitutional right to peaceably assemble and demand redress of grievances and we were in no mood to obey any unconstitutional limitations on our political freedoms. But SCLC, CORE, and SNCC were all flat broke and deeply in debt from the costs already incurred by the march. There was no money to bail out hundreds of arrestees, let alone thousands — or tens of thousands.

If the cops attacked the march and dispersed the throng into downtown, there was no hope whatsoever of maintaining nonviolent discipline. If looting and arson broke out there was no doubt in anyone's mind that the cops would open fire with all the weapons at their command. Dozens would be killed, hundreds wounded. Hundreds more would be arrested for violent felonies, be tried by all-white juries and face long prison sentences. And, of course, there would be enormous negative political ramifications if a nonviolent demonstration "led by Martin Luther King" turned into a violent urban riot — regardless of the provocation.

So another compromise was worked out by march leaders and white officials. The new "no-protests" law would be quietly ignored and we could hold our rally in the large Capitol parking lot — so long as we did not get too close to the actual building itself. In other words, we could protest on Capitol grounds but not *touch* the holy building or *defile* the grass lawn around the monument to white womanhood.

As we poured onto the Capitol grounds an army of cops armed with rifles and tear gas grenades — state troopers, county sheriffs, Jackson police, and state game wardens — formed a shoulder-to-shoulder ring around the building to prevent us from encroaching on their sacred space. Mississippi National Guard soldiers with rifles and fixed bayonets protected the front lawn and the Confederate-women memorial from our vile selves.

Today, when I think about that sick and obsessive effort to prevent us from "profaning" the Capitol with our very presence — a Capitol built in part with Black labor and Afro-American taxes — the insult still makes me angry. Yet, now with the benefit of years and wisdom, I know that the march leaders who engaged with the white power structure and made mutual compromises did the right thing (though I would not have said so at the time).

Violent confrontations and police outrages are not the goal of nonviolent direct action, though enduring them may sometimes be the price of moving the struggle forward. We were trying to accomplish real social change, and forcing the state of Mississippi to accept our right to protest at the Capitol was an important advance. Provoking a bloodbath by trying to push our way through the cops and guardsmen to reach the steps or rally on the lawn would have gotten a lot of people hurt — possibly killed — an irresponsible action that would have been seriously detrimental to the Freedom Movement's long-term goals.

At the time, though, I was simply too exhausted and enervated from the heat to give a damn one way or the other. My chunk of ice had long since melted, the late afternoon sun was harsh, and my feet were swollen and sore. I think most of the other marchers felt the same. I sat down in the shade of a tree and rested against the trunk. I'm sure the rally speeches were great and inspiring, but the sound system was so inadequate I couldn't understand what was being said and I was woozy from the heat. I just dozed off.

To the American mass media, the only lasting significance of the Meredith March was the emergence of "Black Power" as a controversial slogan that they proceeded to demonize. As *Newsweek* put it, "Freedom Road has taken a disconcerting turn." Yet for myself and other civil rights activists whose boots were on the ground, it was the liberal mass media who had taken a "disconcerting turn" over the previous year. A turn away from objective reporting and towards stoking white fears of urban violence and "Black militants." A turn towards hyping the "white backlash" of resentment against civil rights and Black social and economic gains.

To this day, some historians still echo the mass media and dismiss the Meredith March as of little interest or consequence because it did not become the tipping point for new national legislation like Birmingham and St. Augustine or Selma and the March to Montgomery. But those specific events did not, in and of themselves, force Congress to act. It was the cumulative effect over time of the Freedom Movement as a whole that won new legislation and court rulings. Yes, those famous tipping point events were important, but so were hundreds of other efforts, including the Montgomery Bus Boycott, lunch counter sit-ins, Freedom Rides, Freedom Summer, and local campaigns across the South in places like Greenwood, Gadsden, Orangeburg, Durham, Cambridge, Danville, and dozens of other locales.

Moreover, the real power and ultimate effect of the Freedom Movement can't really be measured in legislation and judicial rulings. There had been laws and court orders in the past, but the realities of Afro-American life in the South had not changed. What transformed race relations in Dixie was the effect of the Freedom Movement on the people themselves — both Black and white. Segregation ended because Afro-Americans simply refused to accept it any longer and the Movement brought them together and gave them political and legal tools to make that refusal stick. In that sense, even though our Luverne, Alabama sit-in and Brantley confrontation had received not one sound bite or column inch in the media, they were as important to forcing changes in Crenshaw County as were the laws passed in Washington DC — maybe more so.

When evaluated in that context, the Meredith Mississippi March was just as significant and important as any of the other large-scale campaigns and protests of the era because it directly affected those who participated in it, observed it, and had to respond to it. And that includes members of the white power structure who were forced to meet with, negotiate with, and make concessions to Afro-American leaders whose power derived from the Freedom Movement.

The Meredith March also directly sparked a Grenada Freedom Movement, provided a jolt of activity for the MFDP in Greenwood and throughout the Delta, revived movement activity in Canton where the boycott of white merchants continued through the summer along with weekly protest marches, and it spurred Black voter registration throughout the state. The following year, 1967, was an election year, and more than 20 Afro-Americans were elected to public office for the first time since Reconstruction, including MFDP member Robert Clark of Holmes County in the Delta, who became the first Afro-American elected to the state legislature in living memory.

The Missing Word

Nowadays I consider myself more a writer than a protester, and as a writer I love the English language. I love its richness, its breadth, its depth. Yet for all of that, there's a word that's missing. We know and hold an important concept for which English does not provide a word.

Like many civil rights veterans I am quite critical of the way the Freedom Movement is taught in schools and presented by the media — almost always in terms of the Supreme Court putting the cause into motion with a bold ruling, one or two charismatic leaders, a handful of famous protests in a few well-known places, some tragic martyrs, and the gracious largesse of magnanimous legislators. Or, as Julian Bond critiqued it so succinctly, "Rosa sat, so Martin could march, so Obama could run."

But we who were there know that without the activity, determination, and courage of hundreds of thousands of men and women of all ages in cities, towns and hamlets across the South — and across the nation as a whole — there would have been no court rulings, no movement, no famous leaders, no new laws, and no change. We know that it was the Freedom Movement that made the leaders, not they who made the Movement. Martin Luther King did not create the Montgomery Bus Boycott, the boycott created Dr. King.

For us, the movement we participated in was above all a mass people's movement — people nonviolently coming together to make history for themselves. What was fundamental and profound about that struggle was the central role played by men and women, boys and girls, transforming their own lives for themselves through extraordinary courage. For us, these non-famous folk who are so consistently overlooked or undervalued by mainstream history were the heart and soul, blood and bone of the Freedom Movement.

When speaking of these unsung warriors — people like the Wests in Selma, Richburg, Kolb, and Greene in Crenshaw County, the teenage marchers in towns and hamlets across the South, and so many others — we sometimes use terms like "ordinary" or "regular" to distinguish them from those who were famous and well-known. But that's wrong. There was nothing ordinary about the men and women who risked all to defy white supremacy by lining up to register at the courthouse, or who sat on their porches with shotguns guarding us from night-riding terrorists, or the young girls and boys who defied dogs and fire hoses and filthy jail cells to march for freedom. Regular? No way.

No, the ordinary people took counsel of their fears and stayed away from "that mess." Regular people didn't go on freedom rides, or sit-in at the five & dime, or defy Bull Connor and Sheriff Clark. Nor did ordinary people sacrifice their scant dollars to pay bail bonds, or their evenings, weekends, and precious hours with their families to attend meetings, circulate petitions, and knock on doors. And regular people didn't share their homes and what little food they had with strangers like me, whose very presence put them and their families at deadly risk.

Selma, Alabama had one of the largest local movements in the South. Because of a court-ordered appearance-book system we know that somewhere around 15% of eligible Dallas County Blacks attempted to register during a time when it was hard, humiliating, and dangerous. Fifteen percent doesn't sound like much, but it was way more than most local movements ever achieved. Across the South, whether it was 2%, 10%, or 15%, those brave few who risked life and livelihood by daring to defy white supremacy were neither "regular" nor "ordinary" — and we should not refer to them as such. But if "ordinary" and "regular" miss the point, what word do we use?

Perhaps Bob Moses of SNCC comes closest with his term "unexpected actors," referring to those who for reasons of race, class, and gender are assumed by our cultural gatekeepers and intellectual notables to be drones and followers rather than agents of social change. But for those of us familiar with Howard Zinn's *People's History* they were *not* unexpected. Down through the generations there have been many people's movements that changed history — movements carried in the hearts and on the backs of thousands, tens of thousands, and hundreds of thousands. The abolitionists, the women's suffrage marchers, striking workers in the 1930s, and so many others who changed the economic and social face of America.

But as with the Freedom Movement, when *that* history of social struggle is taught (if it's taught at all) it's also presented in terms of the famous few, not the unsung many — John L. Lewis and Walter Reuther, Susan B. Anthony, William Lloyd Garrison, Harriet Beecher Stowe, and (hopefully) Frederick Douglass & Harriet Tubman. But not the labor rank and file who walked those dreary picket lines, nor the courageous suffrage hunger-strikers being force-fed in prison, nor the embattled sharecroppers trying to defend their land, nor those who risked their lives on the underground railroad. They too were neither famous, nor "ordinary," nor "regular." What do we call them?

For some of us, social and political causes are the major focus of our lives, and for us words do exist. We're called "activists" or "community organizers" (and, yes, sometimes "troublemakers"). But we alone do not make history, we are always too few. History is made and changed when the fives and tens and fifteen percents of not famous, not ordinary, not regular people stand up for justice. The thousands of children who marched into Birmingham jails, the thousands of adults who lined up outside county courthouses, the thousands of men and women who housed and guarded people like me at night.

The culture promulgated by our schools and mass media imply that history and change are made by important individuals — kings and presidents, tycoons and innovators, wealthy thieves and violent terrorists. But never by masses of non-famous people who show up and nonviolently take a stand. We who participated in the Freedom Movement know how wrong that is.

What we don't have is an adequate word for those people.

Mississippi Goddam!

Hound dogs on my trail
School children sitting in jail
Black cat cross my path
I think every day's gonna be my last
Alabama's gotten me so upset
Tennessee made me lose my rest
And everybody knows about Mississippi
— Goddam!
From "Mississippi Goddam!" by Nina
Simone

A Century From Freedom ~ 1966

Before I-55 was completed, U.S. Highway 51 was the main highway between Jackson and Memphis. Halfway between those two cities is the town of Grenada, the seat of Grenada County. The county's western side dips down into the rich, flat cotton country of the Mississippi Delta while the hilly eastern portion is partially flooded by Grenada Lake. Local lore had it that both were named after the province and city in Spain, but folk pronounced the names more like the hand-thrown military weapon than any location named in Spanish geography.

Grenada had always been a segregation stronghold. In May of 1966, both town and county still lived as if it were 1866. Blacks still sat at the rear of the Greyhound buses that briefly paused each day at the depot. In flagrant violation of the Civil Rights Act, Afro-Americans were not permitted to enter the library at all. Nor could they eat at the white diners or lunch counters. White women worked behind the desks and cash registers of downtown Grenada, Negro women pushed mops and scrubbed toilets in the homes of their white employers.

Over the previous century there had been a number of racial lynchings — four in one day in 1885. Fear still ruled the Afro-American community and Blacks didn't get "uppity" in Grenada, not if they wanted to survive, not if they wanted to stay. For Afro-Americans, society was still ruled by the edict of Supreme Court Justice Roger Taney in the infamous 1857 Dred Scott decision that, *a negro of the African race had no rights which a white man was bound to respect.*

A Black man risked a beating, arrest on a trumped-up charge, or even death if he looked a white man in the eye, questioned or challenged a white person in authority, or simply failed to step off the sidewalk into the gutter to let a white woman pass by. And Black women lived with the daily knowledge that under the southern doctrine of "paramour rights" white men could sexually assault them with impunity.

Though its population was barely 18,000, like all Mississippi counties Grenada was large enough to contain two separate and distinct worlds — one Black, one white. About 8,000 people lived in Grenada town. Most of the city's land was occupied by whites and their white world was one of paved, tree-shaded streets with sidewalks, lush green lawns, and red-brick homes. Grenada's Afro-American population lived on the periphery, mostly on the north and west edges with a smaller isolated district on the east side. Their Black world was one of dirt lanes — dusty in the summer, muddy in the winter — with small weather-beaten "shotgun" shacks jam-crammed side by side on every square inch of available land. No lawns, no sidewalks, no streetlights, no sewers, and no storm drains.

With many Afro-American adults gone north to seek work, whites had a slim 51-49% majority in the county and a similar narrow margin in town. But the Black population was skewed towards children too young to vote and the elderly too old to get to the polls or too poor to pay the poll tax, so even if Afro-Americans were allowed to register without difficulty whites would still have a solid 57-43% voting edge. In actuality, few Blacks were allowed to register, and fewer still dared show up at a polling place to cast a ballot. Of 4323 Afro-Americans eligible to vote in 1961, only 61 (1.4%) were registered, while 95% of the 5792 whites were listed on the voting rolls.

In 1966, almost everyone in Grenada County was born and raised in the area. People seeking economic opportunity migrated out and almost no one moved in. Poverty was deep and widespread. Only half the population had steady year-round jobs — mostly related to agriculture. The federal "poverty line" for a family of four was an annual income of $3300 or less (equal to a bit over $25,000 in 2018). The median income for

Black families was $1400 (equal to about $11,600 in 2018), less than half the official poverty rate, meaning that the great majority of Afro-Americans lived in poverty. For whites, the median income was around $4300 (equal about $38,000 in 2018), putting the great majority of them well above the poverty line.

There had never been much significant Civil Rights Movement activity in the county; it was considered too tough a nut to crack. Freedom Summer did not touch Grenada because no local leader or church could be found to sponsor a project or house a freedom school. The NAACP was moribund and a brief organizing effort by SNCC in 1965 had been swiftly suppressed.

At three o'clock in the afternoon of June 15 — while I was still in Alabama, having not yet been sent to join it — the Meredith Mississippi March Against Fear (and with it, the 20th century) came striding down Highway 51 into Grenada. The white power structure knew it was coming and they had a plan — make soothing promises and see to it that those "outside" marchers had no issues to demonstrate about. They assumed that as in the past their local Afro-Americans would "stay in their place." As City Manager John McEachin explained to a reporter, "All we want is to get these people through town and out of here. Good niggers don't want anything to do with this march. And there are more good niggers [in Grenada] than sorry niggers."

> [Unlike most Mississippi towns, Grenada had a "city manager"
> form of government. The City Council hired a professional to run
> the town and the position of mayor was largely symbolic.]

McEachin's confidence notwithstanding, Grenada whites were bitterly divided over how to contain and kill this Black challenge to white supremacy. One faction — the "hardliners" — remained committed to the traditional methods of jail, police violence, white terrorism, and economic retaliation that had maintained segregation in the Deep South for generations. The other group — the "racial moderates" like McEachin — wanted to avoid actions that might provoke federal intervention, or attract negative attention from outsiders, or risk fanning the flames of resistance. They favored the more sophisticated strategies and tactics of chicanery, misdirection, divide and conquer, and wearing the Freedom Movement down through attrition.

In the short run, McEachin's plan failed — utterly and spectacularly. Grenada's Black community responded to the Meredith March with enormous enthusiasm, greater than any town on the entire route except for Canton a week later. A tidal wave of local Blacks — women, men, young, old — poured out from their shanty shacks to join the march when it turned off Highway 51 and headed up Pearl Street towards the center of town. So many that an amazed state trooper told a reporter that, "about a mile of niggers," were marching up towards the town square.

Like so many other southern towns, Grenada was built around an open, park-like central green. The streets surrounding the green made up the "downtown" business district — known as the "square" — with stores, offices and public buildings fronting on wide sidewalks. In Grenada's case, the courthouse wasn't located on the green itself but rather across the aptly named Green Street. The park did, however, hold the obligatory Confederate war memorial, a soldier statue on a tall pedestal.

When the Meredith marchers accompanied by hundreds of Black Grenadans reached the square, they held a large voter rally on the green. To a roar of Afro-American approval, Dr. Robert Green of SCLC placed a small American flag on the Confederate War Memorial statue, saying, "We're tired of seeing rebel flags. Give me the flag of the United States, the flag of freedom!"

Local whites were outraged and aghast at his "defilement" of their sacred memorial to those who had died to maintain slavery. And from the floor of the U.S. Senate the next day, Mississippi Senator James Eastland declared, "I would not be surprised if Martin Luther King and these agitators next desecrate the graves of Confederate soldiers and drag their remains through the streets."

After the rally, Afro-American men and women lined up at the courthouse to become voters. They were registered by four Black registrars who had been temporarily hired by the county under McEachin's "give-them-no-excuse" plan. When the Civil Rights Act had outlawed segregation back in 1964, the courthouse toilet signs had been quickly changed from "White" and "Colored" to "#1" and "#2," though, of course, any Afro-American who dared use #1 would quickly suffer the consequences. Now, while white onlookers and courthouse officials seethed in fury, grinning Black citizens made use of #1 for the first time in their lives.

Later that evening, Fannie Lou Hamer led the mass meeting in freedom songs and Dr. King told them, "Now is the time to make real the promises of democracy." He asked them if they wanted him to return with SCLC when the Meredith March was over. They did.

But after the march and its attendant reporters and TV cameras continued on its way the following day, Grenada reverted to its traditional "southern way of life." The Afro-American registrars were quickly fired and the little American flag placed on the Confederate memorial was torn down by furious whites. The power structure immediately revoked the promises they had made in response to the march, including desegregation of public facilities as required by the Civil Rights Act — a law that clearly had not yet come to Grenada, Mississippi.

Several members of SCLC's field staff, however, remained behind to continue the voter registration drive and help local leaders build an ongoing movement. Within a few days some 1300 Afro-Americans were registered, many times the number of Black voters in the county before the march arrived. It was then discovered that more than 700 of those just registered at the courthouse had been tricked. By some mysterious quirk of local law, all residents of Grenada town had to be given a slip of paper by the registrars at the courthouse which they then had to take to City Hall so that they could vote in city elections. No one had been given those slips, or informed that they had to register twice, so they still had no vote in municipal elections. With the numeric margin of whites narrower in town than in the rural areas, the power structure wanted to be certain there was no chance of any Blacks being elected to city government. When the trick was finally discovered all the city voters had to be re-registered.

Once the Meredith March was deep in the Delta — too far to return — Black SCLC staff members were arrested for the crime of sitting in the "white" section of the Grenada Theater. Police and sheriffs deputies resumed their traditional tactics of intimidation and retaliation and newly registered Afro-American voters were fired from their jobs and evicted from their homes. But by now Grenada's Black community had tasted freedom and they were determined not to back down. In a well-attended mass meeting they voted to form the Grenada County Freedom Movement (GCFM) and affiliate with SCLC. The GCFM was led by Rev. Sharper T. Cunningham and its initial goal was continued voter registration and enforcing the Civil Rights Act of 1964 by desegregating those businesses and public facilities that remained "white only."

When the Meredith March ended in Jackson, I returned to Alabama with Albert Turner and briefly resumed maintaining contact with local leaders in Perry, Hale, and Marengo counties. Over in Mississippi, SCLC sent additional staff into Grenada just as King had promised, including national-level SCLC leaders like Hosea Williams, Andrew Young, and Dr. King himself, who split his time between Grenada and the Chicago Freedom Movement's ferocious battle for open housing.

The conciliatory scheme to ease the Meredith March through town had failed to prevent the eruption of a widespread local challenge to white authority. That failure strengthened the hand of the hard-line group who favored Mississippi's traditional "knock 'em in the head and toss 'em in jail" methods of social control. With the hardliners now back in control, violence and arrests were the order of the day. GCFM efforts were met with adamant opposition from whites determined to return Grenada to the Jim Crow racial order of the past.

On July 4th, SCLC workers and local activists were invited to a barbecue in the rural Sweethome area by an Afro-American woman who was posing as a Movement supporter. After they arrived she called Sheriff Suggs Ingram and had 27 of them arrested for "trespass" in what was obviously a setup. Three days later, a march protesting those arrests was broken up by the cops and more than 40 were arrested for violating a local parade ordinance.

> [Throughout the South, such unconstitutional parade ordinances were frequently used to suppress nonviolent protests. The local authorities refused to issue parade permits to civil rights groups and the cops could unilaterally declare that almost any kind of protest was an illegal "parade" — even if everyone was walking by the side of the road or on a sidewalk without blocking any traffic. White officials knew the ordinances would eventually be overturned on Constitutional grounds in the courts, but that would take time during which they hoped to choke off protests and suppress Afro-American freedom aspirations.]

Meanwhile, up in Chicago, SCLC's efforts to end residential segregation were being met by savage violence. Two fierce fires burning simultaneously, one North one South, stretched SCLC staff and finances to the breaking point. With half the Grenada staff in jail and Chicago an ever-expanding vortex of protest and violence, SCLC headquarters in Atlanta sent out a call for reinforcements. I volunteered for transfer to Grenada and arrived late on Friday, July 8th.

J.T. Johnson was SCLC's Grenada Project Director. He was in command when Executive Staff members like Hosea Williams or Andrew Young were not in town. At that time, the number of SCLC field staff assigned to Grenada fluctuated between 10 and 15 or so, most of them Afro-American with 3 or 4 whites — now including me.

Machine Guns & Draft Cards ~ 1966

My first full day in Grenada was Saturday, July 9th.

Mass meetings were usually held in Belle Flower Missionary Baptist Church on Pearl Street, a stone's throw from Highway 51. Belle Flower (sometimes referred to as Belle Flowers, Bell Flowers or Bellflower) was said to be the third oldest Black church in Mississippi. The meeting that afternoon voted to begin an "integrate everything" campaign to make Grenada an "open city." To that end they adopted 51 demands including desegregation of public facilities, Afro-American voter registrars with neighborhood and evening registration, and equal employment by government and private businesses. [*]

Teams composed mainly of high school students were sent to test Civil Rights Act compliance at diners, motels, the library, and the municipal swimming pool. Most places complied with the law, but the pool was permanently closed rather than permit Black kids to swim with white kids.

The open city campaign continued for weeks with integration testing and lawsuits filed under the Civil Rights Act against non-complying establishments. The swimming pool remained closed because the thought of white girls and Black boys in close proximity to each other while wearing nothing but swimsuits was simply unacceptable to white adults. Other than that, the campaign was largely successful — at least in the technical sense that Blacks willing to defy white hostility and the threat of later retaliation could ask for, and receive, service at most establishments without being arrested. As a practical matter, however, most Afro-Americans chose not to run such risks so the customs of race segregation in Grenada remained largely — though not entirely — intact.

Later that afternoon, I was standing near the church when a pickup truck drove up and one of the two guys inside opened fire with a machine gun. As trained, I instantly dropped to the dirt. His targets were two other Freedom Movement activists and a Justice Department official. The car they were standing next to was shot full of holes but they managed to dive to the ground in the nick of time and were not hit. The shooter was arrested a few blocks away — but only on a minor unrelated charge rather than assault with a deadly weapon. An all-white jury later acquitted him.

That evening a pair of FBI agents asked to meet with me. I assumed, of course, that they wanted to know what I had witnessed regarding the attempted assassination of a government official (and, oh yes, a pair of civil rights workers too). As it turned out, the only thing they asked me

---

[*] See www.crmvet.org/docs/grendocs.htm for the text of the 51 demands and other documents and reports from the Grenada Freedom Movement of 1966.

about was my draft status. They demanded to see my draft card. They seemed quite disappointed when they discovered that I had a valid "1Y" classification and that I wasn't a draft dodger on the run who they could apprehend.

Under the Selective Service system in 1966, men with "1A" classifications could be drafted into the army at any time, but those with a "1Y" status like me were essentially exempt. The "1Y" classification was for those "mentally, morally, or physically unfit for combat except in cases of extreme national emergency." In other words, if an invasion fleet of Viet Cong rowboats appeared off the California coast I might be drafted — otherwise not. Since I had never been given either a physical or mental exam I assumed my draft board considered me *morally unfit* to fight in Vietnam — no doubt because of my civil rights arrests.

Unbeknownst to me, however, ten days after my chat with the FBI my Los Angeles draft board suddenly and without explanation decided to reclassify me "1A." The first I learned of it was when I received an order to report for my pre-induction physical — next stop Vietnam! Since they were still sending mail to my old California address where it was forwarded by friends, first to Selma, and then finally to Grenada, I didn't receive their various notices until the dates had passed. Much confusion ensued.

I had no intention of fighting a war I profoundly opposed on both moral and political grounds, so I filed for Conscientious Objector status. Since I was working for Martin Luther King and had supporting letters from people like Andrew Young and Hosea Williams, to say nothing of a thoroughly documented two-year record of advocating, teaching, and practicing nonviolence, I had a good case — which I eventually won.

The timing, though, was striking. I had been classified "1Y" in September of 1964, no doubt because of my arrests at the Van de Kamp's protests. I continued my Freedom Movement activity over the following two years with more arrests in Selma. Clearly there had been no noticeable change in my "immoral" behavior. Then, just ten days after the FBI interrogated me about my draft status rather than the shooting they were supposed to be investigating, my draft board reclassified me "1A" without explanation. Under the Selective Service rules, had I known about the reclassification I would have had ten days to appeal it. Precisely ten days after being reclassified "1A," I was called up for induction. What a marvel of bureaucratic efficiency!

FBI Director J. Edgar Hoover's obsessive racism was by now well known to everyone active in the Freedom Movement. His bureau was a segregated, white-only institution that employed not a single Black,

Brown, Asian, or Native American agent. His open hostility to the Civil Rights Movement was notorious, as was the explicit racism and support for segregation evinced by many southern FBI agents who worked hand-in-glove with local law enforcement and the White Citizens' Councils.

Across the South in 1966, men who were active in the Freedom Movement were being drafted into the military as a way of removing them from the communities they were organizing. So the feeb's action in my case was part of that broader pattern of anti–civil-rights racism and using the draft to cripple the Movement. And on a personal level, it reminded me of how they used to follow my parents from job to job informing employers about the dangerous "reds" they had on the payroll, which would then result in immediate termination.

Decades later I obtained my FBI file through the Freedom of Information Act but all the pertinent information was blacked out, so I can't prove that the FBI reached out to Draft Board 102 with a "suggestion" that they reclassify and draft me forthwith. I can't prove it, but I believe it.

Sunday the 10th was my second day in Grenada. After church, we protested the attempted murders with a support rally in front of the county jail where those who had been arrested on the July 7 march were still incarcerated. Since the unconstitutional parade ordinance still barred marches, we "drifted" downtown in small groups from Belle Flower church six blocks away. When the signal was given, about 50 of us quickly gathered on the lawn around the flagpole flying the "stars and bars" of the Mississippi state flag and commenced singing freedom songs as loud as we could so the prisoners inside could hear us and know we hadn't forgotten them. The jail was adjacent to the northside Black neighborhood and about 250 Afro-Americans observed our action with smiles and indications of support.

As was normal throughout the South, Black kids too young to risk arrest as demonstrators acted as freedom scouts. They soon reported that a force of Mississippi State Troopers in full riot gear were forming up behind the courthouse across the street, so we quickly ended our rally. Most of the protesters retreated to the church while a few merged with the bystanders. Some of us from SCLC dodged into a neighboring building and up to the second floor where from windows we could observe the scene.

When the troopers charged around the corner there were no demonstrators to arrest or assault. Clearly disappointed, they turned on the crowd of Afro-American onlookers, brutally beating them with rifle butts and chasing them in all directions. As had been the case in Canton, troopers seemed to prefer beating people with their rifles and shotguns while city cops and sheriffs favored the more traditional billy clubs — a pattern we experienced often in the months to come.

Up on the second floor we crouched down, peeking out the windows. Well, the Black SCLC staff members did. They didn't want me to do so because the sight of a white face at the window of an Afro-American building would give away our position and the cops would come charging in after us. I understood that, yet I couldn't prevent myself from attempting to grab a quick look at what was happening. Fortunately, the other staff members instantly pulled me back. We had to wait more than an hour for the coast to clear.

On the Square ~ 1966

Though it had been in existence for less than a month, the Grenada County Freedom Movement (GCFM) had already established a tradition of daily mass meetings in Belle Flower Baptist Church, usually in the evening. At that night's meeting, a "blackout" (boycott) of Grenada's white merchants was announced to protest the arrests and beatings and to enforce the 51 demands.

Throughout the South, Afro-American boycotts of white-owned stores had proven to be one of the most effective Freedom Movement strategies. In rural counties like Grenada where few Blacks owned cars, Afro-Americans were more likely to shop locally than the more affluent whites who could drive to larger urban centers where selection was greater and prices lower. By the same token though, the lack of market alternatives made boycotts hard to sustain by poor Blacks who had to obtain food and clothing for their families, so they were not undertaken lightly.

The next day in Oxford, Mississippi, some 50 miles to the north, federal district Judge Claude Clayton declared that the "parade ordinance" was unconstitutional — a victory that elated us. We began sending small teams of three or four people to picket the downtown stores, and that afternoon the white power structure published our 51 demands in the local paper with a statement that claimed no one in Grenada discriminated (heaven forbid) and then declared: "Demands, threats and intimidation are not proper, appropriate, or acceptable means of accomplishing anything, and any and all such tactics will be ignored. There will be no concessions of any type whatsoever, likewise there will be no acceding to any such demands."

On the following day, Wednesday the 13th, with the "parade ordinance" now overturned, a large picket line was sent downtown to enforce the blackout. All 45 pickets, including a couple SCLC staff, were arrested for some reason that was never clearly explained. As with the Queen of Hearts from *Alice in Wonderland*, in Mississippi the rule was "arrest first, figure out charges later."

SCLC was still paying off the costs of the Meredith March and didn't have much money for bail, so the idea of large picket lines was shelved in favor of small picket teams. Small groups were more vulnerable to attack or harassment by hostile whites but less likely to be arrested, and if they were busted fewer needed to be bailed out.

Because of their vulnerability to white violence, small picket teams were deemed too dangerous for white SCLC staff members like me. Grenada whites considered us to be "commie race traitors," and our presence on a small boycott line would provoke them to violence which would result in the pickets being busted for "disturbing the peace." So J.T. took me off picket duty and assigned R.B. Cottonreader, an Afro-American staff member, to coordinate and lead the pickets while the rest of us — both Black and white — canvassed door-to-door in the Black community.

On Thursday the 14th we urged people to attend a special afternoon mass meeting and then join a mass march — the first since the "parade ordinance" had been overturned. The mass meeting was well attended, and more than 200 people joined the march up to the square led by Hosea Williams of SCLC. By big-city standards, 200 people may not sound like much, but in a small rural town with only a few thousand Afro-Americans of high school age or older, for that many to defy a century of social conditioning and the very real threats of economic retaliation, police repression, and Klan violence was significant.

Within the GCFM, the formal leadership positions were all held by men though much of the actual leadership *work* was done by women out of the public spotlight. Male leaders, both local and SCLC, led the marches, but women and children formed the bulk of the protesters. Most of those marching were high school students, with girls outnumbering the boys.

While enraged whites might spontaneously assault a small picket line of a few protesters, the social psychology of crowds meant that mass marches were — for the most part — only vulnerable to attack by large mobs incited to violence by Klan or Council leaders with the cooperation, or at least acquiescence, of the cops and courts. So white activists like me were allowed to participate in marches even though we were barred from small pickets.

Two by two we marched on the side of the road (no sidewalks in the Black community) so as not to be accused of blocking traffic. I was assigned as a march marshal to the rear of the column. My job was to move up and down alongside my portion of the line, keeping people caught up and being on the lookout for trouble. Since protest actions with as few as 40 or 50 participants had resulted in arrests, we were all tense, expecting to be jumped at any moment by cops or Klan, but nothing untoward occurred.

When we reached the square and entered onto the green we discovered that a dozen or so Black inmates from Parchman Farm prison had been brought in to prevent us from again "desecrating" the holy statue. Parchman was justifiably notorious as one of the most brutal penitentiaries in the nation, and under the hard-eyed watch of heavily armed white deputies, the prisoners stood shoulder to shoulder around the pedestal, obviously under orders to attack any protester who approached. White officials and cops were present in force, grinning and joking. They clearly relished the symbolism of Black prisoners beating Afro-American protesters to defend a memorial to Confederate soldiers who had died fighting to maintain slavery.

For our part, we all understood the terrible punishments that those inmates would suffer if they failed to violently prevent us from "defiling" the statue with another American flag — or with merely the vile touch of an Afro-American protester. SCLC leader Hosea Williams cautioned us to leave them alone and we held our rally well away from the memorial and its coerced defenders.

That was the first march in Grenada that wasn't blocked or smashed by the cops since June 15 when the Meredith March had passed through. In that sense it was a victory. But I was so furious at the tactics of the white officials — so typical of the vicious, petty cruelty inherent in white supremacy and segregation — that it didn't feel like any kind of accomplishment.

The white power structure's use of Parchman prisoners to guard the statue was reported in the northern press with condemnation and ridicule. After a couple more marches they stopped using the prisoners and we held many of our rallies near the monument. But knowing they would bring the inmates back, and not wanting to place them in a such a cruel position, we chose not to actively "defile" it with American flags.

When our rally ended, Black Grenadans lined up to register to vote at the courthouse across the street. But Sheriff Suggs Ingram refused to let more than three at a time enter the building. Whites were not subject to any such rules, they could enter and leave freely. Since small Afro-American groups were vulnerable to arrest, attack, and intimidation GCFM leaders rejected his demand. No one entered the courthouse and no one was registered.

The next day we held a similar afternoon march, and that evening after the mass meeting in Belle Flower we staged a dangerous night march up to the square and then through the northside Afro-American neighborhood. We started with about 250 marchers, others joined us along the way, and there were more than 600 by the time we rallied outside the Chat & Chew Cafe on Union Street. That soon became our normal custom: different kinds of Movement activity during the day such as boycott leafleting and picketing, door-to-door organizing, workshops and training, then an evening mass meeting and a night march to the square with a rally at the courthouse or on the green. Sometimes followed by marching through the Black neighborhood with another rally on Union Street.

The Chat & Chew was the only Afro-American–owned cafe in the northside Black community and therefore the only safe place for white civil rights workers. There were a couple of Afro-American eating establishments in the downtown area, but the first time I tried to grab a bite at one of them I was spotted through the window by angry whites on the street and had to escape out the back way as they gathered to come in and drag me out for an old-fashioned southern whupping.

Chat's was in an old wooden building with warped plank floors. They had pretty decent burgers, but their real speciality was deep-fried catfish sandwiches, which were really good. I'd never eaten catfish before, but commercial catfish ponds were beginning to replace some of the Delta cotton patches and it was becoming a low-cost food staple across the state.

Over the next week, downtown boycott pickets continued to be harassed and sometimes arrested, but our marches were not interfered with. There were still a dozen or more members of the SCLC field staff permanently assigned to Grenada but that was barely enough to keep up with the work. For the most part, local students handled the picketing, sometimes with the help of SCLC organizer R.B. Cottonreader, but often on their own. Since I mainly did door-to-door canvassing for the mass meetings and voter registration, I wasn't arrested. Which was fine by me, I had already enjoyed the hospitality of the southern penal system in Selma, Alabama and that had been quite sufficient.

By now I was being hosted by an Afro-American woman in her small wood-plank home on Newsome Alley around the corner from the Chat & Chew on Union Street. It took a lot of courage for an elderly woman living alone to open her door to a freedom worker. She let me use the little room that her children had once occupied, and I slept on an old iron-frame bed with a thick feather mattress in a muslin cover. Each morning she fed me breakfast of grits, bacon, and biscuits & gravy, and if I hadn't had dinner by the time I returned in the evening she always warmed something up, so I never went to bed hungry.

On Friday, July 22nd, the federal judge in Oxford ruled in our favor, issuing a sweeping injunction commanding the white power structure to accept that Afro-Americans had First Amendment rights, ordering the cops to stop interfering with legal protests, and instructing them to protect demonstrators from terrorist attacks by the Klan and other racists.

Included in his injunction were rules of conduct that *we* had to obey. He required us to march two by two on the side of the road or on sidewalks and obey all traffic rules. He also ordered us to break our marches into sections of 20 people with 20 feet between each group. Since we had to obey traffic rules anyway, the additional public benefit of the groups-of-20 rule eluded us, but we generally followed it — except when we had to close up tight for self-protection against mob attack.

Grenada's white community reacted to Clayton's ruling with raging fury. It was hard to tell who they hated more, the "damn Yankee" federal government daring to tell them how to treat their "nigrahs," or us racial troublemakers challenging the tranquility of their Jim Crow "southern way of life." The judge and other federals, however, were distant targets, well protected by armed law enforcement. We, however, were near at hand — and nonviolent.

In anticipation of our Saturday night march on the 23rd, more than 700 angry whites gathered on the square, visibly ready to attack us with baseball bats, chains, and steel pipes. We figured that some of them probably carried concealed knives and guns. Our young scouts reported that, judging by license plates, several carloads had come in from Klan strongholds like Neshoba County and the Pearl River area in the Southwest corner of the state. Large mobs like that don't form spontaneously. Someone with political clout has to organize and mobilize them, but no one was claiming responsibility. And by now it was quite clear that county Sheriff Suggs Ingram had no intention of protecting us from his white constituents. Not that night. Not ever.

The normal Mississippi practice was to station one or two state troopers in each rural county, but since the beginning of the month the

Grenada contingent had been reinforced to a couple dozen troopers in order to suppress protests and enforce the recently overturned "parade ordinance." Now under court order to protect rather than attack us, their commander said he had been "caught by surprise" by this "unexpected" hostile mob. He claimed he didn't have enough men to guard us if we marched, but he promised that if we canceled on this night he'd bring in enough reinforcements to protect our marches on the following nights.

We took his promise of future protection with a large grain of salt but agreed not to march that Saturday night. When the white mob realized we weren't going to walk into their ambush they began advancing down Pearl and Cherry Streets toward Belle Flower where we were holding our mass meeting. To their credit, the troopers did hold them a block away so they couldn't attack the church.

On Sunday the 24th, an even bigger mob of whites again gathered on the square to assault our march. Reporters estimated it at over 1,000, armed with bats and clubs. Again the troopers said they didn't have enough men to protect us and again they asked us to cancel the march. No way. We knew that if we let them continue to intimidate us we'd never be able to march again.

About 200 of us strode out of Belle Flower along Pearl Street towards the square (the groups-of-twenty rule made our numbers easy to count). Under Clayton's rules, a few march marshals were exempted from walking two by two and allowed to patrol up and down the line, so I was in my usual marshal spot, responsible for the three sections at the rear of the column. As a general rule of thumb, when a nonviolent protest march encountered a hostile mob the most dangerous spot was usually the front, because that's where the most enraged assailants would attack first, but rear guard was the next-most vulnerable because, like beasts-of-prey, mobs would often assault a retreating line that they could attack from behind.

Usually we exuberantly sang our freedom songs but on this night we were silent. Silent and scared. Scared but determined. We were welcomed to the square by shouted curses, jeers, and hate-filled epithets. In addition to the enraged cries of "nigger," "nigger-lover," "commies," and of course "race traitors," so familiar to me from Los Angeles and Alabama, there was now a new racist battle cry of "white power!"

We saw only a handful of troopers plus a few cops and deputies who seemed more interested in socializing with members of the mob than restraining them. Instead of crossing the street onto the central green for our usual rally we took the whites by surprise, striding rapidly past the courthouse and then turning right on 1st Street to exit the square before the mob realized we weren't going to stop. They had been waiting for us to begin our rally before charging into us — which the almost total absence of law enforcement eloquently invited them to do.

When they saw we were escaping they chased after us but were blocked by the few troopers on hand. Unable to get at us, they then attacked news reporters and a TV crew, beating them and smashing their cameras. On Monday, the national media, both print and broadcast, featured the mob violence of the evening before in a glare of negative publicity.

The ideological divisions within the Grenada white power structure were mirrored by similar conflicts at the state level. Both locally and in Jackson, hardliners still believed they could beat Blacks back into Jim Crow submission, so police and mob violence suited them down to the ground. Meanwhile moderates were trying to soften the state's image so as to attract northern investment. The beating of newsmen and smashing of cameras generated intense negative publicity and that temporarily strengthened the moderates.

With the moderate faction back in the ascendancy, trooper command must have convinced their higher-ups that bluffing us out of marching wasn't going to work, so they sent in a whole company of troopers with orders to suppress mob violence. They assured their white constituents that if they deprived the press of dramatic newsworthy events — such as mob violence against reporters and cameramen — the reporters would leave. And that without national publicity in the northern media, Afro-American protests in Grenada would dwindle away to nothing — leaving the old order of tranquil white supremacy restored. So the moderate local white leaders urged their constituents to stay away from our marches.

On Monday night, the 25th, the white mob on the square was just half the size of the previous evening, perhaps around 500 or so, and close to 100 troopers were out in force to prevent any photogenic violence. Some 220 of us marched around the green ignoring their shouted jeers, insults, and threats and the occasional rocks and bottles hurled our way. The next night, no more than 100 whites were present and we outnumbered them, so we resumed our rallies on the green under the protection of the troopers. By the end of the week, the general pattern of daytime boycott leafletting and picketing, canvassing and organizing, nightly marches to a square empty of hostile whites, followed by a rally on the green or a voter registration rally in a Black neighborhood had reasserted itself — organized mob violence had failed to halt our daily protest marches a clear Movement victory.

Though we didn't know it at the time, this series of events set a pattern. We or the courts would do something that infuriated the segregationists, the hardliners would temporarily wrest political control from the moderates and they'd mobilize a white mob to attack both us and the press. After two or three days of brutal violence and subsequent media condemnation, the moderates would be re-empowered, the governor would send in state troopers to control the mob, and the hardliners would tell their violent supporters to stand down for the time being. When the violence stopped, the TV cameras would leave and we'd be back to marching around an empty square — until we did something that provoked a new wave of violence.

Over the next week we continued our boycott picketing, voter registration, and nightly marches to the square. Yet the power structure's "no audience" scheme didn't mean an end to repression. The local police and sheriff's deputies increased their harassment arrests for alleged traffic violations, "disturbing the peace," and other trumped-up charges. SCLC staff member R.B. Cottenreader was arrested for "touching" a white lady while picketing, the driver and three passengers were arrested for their car being in the intersection when the stoplight changed to yellow, and so on. (It was common in the Deep South for civil rights activists behind the wheel *and their passengers* to be arrested for minor traffic infractions rather than just given a ticket.)

In early August we received a welcome sign that the boycott was having an effect. On Friday the 5th, bogus "Boycott Over" leaflets mysteriously appeared in the main Afro-American neighborhoods. No one was fooled and the blackout continued.

That evening there was a fund-raising party in Grenada's Tie Plant neighborhood with entertainment by SCLC's Freedom Singers. Not being an alcohol drinker, I went home after their set. Around midnight, troopers and police surrounded the Collins Cafe where the party was being held and blocked all the roads leading into the area. They shot tear gas into the building and arrested about 50 people on various charges such as "possession of liquor" and "drunk and disorderly."

[Grenada was a "dry" county, which meant that in the time-honored southern tradition local lawmen enriched themselves by collecting regular bribes from bootleggers of both races. Which meant that they knew from the Afro-American bootleggers when and where parties were planned. In some cases, that worked to the movement's advantage as a covert communication back channel to the police and sheriffs. And on occasion Black bootleggers were able to talk the cops into releasing someone who had been arrested by error or misunderstanding — "Come on, Sheriff, that child wasn't picketing, she was going to visit her auntie."]

At our mass meeting the next day people voted to update the 51 demands of July 9 with additional demands related to police repression and freedom of speech and assembly. We also added dropping the charges against those arrested the night before. Evidently this convinced the hardliners that their "no audience" strategy was failing to weaken the Movement. So once again their strategic pendulum swung back towards violence. *

Faulkner Nailed It ~ 1966

By the end of July, Grenada Mississippi was becoming increasingly dangerous. The racists who had fired a machine gun at a government official and civil rights workers had been acquitted on all charges by an all-white jury. Klansmen who had been seen inciting the mobs on the square were prowling about and becoming ever more menacing. It was too risky for white freedom riders like me to canvass out in the rural areas, and even in town the sense of imminent threat was palpable.

State troopers might be under orders from a federal injunction to protect our marches, but it was clear they had no intention of guarding individuals from KKK terrorism outside the marches. The home where I boarded was on Newsome Alley just a block off Highway 51. Though it was in the heart of the Union Street Afro-American neighborhood, it would be a quick and easy target for a Klan night raid. So I decided to buy a pistol for protection. I already knew how to shoot. My dad had given me my first rifle when I turned 12. By high school age I was a paid-up member of the National Rifle Association and shot competitively on an NRA-sanctioned rifle team.

Stores selling guns were plentiful in Grenada and the surrounding Mississippi counties, but they were all owned by hostile whites who we were boycotting. And after my experience with Chief Raupach and his shoebox of dossiers in Crenshaw County, it seemed likely that a gun store owner might recognize me and report back to both cops and Klan.

My friend Richard Thompson from L.A. CORE and N-VAC was another white civil rights worker. He was now on the CORE field staff

---

* See www.crmvet.org/docs/grendocs.htm for the text of the revised demands and other documents and reports from the Grenada Movement.

working in Claiborne Parish, Louisiana, a five-hour drive from Grenada through Greenville and Monroe, so I decided to visit him and buy some protection in a different state.

He took me over to the nearby town of Minden where he wasn't well known and there were several stores and pawn shops selling a wide array of firearms. No state identification, background check, or paperwork were required — it was simply cash on the counter and walk out with your piece. I bought a used Beretta Puma semi-automatic pistol and a couple of extra clips. It was a compact weapon that fit easily into my pocket or the attaché case I used for flyers and other written materials. While I never carried it on a protest or at a Movement meeting, its presence was a comfort at night on the table beside me or when I was driving through rural areas.

In preparation for going South I had read a number of books. The most useful was *The New Abolitionists* by Howard Zinn which oriented me to Civil Rights Movement realities and organizational strategies and tactics. For understanding the sociology and psychology of Jim Crow and the southern way of life, the ones that proved most helpful were *Killers of the Dream* by Lillian Smith because it explored the intense, intimate intersection of race, gender, and misogyny, and the novels of William Faulkner — novels that to at least a degree prepared me for the twisted, psychological weirdness that white supremacy and Jim Crow segregation imposed on southern society and relationships between Blacks and whites.

Richard and I returned to the village of Homer where he was based, and later that evening he told me an interesting story. One day he'd been at the freedom house when a white guy pulled up in an old car and knocked on the door. Dressed for farm work, he was middle-aged, with dry leathery skin. In other words, the kind of guy who a lot of folks called a "redneck" and who looked and dressed no different than most Klan members.

"You the civil rights?" he asked Richard.

"Yes," replied Richard cautiously, ready to slam and lock the door if he needed to.

"Well, I need your help," the guy told him. Which, as you can imagine, surprised the hell out of Richard, who then invited him inside.

"I been to the sheriff and the mayor," the guy told him, "and they won't do nuthing. The judge neither. Won't nobody help me, so I come to you."

He went on to explain that in addition to the farm where he lived he owned a second piece of land where a new dam was being built to create a recreational lake. His property would be on the new lakefront. A wealthy local landowner wanted to buy up his parcel to develop a fishing lodge but he didn't want to sell — at least not at the price being offered — and he had refused several times to accept ever more insistent demands.

He had long been renting out that land to an Afro-American tenant farmer. Recently the wooden shack on the property had burned down, killing his tenant. He was convinced the fire was arson, deliberately set to force him to sell. That got his dander up, and the murder of his tenant also irked him. As he put it, "He was the best durned nigger I ever had." So he went to the authorities, who refused to investigate the fire as a possible arson.

"Now, you don't have to just take my word for this," he assured Richard. "I got proof." He showed Richard a map marked with the location of his land and the anticipated shoreline of the new lake. He also had a clipping from the local paper describing the fire and the man's death as "accidental." Then he asked Richard to follow him out to his car where he opened up the trunk and there in a white enamel washbasin were the charred bones of his dead tenant.

Now don't tell me that Faulkner's tales weren't based in the nitty-gritty realities of the "southern way of life."

Speaking of which, years later I was told by SNCC worker Bob Weil about his meeting an elderly Black woman in a shack near Oxford, Mississippi who spoke in exactly the same kind of stream-of-consciousness language — the voice — that Faulkner wrote in. Turned out she had been a domestic servant in Faulkner's home and, as was quite common in the South, had helped raise him. And that she had known, and talked to him about, many of the real people his characters were later based on. So far as I know, she never received a word of credit in any of Faulkner's books.

Anyway, Richard told the farmer guy there wasn't anything that he as a CORE activist could do himself, but he sent him on to the ACLU down in New Orleans. He never heard from him again. The next morning I drove back to Grenada with the attaché case containing my Beretta on the seat beside me. Thankfully, that I never had to use it.

Battle for the Ballot ~ 1966

Back in mid-July, federal voter registrars had been sent to Grenada under the Voting Rights Act.

[In the language of the Voting Rights Act, federal officers assigned to enforce it were officially known as "examiners" rather than "registrars." But in common usage, everyone referred to them as "registrars."]

The federal registrars operated out of the post office on the square with little success. In two weeks only 22 Afro-Americans were added to the rolls, an average of two per day.

The reason was obvious — Blacks were afraid to go into the downtown area. Most of the Afro-Americans willing to defy white supremacy by registering to vote were boycotting the downtown stores, so they were no longer shopping on the square. Police and state troopers were harassing, and sometimes arresting, anyone they suspected might be intending to hand out boycott flyers or picket a store. And white racists were on the prowl ready to attack "troublemakers," who in their view meant anyone with a dark skin. So as far as most Afro-Americans were concerned, the federal registrars were located in a zone of hostility and danger.

We explained those realities to the federal registrars and suggested they set up shop in a Black neighborhood where they would be warmly welcomed. The registrars claimed that they *had* to work out of a United States government office and the post office on the square was the only federal presence available. That was bullshit — and everyone knew it. Legally, they could operate wherever they chose and in many other counties federal registrars operated out of Afro-American churches, stores, community centers, and so on.

Off the record, the registrars let us know they were under orders from their supervisors in Jackson to have no association with us or any appearance of being allied to the Freedom Movement in any way, shape, or form. The local white power structure understood the social dynamics of violent racism as well as we did, and they were using their considerable political power and influence with officials in Jackson to ensure that the registrars remained downtown where they would have minimal success.

We filed complaints, and I guess the SCLC office in Washington began contacting supporters in Congress and rattling some administration cages because on Monday, August 8, the registrars changed their minds and moved their operation to the Chat & Chew on

Union Street in the heart of the main Black community. On their first day there more than 300 people showed up to get registered, including many who were finishing up the registration process started at the courthouse back in June but not completed because of the double-registration trick.

We were elated. The white power structure, however, was furious. To them, shifting the registrars into the Afro-American community was evidence of *sinister collusion* between defiant Blacks and a hostile federal government. They understood as clearly as we did that large numbers of Black voters would ultimately doom their traditional methods of maintaining Jim-Crow–style white supremacy. Since whites held narrow population majorities in both county and city, they were confident that Blacks could never elect an Afro-American sheriff or judge, but Black voters might be able to elect one or two county supervisors or city council members from Black-majority beats and wards.

And in city and countywide elections, Blacks might end up holding the balance of power between competing white candidates. If that came to pass, sooner or later whites challenging incumbent officeholders would begin advocating policies and offering concessions aimed at winning the support of Black voters — thus eroding the complete exclusion of Afro-Americans from all aspects of political power. That wouldn't usher in any dawn of full-on Black Power, but it would definitely mean an end to white-only power. So within the local power structure the hardliners once again took control. If they couldn't block Black registration though tricks and ploys they'd return to their traditional methods of violence and intimidation.

Rather than our usual march to the square, on the night the registrars set up shop on Union Street we staged a voter registration rally in front of the Chat & Chew. The crowd soon swelled to over 500, with Movement leaders speaking from the roof of a parked car. Since there were no streetlights in the Black community, the only illumination came from the flickering light of Chat's business sign.

Union Street was narrow, just one lane in each direction, and back then that block was hemmed in by buildings and rental shacks. There was no way so many folks could gather without blocking traffic — which wasn't really an issue because whites rarely drove into the Black community at night and Blacks had no problem using another street to go around. Nevertheless, the cops ordered us to clear the road. We did the best we could, squeezing open a single-car lane through the middle of the throng even though there were no drivers attempting to use it.

I was one of the protest marshals trying to keep the car lane open. Suddenly there was some unintelligible shouting through a blurry bullhorn followed almost immediately with the now familiar *Pop! Pop! Pop!* of tear gas canisters exploding all around us.

As with the Canton attack in June, I again experienced searing smoke, burning eyes, and crushing lung pain. Troopers in gas masks loomed out of the darkness and chemical fog to smash people with their rifle butts, while sheriffs and cops flailed away at anyone in reach with their clubs. We all fled as best we could. Later that night, I was in SCLC's little office at the back of Belle Flower compiling a list of more than 20 people injured badly enough to require medical attention. Afterwards, unable to sleep, I wrote one of the only two poems I've ever written:

MISSISSIPPI VOTER RALLY

Hot, drippy evening,
*   red & yellow bars of neon light.*
A crowd of dark shadows
*   defiantly standing in the Mississippi night.*
Car roof buckles under the weight
*   of silhouetted shadows against the neon.*
Courage and song rise up from
*   the surrounding sea of unseen folk*
*   engulfing us like a warm friendly ocean.*

Helmets advance out of the dark
*   fearsome, their long false faces*
*   hideous masks of death.*
A shouted command, choking fumes,
*   explosions,*
*   screams,*
*   terror.*
Can't breathe, can't see.

The warm ocean scatters like
*   spilled quicksilver.*
Blindly running, blindly escaping.
Clubs thud against fragile flesh
*   as helmets leap out of the night,*
out of the agonizing blinding fog
*   to fall on helpless innocence.*

Quiet, echoing quiet,
*   the damp Mississippi night closes in*
on homes strangely dark.
Black shadows peer from dark windows
*   as the Mars-men patrol*

their temporarily conquered territory,
boots echoing off stony-faced homes.

Inside, in the dark, human blast furnaces
  forge inner resolve.
Hammers of rage pounding out determination,
  tomorrow... tomorrow... tomorrow...

The next evening, Tuesday, August 9th, we came back and again held a voting rally at the Chat & Chew. People were afraid of another tear gas attack so the crowd was noticeably smaller — a bit under 300. Our lawyers had complained to Federal Judge Clayton in Oxford about the troopers and cops violating his injunction against interfering with a lawful protest, and so on this night they didn't attack us.

Instead, a crowd of angry whites — young men mostly — suddenly appeared at the corner of Union St. and Highway 51, which at that time was called Commerce Street (today it's Martin Luther King Blvd). This was the heart of the Black community and no group of hostile whites had ever shown up there to harass a civil rights gathering. They'd obviously been mobilized and organized by someone — Citizens Council, Klan, or someone else, we didn't know. They gathered less than 50 feet from our rally and began pelting us with rocks and bottles thrown over the heads of the few cops standing between the two groups.

As required by Clayton's injunction, we had informed the authorities of our intention to march up to the square from the Chat & Chew. About 280 of us, mostly high-school-age girls and boys and adult women, led by a small number of adult men, marched over to Pearl Street and then up Pearl past Belle Flower for our normal route downtown. In reluctant obedience to the court order, the troopers cleared a path for us through the throng of hostile whites — who then raced up Cherry Street to reach the square before us.

When we got to the square it was occupied by 750 or so whites including those who had attacked our rally on Union Street. Half of them were actually on the green where we usually held our rallies, the remainder were across the street on the sidewalks. At least two formations of riot-equipped troopers were standing around but they didn't seem interested in taking any action. For their part, the local lawmen seemed quite friendly to the angry mob. In an article the next day, Jack Nelson of the *Los Angeles Times* quoted Grenada County Sheriff Suggs Ingram as saying, "Now you're going to see a show."

As usual we were walking two by two in groups of 20 with a few march marshals like me paralleling the line. We quickly closed up, eliminating the section gaps required by Clayton's march rules — if he didn't like it he could lump it. Holding ourselves in a tight disciplined formation was our best protection. Each marcher's body was partially protected by those pressing in close from front, behind, and one side. If the racists attacked with clubs and fists they had to assault the column as a whole rather than ganging up on individuals as they normally preferred. And by singing our freedom songs as loud as we could, we not only bolstered our courage but manifested our presence as a unified group rather than a collection of individuals.

As we neared the central green the mob began bombarding us with hurled bricks, rocks, bottles, and exploding cherry bombs. I and the other marshals did what we could to knock the flying missiles aside and dodge those we couldn't block. Our job was to hold everyone together and keep the formation tight, because if they managed to break into our line and scatter us we'd be stomped.

"Hold tight, hold tight," I kept shouting over the massed singing. "Keep moving, keep moving!" Of course, nobody needed my shouted instructions, by now they were all experienced protesters. But tightly packed against each other with their heads down and faces pressed for protection against the person in front of them, they couldn't see what was happening around them, and the commands shouted by us marshals let them know the line was still intact and discipline holding.

Suddenly a band of whites on the green charged against us, shrieking rage and hitting people with pipes and sticks. "Niggers! Niggers! Kill the niggers! Kill 'em! Kill 'em!"

As a white freedom rider and a marshal outside the line, I was an easier target than those paired up and tightly packed. When they swarmed us, I pressed myself tight against the march line's flank, holding on to two marchers as strong as I could. They clasped their arms around my waist to keep me from being pulled away. With my head down and my face buried in their shoulders for protection, I wasn't able to recognize who they were — they were fellow freedom fighters, that's all that mattered. As the swirl of racist thugs surged by me I was punched and kicked and struck by their clubs, but they failed to knock me down or drag me apart from the others.

As more and more whites charged at us with bats and clubs, we couldn't reach the green or hold our ground in the street. We were forced to retreat to the intersection of Green and Doak streets at the northwest corner of the square, and then up Green towards Pearl Street.

The 50 or so state troopers watched it all but did nothing to deter the white violence. From past experience we knew they were waiting for some tiny sign of defensive violence on our part as an excuse for arresting all those who dared to challenge the southern way of life. They must have been bitterly disappointed that none of us provided the pretext they were waiting for. One of the lawmen threw a tear gas bomb into our line. With the mob still hounding us, we didn't dare scatter, so we had to just hold our breath and walk through the poisonous fumes.

In good order, with our column solid and our songs still repelling their racist hate, we retreated from the square and headed back to the Chat & Chew on Union Street. The mob began to follow us and finally the troopers bestirred themselves. They formed a line across the road between the tail end of our march and the jeering, howling segregationists. With their rifles and shotguns resting upright on their hips they faced us rather than the violent whites behind them. A posture that declared to all and sundry that they saw themselves as protecting the square and white supremacy from defiant but nonviolent Afro-Americans demanding justice. Which, of course, was exactly the case. From behind the troopers, the whites continued to hurl their missiles at us over the heads of the lawmen for as long as we were in range.

Some of the marchers were bruised and bleeding, but just one person needed hospital care — testimony to the effectiveness of nonviolent discipline and training that carried 280 protesters, mostly women and children, through an attack by a violent mob of more than 750 racists. For myself, I was badly bruised, had a painful knot on my skull and some bloody cuts, but was not seriously injured.

The next evening, Wednesday, August 10, we again rallied outside Chat's on Union Street. Again a white mob formed at Union and Commerce, this time armed with large slingshots that they used to shoot lead fishing sinkers, sharp links of steel chain, and exploding cherry bombs at us — missiles that sailed over the heads of the troopers to draw blood and inflict injury on us. We feared that someone might lose an eye but fortunately that didn't occur though half a dozen people were injured.

After the bloody assault of the night before, this rally was even smaller than Tuesday's. But it was almost entirely made up of adult Black men who had turned out to face mob violence in place of their wives, mothers, sisters, and daughters. This was extraordinary. Throughout the South, Afro-American men were the most vulnerable to white violence and retaliation, far more so than women and kids. Black men were the ones most often lynched or assassinated by the Klan, they were the ones the cops arrested on phony charges and sentenced to years in prison. And it was Afro-American men — the family breadwinners — who were most likely to be fired from their jobs if they participated in a protest.

But on *this* night, in *this* small Mississippi town, *these* Black men were determined they would not be driven off the square by white violence. They would not retreat from the green. They had told the women and kids to stand aside so they could step up. They understood and accepted the necessity of nonviolence, some reluctantly so, others with more commitment. They were ready to endure whatever they had to endure in order to resist — nonviolently. To enforce this, Afro-American SCLC staff members moved through the crowd collecting knives and a few pistols that some of the men had brought with them. As a white activist, it was not my place to do that.

As it happened though, our project director J.T. Johnson and the other senior SCLC staff members assigned to Grenada were now in Jackson for the Tenth Annual SCLC Convention. The fact that Dr. King could hold a convention in Mississippi and be welcomed by the new mayor was incontrovertible evidence that the Freedom Movement was defeating old-style Jim Crow white supremacy across the South — even if Grenada had not yet received the memo.

But rather than let us handle this mob violence crisis on our own, some SCLC functionary decided to send in a temporary project director who had a great deal of direct action experience in other states but had never been to Grenada before. Led by the temporary director, about 250 of us, almost all adult Black men, marched up towards the square.

Again, a furious white mob outnumbering us three to one was waiting. But state officials in Jackson, reeling from yet another round of atrocious publicity from the previous attacks, were desperate to prevent a third outbreak of racist violence. They sent in more troopers and a posse of state game wardens with new orders from the governor. When the whites opened up on us with their rocks, bottles, cherry bombs, and slingshots, they began maneuvering in formation to force the mob out of the square.

Unfortunately, the new march leader was unfamiliar with the situation and previous events. He thought the police were setting a trap, that they were clearing out the mob so they themselves could smash our line with gas, clubs, and mass arrests without worrying about hurting local white folk. So as the mob was being pushed out of the square to the south and east he led us west back to Belle Flower. The square was left empty of everyone except law enforcement.

Afterwards, there was enormous disappointment and frustration over retreating from the square, particularly among the Black men who had worked up their courage and defiance to a peak, came out to march — nonviolently — into a racist mob and then been undercut by a mistaken decision. Most of those men never marched again. On the next march, and all the marches that followed, the pattern of a few dozen men leading hundreds of women and students reasserted itself.

For a time I was angry at that leader and even more so at the higher-ups who placed over us someone unfamiliar with the situation. But when the convention was over and J.T. resumed his project director position, the temporary director stayed and continued to work in Grenada, where he showed himself to be a brave and effective organizer — and a good leader. In time I came to understand that he had led us off the square not out of personal fear but out of responsibility for the safety of the people he was charged with caring for.

And I also understood that while his error had unhappy consequences, the self-discipline that resulted in the rest of us obeying his order to retreat even though we disagreed with it was the very thing that in the long run kept us safe and united. It was that kind of self-discipline — even in the case of a mistake — that was the foundation on which Freedom Movement victories were won.

Meanwhile, the white power structure continued trying to prevent Afro-Americans from registering to vote. A few days earlier they had resurrected an old ordinance forbidding gatherings at the courthouse, but since voter registration was now being done at the Chat & Chew, the courthouse was no longer our focus. So on Thursday the 11th, the Grenada City Council passed a new law forbidding any public gatherings on the green.

Apparently they also decided to give their "no audience" strategy another try because no whites showed up to harass our voter registration rally at Chat's and only a small handful of hecklers were on the square when we arrived — too few to even be called a gang, much less a mob. The cops blocked us from walking on to the square, so we marched around it a few times singing our freedom songs — we felt like Joshua marching around Jericho.

When we marched up to the square on Friday evening there were no white hecklers at all. One of SCLC's Executive Staff leaders from Atlanta was in town and he told us that without dramatic violence to film and write about, the TV cameras and reporters were going to depart as they always did. He ordered some of the SCLC staff to try pushing our way onto the green *through* the cops. I and another staff member refused.

It seemed an artificial, ego-driven publicity stunt to me, and that wasn't enough to motivate me into getting my head split open by police billy clubs. While the march circled around the square, some of other staff members did try to get on the green. They were shoved off by the cops and seven were arrested.

As we began to leave the square a formation of troopers suddenly charged against the rear end — I have no idea what their excuse was. A number of marchers were injured, including Emerald Cunningham, age 14, a polio survivor who was unable to run or dodge. They brutally beat her in the back with their rifle butts. I was in my usual spot as rear guard marshal and I also got clobbered. As it turned out, I'd have been safer if I'd agreed to be one of those arrested for trying to get on the green.

I and the other guy who had refused to participate in what I continued to view as an egotistic publicity stunt were ordered by that SCLC official to report to SCLC headquarters in Atlanta for "disciplinary action." The other guy went. I didn't. It was well known in the Freedom Movement that while SNCC and CORE were egalitarian, SCLC was hierarchical. Yet it wasn't as rigidly structured as it sometimes appeared from the outside. I just continued on in Grenada doing my work. After a week or so that officer told me that since I obviously wasn't going to obey him, I should stay in Grenada. The other guy returned to duty after a week of boredom in Atlanta.

That particular SCLC leader remained annoyed with me for quite a while, but other than that my disobedience resulted in no further consequences — I'm not sure why. It may be he knew he had been wrong. He ordered no further attempts to provoke dramatic action by pushing on to the green, and soon the press departed. J.T. and the other SCLC staff members didn't condemn me for my refusal, nor did they insist that I be sent away. And their silent support probably carried a lot of weight. And I suspect that local leaders and local folk who knew me quietly supported me behind the scenes.

After that Friday night attack on the tail end of the march, the normal routine settled back in. Day after day I continued canvassing door-to-door, doing office and research work, and representing SCLC at small house meetings. Every evening 200-300 of us would participate in the nightly mass meeting and then march up to the deserted square and circle around the green a few times before returning to the church. We were always relieved to find the square empty of hostile whites, but it was kind of eerie protesting in a square containing no one but ourselves and the cops.

A Mississippi Trial ~ 1966

On Monday August 22nd, we held our normal nightly march. It seemed no different than any other march. On the following night we began our pre-march mass meeting in Belle Flower as usual, until latecomers reported that the cops had surrounded the church. An SCLC staff member, I think it might have been Leon Hall, left the building to find out what they wanted. He was immediately arrested, apparently on some kind of warrant. Project Director J.T. Johnson followed and he too was busted. Nobody knew why.

Hosea Williams was in town that night as the featured speaker. He told the meeting they were trying to pick off the leaders and he assumed he was the prime target. He instructed everyone to line up at the two doors and all the side windows which were all wide open in the muggy heat of an August evening. At his command everyone was instructed to nonviolently flood out from all possible exits and scatter as fast as they could to limit the number arrested. Anyone nabbed was to go limp, but not otherwise resist.

It was a good plan and it worked quite well — except for me. In the darkness only about a dozen people were arrested, but as one of the few whites trying to escape in the darkness, I was easily spotted and quickly nabbed.

As I was hustled off to the Grenada County lockup I asked the arresting officer what I was being arrested for. He answered by hard-jabbing his billy club into my gut. I interpreted that as an indication he wasn't in a conversational mood. At the jail we all were treated to the usual hospitality that Mississippi police extended to civil rights troublemakers — kicks and punches, being slammed up against the wall, enthusiastic frisking for concealed weapons or subversive literature, and all the other little flourishes by which they expressed their opinion of us.

We were jam-crammed into small cells. Two or three days went by and we still hadn't been told what we were charged with. For some reason we weren't bailed out. No phone calls were allowed. Just a dozen of us stuck in the slammer with lousy food, no showers, and no clue as to what was going on. And of course, no "Miranda rights" to remain silent or be represented by an attorney — those rights didn't exist in 1966.

Finally, someone showed up and introduced himself as our lawyer sent from the ACLU office in Jackson. He was one of the volunteer lawyers who came down from the North on their summer vacation to defend civil rights workers. He'd just arrived in Mississippi from, I think New York, and we were his first case. I can't recall his name other than it was a very Jewish name, so I'll just call him Israel Feldstein (a name I'm making up).

"I've been sent to represent you in your trial today," he told us. That was the first we'd heard about a trial date.

"What are they charging you with?" he asked us.

Okay, confession time. The honest truth is that we were bored, frustrated and downright grumpy. "You're the lawyer, why are you asking us what the charges are?" someone responded in a surly tone.

"They're holding you for days and they haven't told you the charges?"

He was clearly surprised and I remember thinking to myself, *Jeez, what planet is this cat from? Welcome to Mississippi, Izzy.*

"Okay," he assured us, "the first thing I'll do is find out the charges."

"Right, you do that. Good idea!"

A few minutes later they marched us into court. As project director, J.T. sat with the lawyer while the rest of us were seated in a row behind their table. True to his promise, Izzy right off asked what the charges were and the prosecutor read out this long list of crimes like insurrection, riot, sedition, disturbing the peace, disorderly conduct, and so forth — I can't remember them all but it was a very impressive list.

The prosecutor then got up to commence his case, but Izzy interrupted. "Excuse me, your Honor, but where's the court reporter? There's no one taking a record.

The judge slammed his gavel down and shouted at him, "I don't need no God damned kike telling me how to run my court! You want a court reporter? You pay for him yourself!"

Of course, even if we had had the dough (which we didn't), all Mississippi court reporters were white and even if there was one in Grenada it was unlikely he would offend the judge by working for civil rights supporters in a case where his presence wasn't mandated by law. And for all we knew, the nearest Black court reporter might be in Memphis.

Moreover, I don't think Izzy had ever been called a "kike" in a court of law before — certainly not by the judge. This was clearly a new experience for him. But though he most likely grew up as some scrawny Jewish nerd from the Big Apple, you don't mess with Manhattan. He had some game and wasn't going to be intimidated. "Well, if that's the way it's gonna be, your Honor, we want a jury trial."

This particular judge was on the lowest rung of the judicial ladder, he was only authorized to try the most minor of cases — those that used six-man juries. (Women, emotionally frail and prone to the vapors as they were assumed to be, were not permitted to sit on Mississippi criminal case juries in 1966.)

The judge grinned. Lounging around his courtroom were a dozen or more of the regular courthouse loafers, good ol' boys all well known to him. "Tom, Billy-Bob, Frank, Mo, George, Gumby, you're appointed to jury duty. Get in the box."

I guess Izzy realized that there wasn't going to be any questioning of potential jurors for bias, so he said nothing as the judge asked the jury, "You all swear to do your duty?"

"Oh, yeah, right Judge. You bet."

The prosecutor then called Suggs Ingram, the sheriff, as his first witness. "Sheriff Ingram, please describe to this honorable court the criminal behavior you observed these felons commit."

"Oh, they committed insurrection, they was riotous, they disturbed the peace..." He just reiterated all of the charges in verb form.

The prosecutor nodded wisely and then said, "Thank you, Sheriff Ingram. No further questions."

The judge asked Izzy, "Do you want to cross-examine?"

"How can I cross-examine? He hasn't said anything yet." But seeing that the judge was about to dismiss the witness, Izzy got up and asked Suggs, "Sheriff Ingram, could you describe what the defendants did?"

So Suggs started going into his "Well, they was riotous and they..."

Izzy interrupted him. "No, no, Sheriff. Could you please explain what they actually did? What were their physical actions?"

The light dawned on Suggs's face. "Oh, they started singing on the south side of the telephone building." There was triumph in his voice. He knew he had us now.

Izzy, of course, had no clue what the bejeezus Sheriff Ingram was talking about, so he consulted briefly with J.T., who I assumed explained to him that we were under Judge Clayton's federal injunction prohibiting us from singing in residential neighborhoods. We could only sing in the downtown area and evidently the Grenada authorities were now claiming that the south side of the telephone building was somehow "residential," though once we had turned the corner we would clearly have been "downtown" (such as it was).

I don't think anyone had ever formally notified us that that portion of our normal march route was "residential," so we had simply made the assumption that since the telephone building wasn't anyone's home it wasn't "residential," and once we reached it we could start singing. Izzy then clarified with Suggs that the only thing that we were accused of actually doing was singing on the south side of the telephone building — a heinous crime to be sure, but one deserving charges of insurrection and riot? Apparently so, in Sheriff Ingram's opinion.

When Izzy finished with Sheriff Ingram the judge asked the prosecutor if he had any further witnesses. In yet another stellar example of Mississippi's swift and efficient dispensation of justice the prosecutor replied, "No, Your Honor, we rest our case."

The judge turned to Izzy. "Is the defense ready to present its case?"

"Your Honor," replied Izzy, "I can't present a defense because there's been no prosecution. The only thing my clients are accused of actually doing is violating a federal injunction. But they're not charged with that because this court has no jurisdiction. So there's no prosecution case against which I can present a defense because no evidence of any crime related to the charges has been presented. Therefore, I move for an immediate dismissal of all charges."

The judge didn't even bother waiting for the prosecutor to demur. "Motion denied. Is the jury ready to render its verdict? You won't need to withdraw or consult, will you?"

All the jurors shook their heads, murmuring, "Oh no, Your Honor, we're ready."

"What's your verdict, then?"

"Guilty Your Honor."

He immediately sentenced us to ten days in jail or fines of $100 each (equal to around $775 in 2018), which was the maximum penalty his court was allowed to levy. Izzy filed notice of appeal and we were released on bail.

As it turned out though, our lawyers later dropped that appeal because if we had won it our case would then have been retried before a higher-level judge who could have sentenced us to a year in prison if we were convicted. Since we had filed complaints against that particular judge for the role he played in leading a white mob that brutally assaulted Black schoolchildren attempting to integrate a previously white-only school, everyone concluded that appealing our $100 fines was probably not a brilliant idea.

By that time though, it was more than a year later, the fall of 1967, and I was back in California attending San Francisco State College. SCLC was broke and hoped to recover the appeal bond money they had put up, so they wanted me to either send them $100 to pay my fine or return to Mississippi to serve my ten-day sentence. But they didn't know how to reach me. So Rev. Jesse Jackson called my Mom in Connecticut, explained the problem, and asked her for my address and phone number.

"What? Are you crazy?" she responded with her usual diplomatic tact. "I'm not going to tell you where my son is!" She and Jesse then got into it, but she refused to give him my contact info because she was afraid that I would actually go back to Mississippi and be jailed out of some sense of political principle.

When she got around to informing me of this I was quite offended. By then I was a radical SDS "revolutionary." No way in hell was I going to supinely kowtow to "the man" by submitting to a racist kangaroo court, paying any police-state fine, or voluntarily surrendering myself for incarceration. Even though I'd been quite the idealist for the previous four years, I felt she should have intuitively grasped the new, more militant me and given Jesse my contact info so I could have personally refused him. Ah, such is the passion of youth.

The School Crisis ~ 1966

Not long after that trial, Afro-American parents began filling out "Freedom of Choice" forms for the court-ordered school desegregation of Grenada County's two "white" schools — John Rundle High and Lizzie Horn Elementary. They were adjacent to each other on South Line Street, a white neighborhood just a few blocks from Belle Flower and in easy walking distance from the main Afro-American community.

After the Supreme Court's *Brown v. Board of Education* decision in 1954, segregationists in the Deep South had been allowed to retain their separate and unequal white and Colored school systems. For ten years the court's "all deliberate speed" policy had allowed the South to almost entirely circumvent *Brown* by admitting just a token handful of Blacks to selected white schools in a few locales. But the Civil Rights Act of 1964 called for cutting off federal funds from segregated school systems. Without those federal dollars, southern politicians would have to either close schools or significantly raise taxes — neither of which would sit well with white voters. So most of them reluctantly realized they had to begin accepting at least a *few* Afro-Americans into *all* of the formerly white schools.

Yet they still hoped to retain their separate and unequal dual systems — one white, one Colored. For the ruling elite, it wasn't just that they wanted to limit social mingling between the races, it was also a matter of restricting as many Afro-Americans as possible to the kind of "sharecropper education" that limited them to menial, low-paid, and highly-exploited occupations like field hand and domestic servant.

To ensure that federal dollars continued to flow from Washington, while simultaneously keeping the great majority of Afro-American students in segregated schools, they devised "Freedom of Choice" plans. Under those plans, parents were legally "free" to choose which school — white or Colored — their children were to attend. Everyone knew, though, that Black parents who choose a white school faced firings, evictions, foreclosures, boycotts organized by the White Citizens' Council, and violent terrorism from the Ku Klux Klan.

Since few Black families could risk losing their job, home, or business (to say nothing of their lives), white political leaders across the Deep South were confident that just a few Black children would enroll in formerly all-white schools. Those few would then face harassment and humiliation by administrators and teachers — and implacable hostility and abuse from the white students who would outnumber them hundreds to one. Unrelenting pressure on Afro-American students and their families could then be counted on to force many (in some cases all) to "freely choose" to withdraw from the white school and go back to the Colored school.

Such "Freedom of Choice" plans allowed southern whites to piously claim they no longer practiced racial discrimination and that Afro-Americans simply didn't want integration because they were "freely choosing" to send their children to the segregated Colored schools. Since Afro-Americans were no longer *legally required* to attend Colored schools, officials argued they were in compliance with the Civil Rights Act and therefore should continue to receive federal education funds. From 1964 until 1968 when "Freedom of Choice" plans were finally ruled illegal they effectively perpetuated segregation in public school systems across most of the South.

But not in Grenada Mississippi.

Grenada had been one of those die-hard segregationist strongholds that refused to allow any school integration at all despite *Brown* and the Civil Rights Act. Which is where matters stood when the Meredith March and the 20th century arrived in June of 1966.

The newly-formed Grenada County Freedom Movement asked the NAACP Legal Defense Fund to file a lawsuit demanding that Grenada cease operating its completely segregated dual white and Colored school systems. Presented with an open-and-shut case of flagrant violation of both the *Brown* decision and the Civil Rights Act, a federal judge quickly ruled that Grenada schools had to be desegregated forthwith — by September!

The Grenada school board responded with a "Freedom of Choice" plan, no doubt expecting to end up with just a handful of Black children attending the two white schools. But Grenada now had a powerful and well-organized local movement to support Afro-American parents, assist them in resisting intimidation, and provide timely legal aid. And SCLC's Washington office stood ready to make sure that both the Justice and Education Departments diligently enforced federal law.

On Monday, August 29th, we organized hundreds of students and parents to march together en masse to pick up the "choice" forms. By Thursday, September 1st, some 450 Black kids had turned in forms choosing to attend the white schools — an enormous number, not just for Mississippi but for the entire Deep South, where most white schools still had less than a dozen Afro-American students (if they had any at all).

Whites in Grenada were aghast — and *enraged*. Hecklers began returning to the square to harass our marches for the first time since the voter registration violence two weeks earlier. Day by day, the number of hostile whites shouting hate and fury rapidly increased. Though tension was clearly rising, few police or troopers were present.

Friday, September 2nd, was supposed to be the first day of school, but at the last minute the school board postponed it for ten days, citing the burdens of "paperwork." Nevertheless, that evening the white high school played its first football game of the season. Football was an essential element of the Mississippi high school experience, so some of the Black kids who had registered to attend Rundle High showed up to support the Rundle Bulldogs. They were attacked by white students, beaten, and their car windows smashed with baseball bats. So much for school spirit.

It was a brutal attack and I filed a field report on it, but we in SCLC were so focused on the rising tension and hostility confronting our marches up on the square that we failed to take sufficient note of it — or to consider what the attack might portend.

> Fri- 8/2/66 Field report, Bruce Hartford
> Friday night the formerly white high school (John Rundle) had it's opening football game at the stadium. Two car loads of Negroes went out to the stadium to go to the game. They were assaulted by gangs of white teenagers who were waiting outside the stadium in case any Negroes tried to get in. Pat Lock, Constable of Beat-5 drew his pistol and smashed in the windows of one of the cars. Local youth leader Robert Johnson was beaten by the mob. Later a Negro man was driving by the stadium and the teenagers began to throw rocks at his car he sped up to get away and was arrested by state troopers on a traffic charge. [22]

Segregationists used the ten-day delay to wage a fierce campaign against Afro-Americans, coercing them to withdraw their children from the two white schools. Some parents were fired from their jobs, others evicted from their homes. Black families and Movement activists were plagued with racist phone calls filled with curses, obscenities, and explicit death threats. Most folk responded by quickly hanging up, but Afro-American men who listened to the call were treated to graphic descriptions of how they would be castrated with rusty razor blades, and Black women were regaled with detailed descriptions of the brutal, savage rape soon to be inflicted on them — traditional aspects of "southern gentility" that might not be as well known in the North as mint juleps and ostentatious chivalry.

After being attacked by a white man while picketing a downtown store, SCLC staff members J.T. Johnson and R.B. Cottenreader filed an arrest warrant against him. They were then arrested when their white assailant swore out a counter-warrant against them. One of our SCLC cars was firebombed, and when SCLC staff member Willie Bolden tried to talk to a police official about the escalating violence he was arrested on some vague charge.

Activists walking on the streets in the Afro-American community were now at risk. One day I was on Cherry Street, headed back toward Belle Flower after a catfish sandwich at Chat's, when a pickup truck came screeching to a halt next to me. The driver, a hefty white guy, leapt out, knocked me down, and when I curled up in the nonviolent defense position he kicked me again and again.

His son, maybe 10 or 11, jumped out and began stomping on my glasses which had fallen on the pavement. "Daddy, Daddy, they won't break!" he shouted. Damn straight. On one of my visits to my parents in New Haven I'd had a special unbreakable pair of industrial-strength safety glasses made. He was able to damage the plastic frames but not the lenses. After a couple of minutes they both got tired, returned to their truck, and drove off — their civic duty for the day accomplished. I wasn't injured, just the usual bruises and scrapes, so I dusted myself off and continued to our office in the back of the church.

At night, as the old saying went, I "slept with one eye open" — and my Beretta beneath my pillow. (Metaphorically speaking of course. Trying to sleep with a pistol actually under your pillow is quite uncomfortable.)

To support students and parents we doubled up, marching to the square in the afternoon and evening. Day after day and night after night, 200–300 courageous activists marched and marched again. Day after day and night after night the white mobs grew larger and angrier, hurling objects at us and attacking with fists, bats, chains, and steel pipes. Though cops and troopers were under court order to restrain violence and protect us from mob attack, the reluctant, half-hearted, and pro forma gestures they made in that direction were clearly no more than a pretense. Neither we nor the mob took them seriously — we were on our own.

This racist campaign of intimidation, retaliation, and violence was obviously being organized and orchestrated by someone — but who? Klan? White Citizens' Council? Elected officials? Clearly, whoever was behind it wanted Black parents to ponder what might happen to an isolated Black child in a white school surrounded by hostile teachers and students.

We refused to back down. On Thursday, September 8, the Grenada County Freedom Movement defiantly issued a new, more comprehensive set of demands. The original July 9 demands had focused on various kinds of segregation. A month later, the August demands concentrated on ending specific police abuses. The new September demands reflected a growing conviction among local leaders and activists that the root issue was power — political and economic. The GCFM goals were reformulated into a broad, category-by-category demand for economic justice and a fair share of political power in Grenada. The phrase "Black Power" wasn't used but it was a clear step in that direction. [*]

On the Saturday afternoon before school opened only 160 people showed up to march, noticeably fewer than normal. As usual, they were mostly women and high school kids. When we arrived downtown for the afternoon march we saw that whites greatly outnumbered us — and they

---

[*] See www.crmvet.org/docs/grendocs.htm for the text of the August demands and other documents and reports from the Grenada Movement.

had a new tactic. Instead of gathering on the sidewalk around the perimeter of the square to shout abuse and hurl objects, the segregationists were now parading around the green themselves in the street where we normally marched now that the green itself was off limits. We fell in behind them with a narrow gap between the two groups, and both groups circled the green several times, one behind the other.

That evening when our second march of barely 200 reached the square after dark the whites were again parading, but now they had thinned their line to completely surround the green. So our march circled around the green parallel to their march — side by side as it were (though not, of course, in solidarity with each other). Their proximity made it easy for them to dart into our line, and a number of our people were attacked, including SCLC staff members Alphonzo Harris and Mike Bibler.

The segregationists had the edge in violence but we were superior in song and spirit, easily drowning out their racist chants and their pitiful attempts to sing *Dixie* against our *Oh Freedom*.

On Sunday afternoon, the day before school was to open, we didn't march due to church services but some 200 of us grimly gathered our courage and headed for the square in the evening. Again a large crowd of hostile racists far outnumbered us. But they'd abandoned their counter-parade strategy and resumed heckling and throwing rocks and bottles from the sidewalk around the square. Since there was no communication between whites and Blacks in Grenada, we could only speculate on why they did or didn't do this or that. Perhaps marching in even loose formation was too disciplined for them and they preferred to mill around as a mob and share whiskey from bottles concealed by brown paper bags.

Most of the hostile whites contented themselves by shouting their racist hate and hurling rocks, bottles, and cherry bombs at us, but half a dozen of the most violent suddenly charged into our line, beating R.B. Cottonreader and others before pulling back. Among those injured was SCLC staff member Lula Williams, who was attacked by a white woman who repeatedly clubbed her with a furled umbrella.

Despite our efforts, economic retaliation and the escalating violence were having the desired effect. Threatened by loss of jobs and evictions and fearing for their safety of their children, the parents of some 200 of the 450 Afro-American students who had registered for the white schools "freely chose" to withdraw their kids and re-register them at the Colored schools. But to segregationist fury, some 250 Black elementary and high school students remained committed to integrating the previously all-white Grenada schools.

Mob Terror & the Courage of Children ~ 1966

Monday, September 12, was the first day of integrated school. A furious mob of more than 500 white supremacists surrounded the two formerly all-white schools, determined to block Black children from entering.

This was not a spontaneous outburst of rage, it was a well-organized attack with visible leaders — one of whom was Judge Ayers, the Grenada Justice of the Peace. Rather than protecting children from violent attack, almost every elected official and lawman from Grenada City and County was present to defend segregation. Scouts in pickup trucks with two-way radios patrolled the nearby streets, targeting "action teams" against Black children ranging in age from 6 to 17 who were walking to school. And judging by their license plates, racists from all over the state had converged on Grenada, many of them no doubt Klansmen.

Some cars carrying Black children managed to drop their kids off, others were blocked and attacked by the mob who smashed windows with baseball bats and steel pipes and then battered those inside.

The majority of the 250 or so Black students who were still determined to integrate the white schools came from the northside Afro-American neighborhood around Belle Flower where the Freedom Movement had its strongest base. Most of them were walking to school in ones and twos when they were set upon by roving bands who beat them with clubs, chains, bullwhips, and pipes. A white woman tripped Richard Sigh, age 12, with her umbrella, men then kicked him and beat him with pipes, breaking his leg at the hip. Another young boy was forced to run a gauntlet of cursing men, blood sheeting down his face. "That'll teach you, nigger," yelled one of the whites attacking him. "Don't come back tomorrow!"

A reporter overheard a white woman watching a gang of men whip a pig-tailed elementary school girl murmur to herself, "How can they laugh when they are doing it?"

The few cops in the area did nothing at all to halt the violence. A contingent of riot-equipped state troopers loitering around the corner took no action. FBI agents stood by writing in their little notebooks. They made no effort whatsoever to enforce the federal desegregation order, or the Civil Rights Act, or the U.S. Constitution, or to protect innocent children from brutal attack. When asked by a reporter what they were doing, one replied that they were "investigating" to "determine whether any federal laws or court orders had been violated."

Braving the danger and violence, almost a third of the 250 Black kids managed to make it into the temporary safety of the school buildings. The mob didn't follow them inside — probably out of concern that in narrow building corridors white children might accidentally be injured by their violence.

The remaining Afro-American children, bruised, bleeding, and terrified, retreated back to Belle Flower, which now resembled a war zone first-aid station more than a place of worship. In a total failure of foresight, we had made no preparations for anything like this — nothing at all. Other than singer Joan Baez and nonviolence advocates Ira and Susan Sandperl who were volunteering in Grenada to support the Movement, there were no outside observers. Nor were there any MCHR volunteer doctors or nurses on hand to care for the wounded. SCLC staff and parents had to pitch in with emergency first aid and ferrying the badly injured to a hospital in the all-Black town of Mound Bayou more than an hour distant.

Given the long history of anti-integration mob violence ranging from Little Rock to New Orleans, Clinton to Tuscaloosa, there was no excuse for our failure to anticipate the possibility of a mob attack on Black schoolkids. Looking back, all the warning signs and portents were there for us to see, but we had become so fixated on our marches as the danger point that it never occurred to us that children going to school might be so brutally attacked.

Back on South Line Street, reporters and photographers were still trying to cover the first mass integration of a Mississippi school system. Most of them were southerners themselves but that didn't prevent them from being viciously set upon by the enraged white mob. Bloody and battered, they too fell back to the precarious safety of Belle Flower.

Mississippi counties are divided into districts, called "beats," each of which elects a constable who is sort of a junior sheriff. Beat 1 included the town of Grenada, and its constable was Grady Carrol. Of all the county's lawmen, he was the most hostile to Afro-Americans, the Freedom Movement, and the news media. "Some of the newsmen needed a cleaning," he later explained to a New York Times reporter. "If they tell a lie, they need a whupping from anybody who wants to give it to them."

Later that day, Mississippi Governor Paul Johnson "deplored" the assault on local southern reporters and photographers, "It is bad enough for hoodlums to attack with the intent to do violence upon any news personnel. For the ignoramuses to attack our own people is unforgivable." He made no mention of adult men savagely clubbing children.

My assigned post that day was in the SCLC office at the rear of Belle Flower, manning our typewriter and noting down reports as they came in while others worked the phones alerting Atlanta, the Justice Department, and the news media. Normally we were happy to let journalists use one of our two phones, but that day we needed both lines to respond to the crisis, so they had to make do with a wall-mounted pay phone in the hallway. I remember one nationally famous TV reporter from a major TV network with blood dripping down his face and staining his suit. I won't mention his name, but he was screaming hysterically at someone on the other end that he wasn't going to set foot outside of the church until they provided him protection.

What about protecting school kids, I thought to myself but refrained from saying aloud.

A bit after 9:00am, Black SCLC staff members led the children who had retreated to Belle Flower on a march back to the two schools. Many of the student integrators were veterans of mass marches to the square, familiar with the group tactics of nonviolently enduring and prevailing over white violence, and the hope was that those techniques might get the kids through the mob. Since the purpose of the march was to protect the students and see them safely to school, the few white SCLC staff members, Joan Baez, and the Sandperls were asked to stand aside because it was thought that the presence of white allies would incite the racist segregationists to even greater fury.

I was despondent at being left behind. Those kids were my friends and I wanted to face the mob with them. I felt ashamed and guilty watching them march courageously into danger without me. But I knew that the argument against including us white "race traitors" was valid, so I accepted the decision and manned a desk instead of assuming my usual march marshal role. Though I hated it, it was the right thing to do. As I've mentioned before, self-discipline was one of the Freedom Movement's great strengths, one that unfortunately some of the movements of the later '60s tossed aside.

Alerted by the cops, the mob was ready and waiting for the march, brutally attacking en masse. The SCLC staff members leading the line were targeted and beaten, some so badly they had to be hospitalized. Emerald Cunningham, the girl lamed by polio who walked with a pronounced limp and who had previously been attacked by troopers up on the square, couldn't escape. She was beaten down in the street, kicked, and clubbed with a lead pipe. A Klansman held a pistol to her head, "Nigger!" he screamed, "I'll shoot your brains out!" She had to be hospitalized for her injuries, as did other children with broken bones and bloody wounds.

A police officer watched the whole incident and laughed. FBI agents took notes — no doubt to aid their "investigation" into the possibility that someone might be violating a federal court order.

Finally, though, the local cops did move into action. They arrested SCLC member Lula Williams for "felonious assault," based on a complaint by the white woman who had beaten her with an umbrella the previous evening during the march to the square. Grown men who brutally assaulted Black children with baseball bats and steel pipes were allowed free rein, but Lula was held on $1,000 bail (equal to $7,600 in 2018).

Meanwhile, the 80 or so Afro-American kids who had managed to elude the mob earlier that morning were now trapped inside the two schools, surrounded by violent whites on the outside and threatened by hostile white students and teachers on the inside. That first-day session was scheduled to end at noon, by which time the mob had grown larger as they waited for Black children to be forced out through the doors by the school authorities.

Desperate to protect the kids from the white mob, SCLC staff, local movement leaders, and Black parents tried to reach the schools before the noon closing but were halted by rifle-armed Mississippi State Troopers who were blocking the surrounding streets. The troopers barred Afro-Americans, but gave free access to whites. Meanwhile, a truckload of club-wielding white men turned their attention downtown, attacking R.B. Cottonreader and a group of boycott pickets, injuring several.

At noon, one of the principals summoned all the white girls and the younger white boys to a location in the school where they'd be protected and safe. The older white boys were allowed to leave, either going home or joining the mob. Then he ordered the Black boys and girls of all ages out of the building, forcing them into the mob which viciously assaulted them. Dedicated freedom marcher Dorothy Allen, age 16, had to race through a gauntlet of violent attackers, as did Pointdexter Harbie, beaten bloody in the face. A Black child's skull was fractured, sending him and others to hospital with broken bones and internal injuries.

As Nina Simone sang it so well, "Mississippi Goddam!"

[As an historical side note, Dianna Freelon, then 16, was one of the children attacked and beaten that day by the white mob. In 2004 she was elected mayor of Grenada in an election where two white candidates split the white vote. She served one term in office before whites coalesced around a single challenger to oust her.]

No communication channels existed between the Black community and the white power structure, so there was no dialogue of any kind. For hints and clues about what the whites were thinking and planning we relied on rumors passed to us by Black maids and janitors, who reported what little they overheard from their bosses.

For their part, the white power structure relied on their Afro-American snitches to inform them of what we were up to and why. Some of those snitches were motivated by money or favors, others were coerced by blackmail. The Black snitches were able to attend our mass meetings and some of them might have had access to the deliberations of SCLC and GCFM leaders. Yet I suspect they tended to tell whites in power what they thought the whites wanted to hear rather than annoy them with unpalatable truths. In any case, we always assumed that we lived and worked in a fishbowl with no expectation that anything we did or planned could be kept secret from "The Man."

According to our janitorial sources, that evening hundreds of furious whites jammed the City Council meeting to rage against school integration and even the minimal (mostly imagined) passive protection that police presence had granted Black children. "You get the highway patrol out of here and in twenty-four hours there won't be a nigger left!" shouted one man.

To placate the hardliners, who were obviously once more back in control, the Council fired "moderate" City Manager McEachin, who had originally devised the failed strategy for easing the Meredith March through Grenada without sparking protests by local Afro-Americans. Based on what we could glean from the rumors passed on to us, he was purged because he exhibited insufficient enthusiasm for mob attacks on children.

Later, a huge white mob numbering more than a thousand filled the square waiting for our regular march. But by then the national news media was breaking the story of school children and reporters savagely attacked by white racists while law enforcement did nothing.

Once again, that put pressure on state officials in Jackson. The officer in charge of the state trooper contingent promised that if we didn't march that night his men would protect the children going to school the next day. Of course we put no faith in his assurance, we'd heard that "we'll protect you tomorrow" song and dance before. But more than 100 of the 250 kids who had tried to attend the white schools were still determined to persevere despite the danger and we knew we had to do whatever we could to help protect them — even if it meant grasping at straws. So, based on a promise we trusted not at all, we reluctantly agreed to cancel the march.

We put out the word that no Afro-American students should walk to school on their own. Next morning, Tuesday the 13th, more than 100 courageous Black elementary and high school students gathered at Belle Flower to be driven by Afro-American adults willing to risk mob assault and damage to their cars. Again the white mob had the schools surrounded and again they attacked any Blacks who approached, smashing car windows with baseball bats and steel pipes. State troopers, local lawmen, and FBI agents again watched the violence and again did nothing to stop it. At least 10 kids were seriously injured and many vehicles were damaged. Yet despite the violence, a good portion of the students managed to maneuver through the mob, enduring the blows and curses to defiantly enter the two school buildings.

A swarm of journalists and TV crews from around the world were now recording the mob's every action and law enforcement's utter inaction. Again, reporters and photographers were attacked. Again, the cops did finally bestir themselves to arrest someone — SCLC staff member Major Wright, who was on the sidelines, observing and reporting back to us. He was busted for "trespass." A civil rights lawyer, also there to observe, began speaking to Constable Grady Carroll, who called over members of the mob, who then rushed in and beat the lawyer with fists and clubs.

Meanwhile, out in the world, reports and TV footage of Monday's mob attack on schoolkids were being printed and broadcast across the globe. Intense political pressure from business interests both inside and outside the state was now coming down on Mississippi and its governor. Around noon, word began to circulate that he had *finally* ordered the troopers to actually protect the children. That word was passed to the mob leaders. Obedient as ever to the white powers-that-be, the violent throng around the schools quickly dwindled down to a few disgruntled diehards.

Classes ended around 3pm. Led by Dr. King, who had flown down from Chicago, a hundred or so Black adults and civil rights workers marched out of Belle Flower in as large a group as we could muster to escort the students through the mob that we assumed was still lurking in ambush. This time white SCLC staff and volunteer supporters were allowed to participate.

Rifle-armed troopers stopped us at their barricade a couple of blocks from the two schools. Their orders were that no one but students and parents were allowed through. They assured us that from now on they would prevent attacks on the children. We had no reason to believe them (and every reason not to), but there was no way we could force our way through a heavily armed blockade.

We waited anxiously until the kids safely came out through the barricade and told us that the mob was gone. We all marched back to Belle Flower together singing freedom songs and feeling victorious at having survived a second day of integrated school with pride and dignity.

Later that afternoon, an Afro-American who worked at the tiny local airport came to the church with an amusing story. Constable Grady Carroll had heard that two plane loads of newsmen were flying in on a pair of private jets. He gathered his posse of thugs and toughs to give them the kind of welcome he had been handing out to reporters and photographers at the schools.

It didn't go as planned though. Instead of tweedy writers, a dozen hefty, tough-looking guys in casual attire stepped off the plane. They didn't appear to be worried about trouble from Grady's gang. In fact they seemed to be looking forward to it — eagerly. Grady and his posse slunk away without a word. A TV producer we were friendly with clued us in. Two of the three broadcast networks had reached out to Mayor Daley of Chicago who was happy to oblige the gatekeepers of public opinion. At his request, a band of Chicago cops had "voluntarily" taken "leave of absence" to protect network camera crews from mob attack.

That night the evening march was small, only 170 or so and as usual mostly women and children. Wounds and injuries prevented some of the regular protesters from participating and others were frightened by the mob. Those who did march concealed their fear behind a shield of spirited singing. When we reached the square a throng of 500 or more whites were waiting for us with rocks, bottles, bats, and pipes. No cops or troopers were visible. None at all — a silent but eloquent invitation to mob violence. As we circled the green we were bombarded by a hail of thrown missiles and links of steel chain shot from slingshots.

Back in those days, TV cameras capable of filming at night were big, bulky contraptions that had to be strapped to the cameramen with struts and braces making it almost impossible for them to run or dodge attacks. Covering the action on the square were two TV camera crews, each one surrounded by six Chicago cops who were hunched down like linebackers ready to spring out against anyone who threatened the photographers who were filming over their heads. They moved in unison as a squad, like a football team's defensive line. We, of course, had no such protection. But we found their antics amusing.

Singing our hearts out, we circled the green two or three times. By the end, a number of us were bleeding from stones and chain links. I was in my usual position as the rear marshal and I kept expecting the mob who so outnumbered us to physically assault our line. But somehow in the face of our unity and singing most of them were psychologically unable to do so — at first. On our third lap around the green a gang of enraged whites suddenly charged into the front of the line with clubs and fists swinging. The tightly packed protesters took the blows on their shoulders and raised their arms to protect their heads as they kept on marching. A squad of troopers reluctantly came around the corner to push the attackers away and hold them back.

On Wednesday morning, September 14, some 86 children of all ages were still willing to brave the mob and the implacable hostility of white students and teachers. They were determined to win at all cost, to defeat their white racist enemies and not give an inch. This was not, of course, out of any great burning desire to sit next to white children in class. Rather they were simply fed up with being treated as inferior, being told they weren't "good enough." They understood, respected, and deeply appreciated the academic fundamentals and self-pride that courageous Black teachers surreptitiously taught them in defiance of Mississippi's white education authorities. But they were no longer willing to endure the kind of "sharecropper education" that the state forced upon the segregated Colored schools.

The previous day, while the mob was attacking cars carrying Afro-American kids, the police were carefully noting down the license plates of those driving children to school. For the rest of the day cops harassed them with bogus citations for imaginary traffic infractions. So our new strategy was to assemble at Belle Flower and march with the children to school en masse. The march was stopped at the trooper barricade two blocks from the schools. Though there were some white hecklers nearby, there was no mob. None of the children were attacked as they approached the school doors. The small march to the square that night was well protected by troopers and the waiting mob was subdued, limiting themselves for the most part to verbal abuse.

Movement lawyers had, of course, immediately complained to Judge Clayton in Oxford about mob violence thwarting his desegregation order. Classes were canceled on Thursday the 15th so that school officials could appear in federal court. The next day he issued a sweeping injunction ordering the county and city of Grenada and the state of Mississippi to protect children on their way to and from school. For this "intrusive federal interference with states' rights" he was roundly condemned and vilified by white politicians.

Now that troopers were finally protecting students from mob attack, some 160 kids showed up at Belle Flower for the Friday morning march to school. But 25 were sent home by school officials because of minor technicalities in their paperwork. That evening there was no mob in the square waiting for the night march. We didn't know whether the white power structure had gone back to its "no audience strategy" or they were having trouble keeping their mobs mobilized.

We of SCLC, local Movement leaders and activists, and the Afro-American community at large were all buoyed up by a sense of great achievement. Black Grenadans had defied and endured daily assaults at both school and square from raging Klan-led mobs. Now the mobs were gone while we were still marching and Black kids were still attending the white schools. On Sunday, Dr. King addressed a mass meeting jam-packed with more than 650 people. Three times the normal 200 or so participated in the night march to the square including many adults who had never marched before. Afro-Americans saw it as a victory march — and so did many whites though they refused to acknowledge it. It felt good, it felt really, really good.

Over the next week some of those rejected for technicalities were able to get enrolled, others weren't. When it finally settled down, out of the 450 Afro-Americans who had first asked for "Freedom of Choice" transfers in September, about 150 ended up attending the two white schools. While 150 was only a third of the original number, it was far greater than the number of Blacks attending any other integrated school in Mississippi.

On Saturday, September 18, the FBI arrested 13 whites on conspiracy charges for organizing the mob attack on the first day of school. One of them was Judge Ayers who had jurisdiction over many of the civil rights arrest cases in Grenada. He was the one we would have had to appear before had we decided to appeal our "singing on the south side of the telephone building" conviction.

A year later, in 1967, those 13 racists were finally tried in federal court for mobbing schoolchildren. The evidence was overwhelming. The kids identified their attackers from the witness stand. Under oath, two white policemen gave reluctant testimony against the defendants, as did the principal of the white high school. The defense arguments offered to refute the charges were utterly pathetic, some of them claimed they weren't there that day despite overwhelming evidence to the contrary. One man who was accused of kicking a Black child in the face told the court, "The boy fell down at my feet and grabbed at my breeches — when the boy grabbed my leg I fell backward and my leg went up."

It took only 30 minutes for an all-white jury to acquit each and every defendant on every single charge.

Grappling With Poverty ~ 1966

From its commencement in early July, the "Blackout" boycott of Grenada's white merchants had been highly effective, cutting deep into their sales and profits. But groceries were our weak link in sustaining it. The few Black-owned stores were small "mom & pop" operations whose product selection was far smaller than at Pak'N Sak, Grenada's main grocery store (white owned, of course). And because the small Afro-American stores were overcharged by white wholesalers their prices were higher. The nearest town with a large market was Greenwood a 45 minute drive each way. Some Afro-Americans in Grenada had cars but many did not, nor did they have spare coin to share the cost of gas. So a good number of Black families simply had no choice but to sometimes shop at white-owned markets.

SCLC leader Hosea Williams proposed that members of Grenada's miniscule Black business and professional strata build an Afro-American owned "supermarket" to compete with Pak'N Sak. With seed money from the United Auto Workers union plus stock purchased by local folk, B&P Enterprises Inc. (for "Business & Professional") came into existence. The board of directors consisted of Rev. Sharper Cunningham who was pastor of Belle Flower and the main GCFM leader, a principal of one of the two Colored schools, a Black teacher, and the coach of the Black high-school's football team.

An empty lot at the north end of Main Street near the Yalabousha River bridge was purchased from an Afro-American landowner. Supervised by SCLC staff member Jim Bulloch (a former engineer), construction work on a 6600 square-foot concrete block building was begun. (For comparison, today's modern urban "supermarkets" average around 40,000 square feet, but a typical Black-owned "mom & pop" store of the 1960s was usually between 200 and 500 square feet, so the label "supermarket" was not an exaggeration for that time and place.)

Building a Black-owned market fit into a broader context of addressing poverty and unemployment through economic development, political organization, coops, and unions, that the Freedom Movement as a whole was beginning to address. By '66, it was clear that overt, legally-sanctioned segregation would soon be ended (or at least greatly diminished) and Afro-Americans would be registered to vote in large numbers. But most Blacks were still going to be poor and economically dependent on whites. As Hosea and many other SCLC leaders saw it, one way to address economic issues was to build up an Afro-American middle-class of business owners who would serve their community and provide decent jobs to other Blacks. (By contrast, Dr. King was moving towards building a broad political campaign against structural inequality and the economic roots of poverty.)

Elsewhere, SCLC was experimenting with a variety of economic-oriented programs. Led by Jesse Jackson, "Operation Breadbasket" in Atlanta and Chicago used the threat of consumer boycotts to force white employers to start hiring Afro-American workers. And back in the Alabama Black Belt, Albert Turner was organizing the Southwest Alabama Farmers Cooperative Association (SWAFCA) to empower and sustain Black landowners.

In Louisiana, Alabama, and other areas of Mississippi, similar economic empowerment efforts by SNCC and CORE were being undertaken within the ideologic framework of "Black Power." SCLC didn't use that terminology but rhetorical aspects aside, the actual programatic content of our efforts were not markedly different from those of CORE and SNCC.

In my own way, I too was trying to address economic injustice and inequality. Since I was not assigned to the supermarket project I began looking into the upcoming ASCS election — which everyone referred to as the "cotton vote."

The Agriculture Stabilization & Conservation Service (ASCS) was the U.S. Department of Agriculture (USDA) agency that distributed cash subsidies, crop allotments, low-interest loans, and other farm-related benefits (today it's called the Farm Service Agency). County-level ASCS committees were the ones who made the actual decision as to who got what (if anything). In the Deep South, those committees were all-white and their division of benefits between white and Black and rich and poor was profoundly unfair. As SNCC organizer and civil rights attorney Don Jelinek later described it:

> The cotton allotments allocated to Blacks was less than that for whites, and less than strict formulas required. The subsidy payments for Afro-Americans wasn't paid at all, or was underpaid, or paid directly to the company store for the plantation owner to "adjust their account." The net result was that a white farmer and an Afro-American farmer could own or farm equal amounts of equal quality adjacent land, but the white would prosper while the Black went bankrupt and ended up working for the white. [22]

In 1964 and 1965, SNCC and CORE activists in Mississippi, Alabama, and Louisiana had organized campaigns to elect Afro-Americans to those county committees — with no success, not even in counties where Black farmers heavily outnumbered whites. In every state and every county, ASCS and USDA officials colluded with white landowners to blatantly rig the vote. Again in 1966, Movement organizers were waging ASCS campaigns in Mississippi counties neighboring on Grenada. By now SCLC's prohibition against whites canvassing in rural Grenada County had been relaxed, so I obtained materials from the Mississippi Freedom Democratic Party in Jackson and began meeting with Black farmers and sharecroppers about the upcoming ASCS election.

But between the school crisis, the supermarket project, the ongoing blackout, and continuing voter registration work, SCLC in Grenada County was spread thin. We didn't have the resources to take on the kind of major effort that an ASCS campaign would require. Since it wasn't something I could do on my own I had to drop it. And in the end, none of the much larger efforts by SNCC or CORE in other counties were able to overcome the ruthless chicanery of USDA officials who worked hand-in-glove with the plantation owners to maintain the status quo. (Racial discrimination by the USDA was so blatant that in later decades lawsuits by Black farmers against the agency resulted in compensation awards totaling more than a billion dollars.)

At the same time that white mobs were attacking schoolchildren in September, Pak'N Sak grocery filed a lawsuit demanding $960,000 damages for "lost business" due to the blackout (equal to around $7,500,000 in 2018). The named defendants were SCLC staff and GCFM leaders, three Afro-American churches, and all of the Black taxi drivers. I was one of the individual defendants named in the suit.

Under Mississippi law at that time, consumer boycotts were illegal. Economic boycotts by the White Citizens' Council against establishments that tried to operate on an integrated basis were never prosecuted, but "blackouts" and selective buying campaigns by Blacks protesting segregation and discrimination faced legal suppression under the law. In our view, the boycott law was an unconstitutional violation of free speech — and it was clearly enforced in a racially biased manner. So we had defiantly violated that law as an act of civil disobedience.

The lawsuit hearing began in early November. We were accused of organizing a consumer boycott of Pak'N Sak because of their segregation policies, their discriminatory hiring practices, and their general support of white supremacy in Grenada — true that. Had we been in a federal court, our constitutional and selective-prosecution arguments might have carried some weight, but we were being sued in a local Grenada County court, and the hearing was the same kind of farce as my trial for singing on the wrong side of the telephone building.

A.G. Allen, the owner of Pak'N Sak, testified as the plaintiff (in other words, the prosecution against us). Under oath he admitted that he knew only three or four of the seventy or so people he was suing, had *never actually read* the suit, did not know who had written it, and knew nothing about the specific incidents alleged in it. Obviously, he and the lawsuit were being used by the white power structure to crush the boycott, prevent establishment of an Afro-American owned store that might compete against white-owned businesses, and financially cripple SCLC and the churches that were supporting the Movement.

Despite Allen's shaky testimony, the judge immediately ruled against us and issued an injunction prohibiting all boycott activities.

Movement lawyers appealed, but while we waited for the appeal to slowly work its way through Mississippi's judicial system the injunction remained in force. It prohibited leafleting or picketing to maintain the blackout and as a practical matter it wasn't possible to mount a sustained civil disobedience campaign to resist it. Activists who had previously been arrested for violating the anti-boycott law had been bailed out while their cases were successfully appealed on constitutional grounds, but when someone was arrested for violating an injunction, bail and appeals weren't allowed. So anyone arrested for violating the injunction would remain in the slammer indefinitely until the judge (in his infinite mercy) decided to let them go.

Some of the militant student protesters were willing to face indefinite incarceration — but not enough to "fill the jails" which is what it would have taken to successful stymie the injunction. So we had to halt boycott picketing and leafletting. Without a Movement presence downtown the boycott waned and faded away — which was, of course, what the white power structure intended.

Meanwhile, the day-to-day grind of Movement work continued. Using a six-page "community survey" form, I canvassed door-to-door during the day. The form had questions about all sorts of information that might be useful to an organizer — names, addresses, economic matters, health, education, housing, church membership, and so on. Of course, no one had personal computers back then and there was no way to process, collate, or use most of the data we collected, so the survey was really just a pretext for long conversations with people about the details of their lives, their problems, and the issues that concerned them. In other words, the nuts and bolts of traditional one-on-one, face-to-face community organizing.

Out of that canvassing I began organizing a Poor People's Committee. As was customary at that time, its titular head was a male minister (there were no female clergy in 1966), but all the active members and the real leaders were women — Mamie Wilmington, Senora Springfield, Essie Mullin, and Bulah Washington. Within a couple of weeks an average of 15 women were meeting regularly to discuss the economic issues that affected their lives and that of their neighbors. A few were schoolteachers, most of the others were maids or low-wage workers, but all of them were able to read and write fairly well, and their main concern was helping those lower down on the economic ladder than themselves.

Without question, Mississippi's welfare system was one of the very worst in the nation — deliberately so. It was designed to keep large numbers of poor Afro-Americans in such desperate economic straits that they would work for starvation wages on the cotton plantations during the short planting, chopping, and picking seasons — either as sharecroppers or day laborers. Since its purpose was labor force management rather than any effort to help people improve their lives or climb out of poverty, the state welfare system combined with the federal surplus "commodity" food program barely kept recipients alive on a few cents a day while forcing them to live in sharecropper shacks hardly different from slave-era hovels.

Every election cycle, the state's white power structure railed against "those lazy welfare bums." But for decades they themselves had been the chief beneficiaries of the tax-funded welfare system, because it maintained in place their seasonal labor force — at no direct cost to them. Had there been no welfare system they'd have had to pay their seasonal workers enough to survive year-round.

But now a fundamental shift was underway. The fields were being mechanized and the planters no longer needed large numbers of seasonal workers. The White Citizens' Council was providing them with low-interest loans to invest in machines and chemical weed killers that could do the work more efficiently and at lower cost than the abysmally low wages they paid their "field hands." And at the same time those same Black "hands" were beginning to register to vote, which threatened the land-barons' political domination.

So the old welfare system was no longer politically or economically beneficial to the wealthy planters — those who Dr. King referred to as "Bourbons." Now, instead of maintaining sharecroppers and field hands on the land, the Bourbons sought to drive them out of the state. Ever sensitive to shifts in the political winds, welfare officials were now intensifying their efforts to deny or cut people's benefits, and they didn't hesitate to ignore their own rules and regulations to do so.

Grenada, both city and county, was part of that pattern. As soon as Afro-Americans in Grenada began demanding their human rights, local authorities stepped up efforts to economically force them out of the county.

From Marian Wright (today Marian Wright Edelman) at the NAACP Legal Defense Fund in Jackson, I obtained a 70-page handbook explaining in plain English what Mississippi's welfare laws and rules were and how to oppose and appeal illegal or capricious denial of benefits. During the day I and members of the Poor People's Committee met with Afro-American welfare recipients about their experiences with the welfare department. And night after night the ladies of the committee studied the handbook and discussed how to use the information.

We formed three working teams. The first continued to reach out to welfare recipients, noting down their stories and problems, and preparing factual information for a U.S. Civil Rights Commission hearing scheduled for Jackson in 1967. The second team handled written correspondence and appeals with the welfare agency on behalf of recipients who had been unfairly treated. The third team, composed of the most bold and courageous women, accompanied applicants and recipients down to the welfare office to help them fill out the forms and to ensure that they received fair treatment and the benefits they were entitled to.

I did not accompany them when they went to the welfare office. My presence as a white "race traitor" would have provoked rage from the officials and possibly violence or arrests. And I knew it was crucial that the committee ladies confront and overcome the authorities on their own. Which they did. Their first victory was forcing the officials to obey their own rules allowing our advocates to accompany both applicants and people appealing decisions all the way through the process. With defiant courage they demanded that they be allowed to attend interviews and hearings and to help people with their forms — and they won! They, and the Afro-American community at large, were so proud of that victory.

Though the B&P supermarket endeavor was now more or less in limbo because of the lawsuit and lack of funds, it was still SCLC's primary economics-oriented effort in Grenada, so I was pretty much on my own with the Poor People's Committee. SCLC officials in Atlanta didn't oppose what I was doing, but neither did they support it with additional resources. The truth was that I was working the opposite end of the economic spectrum from SCLC's traditional focus on preachers, teachers, landowners and businessmen, and some of the Atlanta-based leaders seemed a bit bemused at the idea of working with people on welfare rather than the Afro-American leaders and elites they personally felt more comfortable with.

On the other hand, while I don't know if Dr. King was aware of what I doing (I doubt it), we all knew he was turning his attention towards poverty and developing ideas and plans that would eventually lead to the Poor People's Campaign. I suspect that was the one reason no one in the SCLC hierarchy ever questioned or openly opposed my work around welfare rights.

The Poor People's Campaign was Dr. King's last great effort and the one he was working on when he was killed. I believed then, and still do to this day, that King's assassination was planned and facilitated by powerful members of society and government because he was opposing the Vietnam War and trying to build an interracial coalition of the poor to fight for economic justice. No one I knew in SCLC — then or now — believed the "crazed lone gunman" assassination theory put forward by the FBI and other government officials.

Grit & Determination ~ 1966

As the summer heat waned and the weather turned to fall we continued to hold our nightly marches, but the number of participants gradually dwindled down to 100 or less. People were tired, worn out with protests, tension, arrests, danger, and economic retaliation by whites. And they were discouraged by the slow — essentially nonexistent — pace of change since "The Movement" had come to town. Despite the steadily rising number of Black voters, all aspects of power still remained exclusively in white hands. Every cop, public official, bureaucrat, and clerk was still white. And nothing had improved economically for Afro-Americans, while many had been fired or evicted as punishment for their Movement activity.

What *had* changed though — and profoundly so — was the Black community itself. Where once fear, subservience, and a sense of inferiority enforced by social custom, law, and violence had been dominant, now courage, pride, and self-respect were on the rise. Even Afro-Americans who personally took no active part in the Freedom Movement felt the change. And so too did whites who fought it, and resented it, but had no choice but to accept it because despite their ruthless efforts the old days of

Jim Crow–style white supremacy were dying — killed by Black men and women, girls and boys who simply refused to endure it any longer.

Thursday, October 6th, marked the 100th mass march of the Grenada Movement. We made a special turnout effort and some 170 people participated. In defiance of the ordinance forbidding such activity, we held a rally at the courthouse. When the cops looked like they were about to bust us we quickly left. Spirits were temporarily lifted, but the persistent problem of dwindling participation remained.

On Saturday the 8th, for the first time ever not enough people showed up at the nightly mass meeting to hold a march. Our sense was that 75 was the rock-bottom minimum number we had to have for safety. If we didn't have at least that many we'd look so weak as to invite attack from spontaneous groups of hostile whites. Over the next ten days small marches of between 75 and 100 were held, but twice more we had to cancel for lack of marchers.

It was frustrating, painful, and deeply discouraging to watch the Grenada Movement's direct action phase wane away. As with the N-VAC campaign against Van de Kamp's in 1964, we were now reaching the limits of sustained direct action. We knew that if some crisis or atrocity temporarily reenergized people we might be able to resume protests for a while around that particular issue, but daily mass meetings and marches as a way of involving people in the Freedom Movement had run its course. We heard that McEachin had been rehired as City Manager, an indication that our faltering numbers and canceled marches had once again put the white "moderates" in ascendancy over the hardliners.

And at the same time, broader social currents were weakening SCLC as an organization. Nationwide, the urban uprisings, Black Power controversies, and the Freedom Movement's shift of focus towards issues of northern-style segregation, economic justice, and opposition to the Vietnam War were reducing financial contributions from white liberals. By summer's end it was clear that Dr. King and SCLC had suffered a strategic defeat in the Chicago Open Housing campaign. Too many of the northern liberals who had supported campaigns against southern segregation were unwilling to back desegregation efforts in their own back yard.

Moreover, King's growing prominence as an opponent of the Vietnam War was alienating important institutions and power brokers including national leaders of the Democratic Party and President Lyndon Johnson himself. With SCLC now struggling financially, bail money was no longer available for large, sustained civil disobedience campaigns, and the number of staff assigned to Grenada had dropped to fewer than half of those who had been there during the summer peak.

Meanwhile, the Afro-American children in the white schools were enduring intense, unremitting harassment aimed at pressuring them to drop out and resume their Colored education. While they no longer faced attack by white mobs outside the buildings, inside they were faced with daily battles for dignity and survival. White kids freely kicked and pushed Black kids in the halls, threw objects at them, cursed them, and called them "nigger," "jigaboo," "coon," and other insults.

School authorities did nothing to curtail student behavior or protect Afro-American children. White boys were allowed to carry knives, saps, and other weapons, but nonwhites were suspended for doing the same. Whenever an Afro-American student had any kind of conflict with a white, the Black was punished — by mid-October, 40 had already been suspended or expelled as "troublemakers" — while the white kids got a wink and a nod from administrators and teachers.

Knowing what they faced, the young Afro-American school integrators dreaded going to school each day. By mid-October, 60 of the 150 or so who had managed to enroll at the beginning of the term had been driven out by indignities, physical attacks, harassment from teachers and administrators, and economic retaliation against their parents. But with raw courage, grit, and determination some 90 or so Black children still held out. They picked up their books each morning and walked into what had for them become halls of hell.

On Tuesday, October 18, there were two new incidents. At Horn Elementary an Afro-American boy had been sitting in the cafeteria with some white students. The principal ordered him to move and sit with the other Black kids. When he refused, the principal yanked him from his seat, ripping his jacket. At Rundle High the same day, Dorothy Allen — one of the most courageous and dedicated of the young freedom marchers — was punched by a white boy. She hit him back and was taken to the principal who ordered her to bring her mother to school the following day — an indication that she was about to be expelled.

That evening, we called an emergency meeting of parents to discuss what to do about the violence and harassment at the white schools. More than 100 parents showed up. They decided to send a delegation to accompany Dorothy's mother to see the principal and to ask for formal meetings between parents and teachers. Twenty of those present courageously agreed to be part of the delegation.

On Wednesday, the principal refused to meet with the parents delegation or to set up any future meetings. He adamantly denied that any pattern of discrimination or abuse existed. He claimed he was willing talk to *individual* parents about *specific* problems, but he refused to acknowledge the existence of issues affecting Afro-American students as a group. Nor was he willing to meet with more than one set of parents at a time. In other words, mothers and fathers of one child with a complaint could come before him as lone supplicants in traditional Jim Crow fashion, but not if they brought along anyone else to support them — or anyone who might later become a witness in a court of law.

That night the mass meeting was well attended for the first time in weeks. They decided to try to meet with the principal again on Thursday and if he refused, the Black students would walk out in protest on Friday. That night, more than 200 joined our march to the square, the largest number in some time.

On Thursday, the principal again refused to meet with any group of Black parents. On Friday at 10am the remaining 90 or so Afro-American students in the two white schools defiantly walked out to protest continuing abuse and harassment. Some 180 students at the two Colored schools also walked out in sympathy. Later that afternoon, another delegation of parents tried to talk to both the principal and Grenada School Superintendent Wilborn, but troopers prevented them from reaching the campus — the first time that parents had ever been blocked.

Over the weekend, parents of the Black kids who walked out of both the white and Colored schools were notified that their children were suspended for ten days until November 1st. On Monday the 24th, there was a morning march of more than 200 parents and students to the white schools to protest the suspensions. The few SCLC staff members left in Grenada were spread thin, so thin that only three (not including me) were assigned to accompany the marchers.

When the march column was stopped by state troopers, they knelt down to pray. All 200 of them were arrested on some vague charge. Grenada didn't have cells for large numbers of arrestees, so those older than 15 were forced into open cattle trucks and taken to the notorious Parchman Prison an hour's drive into the Delta. Some of the younger kids were shipped to the Greenville jail, an hour and a half away, while others were locked up in Grenada City and County jails. The very young kids were released to their parents.

That afternoon another parents' delegation tried to meet with the principal of Lizzie Horn Elementary. He told them he "didn't want to talk to no niggers." On Tuesday the 25th, yet another delegation was turned away, and when they sat down on the sidewalk in protest some 30 or so were arrested.

Inside the prison cells, SCLC staff members Major Wright, Herman Dozier, and Bill Harris were brutally beaten by cops and guards, and Lester Hankerson never fully recovered from the savage assault he was subjected to. Tom Scarbrough, an agent of the secretive Mississippi Sovereignty Commission, was in Grenada covertly working with the white power structure to stymie and destroy the Freedom Movement. In one of the reports he wrote to his superiors in Jackson he noted:

> "It is said they can't let [SCLC Director J.T. Johnson] out of Parchman because he's so beaten up he couldn't get up to get out." [23]

The beatings and arrests sparked an expanded boycott of the Colored schools as more and more Black students walked out in protest. More people were arrested on Wednesday and that night our march to the square just barely met the threshold of 75 because so many activists were now locked up in Parchman Prison and jails in Grenada, Greenville, Batesville, Water Valley, and Oxford.

By now our attorneys were back in court before federal Judge Clayton in Oxford informing him of the adamant white resistance to his school desegregation decree. He refused to order our people released from jail (as he legally could have), but our lawyers indicated that a deal was being worked out behind the scenes to release most of those arrested. The next day all the students were released without bail. Bail on the local adults was reduced to $54 each (equal to a bit over $400 in 2018) but the charges against them were not dropped. And all the incarcerated SCLC staff — more than half of those assigned to Grenada — remained in the slammer because SCLC didn't have the cash to pay their much higher bail.

By this time, 2200 of the 2600 Afro-American students enrolled in the Colored schools were boycotting classes. White school officials were, of course, pleased that the 90 school integrators were both refusing to attend and under suspension. But having over two thousand Black kids out of school posed a serious problem because funding from the state was based on average daily attendance, so the student strike was costing them money. And having so many angry youths roaming free on the streets and potentially joining the ongoing protests and marches worried local authorities — as well it should have.

On Saturday, October 29, all those remaining in jail were finally bailed out, but white terrorism was again on the rise. SCLC project director J.T. Johnson and SCLC staff member Robert Johnson were shot at by a hidden sniper — fortunately his aim was poor and no one was hit.

Some 160 people participated in our march to the square that night. Unable to sleep because of nervous tension, I pecked out my second and final poem on the old typewriter in our office at the rear of Belle Flower church:

GRENADA MARCH #107

Echoing songs on the square
White breath in cold night air
Black shadows, two by two
Marching strong, me and you.

> *"Oh freedom, Oh freedom*
> *Oh freedom over me...."*

Beneath a lonely streetlight
Children singing out at night.
The mobs are gone, for this time
And tension eases down the line.

> *"...and before I'll be a slave*
> *I'll be buried in my grave*
> *and go home to my Lord*
> *and be free-oh and be free..."*

Standing silent round the square
Troopers watch with hard, cold stare.
"Niggers on the march again.
Will they never end?"

"...No more gassings, no more beatings
no more jailings, over me..."

Around, around, the square we stride
Cold air filled with freedom's pride.
We'll keep marching side by side
till freedom gates are opened wide.

> *"...and before I'll be a slave*
> *I'll be buried in my grave*
> *and go home to my Lord*
> *and be free-oh and be free."*

It's quite on the square again
As one-oh-seven comes to end.
Proud, we march down Pearl Street
Back to church where we meet.

As you can see, I lack any shred of poetic talent but I was moved to say something and that's how it came out.

On Monday, October 31st, Judge Clayton began hearing our complaint about the school situation. Superintendent Wilborn admitted under oath that almost the entire Afro-American student body was boycotting the Colored schools and all the Black kids registered at the white schools couldn't return to class even if they wanted to because of his blanket suspension order.

At Clayton's request, our side agreed to call off the boycott on his assurance of a fair resolution of the issues. Black kids returned to the Colored schools but Afro-American students were stilled barred from the white schools. That night was Halloween and we said we considered it too dangerous to try marching to the square. In truth, with emotions cooling over the judge's promises, we didn't think we would have the minimum of 75 marchers we needed. In reluctant recognition of painful realities, we announced that henceforth we were discontinuing nightly marches in favor of marches "as needed."

The court hearing continued for the rest of the week and on Monday, November 7, Clayton issued his order. Parents and students were prohibited from demonstrating at the schools or organizing boycotts. The school system was ordered under threat of contempt to treat everyone equal regardless of race and to protect children from "violence, intimidation, or abuse." The superintendent was ordered to set up meetings between parents and teachers, but he was not required to meet with group delegations. A complaint system was put into place to handle disputes. While this was not a total triumph — and in fact, from our point of view it had serious shortcomings — it was viewed by both Blacks *and* whites as a victory for the Freedom Movement.

On paper, Clayton's ruling sounded fair and reasonable, but as with so many federal court orders in the South it failed to take into account the grim realities of racism, violence, and intimidation that Afro-Americans in Grenada faced. Under the details of his order, before Black parents could bring a complaint to him they had to first meet with the teacher to ask for resolution, then if that failed meet with the principal, and after that the superintendent. In real life, however, it required an act of defiance and courage (plus time off from work) for an Afro-American parent to confront *any* white person in authority over any complaint or grievance. And complainers were marked by whites as "troublemakers" who then become targets for retaliation.

So as a practical matter, Clayton's fine words had only a limited effect in reducing abuse in the white schools and the harassment continued. On December 20, Freedom Movement lawyers Iris and Paul Brest and Marian Wright sent a report to the parents of the school integrators:

> Lawyers from our office spent Friday and Saturday speaking to many of the children still attending the formerly white schools in Grenada. And this is what we found. The Court's order requires the schools to protect your children "from violence, intimidation, or abuse." Your children tell us that in the last month-and-a-half, they have been subjected to all sorts of violence, intimidation, and abuse:
>
>> Every day white students kick and push your children, throw papers and spitballs at them, curse at them and call them names. Often this happens when a teacher is present, but the teacher does nothing to stop it.
>>
>> One child was so badly injured when a white boy threw a metal object at him that he was hospitalized at Mound Bayou, and may require further treatment.
>>
>> White students bring knives, brass knuckles, and other weapons to school. At least one white boy has actually pulled a knife on a Negro child. Some teachers and other school official continue to abuse the Negro students by calling them "niggers," and by making other derogatory comments.
>>
>> At least one teacher has explicitly urged the white students to inflict physical harm on the Negro students.
>>
>> Some teachers continue to make the Negro students sit together, in a segregated group.
>>
>> Some teachers refuse to allow Negro students to recite in Class, and ignore them when their hands are raised.
>>
>> Some teachers grade the Negro students unfairly, giving them low grades even when they do well.
>>
>> Several Negro students have been suspended because of arguments or fights with white students; the whites were not suspended.
>>
>> All the Negro children who were suspended from school during the week of October 24, were failed in all their courses for the second six-week period.
>
> Excerpted from report of 12/20/66 [24]

At the end of November all the Afro-American school integrators who had walked out of the white schools and been suspended in October were given "Failing" grades for that period. But criminal charges against those under age 13 who had been arrested for marching or picketing were dropped. Those over 13 pled "Not Guilty," with no date set for trial. So far as I know, no trials of any of those arrested for protesting the treatment of Black school children were ever held.

Grenada Today ~ 2018

November 8 was election day in 1966. In Grenada County some 1300 votes were cast for Clifton Whitley, a Black man running for the U.S. Senate on the Mississippi Freedom Democratic Party (MFDP) ticket. James Eastland, the white incumbent, received around 3000 votes. Given the county's racial polarization, we interpreted those numbers to mean that more than 1300 Blacks went to the polls that day. While that Afro-American vote was only 30% of the total, for a county that had no more than a handful of Black voters before the Meredith March just four months earlier, it was a huge step forward. (Eastland, of course, won the state-wide election as everyone knew he would.)

Over the cold wet winter that followed, sporadic violence, intimidation, arrests, and racial tension continued, but at a lower level than during the summer and fall. We held occasional marches to the square of 75–200 people but daily direct action protests were no longer possible. After months of constant protests, jailings, and beatings, on most nights we simply didn't have the minimum number of 75 for a march. So the direct action phase of Grenada County's freedom struggle faded away as all such protest campaigns inevitably do — though the threat of resumed demonstrations on the part of the Afro-American community remained at least a theoretical restraint against unbridled excesses of white power.

With the injunction still in force it was impossible to sustain the boycott, so that too dwindled away. The B&P supermarket was never built and the land remains an empty lot today. Yet though the protest marches had come to an end, the legal work of defending those arrested and challenging the boycott injunction and the supermarket lawsuit in court continued. As did voter registration, political education, and organizing.

In the months and then the years that followed, Afro-American voter registration rose steadily until registration rates for both Blacks and whites were more or less comparable. But whites continued to hold a numeric majority and the electorate remained racially polarized — in 2016, Trump the Republican candidate won 57% of the vote, almost all of which were cast by whites, while Clinton the Democrat received 42%, almost entirely from Afro-Americans. In 2018, the U.S. Senate race resulted in a similar 57% to 42% split.

Yet even though Afro-American voters in Grenada continue to be outnumbered by whites, in the ordinary course of civic government Afro-Americans now have a voice. Over time they became numerous enough to first influence city and county elections and then elect Black candidates from wards and beats with Afro-American majorities. Today, two of the five county supervisors are Black and the city council shows similar racial diversity. Most of the streets in Afro-American neighborhoods are paved and some have sidewalks. There are Black men and women working in government offices and wearing badges in patrol cars. All of which had been utterly unthinkable before the Freedom Movement marched into town on June 15, 1966.

Where once more than 70% of Grenada's Afro-American population lived in poverty, today only a third of them exist below the federal poverty line. By comparison, just 17% of the white population is officially "poor," a ratio not all that different from the 1960s. The town's Black neighborhoods are now filled with empty lots where once impoverished slum shacks were jam-crammed side by side on muddy lots. The narrow Union Street block where Chat & Chew used to do business, and where we held our voter rallies squeezed into the narrow street by storefronts and porches, is now mostly open — and devoid of businesses.

The drop in Black poverty (as officially defined) can be traced mostly to the ending of the old Jim Crow, hand-labor system of plantation agriculture which relied on masses of Black field hands enduring a form of feudal-like peonage. On the other hand, at least some of the increase in Afro-American income levels can be attributed to the Freedom Movement's partially successful campaigns against employment discrimination and exploitation. Today, for example, Blacks are paid wages rather than miniscule "shares" or plantation store "credits." While steadier, better-paid jobs are still more likely to be filled by whites, and lower-wage and part-time employment is the lot of most Afro-Americans, the number of Blacks with middle-class jobs and livelihoods has significantly expanded since 1966. And not just in numbers, but also in the types of occupations now open to Afro-Americans, such as store manager, municipal employee, utility lineman, and so on.

When the Freedom Movement arrived in Grenada in the summer of 1966, both county and town were rigidly segregated into separate and distinct worlds — one Black, one white — a separation ruthlessly enforced by custom, law, economic power, and terrorist violence. Today in 2018, most Grenadans still live in racially separate worlds, but now that separation is primarily the result of custom, social pressure, and economic barriers rather than naked force. White and Afro-American students, for example, tend to patronize the local movie theater on different nights, and during the sweltering summer season it's mostly Blacks who use the public swimming pool while whites pay $195 for the private Kiwanis pool.

Grenada's public schools are now fully integrated, with Afro-Americans a slight majority. The children of affluent whites attend the private Kirk Academy while white kids from less well-to-do families share academically integrated but socially self-segregated public school classrooms with Blacks. Even by Mississippi's low standards, Grenada public schools are underfunded, and just a bit over half of those who enter high school end up graduating with a diploma. Private tuition at Kirk, which was founded in 1966 at the time of the school integration crisis, is close to $5000 per year, 98% of its students are white, and it prides itself on offering a "Christian-based" education.

Yet while social segregation, discrimination, and racial disparities in income, education, and political power still persist, life for Afro-Americans in Grenada has fundamentally changed for the better. Today, Black Grenadans are part of *"We the People"* with enough political power to force both the power structure and whites in general to acknowledge their civic rights and respect their human dignity. For younger generations who grew up assuming that such is the birthright of all Americans that may not sound like much, but it's a far cry and a huge step forward from a society founded on Judge Taney's edict that *a negro of the African race had no rights which the white man was bound to respect.*

And a Song Shall Rise

Sometimes I'm asked, how did we endure? And what kept us going? My answer is — freedom songs and freedom singing. Freedom songs and freedom singing were our most effective nonviolent weapon, and the songs and the singing were the psychic threads that bound us into a tapestry of purpose, solidarity, courage, and hope.

> The songs spread our message,
> The songs bonded us together,
>   The songs elevated our courage,
>   The songs shielded us from hate,
>   The songs forged our discipline,

The songs protected us from danger,
And it was the songs that kept us sane.

Singing those songs suffused each of us with the summed power of our whole. And not just on picket lines and freedom rides but day to day in the community as a whole. They wove into a single Freedom Movement the adults who sang them in mass meetings, the young militants who carried them into jail, and the impoverished maids, laborers, and sharecroppers who raised them in small circles of courage surrounded by seas of hate and danger.

Freedom songs were the vows we made, each to other, to stand side by side through all that we had to endure. They were the pledges we took to struggle together for justice and freedom. As the furnace-fire turns iron into steel, singing our shared songs forged bonds of loyalty that for many of us have not withered with age over more than five decades. I'm writing this in the season of the 50th anniversaries and at every reunion, for many of us, singing those songs together still brings tears of joy and remembrance to our eyes.

The songs also carried and shaped our message. College teaches us that political movements are primarily about the intellectual content of statements, speeches, positions, and proposals. But what the Civil Rights Movement taught me was that social and political struggles — popular mass movements — are as much, or more, about emotion as they are about ideology and it was our songs that released and expressed that emotion.

The songs inspired and encouraged us, yes, but they were also consciously used as practical tools for focusing and guiding the emotional contours of events, meetings, protests, even jail time. Different songs, different verses of the same song, and differences in the tone and style of the singing all evoked different responses. Like an artist using color to alter the mood of an image, skilled song leaders sensitive to the moment used freedom songs to shape and direct the emotions experienced by both ourselves and those within the sound of our voices.

And on occasion the songs even protected us from imminent violence. Time after time on the Grenada Square when we were confronted and outnumbered by Klan-led mobs armed with baseball bats and steel pipes, our songs held us together. And often — not always, but often — our singing literally prevented them from charging into us with their clubs swinging. I know that sounds impossibly mystic and fanciful, but it's true. I saw it. I experienced it.

I so vividly remember those night marches during the school crisis when white mobs filled the outer perimeter of the square. The most angry and hate-filled were clustered along the Doak Street side. As we marched around the green singing with every ounce of energy and passion we could muster we had to circle again, and again, and again, past that one spot where they were most intensely trying to break into our line. Most of the time they couldn't do it. They simply couldn't do it. In some way I can't explain our singing and our sense of solidarity created a kind of psychological barrier between us and them, a wall of moral strength that they couldn't physically push through to attack us with their clubs and chains, as they so obviously wanted to do.

It wasn't visual, it wasn't something you could see, but I could sense that our singing and our unity was holding them off, pushing them back. It was most obvious when we passed that wedge they made on the north side of the square. The Klan leaders surged forward off the sidewalk and into the street, trying to push into us. They got within a few feet of us, but they couldn't get closer. By our singing, we psychologically pressed them back. Most of the time, the only way they could strike at us was to bombard us from a distance with thrown rocks, chain links, and cherry bombs. But if for some reason we stopped singing, even for just a moment, it was like a bubble broke. Then they charged into us with clubs and fists swinging.

Grenada wasn't the only place I saw and experienced that kind of song-power. I saw the same thing that cold January night in 1964 when we held the Wich Stand picket line between white teenagers hurling eggs and verbal abuse at us on one side and a furious throng of neighborhood Afro-Americans on the other side. To this day I'm convinced that it was the psychological barrier we built with our singing that kept the white teenagers from charging into us and neighborhood Blacks from rolling over us to get at the white racists.

Freedom singing, however, was different from performance singing. Participation was its essence — not the entertainment quality of the music. Everyone was expected to sing. I won't hide this, I can't sing a lick. I'm tone-deaf. In fact, I was notorious as the worst singer in N-VAC and later the worst singer in SCLC. But I sang loud, and when danger threatened I was often the one who led the singing, not because of the (off-key) quality of my voice, but because I knew how to use song as a tactical tool, which is what was needed in those moments.

Song was also one of our most powerful and effective organizing tools. All human communities are riven with divisions — personal, social, political, religious, cultural, class, gender, age, sexual-orientation, and of course race. Building unity across these many divides is hard. Really hard. Rich and poor, elite and "no account," don't mingle easily. Individuals might be at odds with other individuals. Someone from one race or culture may feel unwelcome or out of place in settings dominated by a different race or culture. Singing our songs together helped break those barriers down.

In any established group there's a natural tendency for newcomers to feel like outsiders in cold distant orbit around the warmth of the "in crowd." For the Freedom Movement of the 1960s nothing was more effective in breaking down individual isolation and making newcomers feel welcome than singing freedom songs. And when I was doing voter registration and organizing in the South, time after time folk showed up for the singing and stayed for the struggle.

I am also convinced that singing our songs held us together politically. Looking back now from a distance of more than 50 years, I don't recall much (if any) singing at L.A. CORE meetings. Maybe the general membership meetings ended with "We Shall Overcome," but I don't remember any singing in the work and committee meetings. But in N-VAC and SCLC (and SNCC and the southern CORE chapters, too) every gathering of any size began and ended with songs.

You know, they say that talk is cheap, and of course that's often the case. But talk can also be agonizing, wrenching, and divisive. When our meetings were filled with bitter contention, when jealousy, frustration, and anger poisoned the air, we sang our freedom songs together and somehow eased our discord and reknit our tattered unity, even when the underlying conflicts remained unresolved. And we discovered that beginning a meeting with song started it from a place of unity, and ending every meeting the same way helped keep us together. Perhaps if L.A. CORE had done more singing and less factionating it would not have split in two.

Looking Back on the Freedom Movement

Farewell Grenada ~ 1967

That winter of 1966–67 was cold. Cold and wet. On some mornings there was even a thin dusting of snow on the eaves and frost rime in the muddy streets. We don't normally think of Mississippi as a winter state, but uninsulated, single-plank wood shacks, poorly heated by iron stoves burning scrounged wood scraps provide neither protection nor warmth. It's widely believed that Mark Twain once said, "The coldest winter I ever spent was a summer in San Francisco." Well, as a San Franciscan myself I can attest that the coldest winter *I* ever spent was a winter in Grenada Mississippi.

After long months of stress and tension, by January of '67 my health had deteriorated noticeably. I was physically and emotionally exhausted from little sleep, no small amount of fear, and constant vigilance. My stomach hurt all the time and my weight had dropped to 135 (today I'm at 200 with a gray beard and an old man's paunch). I had become a mental and physical wreck — nervous and jumpy. When I managed to sleep at all, it was only with my pistol on the night table near at hand.

The rest of the SCLC staff and the main local activists were in no better condition. We kept ourselves going on determination, rage, raw grit, and an utter refusal to let each other down by quitting or slowing down our pace.

Our situation was not unique. Across the Deep South, by the end of 1966 most of the long-term freedom riders who were still doing Movement work were equally debilitated. Like us, they were just barely hanging on. We referred to it as "burnout" and described it as "running on fumes." Sooner or later, most civil rights activists in the South succumbed to it. Today I suppose it would be diagnosed as some form of post-traumatic stress disorder (PTSD).

By the beginning of 1967, the Poor People's Committee was doing well on its own, and I knew it was time for me to leave the South. Yet I didn't want to go. I had come to love the people I was working with and the Afro-American community that had embraced me as an ally and a friend. More than that, I had come to love the freedom struggle itself. Being part of a mass people's movement for justice and equality, a cause dedicated to living out the truest meaning of the American creed — *We hold these truths to be self-evident..., Liberty and justice for all, Government of the people, by the people, for the people,* was the greatest experience of my life. I didn't want it to end — but I had no choice. It was time.

Reluctantly, I resigned from SCLC and left Grenada in February, not returning to the South for 40 years.

For a while I remained in touch with the ladies of the Poor People's Committee, who continued to soldier on. I recently came across a copy of a poignant yet noble letter they sent to Dr. King in 1968, a year after I left the South.

Dr. Martin Luther King

January 19, 1968

Dear Dr King first I want to think you for bringing the Movement into Grenada, Mississippi. God should have sent a Moses like you long before now and all the other real god-sent worker that came to Grenada to help us fight for freedom we will forever love Mr Williams Mr Hall Mr. Cottonreader J.T. Johnson and Big Lester and Our Praying brother that lost his life we love them all. We shall forever love Mrs. King your most beautiful wife.

Dr King many of us have worked very hard trying to get our freedom in Mississippi we have spent many sleepless night worrying about our people. I have not been in a white person store since the boycott was put on. I have worked as chairman of the Poor people Committee working [on] welfare problems. We have gotton a many poor family's check started that never would have gotten any help. We was taught the law of welfare by one of the member of your staff Bruce Hartford. I dont mean to ever to ever turn back, no never. Dr. King we need your help. Leon and Cottonreader need you here in Grenada Mississippi we are just about lost on what to do about many thing. We need everybody back in Grenada, and start all ever again like you did the first time you came here.

We have only a few teachers going along with us, they are standing in our way, they have not stop going in the white stores or having the white cars driven by Negroes to bring clothes and food to the home the principle of Willie Wilson [Colored high school] [who] have refused to stop buying downtown. He also carry a gun for his protection if any one say something to him about buying downtown so you can see we need some help or else we will have to do like some of the other city we have got to do something to stop our from going in the white stores. As long as Negroes buy in the white store the whites will never talk with us and they are keeping the poor families that farther from jobs. We need jobs here for poor families, we need an adult training program for adults, one for young woman who is not able to go to college such as typing, IBM secretary and any other worthwhile traning program that will help young Negro men and women to get decent jobs like all others races.

We will never get any where like we are going now so will you and others please come and stay for a few days if you can, you and others. Please escuse the many mistakes I am very tired I have work day and night since the Movement came here and I will never turn back. I may die trying to get my freedom and my sister and brother all over Mississippi. This Grenada can truly say I fought a good fight trying to help free my people. Pray for me and others.

Sincerely yours

Miss Mamie G. Wilmington
Mrs. Essie L. Mullin
Mrs. Senora Springfield
Mrs. Bulah L. Washington

Poor Peoples Committee
Grenada County Freedom Movement ₂₅

Leaving the Civil Rights Movement left me depressed, disoriented, and profoundly bereft. I spent the first couple of days with a friend in Manhattan trying to re-enter normative life — which, it turned out, was a somewhat surreal experience. Suddenly I was surrounded by huge numbers of strange white people and I felt threatened and in danger, though of course there was no reason for such fear. No one was hunting me, no one was hate-staring me, no one was marking and judging my every move and action. But for two intense years, whites had meant *danger* and only with Black folk was I safe.

Eventually I adjusted, spent time with my family, and went on to become an activist in the anti–Vietnam War and student movements. From March of '67 through the end of that summer I worked for the Spring Mobilization Against the War in Vietnam (the "Mobe"), initially on the first mass protest march against the war from Central Park to the United Nations, then as a grassroots anti-war organizer in Brooklyn where at one point we were attacked by a hostile mob that was quite reminiscent of Grenada Mississippi.

In the fall of '67, I began attending San Francisco State College (today University), where I joined Students for a Democratic Society (SDS). For two years I was a "New Left" radical, opposing the war, fighting on-campus racism, and battling the college administration for student rights, all of which culminated in the long and bitterly fought 1968–69 student strike for Third World Studies and increased admission of nonwhite students — the largest, longest, and arguably most successful student strike in American history

For more than a year I lived in Asia as a freelance journalist covering military affairs while helping U.S. Marines publish an underground anti-war GI newspaper called the *Semper Fi*. Later in life, I became a labor activist and one of the founders and longtime officers of the National Writers Union. Today I am webspinner for the Civil Rights Movement Veterans website (www.crmvet.org) and a board member of the SNCC Legacy Project (www.sncclegacyproject.org).

Yet as the decades slipped by the Freedom Movement was never far from my thoughts. It was and still is the touchstone and North Star of my life, and my participation in it remains a source of tremendous pride. I was blessed with the opportunity to share in something profoundly important, not just to me but to America. My part was small, but it was a part nonetheless in a story that would, and does, echo down the generations.

Fifty Years On ~ 2018

The Movement work I did in California, Alabama, and Mississippi had both successes and failures — as did the Civil Rights Movement everywhere. Both North and South, *freedom* was the fundamental goal. *Freedom,* meaning an end to generations-old race-based systems of political, economic, social, and psychological oppression and exploitation.

But effective social change movements can't be built around generalized abstractions. Movements that actually achieve real-life victories can only be built by addressing specific problems and instances of abuse — and by so doing affecting the larger issues. Labor unions, for example, came into being because workers wanted a better standard of living, safer workplaces, and more control over their working lives; but they struck for a 15% pay hike, a health plan, specific safety changes, and a grievance committee. And by winning those demands they altered the broader relations of power and respect between themselves and management.

In the North, our goal was *freedom*, but our specific focus was on eliminating employment discrimination, ending residential segregation, and halting northern-style school segregation. In those endeavors we were only partially successful.

The Civil Rights Act of 1964 and subsequent legislation and court rulings halted *overt, legally sanctioned* race and gender bias in employment. That put a long-desired end to explicit "Colored jobs" and "women's work" occupational categories. But to this day, substantial *covert* hiring and promotion discrimination continues against people of color, women, and those with nontraditional sexual orientations.

Similarly, many overt housing segregation practices and policies on the part of government and business were outlawed by the Fair Housing Act of 1968 and similar state laws. Explicit racial redlining and most restrictive covenants were eliminated, as was *overt* racial bias in rentals and home sales. But *covert* methods of segregation continue to flourish.

Today, people of color who have the money — and the desire to do so — can usually live outside racial ghettos if they are willing to endure the suspicions and prejudices of white neighbors, merchants, and police. But in most northern cities and suburbs the majority of nonwhites still live in racially defined neighborhoods, though the boundaries of those districts are now diffuse and blurry, no longer delineated with the knife-edge sharpness they had in the 1960s.

Against northern de facto school desegregation based on neighborhood districts drawn by race and economic class, our success was minimal. Despite decades of protests, boycotts, lawsuits, and legislative efforts, northern schools continue to be mostly segregated. And though there are exceptions, by and large the predominantly Black and Latino schools are underfunded and underserved, with the lowest graduation rates and the fewest students going on to college. In most urban areas, parents and students know which are the "good" schools serving the white middle and upper class and which are the "failing" schools serving nonwhites and poor whites.

In the South, our goal was *freedom* and our initial demands were eliminating separate white and Colored school systems, eradicating public segregation with its white-only humiliations and restrictions, and ending race-based denial of voting rights. We largely achieved those goals.

In 1857, Supreme Court Justice Taney ruled that *a negro of the African race had no rights which a white man was bound to respect*. For more than a century, Taney's edict was the governing principle of the southern way of life. The Freedom Movement fundamentally altered and ended that system. From Maryland to Texas, the defiant protests, steadfast courage, and resurgent pride of the Afro-American community struck a decisive blow against southern-style white supremacy and old Jim Crow. Race relations in the South were permanently altered for the better.

It was the Freedom Movement that brought the five *Brown v. Board of Education* cases before the Supreme Court. It was the Freedom Movement that compelled them to re-examine *Plessy v. Ferguson* and the doctrine of "separate but equal." It was the Freedom Movement that pressured the court to rule that separate is inherently unequal and that segregated school systems have no place in America. And it was the courage and determination of young school integrators, their parents, and the Freedom Movement who supported them, that finally ended the dual-school system in the South — though not without painful, bitter, and sometimes violent struggle.

Today, *explicit* legally-mandated racial segregation in higher education no longer exists, though race-related economic barriers still persist. For public grade schools, the results are mixed. Yes, the separate and deeply unequal segregated school systems were eliminated. Overt, legally sanctioned segregation was ended. But many whites withdrew their children from the public schools and placed them in segregated private schools (know colloquially as "academies") that still receive varying degrees of overt and covert state support.

Today in some locations such as Selma, public school student bodies are almost entirely Afro-American, in many cases comprising 95% or more of the total enrollment with almost all the white kids attending restricted private academies. In other places, such as Grenada Mississippi, it's mostly just the upper-income whites who send their children to private school while less affluent whites go to the thoroughly integrated — but desperately underfunded — public schools. Throughout the South, the great majority of Black children still receive inadequate educations from resource-starved public institutions controlled by authorities more concerned with keeping taxes low than providing a quality education for the *have-nots* of society.

It was the Freedom Movement that forced Congress to enact the Civil Rights Act of 1964, ending overt racial apartheid in America. That act overturned the thousands of state and local segregation laws that mandated who could sit, walk, drink, learn, shop and socialize where —

and with whom. It also made subject to court challenge the crazy-quilt maze of race-related social customs and segregation traditions that blanketed the South — and elsewhere. Yes, today, whites and Blacks often voluntarily self-segregate, congregating and socializing with those of their own color, but neither sheriff nor court can enforce such behavior, nor suppress those who choose to eat, ride, shop, or play wherever they wish.

It was the Freedom Movement that forced Lyndon Baines Johnson and the United States Congress to enact the Voting Rights Act of 1965 — the most effective civil rights law in American history. The VRA restored to Afro-Americans the voting rights that had been stripped away by the Republican-Democrat "compromise" of 1877. A so-called "compromise" that granted white southerners free rein to use law, economic power, and violent terrorism to deny Black people the right to vote. And by restoring voting rights for Afro-Americans, the Freedom Movement won them for *all* citizens of color.

For generations, racially-motivated murders — lynchings — were an American phenomenon, particularly in the South. And the victims weren't only Afro-Americans. Latinos, Asians, Jews and "undesirable elements" like labor organizers were also subject to "lynch law," both in the South and elsewhere around the nation. Until the Freedom Movement of the 1960s, lynchings were so frequent and so normalized that only rarely did the national media report them. Local papers usually ignored them as well, though in some instances they were covered as if they were a sports event.

Lynching and other forms of violence were foundation stones of the Jim Crow southern way of life. Afro-Americans who in any way questioned or challenged white supremacy risked being brutalized, raped, bombed, and killed. Such racial murders were carried out by one or two individuals, by KKK "action teams," and by mobs. The obvious impunity that the killers enjoyed made plain that to one degree or another lynch law violence was socially-sanctioned by both government and a large portion of the white community. The published photos of smiling children brought to a public hanging or burning by their parents confirms the wide acceptability of racial brutality and murder.

The number of such lynchings can never be fully counted because so many were not reported at all, or reported but not recorded, or recorded but not officially categorized as a racially-motivated murder. But the true scope of racial terrorism in the Deep South was brought to light in July of 1964 when Navy divers searching for Chaney, Schwerner, and Goodman dragged the rivers of central Mississippi and discovered the bodies of eight Afro-American men — three whom had been reported as "missing" and another five who were never identified at all. Eight Black bodies in one month, in one river system, in one portion, of one southern state. You can do the math.

Though it didn't happen instantly, over time the Civil Rights Movement so changed America's culture that today lynching and other forms of racially-motivated violence are no longer socially or politically acceptable — not even in the Deep South. We changed that. Yes, some racially-motivated murders do still occur though their number has been greatly reduced. But when a lynching occurs today it is usually reported and often becomes a mass media sensation. The murder is investigated, the killers are usually prosecuted, and most of the time they are convicted by integrated juries and sent to prison. None of that was the case before the Freedom Movement.

However, against *state* terrorism inflicted on nonwhites and their supporters by police and courts we had less success — though not from lack of trying. Blacks who challenged white authority risked being arrested and imprisoned on trumped up charges, beaten by club-wielding "lawmen," sentenced to years of brutal slavery on southern chain gangs, or shot to death for "resisting arrest" — and so too, on a few occasions, did some of their white allies.

Throughout the '60s we tried to raise public awareness of police brutality inflicted on nonviolent protesters and anyone else with the temerity to defy the southern way of life. We demanded legislative and policy changes. We filed lawsuits against cops and troopers who shot and killed demonstrators and activists — Jimmy Lee Jackson in Marion Alabama and Benjamin Brown in Jackson Mississippi to name just two. But in both North and South the mass media, prosecutors, judges, and juries almost always accepted without doubt or question police justifications and outright lies regardless of testimony from civilian eye-witnesses and news reporters.

It was not until the advent of video-taped evidence in the 1990s followed later by cell phone videos that nonwhite citizens and protesters had a prayer of proving that a particular instance of police violence was wrongful. Without photographic evidence we were unable to expose the vast discrepancies between official statements and brutal reality.

Today, organizations like Black Lives Matter and Dream Defenders — who most Freedom Movement veterans cherish as our political grandchildren — have taken up the fight against racial shootings by law enforcement. It remains a hard struggle even *with* videos and the public awareness created by mass protests. Only rarely are cops who shoot and kill without reasonable cause called to account. But now the fact that they *might* be brought to book is beginning to at least *reduce* "shoot first and justify later" behavior patterns that for generations were deeply embedded in far too many police department cultures.

Taken as a whole then, the victories won by our Freedom Movement decisively ended the Jim Crow southern way of life. They significantly changed for the better both the South as a region and the individual lives of Black and white southerners. To be clear though, *none* of those victories were magnanimously bestowed upon us by benevolent authorities. None of them were spontaneous acts of social compassion on the part of judges or legislators. Rather, they were *forced up from below* by a mass movement of Afro-Americans determined to be free. Veteran SNCC organizer Charlie Cobb later wrote:

> What defines this era is that people and communities began speaking for themselves, making demands for the kind of society *they* wanted instead of standing aside silently while others, sympathetic advocates or white supremacists, spoke for them and of them. What the country began to hear clearly in the mid-twentieth century — or at least could no longer ignore — were insistent Afro-American voices from the grassroots. Through words and actions they refuted any idea that they were indifferent, apathetic, or willing to accede to the myth that they considered full citizenship rights "white folks' business." The public actions of ordinary black people across the South — among them sharecroppers, day workers, small farmers, factory workers, maids, and cooks — who found their own voices made the difference; they defeated Jim Crow. This period culminated with the passage and signing into law of the 1965 Voting Rights Act. [26]

Yet our achievements, important as they were, were not sufficient. There's no question that the human suffering caused by abject, systemic poverty was a fundamental root from which grew the Freedom Movement. The initial demands for dismantling Jim Crow, ending school segregation, and winning voting rights were in part aimed at combating economic misery. But when I joined CORE in early 1963, I was only vaguely aware of economic inequality as a social issue. It wasn't until I went South that the realities of poverty smacked me upside the head. And of all the issues that the Movement awakened me to, alleviating poverty is the one where we had the least success — though not from lack of trying.

Once the Voting Rights Act passed, Movement organizations across the South began seeking ways to alleviate poverty and fight for economic justice. In Mississippi, efforts included the Freedom Labor Union in the Delta, the Greenville Air Force base occupation, a variety of coops and programs, and the Poor People's Committee in Grenada.

My stillborn efforts to elect African-Americans to the critical Grenada County ASCS committee so that Black farmers might gain a fair share of federal agricultural subsidies was part of a multi-year project across Louisiana, Mississippi, Alabama, and Georgia — a project that failed. On the bright side, Albert Turner's far more successful effort to form a multi-county farmers coop in Southwest Alabama was replicated across the region as were craft coops like the famous Gees Bend quilters in Wilcox County. Dr. King's final campaign sought to build a multiracial alliance of the poor to fight on their own behalf for economic justice. He was assassinated in Memphis while supporting the garbage workers strike and his dream of a united Poor People's Campaign died with him.

For the most part, our efforts to win economic justice were either defeated outright or limited and contained by fierce resistance from the power elites and the weight of government opposition at all levels — local, state, and federal. And we were unable to prevent a significant number of Afro-American sharecroppers and agricultural laborers being forced off the land and out of the South — and therefore out of the electorate. Most of them drifted into urban ghettos, joining the ranks of the inner-city poor where they and their descendants remain.

Today, if you drive the back roads of the Deep South almost all the old sharecropper shacks are gone — burned or bulldozed down. Yet across the region, poverty, economic inequalities, significant racial discrimination, and great education disparities still remain. Yes, the Southern Freedom Movement broke down barriers that denied people access to facilities based on race, but income barriers to even basic necessities such as food, shelter, and clothing remain. If they have the money, a Black family can now join the country club, but large numbers of Afro-Americans have no access to decent-quality health coverage for themselves or their children. As a practical reality today, many of the social and economic problems that grew out of slavery and a century of Jim Crow oppression continue to fester.

Nevertheless, despite our inability to alleviate systemic poverty, it's obvious that Freedom Movement successes, and the struggle itself, had immense social and psychological effects on Afro-American communities and individuals — and on people of color in general. As a white man, I'm not competent to describe or analyze those effects, though I certainly sensed them, as did every other white person in America. In 1951, for example, Morton Sobell was jailed during the Red Scare era for spying. When he was released in 1969, his stepdaughter Sydney Gurewitz, a Movement activist in Atlanta, asked him what he found different in society after 18 years in prison. He replied, "Black people look you in the eye, they never used to look you in the eye."

Jean Wiley, a Black freedom fighter who worked in Alabama and the Atlanta SNCC office, later recalled:

> I think there were many successes, but you kind of have to have been there before. When I talk to my son and his friends about it, it's like I'm talking about the 15th century. There were enormous successes, but what amazes me is that the movement could have existed at all given the level of terror and resistance. That's what strikes me most when I think back about it. How, despite that, that you could begin to open up. I think people ought to study the Freedom Rides more than they do because it's inconceivable now, especially to young people, that you couldn't hop on a bus and go wherever the hell you want to go, and sit wherever you wanted to sit without fear of safety. [27]

Ron Bridgeforth who worked for SNCC in Starkville Mississippi, later observed:

> The most fundamental and important change was how we saw ourselves. Agency. The act of going down to register to vote. Changes you. It changes people who see you. It changes how white folks see you. They might kill you for it; they may take your job for it, but other Black folks are always watching very carefully. And everybody's got to make their own journey.

> My wife and I talk a lot about the '60s and how things have changed. She said that we thought we had won. And so we went on about our business of raising families and living our lives. And then you know, the rise of all this reactionary Republican stuff and poverty, starting to wash it all away. Passing all this legislation to take away the rights of women. Passing all this legislation to take away voting rights. And we thought we had won, and we could forget, since you didn't have to remain vigilant.

> And here they come again. One of the things our kids said, this was when [the 2006 incident of racial injustice in] Jena, Louisiana happened, they said, "You didn't tell us about what it took for us to get here, this integration and freedoms and all this stuff that we enjoy. And so we are left unprepared." One of the things we've talked about is that we didn't tell our children, because we didn't want them to be bitter. But one of my theories is we didn't tell our children because we were ashamed [of how we had been treated]. [28]

In *Hands on the Freedom Plow: Personal Accounts by Women in SNCC*, activist Joann Christian Mants of Albany Georgia later described how her involvement in the Movement affected and shaped her life:

> My sister and I sort of huddled behind the older SNCC folk, and they sort of patted us on the head as though they thought we were very cute. I

was fourteen years old. I kept thinking, *This is something else. We are going to be free.* I was not sure where I would fit in, what my niche would be, but I knew I would *do something.* I didn't understand all their words and language then. I was naive and just wanting to be free, wanting all of us to be free. I continued to listen. I learned a great deal from these strange, new-thinking, new-talking, and new-acting SNCC folk. I continued to listen. Eventually I was able to understand them; some of their ideas became my ideas, and then I was able to create some of my own new ideas and concepts. [29]

Also in *Hands on the Freedom Plow*, freedom worker Jean Smith Young sets the record straight about the role of Black women in the Freedom Movement:

> I cannot end without saying something about the controversy over the role of women in SNCC: I never felt discriminated against as a woman in this organization. In fact, I felt and experienced just the opposite. SNCC was a liberating experience for me as a woman. The staff, including Stokely Carmichael, always treated me as an esteemed member of the team and always encouraged me to stretch my wings and fly. In the SNCC that I knew the message was "Do whatever you are big enough to do." [29]

Looking back now across 50 years, I've come to realize that our most significant achievement was changing the culture of what is acceptable in America regarding race. For someone like me who grew up surrounded by the explicit racism and bigotry that so characterized white culture in the 1950s the change is obvious — and profound.

Yes, of course there is still white racism and white supremacy, but in most milieus now (or at least until recently) it's been *covert* rather than *overt*. Where once politicians routinely spewed explicit words of hate on the campaign trail and Senate floor, today racist politicians, celebrities, and opinion makers have to disguise their intent by using "dog whistles" that they piously pretend have no racial significance. Where once the powerful few felt free to plainly speak their bigotry, now a billionaire basketball king is forced to sell his NBA franchise because of a comment no one would have noticed before the Freedom Movement changed America's culture. When I was a kid, racist, sexist, and anti-Semitic jokes, tropes, and memes were common around the dinner tables of white families from the poorest of the poor to the richest of the rich. Now famous TV stars lose their shows because of comments and tweets that wouldn't have raised an eyebrow before the Civil Rights Movement.

Yes, as I write these words I see Trump and the Republican Party enabling, stoking, and using the kind of overt racism we thought we had put an end to 50 years ago. And at age 75 I've returned to the streets to protest it, him, and them. So no, the Freedom Movement did not end racism. But it did for a while force white-supremacist America to lurk below the political surface. For a time. Yet they remained as vicious and hostile as ever, so it's no surprise that demagogues, corrupt politicians, their political operatives, and the corporate power brokers who finance them are now, once again, mobilizing race hatred for their own selfish purposes.

What *has* surprised me in the two years since the election of 2016 has been the breadth and depth of white rejection of, and opposition to, the reemergence of in-your-face racism, misogyny, and bigotry. White participation in anti-racist, women's rights, immigrant-defense, and anti-Trump protests has been far larger than what we saw in the 1960s. Not just the 40,000 who showed up in 2017 on Boston Common to protest white nationalism after the Charlottesville violence, but more importantly the large and small groups of courageous Americans who persistently and steadfastly stand in city, town and village squares across the nation, week after week, month after month, to oppose the politics of hate.

There's no question in my mind that the cultural changes wrought by the Freedom Movement can take at least some of the credit for the number of whites who today resist a return to the bad old days of back-of-the-bus and white-only. And there's no question that despite our many shortcomings the mass Freedom Movement of the 1960s — made up mostly of Afro-Americans — forced fundamental changes in society, culture, and law. Advances that brought people of color into *We the People* and ended centuries-old systems of white supremacy and Black subservience that had been enforced by police authority, judicial power, economic coercion, social custom, and violent terrorism.

So why then, in the late '60s, did I and so many others from the Southern Freedom Movement succumb to frustration, disappointment, and depression? Why did we feel — and in some cases publicly assert — that the Civil Rights Movement had *failed*?

For myself, I think it was the glaring truth that while the Black-led Freedom Movement achieved a social revolution by enlarging *We the People* to include nonwhites and gaining some share of political power on the local level, to this day white power structures of wealth and privilege continue to dominate our economy and government. And the bitter, burning reality of their power and greed sears our souls to this day.

It was inevitable, I think, that we who had fought so hard and held such high hopes would end up dissatisfied with our achievements because the struggle itself awakened us to issues of injustice, poverty, race, gender, and class that were beyond our reach to address. We so desperately wanted to make immense immediate improvements to lives oppressed by white supremacy and economic injustice that we were unable to accept that throughout history it has been *incremental* changes forced up from below by popular pressure that have steadily improved the human condition of the very many against the opposition of the elite but powerful few. What we wanted was the complete elimination of all forms of bigotry, exploitation, and oppression, what we achieved through fierce struggle was hard-won social progress — and so too was it with my parents in the '30s and '40s.

For me personally, despite those many areas where we fell short of our highest hopes and dearest dreams, I still take great pride in the small contribution I was privileged to make towards realizing Freedom Movement achievements. I was blessed by the opportunity to experience and share moments of enormous unity, courage, and exaltation, the memories of which will remain with me all my days — The March on Washington, holding the line at the Which Stand, my first arrest, marching over the Selma bridge and into Montgomery, Crenshaw County and all that occurred there, and the nonviolent war for dignity and freedom that we waged for half a year in Grenada, Mississippi. Never will I touch those heights again — but the memories remain as I have set them down in this manuscript.

Dinner at Hyde Park ~ 1941

Just days before Pearl Harbor, in late November of 1941 my mother had dinner — and a fierce fight — with President Franklin Delano Roosevelt at his Hyde Park mansion. The roots of that tale, however, go all the way back to the early 1930s when my mom and dad became union activists and joined the Communist Party (CP). At that time, Party policy was to form separate unions that competed for members against American Federation of Labor (AFL) unions in the same industry.

After Hitler came to power in 1934, the Party reversed itself. Declaring that it was now committed to a "Popular Front Against Fascism," it sought unity with organizations and individuals it had previously condemned and opposed. Under this revised policy, CP-led unions merged into the new Congress of Industrial Organizations (CIO). One result was that the American Communications Association (ACA) received financial support from the CIO, allowing them to hire more full-time organizers — two of whom eventually met, married, and became my parents.

During the later half of the 1930s, President Roosevelt was struggling to force his New Deal reforms through a recalcitrant Congress and past a deeply conservative Supreme Court dominated by Republican-leaning justices. As part of the CP's Popular Front strategy, from 1934 to mid-1940 they supported FDR while simultaneously criticizing him for failing to go far enough. They assiduously tried to convince him — and the general public — to more strongly oppose Nazi Germany and Fascist Italy. And to give military aid to the embattled Spanish Republic which FDR refused to do. One unintended result of those efforts was my mom having to explain to a mass meeting of Chicago telegraph workers that she really wasn't a Parisian spy or the secret mistress of the French Premier.

And by the late 1930s, with the threat of German and Italian fascism rapidly intensifying, the U.S. Communist Party had switched from its traditional anti-militarist stand to one of support for Roosevelt's effort to enlarge the armed services and increase defense spending for the inevitable war to come. It was conservative Republicans and southern Democrats who were the fiercest opponents of FDR's interventionist foreign policy and his war preparations — some because they were staunch isolationists and others because they openly admired "strongman" authoritarians like Hitler and Mussolini, who crushed unions and suppressed undesirable populations like Jews, Gypsies, homosexuals, and, of course, Reds and labor unions.

As part of their anti-fascist work for the CP, my parents organized boycotts against American corporations, like Ford Motor Company and Standard Oil who were doing business with Germany, Italy, and Japan. Then in August of 1939, Germany and the Soviet Union signed the Hitler-Stalin Pact. Russia's alliance with the Nazis hit the American Communist Party like a thunderclap. My dad once told me how he was picketing against some business selling war materiel to Germany when a truck arrived with a new set of signs. The protesters were ordered to trade their "Anti-Fascist" and "Hitler Must Go" placards for "The Yanks are Not Coming!" and "Stop the War-Mongers" (meaning those who continued to advocate fighting Hitler).

Where previously the CP had stridently called on President Roosevelt to oppose Hitler and prepare America for battle, now they made tacit alliance with his arch-conservative "America First" enemies to oppose him at every turn. The anti-fascist boycotts they had been organizing were immediately dropped and a "perpetual peace vigil" was established outside the White House. Many CP members, particularly Jews, were unable to stomach that 180-degree turn and they left the Party in furious anger. So too did many class-conscious workers who refused to accept any alliance — however temporary or tactical — with the union-busting far right.

I once asked my parents why they remained Party members. Their answer was that they still believed the Soviet Union was a beacon of hope for the world's working class and that it had to be defended at all costs. Depression-era unemployment and poverty were still devastating the nation, racial lynchings were increasing, and unions were under ferocious attack by business interests. Party leaders proclaimed that only the CP could effectively fight the fights that needed to be fought and that sometimes distasteful tactics and unsavory alliances had to be accepted as the cost of eventual victory. In September of 1939 my parents accepted that argument, but as a young activist in the 1960s I found their explanations unconvincing. And since they themselves were long gone from the Party by the time we had that conversation, I don't think they believed it either.

For 22 agonizing months, Party members were at bitter odds with the non-CP leftists, progressives, liberals, and New Deal Democrats who continued to oppose fascism and support Roosevelt. Marriages were sundered and long-term friendships broken beyond repair.

While first Poland, and then Denmark, Norway, Holland, Luxembourg, Belgium, and France fell to German military conquest amidst horrifying atrocities, Party members dutifully defended the Hitler-Stalin Pact and actively campaigned against strengthening the American military or any U.S. involvement the war. They opposed sending aid to embattled Britain, the last European nation still standing against the Third Reich, and they argued against admitting anti-fascist refugees fleeing Hitler's concentration camps. Hearing them describe it 25 years later, I could sense that for my parents it was a dark, bitter, and painful period in their lives that left emotional scars which never healed.

Meanwhile, the American armed forces that Roosevelt was trying to enlarge and rearm were rigidly segregated. Blacks, Latinos and Native Americans were restricted to the most menial jobs and assigned to Colored units led by white officers. There were no Afro-American officers because it was *unthinkable* that a white enlisted man might have to salute or take orders from a Black, Brown, Yellow or Red man.

And as war production rapidly expanded, Afro-Americans and other nonwhites were excluded from the new jobs opening up at defense plants. Employers openly and explicitly stated that they wouldn't hire Blacks or other nonwhites even if they proved they had the necessary skills. The more conservative unions supported such white-only stands, but progressive CIO unions, including my parent's union, opposed race discrimination and called for fair hiring even though that infuriated many of their white rank-and-file members who felt that higher-paying skilled jobs should be reserved for whites only.

In January of 1941, A. Philip Randolph and Bayard Rustin called for a massive Afro-American March on Washington to demand desegregation of the military and an end to employment discrimination in the defense industries. All across the country Blacks, white progressives, and anti-racist unions like the ACA began organizing and mobilizing for that July 1st march. Committees were organized across the country and people began saving their dimes for the cost of transportation to the nation's capital.

The news media predicted 100,000 Afro-Americans were about to descend on the capital. At that time Washington was a thoroughly segregated southern city and DC whites were horrified at the prospect of militant Blacks marching through their streets, attempting to eat at their white-only restaurants, and demanding to stay in segregated hotels.

Caught between determined Blacks on one side and enraged southern segregationists on the other, President Roosevelt offered a compromise — the military would remain racially segregated, but he would issue an executive order barring race discrimination in defense-related industries and he would establish a Fair Employment Practices Committee to enforce that non-discrimination order. Randolph accepted Roosevelt's compromise and called off the march. Progressive unions like my parents' ACA immediately signed pledges to honor Executive Order 8802 and implement Fair Employment Practices.

On June 22, 1941, Germany suddenly invaded the Soviet Union. They named their massive assault "Barbarossa." Within hours, the CP "turned on a dime" (its phrase) and once again began shouting, "Down with Hitler!" "Defend the Soviet Union!" — and of course "All out for the war effort!" From the way my parents later described those events I knew that though they were horrified at the carnage and devastation being inflicted on Russia they were immensely relieved to once again be fighting on the anti-fascist side — except for one little problem.

With France occupied by the Nazis, German bombs devastating London, and American ships being torpedoed in the Atlantic, President Roosevelt asked American unions to sign a "no strike" pledge in the interests of the war effort. And after Barbarossa it wasn't just Roosevelt who wanted to prevent "labor strife" (as it was called) from interfering with the military buildup. The Communist Party issued its own "no strike" edict forbidding members from doing anything that might impede defense production or undercut public support for the battle against fascism. The ACA was one of the first unions to comply, quickly agreeing to forego strikes.

But for years, building the ACA had been at the center of my parents' lives. They'd been organizing and educating, fighting the companies, defending against goons and stool pigeons — month after month, year after year, 10, 12, 14 hours a day, every day. And finally, in the summer of 1941 their work was bearing fruit. Union locals for the telegraph industry had been organized across the nation, the workers understood their rights and were ready, in fact determined, to win a union contract. And if necessary, they were ready to strike.

And the law was on their side. The New Deal's National Labor Relations Act (at the time commonly known as the "Wagner Act") required that companies negotiate with labor unions who won worker representation elections. The ACA decisively won those votes in the telegraph industry. They began trying to negotiate with one of the two major companies — Postal Telegraph or Western Union, I forget which. But the company was stonewalling. Not only were they refusing to negotiate in good faith and sign a contract, they were also refusing to accept the Fair Employment standards, which they were legally obligated to do under Executive Order 8802. They knew that the ACA had signed FDR's no-strike pledge, so they had no reason to fear a walkout and therefore had no incentive to meet with the union or sign a contract.

In their public statements, the companies justified defying both federal law and executive order by proclaiming their high-minded commitment to war preparations. In reality it was all about the money — they didn't want to raise wages or improve working conditions. More and more rank-and-file ACA members were now demanding a strike to force the company to sign a union contract. Which is exactly what militant trade unionists like my mom and dad had been working towards for years. But a good portion of the ACA leadership were Party members and by now most union members were Roosevelt supporters, so everyone was in a pickle. They'd been preaching "union contract or strike" to the membership, now the time had come, and both President and Party were telling them "No."

The ACA's top leadership was summoned to New York for an emergency meeting to figure out what to do. No one had a solution. The company wasn't budging, the workers were demanding a strike, the President was insisting that unions honor their "no strike" pledges, and the Party was adamant that everything had to be subordinated to the needs of the Soviet Union — and if that hurt American workers, tough shit.

By this time my mom had become the ACA's Midwest Regional Director and one of the highest-ranking women in the national CIO staff hierarchy. After hours of fruitless discussion she desperately grasped at a straw. "You know, last year when Mrs. Roosevelt addressed our convention she complimented me on being one of the few women in union leadership. She said if I ever needed anything I should call her. Do you think it's worth asking her for help?"

"Yes! Yes!" the other ACA leaders (all men) shouted eagerly.

So Mom called the White House and reached Malvina Thompson, Mrs. Roosevelt's chief aide, who told her that she was in luck. The Roosevelts were going to be at their home in Hyde Park over the weekend. She invited Mom to come up for dinner on Friday evening and then return to the city on the night train.

My mother still had some of the classy pre-Depression clothes her father had bought for her when he was still wealthy, so on Friday she "dressed to the nines" (as the saying went), donned her leopard-fur coat for warmth against late November snow showers, and took a cab to Grand Central Station. Hyde Park was a three-hour winter train ride up along the Hudson from New York City and she was so nervous she hadn't been able to eat anything all day. She'd just turned 28 and the fate of her union was now riding on her narrow shoulders.

She was met at the station by a Black chauffeur driving a shiny limousine who took her to the mansion. A butler met her at the door and had a maid show her to a guest room where she could wait and "refresh" herself before dinner at eight.

Mom wasn't aware that in high society "dinner at eight" meant that everyone was expected to arrive fashionably late. And as a Communist cadre she was thoroughly trained (well, "conditioned" is probably a more accurate term) to never, ever, under any circumstances arrive late for a meeting. So, dressed in patriotic colors — white silk blouse, pleated navy skirt and red pillbox hat — she arrived in the foyer precisely at 8 o'clock on the dot. The room was empty. No one was there, not even any of the servants.

Too filled with nervous energy to wait patiently, she noticed a large coffee table with an array of current magazines on display. One of them was *New Masses*, a Communist Party monthly publication. Knowing that she'd be quizzed on the contents at her next Party branch meeting, she picked it up and began to leaf through it.

She was reading some article when her concentration was abruptly broken by a mellifluous, instantly recognizable patrician voice behind her saying, "I suppose you think I'm a Communist because I have that magazine?" President Roosevelt had rolled up behind her in his wheelchair and the room's plush rug had deadened any sound.

Mom whirled around and before she could stop herself she blurted out, "Well, I wish you'd act like one!"

"Whatever do you mean?"

And then they went at it, hammer and tongs, she standing for the union, he arguing that he was being attacked from left and right, she charging that his own administration was refusing to enforce the Wagner Act — he countering with the war effort — she the Labor Board — he Germany and the fascists — the Fair Employment pledge — London in flames from Nazi bombs — on and on and on they debated and argued. Other guests began drifting into the room but they were ignored. Years later, my mom described it to me:

> I said, "We supported you on [the no-strike pledge] and what do you think the companies did? They're taking away benefits. And we signed the pledge because you asked for it and now we're having such trouble." He's answering, and we start a fight. It was like arguing with my father. I never realized what I was doing or who I was talking to. Now that sounds silly, but it's true. I was so caught up in what monstrous developments were occurring, where we were in danger of losing the union because of our support of him, and he's telling me that we're not helping him?
>
> And among other things he said, "I want you to know that I'm the best capitalist this country ever had. I know that there would be a revolution or something if I didn't do the things I'm doing with the projects and welfare and helping the people. And I am being called a Communist because of it."
>
> I again said, "Communist? You're nothing like a Communist! [6]

Dinner was announced and they walked into the elaborate dining room still arguing back and forth. Everyone sat down, my mom, the President and First Lady, Princess Marta of Norway, and a table-full of other notables and nabobs. Back and forth, back and forth, they continued to battle until finally Mrs. Roosevelt intervened saying, "Franklin, will you stop tormenting that poor child?"

"Me? Tormenting her?" he exclaimed in faux outrage and then laughed. After that he turned to the exiled Princess Marta to discuss the latest war bulletins from Europe, and that was the end of the exchange between my mom and the President.

When I asked her what they had for dinner, she told me, "I was too upset to eat. I'd just had a fight with the President of the United States and I was terrified that I had muffed our chance to get his help." All during the long train ride back to the city, and then over the weekend, she worried and worried (as I've mentioned before, she was a champion worrier).

Early on Monday morning they reconvened the ACA leadership meeting. "What happened? What happened?" the men asked my mother.

"I don't know, I had a fight with the President."

So she called the White House and again spoke to Malvina Thompson. Thompson told her, "I heard about your discussion with the President. He was quite taken with you. Let me get back to you."

An hour later Thompson called the union office and told Mom, "Don't worry, it's all taken care of." Ten minutes later the head of the company called to say he was ready to sign the contract and begin implementing the Fair Employment order.

Way to go Mom!

Blunting McCarthyism

There is one other Freedom Movement achievement that must be acknowledged. One that is often overlooked, and one that I would be remiss in not calling attention to — our role in blunting the national psychosis known as McCarthyism.

Segregationists and the political right wing labelled us "communists" and accused Dr. King of being a Soviet agent. Sheriff Clark's assertion that, "A communist is any God Damned New York kike that wants our nigrahs to vote," expressed a core McCarthyite dogma, one shared and echoed by many whites — South and North alike.

America's Red Scare pathology ran deep. Throughout the '50s and into the early '60s, any dissent, any protest, any questioning of authority from a progressive or humanist standpoint was seen by many whites as *un-American* — and in many cases as close to treason. Speaking up for racial equality, joining labor unions, supporting the United Nations, participating in "Ban the Bomb" protests, opposing the Korean War, or advocating similar unpopular beliefs were considered *subversive activities* by government officials, academic authorities, a large segment of the media, and a majority of the white populace.

It was the steadfast courage and bold defiance of the Black-led Freedom Movement that drove a stake through the *dissent is un-American* heart of McCarthyism. The contrast between our assertion of human rights for people of color and the violent bigotry of segregationists woke a significant portion of American whites to the fundamental hypocrisy of the flag-waving, right-wing, super-patriots. One of the reasons that Dr. King's famous *I Have a Dream* speech was so historically important is that all 19 minutes of it were broadcast in its entirety, and for those whose hearts were not locked into white supremacy, slanders of Soviet subversion began to lose their credibility.

The Meaning of "Radical"

In 1960, young Afro-Americans in the South faced an unsolvable dilemma. They were no longer willing to live segregated lives as second-class, semi-citizens. No longer would they submit to white supremacy and all it stood for. But every route and avenue of change was closed, every method for redress of grievances blocked. Lobbying for legislation had proved a failure. All attempts at peaceful public protest faced certain arrest, or mob violence, or both. The promise of *Brown v. Board of Education* had been dashed by the "massive resistance" of southern segregationists who defied the ruling — and by a federal government that didn't have the political will to enforce the law of the land.

Back in the 1960s, the overwhelming majority of college students, both Black and white, chose to get their degrees and establish their careers rather than challenge the entrenched status quo with radical action — just as today student loan repayment necessities, hoped-for careers, and other economic realities constrain most youthful idealism into socially sanctioned channels that are largely ineffective.

But in the 1960s a very few, the radical few, chose to *defy* the system and the status quo by in the words of SNCC leader Bob Moses, "standing in a strong sun and casting a sharp shadow." It is they who change the face of the South — and of America.

The young college women and men who challenged the Jim Crow southern way of life faced expulsion by school administrations controlled by white power structures. And those elders who courageously defied white supremacy by trying to register to vote risked their jobs, homes, careers, and lives. Young and not so young, almost all of them came from an Afro-American culture striving for acceptance and respect by a dominant society that — simply because of the color of their skin —

treated them as less than fully human and despised them for false racist stereotypes of laziness, incompetence, and brutish criminality.

Most Afro-American college students of that era were the first ever in their family to attend an institution of higher learning. Their parents were sacrificing to provide them an education. They were proud of making it to college, proud of their educational achievements, and determined to compel white society to recognize them as full American citizens. For them, to be expelled was out of the question, to be arrested and burdened with a criminal record a shame beyond endurance — not only for themselves, but for their families, their churches, and their communities.

Yet in 1960 a few students — a very, very few — in places like Greensboro and Nashville, Atlanta and Baton Rouge, Jackson and Orangeburg dared to start considering dangerous new thoughts that challenged the dominant paradigm. If registering to vote or speaking up meant being expelled from school — so be it. If sitting in at a lunch counter meant jail, they would serve their sentences with pride. If riding at the front of the bus meant facing mob violence, they would endure it. If dropping out to organize communities in the most violent regions of the rural South meant risking their lives, they would brave that danger.

Their words were non-belligerent, their tactics nonviolent, their language inclusive rather than divisive, and their demands "deeply rooted in the American dream." They were determined rather than strident, steadfast rather than dogmatic. At first they wore coats and ties, skirts and heels. Though their attire was conservative they — and their actions — were "radical" in the most profound sense of the term.

And they were willing to pay the piper, whatever the cost. Which was the most radical act of all. The revolutionary Afro-American students of the early '60s understood that there was no safe way to defy segregation and end the Jim Crow system without paying the price and suffering the consequences. The paths claiming to serve both self *and* cause had been revealed as illusionary. There were no clever tricks, no subtle stratagems, no way to defy white supremacy without suffering the penalties erected to enforce it.

And pay the piper they did. In abandoned educations, filthy jail cells, brutal beatings, and crippling injuries, both physical and mental. And for some, sudden violent death. Today, the Freedom Riders of yesterday are considered by many to be heroes, but for every Movement activist who managed to eventually return to school, graduate, and build a successful career in business, politics, or academia there are others who did not. A few achieved great acclaim and even high political office, while most found ways to scrape by on modest incomes while continuing to be activists. And some died homeless or live today in poverty.

After I left the South in 1967, I became a committed "New Leftist" with SDS and other northern groups who proclaimed themselves to be "revolutionary." But the transition from South to North was jarring. What whacked me upside the head when I encountered northern-style political activism was that in the Freedom Movement status and leadership was for the most part based on what you did, what you risked and endured, and your success (or lack thereof) in organizing real people to do actual things that affected their lives for the better. But in the northern New Left, status and leadership was based on the seeming sophistication of your intellectual ideas and the charisma of your rhetoric rather than what you did or accomplished in the real world — if anything.

Most of the intellectual leftists I encountered in committee meetings, coffeehouses, and campus cafeterias were Marxists of one variety or another and all but two or three of them were men. They were highly educated, with copious facts and sweeping theories at their finger-tips. They were self-confident to the point of arrogance and skilled in debate and language — far more so than I. They were utterly secure in their certainties and firmly convinced they were far more ideologically sophisticated than we country bumpkins of the nonviolent Civil Rights Movement, which they contemptuously disparaged as "bourgeois reformism."

To my deep regret, I accepted their premises at face value. Looking back on it now and speaking bitterness from that experience, I reject their assumptions of intellectual superiority and confess to some shame that I allowed myself to be swayed into their orbit.

In the New Left, what was "radical" or "revolutionary" seemed to be defined by fiery speech, complexity of intellectual analysis, and demands for the most extreme remedies and solutions, regardless of any actual chance of actually achieving them. Militant rhetoric and revolutionary posturing were what counted. Seeing an organization leader stand on the stage at an SDS convention and declare "I'm a revolutionary communist!" struck me as terrifically sophisticated and militant at the time, though now with the perspective and wisdom of decades it seems like childish bombast.

I was a young man of 23, and while I remained intensely proud of my service in the Freedom Movement I very much desired respect from the intellectual leftists with whom I was now participating in the anti-Vietnam War and student movements. When I had been part of the Black-led Freedom Movement I wasn't — and did not expect to be — any kind of leader. I was there as an ally to support their struggle. And I had no experience or knowledge that would qualify me to lead anything.

In the North, however, Blacks and whites worked in separate organizations, and in my own pride and arrogance I desired status among the white lefties who I was living and working with. I saw myself as someone with knowledge and abilities learned in four years of hard and dangerous Freedom Movement struggle, experience that I felt qualified me to play a leadership role in the protests that were roiling cities and campuses.

So I adopted their modes and made them my own. I became quite effective at New Left rhetoric and debate — and skilled in competing for leadership in that environment — an achievement I no longer take any pride in, though I did at that time.

In doing so, however, I turned my back on what I should have remembered from the Civil Rights Movement — a movement that rooted its strategies and tactics in the real conditions of the time and place and grounded its appeals and analysis in the actual political aspirations, cherished beliefs, and religious commitment of large segments of the population. Today I see that approach as far more sophisticated and effective than the New Left's abstract theories, Maoist quotations, and intellectual duels of Marxist study groups based on ideologies from distant cultures and different political realities.

As an SDS activist I considered myself an "anti-imperialist revolutionary," but the truth is that in my lifetime the *real* radicals, the real *revolutionaries*, were the young Afro-Americans waging a nonviolent war on segregation and battling for the democratic right to vote in the South. Though they overthrew no governments or economic systems, the changes they wrought in people's lives amounted to a social revolution. They understood, and lived, the true meaning of "radical."

Nonviolent Resistance & Political Power

We of the Freedom Movement didn't protest simply to vent our anger and alienation. The purpose of our actions were to change society. Our sit-ins, Freedom Rides, and mass marches were grounded in an analysis of political reality that led us to the strategy and tactics of Nonviolent Resistance as the most effective means of *winning actual changes.*

We understood that the injustices we opposed were deeper and more complex than simply some bad people with racist ideas. Beneath the surface of segregation and the denial of voting rights lay a white power-structure of wealthy individuals, powerful corporations, and influential politicians who derived great economic and political benefits from systemic-racism. They used political power to establish and maintain the Jim Crow system because it served their interests to do so. Which meant that moral suasion alone would be insufficient. In order to achieve actual change we had to understand what political power is, where it comes from, how it is generated, and how it can be used to force change.

In that context we defined "political power" as the ability to change — or maintain — some aspect of society, government-policy, or the economic system. Obviously, when we think of political power the first thing that comes to mind is government and that's what this essay focuses on. But government is *not the only* means by which political power affects society; culture and economics both *create* and *respond* to political power.

Government exercises power through legislation, spending, court rulings, bureaucratic regulations, police & military force, and so on. Politicians and bureaucrats assure us that they objectively study the issues, and adopt policies and programs based on rational and unbiased judgement for the benefit of all. Unfortunately, that's a self-serving myth.

In real life, the actual content of government policy is largely influenced and directed by political forces from outside government. In other words, while government does generate and wield political power, it mostly *responds* to political power. By analogy, the motor makes a car move, but it's the driver behind the wheel who decides where it goes. Sometimes government decides for itself where it goes, but most of the time it is steered by political pressure — political power — applied to it from the outside.

When we look at political power in the abstract, we see three sources, or kinds, of political power:

- **Violence-power.** The essential nature of violence-power is: *Do what you're told to do and don't do what is forbidden, or you will be jailed, harmed, or killed.* Violence-power can be either actual violence or simply the threat of violence. Military action, police & prison, private security, mob-violence, terrorism, and so on, are all used to control or influence society through their violence-power.

  In a democracy, government is the primary holder and wielder of violence-power, though there are some non-governmental forms such as mob or terrorist violence (the KKK during the '50s and '60s, for example). Most of the time, however, violence-power in America is largely latent, with most political power gravitating to one of two poles: organized money or organized people.

- **Money-power.** Money-power is the *dominant force* in most democracies — particularly the United States. It's the power to exercise corporate control over communications media or to buy PR and advertising to influence public opinion. To grant or withhold monetary investments, or other economic rewards. To bribe politicians with campaign contributions or other enticements. To simply pay people to do X or not to do Y.

  The primary holders and wielders of money-power are large corporations, wealthy individuals, and in some contexts government itself.

- **People-power.** People-power is the only real power that those of us who are neither rich nor at the top of government have. Historically, *only people-power* has been able to — on occasion — consistently check money-power.

  People-power takes many forms: electing/recalling politicians, protests that affect public opinion and change the cultural context, boycotts and other forms of economic pressure such as strikes, "alternative" media that challenges lies and presents different visions, cultural forms such as song, theatre, video, social media and the internet in general that speak truth to power. In the Southern Freedom Movement, for example, our freedom songs were as powerful a force for change as were our protests and the two were inextricably linked.

  In a democracy, the primary wielders of people-power are membership organizations, mass movements, and unorganized individuals acting in concert.

These three kinds of political power are neither separate nor distinct, they are closely related and mutually interactive:

- Violence can be used to coerce popular consent
- Violence (or the threat of violence) can be used to obtain money (taxes, for example)

- Money can elect politicians and manipulate popular consent
- Money can buy violence (government action, private security, strikebreakers, etc)

- People can raise and withhold money (boycotts, for example)

- People can defend themselves against violence (either violently or nonviolently)

Both pro- and anti-gun groups, for example, work to mobilize people-power to influence gun-related legislation. As an example of money-power *buying* people-power, the firearms industry gives major financial backing to membership organizations such as the National Rifle Association. On the other side, wealthy liberals and hundreds of thousands of small-donors fund anti-gun groups.

One way to understand American history — and the current events that shape our lives — is to analyze both past and present in terms of:

1. A broad historic and ongoing struggle between money-power and people-power over who rules and who benefits. Which is why the first rule of investigative reporting is: *Follow the money.*

2. Intermittent conflicts between different money-power or people-power factions. Which is why the second rule of investigative reporting is to ask: *Who benefits?*

Violence-power

With their military, police, and prisons, governments around the world have enormous potential to wield violence-power at all levels of society. Money-power can (and often has) used ruthless violence-power to suppress people and people-power movements or control or overthrow governments.

In the American South of the early and mid-1960s, state and local violence-power exercised through sheriffs, cops, and state troopers was a primary method of maintaining segregation and political control. But at the national level, repressive violence was largely held in reserve except in those few instances when it was used to enforce federal court rulings or suppress spontaneous urban violence. One of the main reasons *we* used *nonviolent* tactics — and loudly proclaimed our nonviolence — was to minimize, and if possible prevent, governmental violence-power from being used in a sustained way to suppress our people-power movement.

The form of government violence-power that was (and still is) most commonly used in America to maintain the status quo is arresting (or on occasion beating or tear-gassing) protesters. In some cases, arrests might be symbolic acts by both sides where people-power demonstrators deliberately provoke arrest to make a political point and government accommodates them to enforce "law and order" and the tranquility of things as they are. But in other cases, large-scale incarceration of nonviolent protesters who are not deliberately courting arrest has been used to quash people-power movements or deny legitimate First-Amendment actions that embarrass or annoy the powerful. The suppression of the Albany Movement in 1961-62 is one example, as is the illegal arrest or detention today of protesters at presidential appearances and political conventions.

Back in the early and mid-'60s, there were Freedom Movement organizations and individuals who on occasion used self-defense against terrorist attacks. Some of us combined nonviolence and self-defense as the situation warranted to defend ourselves from the Ku Klux Klan. But that limited self-defense was the extent of our use of violence-power.

Then in the late '60s and early '70s some leaders and groups — primarily in the North — publicly turned away from nonviolence as the strategy of social change. They heaped scorn on Nonviolent Resistance, glorified guns, and urged "armed struggle" or other forms of *offensive* violence. Such strategies proved short-lived and largely ineffective.

I should mention that when I refer to groups urging offensive violence I'm not talking about the Deacons for Defense and Justice or the Black Panther Party for Self-Defense. The Deacons never glamorized or glorified violence and they were quite clear that they only advocated *defense* against white terrorism. While Panther rhetoric did glorify violence both offensive and defensive, in actual practice they mostly limited themselves to self-defense — which didn't prevent the power structure from using their public embrace of violent revolutionary rhetoric as the political justification for ruthless and police-violence to suppress and destroy them.

And the truth is that in most cases, rhetorical calls for *offensive* violence were little more than posturing. Bombast aside, we had no real access to violence-power in the political sense — then or now. Neither then nor now could we successfully use violence to deter police oppression or ensure justice. We could not then nor can we now wage a successful violent revolution against either Washington or Wall Street. We can't use a pistol to force a slumlord to turn on the heat, or put a corporate polluter in prison, or prevent a friend from being deported, or stop an illegal war, or adequately fund a school system, or ... you fill in the blank.

Those few who actually committed some acts of political violence — or threatened to do so — failed to generate any significant amount of political power or achieve any long-lasting social change. They succeeded only in isolating themselves from potential supporters, and gifting both local and national government with convenient political cover for ruthlessly suppressing them. And that's been the political reality for a long time. As far back as 1900, the Industrial Workers of the World (IWW or "Wobblies") had an adage: "*Watch the man who advocates violence,*" because he was either a dangerous nut case — or a police agent.

Yet, while as a practical matter violence in the U.S. is a form of political suicide, today's music and entertainment media glamorizes violence in ways that encourage us to use it against each other. But fighting with neighbors, abusing spouses, burning local stores, breaking windows, and waging turf-wars against other powerless people only makes life in our communities that much worse — that much more unbearable. Not only does communal violence not generate any political power to improve our lives, it provides convenient pretexts for police suppression, isolates potential allies from each other, and divides us against ourselves in ways that block development of people-power.

Money-Power

In every nation, the goal of money-power is — and always has been — to increase its wealth and power and to prevent social or political changes that might upset a status quo that places them at the top of the heap. Money-power is constant and implacable, it exerts its political pressure 24/7, never resting, never taking a day off. And it is highly effective, the politicians and bureaucrats who determine government policy most often do so in response to the money-power that sets their agenda and guides their actions.

This view of money-power may sound radical to some — and perhaps it is — but it is not a new concept. In 1787, John Adams one of America's Founding Fathers and the 2nd President of the United States wrote: "In every society where property exists, there will ever be a struggle between rich and poor. Mixed in one assembly, equal laws can never be expected." In 1911, Helen Keller, wrote: "The country is governed for the richest, for the corporations, for the bankers, the land speculators, and for the exploiters of labor."

And in November of 1864, Abraham Lincoln wrote to Col. Elkin:

"I see in the near future a crisis approaching that unnerves me and causes me to tremble for the safety of my country. As a result of the war, corporations have been enthroned and an era of corruption in high places will follow, and the money power of the country will endeavor to prolong its reign by working upon the prejudices of the people until all wealth is aggregated in a few hands and the Republic is destroyed. I feel at this moment more anxiety for the safety of my country than ever before, even in the midst of war." — Abraham Lincoln, 11/21/1864

The Occupy Wall Street slogans of 2011 contrasted the non-rich 99% to the wealthy 1% whose average income was around $1million a year in 2018. But if we're making an actual analysis, the truth is that it's really only the top 1/10 of 1% (average income $35million) — or the top 1/100th of 1% of individuals (average income $150million) — who really have money-power in political terms.

And slogans aside, the *primary wielders* of money-power are not wealthy individuals at all but rather global, trans-national corporations. In 2018, for example, the Walmart Corporation had total revenues of $500 billion. That's greater than the total Gross Domestic Products (GDP) of countries like Austria, Norway and Iran. In other words, that single corporation was a larger economic entity than most medium-sized and all small-sized nations. No individual, not even the richest person in the world, can match that kind of economic clout.

Like nations, giant trans-national corporations usually have their own police forces ("corporate security"). Corporations of that size also have their own foreign policies which are separate from and often contrary to the policies of the countries they do business in. And in many cases they use their money-power to shape for their own private benefit the foreign policies of national governments large and small. In some cases, they even acquire their own military by hiring mercenaries or manipulating governments into doing their bidding — the "Banana Wars" of the early 1900s where U.S. Marines were deployed to Honduras and other Latin American nations to protect the profits of United Fruit being clear, classic examples.

Compared to the giant corporations and the wealthiest individuals, people like us don't have money-power in the political sense. We can't buy senators with campaign contributions, or threaten city councils with loss of jobs by closing plants or withholding investments. We don't own or control major media outlets. Nor can we endow opinion-shaping think tanks or university chairs, or finance radio talk shows. And we can't reward government regulators who have served us well by appointing them to cushy directorships as soon as they leave government.

Through advertising and rhetoric the money-power moguls want us to believe that we empower ourselves and achieve happiness by *purchasing* things like clothes, cars, homes, and vacations. But most of us who drive a new car or live in our own home do so through debt, not wealth. And consumer debt doesn't generate money-power — quite the opposite, it makes us vulnerable to the money-power of others.

Yet money-power is not omnipotent. It is rarely monolithic and almost never entirely united around any particular issue. Banks & other lending institutions, for example, are generally "deficit hawks" opposed in principle to government spending because as creditors they hate even the slightest amount of inflation. But the military/industrial complex, the health industry, and construction giants like Bechtel grow rich from government spending which they generally favor so long as the money flows to their sector rather than other sectors with whom they compete for tax-payer dollars.

During the Freedom Movement of the 1960s, money-power interests were split. Local/regional money-power in the South — plantation owners & corporations relying on cheap non-union labor and the local financial institutions that served them — were extremely hostile to the Freedom Movement. Acting through the White Citizens Council, local money-power waged economic terrorism against Blacks who challenged segregation and demanded the right to vote. But elements of national/international money-power saw economic opportunity for themselves in opening up the South to their investment. Goals which required (among other things) a stable rule-of-law and an end to racial "disturbances." Some saw great advantage in breaking the "Dixiecrat" stranglehold on the region's economy and politics. And other elements, such as chain stores like Woolworths, were pressured around segregation issues by people-power consumer boycotts organized by northern students.

So while money-power is enormous, it can be — and has been in the past — defeated by people-power. That's how we won trade unions, Social Security & Medicare, environmental regulations, and health & safety laws.

People-Power

Around the globe, our mass culture of film, TV, song, drama, publishing, internet — both corporate and government produced — glorify and exalt violence-power and money-power and ignore or discredit people-power. That's as true for Bollywood as it as for Hollywood, for London as for Hong Kong, for Moscow as for Cairo. And The *role models* we're given to aspire to are the affluent and super-rich. And *heroes* are men with guns — usually isolated individuals acting alone or with a single sidekick.

Yet in real life, most of us have little access to money-power and even less to violence-power. Yes, we of the 99% can work hard and buy a car, maybe a home, and maybe earn a comfortable life. But few, if any of us, will ever have the kind of wealth from which flows money-power in the political sense. Yes, we can use violence against each other, and today's popular music and media glamorizes individual violence. But we have no access to violence-power in the political sense.

What we do have and *can use* is people-power.

In democracies, government ultimately rests on the consent of the governed — an idea articulated in the Declaration of Independence:

> We hold these truths to be self-evident, that all men are created equal, that they are endowed by their Creator with certain unalienable Rights, that among these are Life, Liberty and the pursuit of Happiness. ... That to secure these rights, Governments are instituted among men, deriving their just powers from the consent of the governed; that whenever any form of government becomes destructive of these ends, it is the right of the people to alter or abolish it and to institute new government, laying its foundations on such principles, and organizing its powers in such form, as to them shall seem most likely to effect their safety and happiness."

Every 4th of July America celebrates this Declaration with fireworks, flag waving, and patriotic speeches. But (not so oddly) almost never do any of the orating politicians actually quote any portion of the Declaration to their audiences — or explain what it means. They would rather not call to our attention our people-power potential.

Yet, despite our rulers' desire that we remain ignorant, docile, and obedient to their commands, throughout our history organized groups of people have successfully used strategies of Nonviolent Resistance to mobilize people-power around a wide variety of issues. People-power movements apply political power to influence government and force it to pass legislation such as the Civil Rights and Voting Rights Acts, affect spending and taxes, regulate abuses, and to provide redress of grievances. The Southern Freedom Movement is the example of people-power that this memoir recalls.

Even more importantly, people-power can also change the social/cultural context within which *all* political power is exercised. Prior to the Freedom Movement, for example, overt, explicit, racism was a common aspect of American society. "Nigger" jokes were on the radio and "Blackface" stereotypes played out on TV. Derogatory racial images were an everyday part of commerce, and politicians used explicit racist appeals in campaigns and cited racist ideology in legislative debates. If you questioned or criticized such overt racism you were, at the very least, considered to be an un-American crank — and probably a Communist.

The Freedom Movement fundamentally changed our cultural context so that what was normal in the 1950s became utterly unacceptable. Other people-power movements made similar profound changes in how our society viewed women and women's roles, how we viewed the global environment, and so on. Today, for their partisan gain the Republican Party and Trump are resurrecting those tropes and memes of racism, misogyny, nativism, homophobia, and so on that we had for a time discredited. And people-power is once again embattled in a raging culture war against them.

Since the end of the Second World War, efforts to mobilize people-power have been somewhat to partially effective in a number of areas — labor, segregation, women, environment, and sexuality issues, for example — and largely ineffective in other areas — foreign policy, war, economic inequality, and so on. In part, this is because money-power is constantly active in influencing government while people-power is intermittent and most of the time largely latent. In part it is because people-power today is often divided. And in part it is because we have failed to fully use the power of Nonviolent Resistance.

Wealth and government maintain their power by making us feel helpless and confused. One way they do so is by telling us that in a democracy it is *only* through elections that *We the People* wield power. But most of the time, candidates are chosen and issues are framed by money-power. Political parties and candidates for office are influenced by money before they are running for office, while they are running, and after they are elected. So much so that few (if any) of the many volunteers who actively work in electoral politics have a voice in selecting the candidates, crafting their positions, or shaping the subsequent legislation.

The only role they offer to most of us is voting on election day — usually for Candidate A who represent the interests of the giant corporations and the wealthy few, or for Candidate B who also represents those same interests but articulates somewhat more "liberal" social policies. Yet historically, people-power can be, and has been, exercised through elections, most recently (to a degree) in the mid-term elections of 2018. But those times when people-power has been powerful at the ballot box have only occurred when there are organizations and movements that educate and mobilize people around their interests *outside* of the electoral process and who do so consistently *between* election cycles.

Which brings us to direct action and Nonviolent Resistance. By and large, the strategies of the Freedom Movement — and the strategies of most successful reform movements — were the strategies of Nonviolent Resistance.

In modern times there have been instances where revolutionary Nonviolent Resistance was used to overthrow authoritarian governments elsewhere in the world — the *Rose Revolution, Arab Spring,* and *Orange Revolution,* for example — but Nonviolent Resistance is more commonly used to reform some aspect of government or society — the U.S. Civil Rights Movement being a case in point.

Whether the goal is revolution or reform, the purpose of nonviolent tactics and strategies is to create a political dynamic that organizes and mobilizes people-power while at the same time limiting and restricting the ability of opponents to suppress the movement with violence or divide and weaken it with money-power.

The *weakness* of money-power is the illegitimacy of actions and policies designed to benefit the wealthy and powerful few at the expense of the many. By mobilizing nonviolent popular action, we use our strength against their weakness. The *strength* of nonviolent people-power is inherent in the word "NO." "No" is the most powerful word in the English language:

No, we won't accept segregation
No, we won't silently stand by in the face of injustice
No, we won't believe the lies of Bush or Trump
No, we won't submit to corporate domination our lives

On the other hand, violence on our part pits our weakness against their strength. In modern society, both money-power and the state are well prepared for political violence with police, courts, jails, military, intelligence agencies, private security, surveillance, internet-tracking, and so on. Violence plays on their field, on their terms, under their rules. Time and again, small violent groups have been ineffective and counter-productive at generating political power. Not because they were small — small nonviolent groups have sometimes achieved great success, the lunch counter sit-ins and Freedom Rides being two examples — but because they tried to rely on violence-power rather than people-power.

To be politically effective using people-power, you have to build *mass* popular support. But in our society, building popular support based on violence won't work for two reasons:

1. **Repression**. The state is well-organized and way over-equipped for suppressing violence. Those in power would prefer that there be no resistance or opposition to their rule. But if there is going to be resistance, they prefer that it be violent because they can quickly

destroy violent opposition. Yet few police forces are trained to effectively contain Nonviolent Resistance. Often it confuses and confounds them because it is so at odds with what they expect and are trained for.

Yes, they can beat and arrest nonviolent protesters, but that often fails to suppress a nonviolent movement or the ideas behind it. Which is why undercover cops & FBI COINTELPRO agents who infiltrated Movement organizations always advocated the most violent acts, and were the most vehement in sneering at and disparaging Nonviolent Resistance — they urged molotov cocktails, rather than peaceful sit-ins.

2. **People fear and oppose violence**. Most people will defend themselves if attacked, but unless driven to utter desperation they won't commit offensive violence, and they don't want their children doing it either. Obviously, you can train and discipline people to do violence — that's why militaries and police have elaborate training camps and academies — but it's not easy.

   Official, state violence may be *As American as cherry pie*, but despite the media's glorification of violence and their definition of *hero* as a *man with a gun*, civil disorder and citizen violence are broadly rejected by all levels of society and only a tiny fraction of the population will engage in it. But if properly organized and led, people will nonviolently exercise their rights to advocate a cause they believe in — boycotting buses in Montgomery, for example, or facing down the Klan, posse, and state troopers in Selma for the right to vote.

So we have this contradiction: Our mass culture tells us that to take effective action you have to be violent, but social change through violence does not work. Nonviolent Resistance breaks this contradiction by providing a method of mobilizing people-power to create social change.

Courage Was the Key

From time to time I'm asked to speak in schools about my experience as a civil rights worker. Below is a presentation I made to a high school assembly as part of their Martin Luther King Day program in January of 2014:

> Courage was the key. Courage was the common thread that bound together all the many events and activities that made up the Civil Rights Movement.

Today, our mass media and popular culture usually portray *courage* as *a man with a gun*. But the Freedom Movement was nonviolent, we didn't use guns or other forms of violence to change society. It was not that we were afraid to fight, nonviolence was by no means safe. Rather, we used nonviolence because *we wanted to win*. In democracies like ours, engaging in political violence is a losing strategy, but nonviolence gave us a *chance* to win — a chance, not a certainty.

Courage is the inescapable requirement of nonviolent resistance to injustice. Yet today our culture tries to make us believe that courage only exists in a context of committing violence — *not true*.

When depicting courage, our culture also tends to portray it as a male trait. Yet it was not just men alone who courageously used nonviolence. The Freedom Movement was made up of men and women, boys and girls. Think of the two most famous names from the Civil Rights Movement — Martin Luther King and Rosa Parks, a man and a woman. When you look at the old photos and newsreels, notice how many women and girls are among those facing the dogs and the fire hoses and filling the jail cells.

Segregation was the rule in the South of the 1960s. The races were separated by law. Blacks and other nonwhite people were forbidden to use white-only drinking fountains, or walk in white-only public parks, or sit at the front of the bus. If they did so, they were arrested. Blacks could shop in stores, but not eat at the lunch counter. In 1960, it was college and high school students who declared, "No, this is wrong and we're not going to accept it anymore!"

In Greensboro, North Carolina, four college students sat down at a lunch counter and said, "We're going to sit here until we're served or arrested." They called it a "sit-in." They said, "If you arrest us, more will come. So many will come you won't be able to arrest us all." And that's what happened. Some were arrested, but more came. This went on for months. When the college students went home for summer vacation, students from Dudley High School continued the struggle until they achieved victory and the lunch counters were desegregated.

Think about that for a moment. Through their courage, high school students very much like you changed the face of their community — and history. High school kids.

In Birmingham, it was college and high school students who stepped up. Led by student body presidents, football players, and cheerleaders, they kept the Freedom Movement alive. Some were beaten, some were bitten by dogs, some were knocked down by fire hoses. But they held true. They didn't give up. So many young people were arrested, that the

Birmingham campaign is now known in history as the "Children's Crusade."

Young people may not have been the famous leaders, but they were the core of the Civil Rights Movement. Most of those who marched and most of those who went to jail were college and high school students — both girls and boys.

Today, people ask us, "Weren't you scared?" We used to sing, "We are not afraid," but we *were* afraid. We were *always* afraid. Courage is not the absence of fear, courage is doing what you know is right even though you're frightened.

But physical courage to face danger and arrest, is not the only kind of courage. It's not even the most important kind of courage that the women and men and girls and boys of the Freedom Movement had to have. Deeper, more important, and often more difficult to achieve than physical courage is *social courage*. The courage to take a public stand for what you believe is right when others among your family, peers, and those in authority over you do not agree. Even when the majority are against you. Even when your friends laugh and jeer and make fun of you.

When confronted with a racist slur, a sexist put-down, a homophobic joke, or an ethnic or cultural sneer it takes social courage to stand up and dissent. To stand against your friends — maybe even your own family — and say, "No, that's not who I am."

The truth is, that for most of us it is harder to stand apart from custom, family, and friends than it is to risk physical danger. Which is why it's often harder to show social courage than physical courage.

You know this from your own lives. How many of you have felt uncomfortable with a bigoted joke or comment from one of your social peers, yet lacked the will to publicly challenge it within your group? How many of you have ever feared to speak up when you knew you should because your friends might mock or laugh at you, or that *you* might become the target of their humiliating insults and demeaning laughter?

Today, those who marched with Dr. King are honored, but that was not always so. At the time, many of our friends and family — Black and white — cautioned us, "Stay out of that mess, don't stir up trouble." Some who thought themselves wise in the ways of the world told us, "Nothing will ever change, and you're a fool for trying." And in one sense they were right, it's always safer to do nothing. But human progress is made by those with the social and physical courage to take a stand. Even if it's an unpopular stand at first.

Every generation has its challenges to face. For my generation, one of our challenges was the Civil Rights Movement. We had our challenges and you will have yours. Every generation must find the social courage, and if necessary the physical courage, to overcome those challenges. What you are being taught in this school is to prepare you for those challenges. But you will have to find the courage to face them on your own.

Two Americas Ever at War With Each Other

The Freedom Movement was not an isolated historical event. It grew out of, and was shaped by, the entire sweep of American history. Its successes and failures can only be evaluated in that historical context.

The strategy, tactics, successes and failures of the Freedom Movement were inevitably influenced by the racial realities of white domination in economics, politics, and culture. But whites were not united, rather they were bitterly divided over the very meaning of America. As I think about it now, I've come to see that America is really two different nations ever at war with each other. One is the America I love and cherish, a multi-racial America that stands for concepts like liberty, equality, justice, opportunity, freedom of thought, and freedom of (and from) religion. It's the America where personal rights are balanced against shared community interests and where social contracts encompass both individual and collective needs.

We can trace the history of my America down through the decades — the Enlightenment of the 1700s, *We hold these truths to be self-evident...*, the abolitionists, *Government of the people...*, the suffragists, *Give me your tired, your poor, your huddled masses...*, the Wobblies and the embattled agrarian reformers, the CIO, the Freedom Movement, women's liberation and gay rights, environmental defense, and today the fight for immigrant justice, reproductive rights, economic equality, and Black Lives Matter.

Standing against my America is another, implacably hostile America that from the get-go embraced — and tried to forcibly impose on others — ideologies of white supremacy, misogyny, nativism, class-aristocracy, religious, ethnic, and cultural bigotry, anti-intellectualism, raw selfish greed, imperialist expansion, and homage and obeisance to wealth and power. This is an America that exalts entitled individualism and unadulterated appetite while spurning compassion for those who are different from themselves — or who are simply poorer.

It's an America that rejects the idea that "shared community" includes people from races, religions and backgrounds other than their own. It's an America that the both despises and fears those who are poorer than themselves. And it's an America that rejects most people whose lifestyles, life choices, or systems of belief fail to conform to a single narrow definition of what is right and proper.

We can trace that America down through the perpetrators and enablers of the Indian genocide, the slave-owning aristocrats, and the witch-burning Puritans; the anti-immigrant Know Nothings of the 1850s, the Ku Klux Klan in its many generations and manifestations, the Darwin deniers and "scientific racists," the anti-Semitic America-Firsters of the 1930s, the White Citizens' Council of the 1960s, down to today's "patriot" militias, neo-Nazis, gay-bashers, and Make America Great Again Trumpites.

There are really two different types of people who inhabit the America of greed and bigotry that I oppose. For many their prejudices and hatreds are deeply held beliefs, but for others bigotry and discrimination are simply convenient avenues for personal wealth and power. For many slaveholders before the Civil War and plantation owners afterwards it was an unshakable conviction that Africans were an inferior race ordained by God Almighty to be the hewers of wood and drawers of water for their betters. For others, that assertion was little more than a self-serving justification and useful counter to those who condemned slavery and the sharecropper system as inherently unjust. And sadly, there's never been any shortage of tycoons and politicians who cynically stoke hatred, racism, and nationalism as their path to riches or political power.

I was never able to tell which of the segregationists we confronted in the 1960s were true believers as opposed to those who were political or economic opportunists — and as a practical matter it made little difference to those who were abused, exploited, jailed, beaten, and shot.

Take Alabama Governor George Wallace for example. An ardent segregationist, he ran for office and governed on a platform of virulent white supremacy. He was our archfoe. Yet once Blacks in Alabama began voting in large numbers, he changed his tune. He apologized to Afro-Americans for the evil he had committed in his drive for political power, and when he successfully ran for governor in 1982 he campaigned for — and received — the Black vote against a Republican opponent running on a traditional white supremacy platform.

In practical reality, the motivation of the haters — true belief or opportunism — makes scant difference to the harm they do to individual victims and society at large. The damage done by Wallace's *white backlash* demagoguery, his calls for *segregation now-segregation forever*, and his *states' rights* ideology continued long after he himself was gone. And to this day his victims carry the scars of the violence, brutality, false arrest, and economic terrorism that he inspired, enabled, and ordered.

Which is why that rather than focus on thoughts and opinions the Freedom Movement of the 1960s primarily focused on modifying racist *behavior* and *actions* by building a political movement that pressured Congress to enact laws, influenced court rulings, and reshaped the cultural norms that determined what was socially acceptable to say or do.

And similarly, just as motivation makes scant difference to the harm done by haters, the progressive motivation of enlightened liberals and progressives provide no guarantee that we and our behavior are inherently immune from the pervasive racism and unconscious bigotry that permeates our entire society. Racist, misogynist, and classist attitudes, assumptions, memes, and mindsets pollute the culture in which we grew up. They surround us all our lives. Inevitably then, our personal mindscapes are contaminated, are harmful to ourselves and others, whether we realize or acknowledge it or not.

Which means that while we fight for justice and equality in society at large, we also have to wage an internal war against our own unexamined biases and damaging behavior. This is true for *all* of us regardless of race, gender, or class, though we who derive benefit from some ingrained and unexamined assumption have the greatest difficulty rejecting it. A responsibility that I don't think anyone ever entirely succeeds at — certainly I haven't — though to paraphrase Rabbi Tarfon, *We are not required to complete the task of healing the world (and ourselves), but neither are we free to avoid it.*

Like a River

American history is a tale of conflict between those two mutually hostile visions, one committed to freedom, justice, and equality; the other to bigotry, greed, and race- gender- and class-supremacy. Down through the generations it's been a harsh and bitter struggle, a political, social, and cultural war waged in the streets, at the ballot box, and in schools, churches, and theaters. It's been *All people are created equal* versus the Trail of Tears; freedom of religion versus anti-Catholicism and anti-Semitism; Frederick Douglass and the abolitionists versus John Calhoun and the *Dred Scott* decision; *a decent respect to the opinions of mankind* versus Manifest Destiny; *unalienable rights* versus anti-labor laws and legalized discrimination; *freedom now!* versus *never!*

My parents were soldiers in that political-cultural war. So was I. So too were all the others who served in the Freedom Movement and subsequent fights for justice and equality. Looking back now, it's clear to me that the America I support has been winning that war, slowly but steadily over generations — though not without temporary setbacks. Today when I and so many others march against the Trump-Republican regime and their resurgent politics of race-, gender-, and class-supremacy we refer to ourselves as the *Resistance*. But as SNCC leader Courtland Cox recently pointed out: "It is Trump and his ilk who are the resistance to the human rights tide of history that has been set in motion over the past decades."

Vincent and Rosemarie Harding were Movement activists and intellects of renown. In his book *There is a River: The Black Struggle for Freedom in America*, Vincent likened the continuous yearning and reaching toward freedom of Afro-Americans to the flowing of a river:

> ... its long continuous movement, flowing like a river, sometimes
> powerful, tumultuous, and roiling with life; at other times meandering
> and turgid, covered with the ice and snow of seemingly endless winters,
> all too often streaked and running with blood. [30]

I now understand that his words apply not just to the Black Freedom Movement but to all human rights struggles throughout world history. When I was young, I naively assumed that social change was like a sports event that would end in victory or defeat. I didn't understand that human progress towards justice and equality is a long journey where each generation passes the torch to the next, and each milestone achieved or setback endured leads inevitably to the next phase of the struggle.

Which is, of course, exactly what happened. Bernice Johnson Reagon of SNCC and *Sweet Honey in the Rock* refers to the Freedom Movement as the *borning movement* of the 1960s because out of it grew the many disparate movements of that era, including:

The student rights and academic freedom movement
The anti-Vietnam War movement
The women's liberation movement
The Chicano rights movement
The environmental movement
The farm workers movement
The gay rights movement
The tenants' rights and other community movements
And so many others.

And to this day, movements for social justice in America — and for that matter, around the world — still take inspiration from the Freedom Movement of the 1960s. Historian and civil rights activist Howard Zinn explained its continued relevance in his 1994 book *You Can't be Neutral on a Moving Train*, when he wrote:

> What the civil rights movement proved ... is that even if people lack the customary attributes of power — money, political authority, physical force — as did the black people of the Deep South, there is a power that can be created out of pent-up indignation, courage, and the inspiration of a common cause, and that if enough people put their minds and bodies into that cause, they can win. It is a phenomenon recorded again and again in the history of popular movements against injustice all over the world ...

> The reward for participating in a movement for social justice is not the prospect of future victory. It is the exhilaration of standing together with other people, taking risks together, enjoying small triumphs and enduring disheartening setbacks — together.

> Note how often ... we have been surprised. By the sudden emergence of a people's movement, the sudden overthrow of a tyranny, the sudden coming to life of a flame we thought extinguished. We are surprised because we have not taken notice of the quiet simmering of indignation, of the first faint sounds of protest, of the scattered signs of resistance that, in the midst of our despair, portend the excitement of change. The isolated acts begin to join, the individual thrusts blend into organized actions, and one day, often when the situation seems most hopeless, there bursts onto the scene a movement. [31]

In Memory of Martin Luther King — A Winter Soldier

In 2018, I was asked to say a few words on Martin Luther King Day by Indivisible San Francisco, an organization advocating mass resistance to Trump and the Republican agenda:

Today we are here to commemorate the birthday of Dr. Martin Luther King who was born on January 15, 1929. He would have been 89 tomorrow.

American history is a history of social change pushed up from below by mass movements of committed citizens: abolitionists, suffragettes, labor and community organizers, civil rights workers, environmentalists, liberated women, proud gays, and courageous immigrants. Yet of all our many public holidays, only one honors that kind of up from below freedom fighter — Martin Luther King Day.

We should begin our MLK day remembrance by recalling an earlier January — January of 1777 when an ink-stained wretch named Tom Paine huddled by a tiny fire in the blood-stained snows of Valley Forge and wrote:

> *THESE are the times that try men's souls. The summer soldier and the sunshine patriot will, in this crisis, shrink from the service of their country; but he that stands by it now, deserves the love and thanks of man and woman. Tyranny, like hell,*

Ever since, those who stand and endure against discouragement, adversity, and defeat have been called "Winter Soldiers." We, the women and men here in this room, Black and white, red and brown and yellow — We are the Winter Soldiers of the unfulfilled American Dream.

Dr. King was a Winter Soldier.

Dr. King was a Winter Soldier, and he was killed in action on April 4, 1968 while supporting a strike of Memphis garbage workers.

When I worked for Dr. King in the mid-1960s we used to joke that we were part of his "freedom army." In that context, Dr. King was the general and I was — at best — just a sergeant. My view of Dr. King was from the rank and file, not from the inner circle. Yet even from that distance, what struck me most about Dr. King was his profoundly humanist vision that united people of all races and creeds. A vision founded in the unkept promise of America, that *"We hold these truths to be self-evident that all men are created equal.*

What struck me about Dr. King was the depth of his compassion for the suffering of all people, of all races, of all nations. What struck me about Dr. King was how much he cared for people, not just people in general as an abstract concept, but people as individuals.

What struck me about Dr. King was his humility. He was profoundly uncomfortable with the adulation that he received, but he consciously used it to move people into action. Yet he never made money for himself, even his Nobel Prize money was put back into the Movement.

Dr. King was often criticized for not being "militant" enough. But what we often forgot — or failed at the time to understand — was that he agonized over every jailed demonstrator, over every beaten voter, over every martyr's death. When we were wounded, he bled. When we were beat, he ached. Later in life I experienced leaders who casually sent others to the barricades without qualms or doubts, and I realized how lucky I had been to be a sergeant in Dr. King's freedom army.

Successful social movements always focus on specific issues as points of attack for much broader goals. The Southern Freedom Movement focused on segregation and voting, but the Movement's vision was much broader than just the limited notion of achieving those two civil rights. The Southern Freedom Movement was really about the overthrow of an entire system of feudal oppression and exploitation that had replaced slavery after the Civil War. Our song and chant was, *Freedom Now!* not *Civil rights now.*

By defining the Freedom Movement as a "Civil Rights Movement," the media limits its scope to that of a modest reform within a benevolent broader system. In reality, it was a fundamental attack on the existing political and economic power structure in the South.

And just as the media distorts the Movement as a whole, it distorts Dr. King by freezing him at the moment in time when he gave his *I Have a Dream* speech at the March on Washington on August 28, 1963. Freezing him in time at *Black & white together,* and *Judging people by the content of their character rather than color of skin.* Over this holiday, compare in your minds the number of times you see images of King on TV saying those words versus the number of times you see him:

Confronting Mayor Daley about urban poverty and racial discrimination in the north.

Supporting workers on strike for economic justice.

Telling students at Stanford: "It's much easier to integrate a lunch counter than it is to guarantee a livable income and a good solid job. It's much easier to guarantee the right to vote than it is to guarantee the right to live in sanitary, decent housing conditions. It is much easier to integrate a public park than it is to make genuine, quality, integrated education a reality. And so today we are struggling for something which says we demand genuine equality.'

Speaking out against the War in Vietnam, and telling America: "A nation that continues year after year to spend more money on military defense than on programs of social uplift is approaching spiritual death."

By freezing Dr. King in time, the media conceals one of the profound truths about him, which that is that he evolved — that he *rapidly* evolved. It's not often mentioned, but like all of us, Dr. King made mistakes and experienced failures. Yet one of the great things about him is that he learned from his mistakes and failures. From the errors he made during the Albany, Georgia campaign of 1962 came the Birmingham victories of 1963 which played such a key role in eventual passage of the Civil Rights Act of 1964.

Out of defeat in the Chicago struggle to end slums in 1966 came the brilliant concept of the Poor People's Campaign in 1967 — an effort to unite people of all races to fight for economic justice. So often we encounter leaders and theoreticians who are so wedded to the correctness of their opinions that they endlessly repeat their failures rather than learn new ideas, new tactics, new strategies. King was not like that. He learned. He grew.

I remember when he spoke from the steps of the Alabama State Capitol at the end of the Selma to Montgomery March. He said, *Though the arc of the moral universe is long, it bends towards justice.* And as I think back on it now, I'm astounded at how far his personal political arc traveled in just 13 short years. From the improvised podium where he stood, he could see the little church in Montgomery, Alabama where he had begun his ministry. On the day before Rosa Parks refused to give up her bus seat in 1955, Dr. King was a socially conventional, politically moderate Baptist preacher. On the day he was assassinated in Memphis 13 years later, he was a global *Trumpet of Conscience*, who was shaking the powers of the world with his calls for social, economic, and international justice.

And that's why they killed him.

Let us be clear about one thing. I do not know of a single Freedom Movement activist who believes the "lone gunman" lie. We all believe that King's assassination was engineered by the power elites for two reasons:

First, because he was uniting poor people across race and ethnic lines around issues of economic justice. Under his leadership the Poor People's Campaign threatened to directly challenge the culture of greed and exploitation on which the wealthy base their power.

And second, by opposing the War in Vietnam he was challenging a foreign policy driven by global corporate expansion and the ideology of neo-colonialism disguised as anti- communism.

Malcolm X was killed for the same reasons. When he returned from Hajj in 1964, Malcolm renounced Black separatism, and said he would work with people of all races. And his first effort was organizing a petition to the UN documenting that the treatment of Black Americans violated the UN Charter and Declaration of Human Rights and demanding that the U.S. be charged with human rights violations.

When Medgar Evers was assassinated in 1963, his widow Myrlie said, "You can kill a man, but you can't kill an idea." And when Dr. King was killed, we said, "You can kill the dreamer, but you cannot kill the dream." And that is true. But it is only true if there are Winter Soldiers with the courage and determination to carry on.

So let me close by taking note of something we often forget when recalling history.

Those Winter Soldiers shivering in the snow at Valley Forge did not know they were eventually going to win. At that time, the Redcoats occupied the major cities and dominated the colonies — only a handful villages and hamlets dared wear liberty blue. The college students sitting in at lunch counters, the freedom riders defying KKK mobs, the children standing against fire hoses in Birmingham, the women and men who marched over the Edmund Pettus Bridge in Selma Alabama did not know they were going to win. There was no easy promise of quick success. The summer soldiers gave up and went home. The Winter Soldiers held on. And that is the essential definition of a Winter Soldier — someone who continues fighting for justice even in the coldest winter.

Dr. King was a Winter Soldier.

It now falls to us to be the Winter Soldiers of the 21st Century.

About the Author

Bruce Hartford joined the Congress of Racial Equality (CORE) in 1963 and for two years engaged in nonviolent direct action against housing discrimination, school segregation, and racist hiring practices in Southern California. In early 1965, he became part of Dr. King's voting rights campaign in Selma, Alabama and participated in the March to Montgomery. As a field secretary for the Southern Christian Leadership Conference (SCLC), in 1965 he directed the Crenshaw County Alabama summer voter registration project. In the summer of 1966. He participated in the Meredith March Against Fear in Mississippi, and until 1967 he was part of the SCLC field staff in Grenada, Mississippi during the long and bloody struggle to end segregation and win voter rights. Today he is webspinner for the Civil Rights Movement Veterans website (www.crmvet.org) and a board member of the SNCC Legacy Project.

www.ingramcontent.com/pod-product-compliance
Lightning Source LLC
Chambersburg PA
CBHW031230090426
42742CB00007B/139